20th Workshop of the Australasian Language Technology Association (ALTA 2022)

Adelaide, Australia
14-16 December 2022

ISBN: 978-1-7138-9102-4

Printed from e-media with permission by:

Curran Associates, Inc.
57 Morehouse Lane
Red Hook, NY 12571

Some format issues inherent in the e-media version may also appear in this print version.

Association for Computational Linguistics
209 N. Eighth Street
Stroudsburg, Pennsylvania 18360

Phone: 1-570-476-8006
Fax: 1-570-476-0860

acl@aclweb.org

Additional copies of this publication are available from:

Curran Associates, Inc.
57 Morehouse Lane
Red Hook, NY 12571 USA
Phone: 845-758-0400
Fax: 845-758-2633
Email: curran@proceedings.com
Web: www.proceedings.com

ALTA 2022

Proceedings of the 20th Workshop of the Australasian Language Technology Association

14–16 December 2022

Flinders University

Adelaide, Australia

Sponsors

Platinum

Australian Government
Defence

Gold

Google

Event Sponsors

Flinders University

MELBOURNE DATA ANALYTICS PLATFORM

THE UNIVERSITY OF MELBOURNE

CROSSING
French Australian Laboratory for Humans-Autonomous Agents Teaming

Introduction

Welcome to The 20th Annual Workshop of the Australasian Language Technology Association and Flinders University.

ALTA is interested in all aspects of language technology, from speech to text, hearing to reading, phonology to morphology, syntax to semantics. Our program reflects this, as does our ongoing coordination with the Australian Document Computing Symposium, which will have a separate stream as well as joint sessions. Participants are welcome to join sessions across the two co-located events.

ALTA is interested in both language and technology, and these days learning is an important aspect of the technology and our keynote speakers will also dig deeper into the human side of language, learning and logic, the tradeoffs between neural learning and symbolic reasoning, as well as the ontological grounding of syntax, semantics and thought. Ed Hovy, from CMU and Melbourne University, will start the ball rolling with a discussion of the limitations of neural NLP and need for reasoning. Stephane Dufau, from CNRS and currently on sabbatical at the University of Queensland, will end the day with a look at how to understanding the process of reading will round off Thursday with a look at how computational models can help us understand the human processes involved in reading, while on Friday a double billing of Thora Tenbrink from Bangor and Barbara Tversky from Stanford will explore how language and thought and behaviour are situated in space and time, and the importance for joint spatial awareness in for properly grounding our understanding of language in humans and robots.

Turning to submitted papers, we had 40 submitted papers (short and long) for formal publication and presentation, as well as allowing for submission of shorter abstracts including work in progress, recently published work or half-baked ideas, for more informal presentation (without publication in the proceedings, and a special session after lunch on Friday). In addition, we once again offered a shared task (with papers from successful entrants published in the proceedings, with a special session before lunch on Friday). We accepted 10 (25%) of the submitted papers for oral presentation and a further 16 (44%) for poster presentation. We will also be presenting a best paper award and a best student paper award in the closing session on Friday afternoon.

After two years of online workshops due to COVID we have made a real effort to allow everyone to come together again in person - and expect close to a hundred in-person attendees across the combined ALTA/ADCS events. In addition, we are allowing on-line participation and will be operating in a hybrid mode with some speakers presenting remotely. For those attending in person, all meals and refreshments are provided and we have a special mentoring lunch for students and mentors as part of our doctoral symposum, mentoring program and tutorial day on Wednesday at our Victoria Square city campus, while the main ALTA workshop and ADCS symposium sessions will be at our Tonsley campus (a bus or train ride away) and our conference dinner will be held at the Tonsley Hotel on Thursday evening.

We would like to thank all the referees, committee members, local organizers and student helpers who have helped this event come together, and in particular we'd like to thank our Platinum Sponsor, the Defence Science and Technology Group, our Gold Sponsor Google, as well as the University of Melbourne, Flinders University, CNRS International Research Lab and CROSSING for their support of the event and its keynote speakers.

Welcome to Flinders, to Adelaide, to South Australia and Australia - our submissions have come from all over the world and we look forward to a rich and rewarding time together. We hope that this hybrid even will be a worthwhile and enjoyable experience for everyone.

David Powers, Jennifer Biggs and Pradeesh Parameswaran

Adelaide and Dunedin

December 2022

Organisers:

Program Co-chairs: David Powers, Jennifer Biggs and Pradeesh Parameswaran
Shared Task Chair: Diego Mollá
ALTA Execs: Maria Kim, Meladel Mistica, Sarvnaz Karimi, Massimo Piccardi, Afshin Rahimi, Diego Mollá
Local Chairs: Richard Leibbrandt, Paulo Santos, Mehwish Nasim, Tina Du, Joel Mackenzie, Maciek Rybinski
Session Chairs: Gabriela Ferraro, Jonathan Kummerfeld

Program Committee:

Abeed Sarkar, Afshin Rahimi, Antonio Jimeno, David Powers, Diego Molla, Fajri Koto, Hamed Hassanzadeh, Guido Zuccon, Hiyori Yoshikawa, Jennifer Biggs, Karin Verspoor, Massimo Piccardi, Mel Mistica, Maria Kim, Nitin Indurkhya, Paulo Santos, Pradeesh Parameswaran, Richard Leibbrandt, Sarvnaz Karimi, Sunghwan Mac Kim, Timothy Baldwin, Veronica Liesaputra, Xiang Dai.

Invited Speakers:

Barbara Tversky, Stanford University
Eduard Hovy, University of Melbourne and Carnegie Mellon University
Thora Tenbrink, Bangor University
Stephane Dufau, Laboratoire de psychologie cognitive (CNRS)

Invited Talks

Barbara Tversky: Mind in Motion: How Action Shapes Thought

I will present a case that actions in space and with the things in it are the foundation of thought, not the entire edifice, but the foundation. To this end, I will bring evidence from neuroscience, from behavior, from language, and from gesture.

Eduard Hovy: On the complementarity of neural and symbolic approaches, and on how to transfer between them

Today's neural NLP can do amazing things, leading some people to expect human-level performance soon. But it also fails spectacularly, in ways we find hard to predict and explain. Is perfection just a matter of doing additional neural architecture engineering and more-advanced training to overcome these problems, or are there deeper reasons for the failures? I argue that trying to understand the nature and reason for failures by couching the necessary operations in terms of symbolic reasoning is a good way to discover what neural networks will remain unable to do despite additional architecture engineering and training.

Thora Tenbrink: Beyond physical robots: How to achieve joint spatial reference with a smart environment

Interacting with a smart environment involves joint understanding of where things and people are or where they should be. Face-to-face interaction between humans, or between humans and robots, implies clearly identifiable perspectives on the environment that can be used to establish such a joint understanding. A smart environment, in contrast, is ubiquitous and thus perspective-independent. In this talk I will review the implications of this situation in terms of the challenges for establishing joint spatial reference between humans and smart systems, and present a somewhat unconventional solution as an opportunity.

Stephane Dufau: How a reading brain works: insights from experimental studies and modelling

Understanding how a human brain processes language in its written form has been at the heart of numerous research efforts over the last century, from the experimental works carried on in the first psychology labs to the use of modern computational models. In my talk, I will briefly review the research domain in an historical perspective and discuss the current concepts that help frame our understanding of our ability to read. I will argue that, in order to deeply represent the interaction between the core reading processes found in perception, attention, and language functions, reading is better investigated with a set of simple models rather than modelled with fully integrated neural networks. Whether computational or not, such simple models are built on basic principles like delta rule and random walks and are constrained by patterns of experimental results from both psycho- and neuro-linguistics. A series of research showcasing the method will be presented, with applications related to Natural Language Processing. More specifically, I will illustrate how text simplification has helped children with reading difficulties read better.

PROGRAMME

14th December (Wednesday) Tutorial, Day 1

09:00	REGISTRATION
09:30 - 11:00	Doctoral Symposium

Improving Care in Clinical Dentistry with Natural Language Processing of Electronic Dental Records
Hanna Pethani
Misinformation Detection via Transfer Learning
Lin Tian
A Discourse-Analytic Approach to the Study of Information Disorders: How Online Communities Legitimate Social Bonds When Communing Around Misinformation and Disinformation
Olivia Inwood
Learning to Adapt Neural Models with Limited Human Supervision in Natural Language Processing
Thuy-Trang Vu

11:00 - 11.30	MORNING TEA
11:30 - 12.30	Mentoring Session
12:30 - 14:00	LUNCH (AND MENTORING SESSION)
14:00 - 14:30	Tutorial (Part 1: Misinformation and Human Perception) Xiuzhen (Jenny) Zhang
14:30 - 15:30	Tutorial (Part 2: Misinformation and Detection) Jey Han Lau
15:30 - 16:00	AFTERNOON TEA
16:00 - 17:00	Tutorial (Part 3: Misinformation Mitigation) Xiuzhen (Jenny) Zhang
17:00	Informal Meet-n-Greet

15th December (Thursday) Day 2

8:15 - 9:00	REGISTRATION
9:00 - 9:30	ALTA/ADCS OPENING

9:30 - 10:30	Keynote 1: Ed Hovy *On the complementarity of neural and symbolic approaches, and on how to transfer between them*
10:30 - 11:00	MORNING TEA
11:00 - 12:30	Session A – (Session Chair: Jonathan Kummerfeld) Presentations are 20 minutes.

Using public domain resources and off-the-shelf tools to produce high-quality multimedia texts
Manny Rayner, Belinda Chiera and Cathy Chua
TCG-Event: Effective Task Conditioning for Generation-based Event Extraction
Fatemeh Shiri, Tongtong Wu, Yuanfang Li and Gholamreza Haffari
Complex Reading Comprehension Through Question Decomposition
Xiao-Yu Guo, Yuan-Fang Li and Gholamreza Haffari
Using Aspect-Based Sentiment Analysis to Classify Attitude-bearing Words
Pradeesh Parameswaran, Andrew Trotman, Veronica Liesaputra and David Eyers

12:30 - 13:30	LUNCH
11:00 - 12:30	Session B (ADCS/ALTA) – (Session Chair: Sarvnaz Karimi) ADCS presentations are 20 minutes and ALTA presentations are 10 minutes.

Investigating Language Use by Polarised Groups on Twitter: A Case Study of the Bushfires (ADCS)
Mehwish Nasim, Naeha Sharif, Pranav Bhandari, Derek Weber, Martin Wood, Lucia Falzon, and Yoshihisa Kashima
Robustness of Neural Rankers to Typos: A Comparative Study (ADCS)
Shengyao Zhuang, Xinyu Mao, and Guido Zuccon
Automatic Explanation Generation For Climate Science Claims (ALTA)
Rui Xing, Shraey Bhatia, Timothy Baldwin and Jey Han Lau
Improving Text-based Early Prediction by Distillation from Privileged Time-Series Text
Jinghui Liu, Daniel Capurro, Anthony Nguyen and Karin Verspoor

14:30 - 15:30	Poster Session
15:30 - 16:00	AFTERNOON TEA
16:00 - 17:00	Session C – (Session Chair: Jonathan Kummerfeld) ADCS presentations are 20 minutes and ALTA presentations are 10 minutes.

Fine-tuning a Subtle Parsing Distinction Using a Probabilistic Decision Tree: the Case of Postnominal "that" in Noun Complement Clauses vs. Relative Clauses
Zineddine Tighidet and Nicolas Ballier
Robustness of Hybrid Models in Cross-domain Readability Assessment

Ho Hung Lim, Tianyuan Cai, John S. Y. Lee and Meichun Liu

17:00 - 17:30	Keynote 2: Stephane Dufau *How a reading brain works: insights from experimental studies and modelling*
17:30 - 18:30	Poster Session
18:30 - late	ALTA/ADCS DINNER @ TONSLEY HOTEL RESTAURANT

16th December (Friday) Day 3

09:00 - 10:00	Keynote 3: Thora Tenbrink *Beyond physical robots: How to achieve joint spatial reference with a smart environment*
10:00 - 10:30	Keynote 4: Barbara Tversky *Mind in Motion: How Action Shapes Thought*
10:30 - 11:00	Rolling Discussion
11:00 - 11:30	Morning Tea
11:30 - 12:15	Session D (Shared Task Challenge) – (Session Chair: Diego Molla) Presentations are 10 minutes

Overview of the 2022 ALTA Shared task: PIBOSO sentence classification, 10 years later
Diego Molla
Context-Aware Sentence Classification in Evidence-Based Medicine
Biaoyan Fang and Fajri Koto
Enhancing the DeBERTa Transformers Model for Classifying Sentences from Biomedical Abstracts
Abdul Aziz, Md. Akram Hossain, and Abu Nowshed Chy
Automatic Classification of Evidence Based Medicine Using Transformers
Necva Bolucu, Pinar Uskaner Hepsag

12:15 - 12:30	ALTA AGM
12:30 - 13:30	LUNCH
13:30 - 15:30	Session E (Abstracts) – (Session Chair: Gabriela Ferraro) Presentations are 20 minutes

Verifying Urarina Language Phonemes With TensorFlow
Michael Dorin and Judith Dorin
A Multi-Faceted Reward for Adversarial Attacks on Text Classifiers
Tom Roth, Inigo Jauregi Unanue, Alsharif Abuadbba and Massimo Piccardi

	Probing of Quantitative Values in Abstractive Summarization Models Nathan White *Zero-shot Slot Filling with Slot-Prefix Prompting and Attention Relationship Descriptor* Qiaoyang Luo and Lingqiao Liu
	Writing Progress in Australian Schools: An Experimental Proof-of-concept Application Charbel El-Khaissi
15:30 - 16:00	AFTERNOON TEA
16:00 - 16:50	Session F (Best Papers) – (Session Chair: Jennifer Biggs) Presentations are 20 minutes
	The Corpus of Australian and New Zealand Spoken English: A new resource of naturalistic speech transcripts Steven Coats *The Role of Context in Vaccine Stance Prediction for Twitter Users* Aleney Khoo, Maciej Rybinski, Sarvnaz Karimi and Adam Dunn.
16:50 - 17:30	Best Paper Award/Shared Task Award & Closing Remarks

Table of Contents

The Corpus of Australian and New Zealand Spoken English: A new resource of naturalistic speech transcripts 1
Steven Coats

Using public domain resources and off-the-shelf tools to produce high-quality multimedia texts . . 6
Manny Rayner, Belinda Chiera and Cathy Chua

The Role of Context in Vaccine Stance Prediction for Twitter Users 16
Aleney Khoo, Maciej Rybinski, Sarvnaz Karimi and Adam Dunn

TCG-Event: Effective Task Conditioning for Generation-based Event Extraction 22
Fatemeh Shiri, Tongtong Wu, Yuanfang Li and Gholamreza Haffari

Complex Reading Comprehension Through Question Decomposition 31
Xiao-Yu Guo, Yuan-Fang Li and Gholamreza Haffari

Using Aspect-Based Sentiment Analysis to Classify Attitude-bearing Words 41
Pradeesh Parameswaran, Andrew Trotman, Veronica Liesaputra and David Eyers

Fine-tuning a Subtle Parsing Distinction Using a Probabilistic Decision Tree: the Case of Postnominal "that" in Noun Complement Clauses vs. Relative Clauses 52
Zineddine Tighidet and Nicolas Ballier

Robustness of Hybrid Models in Cross-domain Readability Assessment 62
Ho Hung Lim, Tianyuan Cai, John S. Y. Lee and Meichun Liu

Specifying Optimisation Problems for Declarative Programs in Precise Natural Language 68
Rolf Schwitter

Improving Text-based Early Prediction by Distillation from Privileged Time-Series Text 73
Jinghui Liu, Daniel Capurro, Anthony Nguyen and Karin Verspoor

A DistilBERTopic Model for Short Text Documents 84
Junaid Rashid, Jungeun Kim, Usman Naseem and Amir Hussain

Generating Code-Switched Text from Monolingual Text with Dependency Tree 90
Bryan Gregorius and Takeshi Okadome

Stability of Forensic Text Comparison System 98
Susan Brown and Shunichi Ishihara

Academic Curriculum Generation using Wikipedia for External Knowledge 107
Anurag Reddy Muthyala and Vikram Pudi

Interactive Rationale Extraction for Text Classification 115
Jiayi Dai, Mi-Young Kim and Randy Goebel

Automatic Explanation Generation For Climate Science Claims 122
Rui Xing, Shraey Bhatia, Timothy Baldwin and Jey Han Lau

Zhangzhou Implosives and Their Variations 130
Yishan Huang and Gwendolyn Hyslop

Evaluating the Examiner: The Perils of Pearson Correlation for Validating Text Similarity Metrics 138
Gisela Vallejo, Timothy Baldwin and Lea Frermann

Can Language Models Help in System Security? Investigating Log Anomaly Detection using BERT 147
Crispin Almodovar, Fariza Sabrina, Sarvnaz Karimi and Salahuddin Azad

A Semantics of Spatial Expressions for interacting with unmanned aerial vehicles 156
Lucas Domingos and Paulo Santos

Enhancing the DeBERTa Transformers Model for Classifying Sentences from Biomedical Abstracts 164
Abdul Aziz, Md. Akram Hossain and Abu Nowshed Chy

Textstar: a Fast and Lightweight Graph-Based Algorithm for Extractive Summarization and Keyphrase Extraction 169
David Brock, Ali Khan, Tam Doan, Alicia Lin, Yifan Guo and Paul Tarau

Contrastive Visual and Language Learning for Visual Relationship Detection . . . . N/A
Thanh Tran, Maelic Neau, Paulo Santos and David Powers

Shared Task (Not Peer Reviewed)

Overview of the 2022 ALTA Shared task: PIBOSO sentence classification, 10 years later 179
Diego Mollá

Estimating the Strength of Authorship Evidence with a Deep-Learning-Based Approach 184
Shunichi Ishihara, Satoru Tsuge, Mitsuyuki Inaba and Wataru Zaitsu

Automatic Classification of Evidence Based Medicine Using Transformers 189
Necva Bolucu and Pinar Uskaner Hepsag

Context-Aware Sentence Classification in Evidence-Based Medicine 194
Biaoyan Fang and Fajri Koto

The Corpus of Australian and New Zealand Spoken English: A new resource of naturalistic speech transcripts

Steven Coats
English, Faculty of Humanities
University of Oulu, Finland
steven.coats@oulu.fi

Abstract

The Corpus of Australian and New Zealand Spoken English (CoANZSE) is a 190-million-word corpus of Automatic Speech Recognition (ASR) transcripts from YouTube channels of local councils and other governmental bodies in 472 locations in Australia and New Zealand. CoANZSE can be used to examine grammar and syntax in Australian and New Zealand spoken English, and because tokens are word-timed and transcripts are linked to videos, it can serve as the starting point for phonetic or multi-modal studies. Two exploratory analyses demonstrate differences between Australia and New Zealand in the relative frequencies of double modals, a rare non-standard syntactic feature, and show that transcripts from Australia and New Zealand can be distinguished on the basis of common lexical items.

1 Introduction and Background

The study of regional grammatical variation in English has been stimulated by new methodological approaches (e.g., Nerbonne, 2009; Szmrecsanyi, 2011) and new sources of data in recent years, with corpus-based statistical analyses coming to the forefront, often utilizing textual data from the Web and social media platforms (e.g., Grieve et al., 2019; Hovy and Purschke, 2018; Dunn, 2019). These studies have provided new insights into the structure and distribution of varieties of English, but corpus-based empirical studies of regional patterns of grammatical variation in contemporary English speech remain few. Corpora of transcribed speech may be focused on specific locations, or may not exhibit sufficient geographic granularity for reliable inferences about regional patterns. Some speech corpora are unsuitable for analyses of contemporary language phenomena as they contain mostly transcripts of speech from older speakers recorded in the middle of the 20th century. Most corpora of transcribed speech are not large enough to capture rare features in grammar and syntax (e.g., Corrigan et al., 2012; Greenbaum, 1998; Du Bois et al., 2000-2005; Anderwald and Wagner, 2007).

The widespread use of Automatic Speech Recognition (ASR) by conferencing and video streaming or sharing sites has made it possible to create large corpora of geo-located naturalistic speech, opening up new possibilities for in-depth studies of variation in English. This paper introduces the Corpus of Australian and New Zealand Spoken English (CoANZSE),[1] a 190-million-word corpus of 56,815 word-timed, part-of-speech-tagged Automatic Speech Recognition (ASR) transcripts, corresponding to more than 24,000 hours of video, from 482 YouTube channels of local councils or other institutions of local governance in 472 locations in Australia and New Zealand. In the following, some existing Australian and New Zealand speech corpora are introduced, then the methods used to create CoANZSE are briefly described. Two example exploratory analyses are provided: the syntactic features of double modals is identified in the transcripts, and a classifier is used to distinguish Australian from New Zealand transcripts. ASR transcripts contain errors, so methods of analysis must be robust for use with "noisy data". The summary notes a few possibilities for future work with CoANZSE and similar data.

For Australia and New Zealand, several corpora of transcribed speech exist. The Australian National Corpus (Cassidy et al., 2012) includes speech transcripts from the Australian component of the International Corpus of English (Greenbaum, 1996), the Monash Corpus of Spoken Australian English (Bradshaw et al., 2010), and the Griffith Corpus of Spoken Australian English (Haugh and Chang, 2013). The geographical coverage of these corpora, however, is inconsistent: the Monash Corpus consists mainly of transcripts of Melbourne speakers,

[1] https://cc.oulu.fi/~scoats/CoANZSE.html

and the Griffith Corpus of Brisbane speakers. In terms of corpus size, existing Australian corpora of speech transcripts are mostly not large enough for research into patterns of syntactic variation.

Several corpora of English speech transcripts have been created from the speech of New Zealanders. The spoken component of the New Zealand International Corpus of English (ICE-NZ) comprises approximately 600,000 words, mainly recorded in the 1990s. The Wellington Corpus of Spoken New Zealand English (Holmes et al., 1998), approximately 1 million words in size, contains transcripts of formal and informal speech, also collected mostly in the 1990s. The Origins of New Zealand English Corpus (Gordon et al., 2007) comprises transcripts of recordings of older New Zealand speakers made by New Zealand Radio in the middle of the 20th century, in addition to recordings made by researchers in the 1990s and 2000s. Transcript corpora from Australia and New Zealand have been used for a wide range of studies, but regional variation in grammar and syntax has not been a consistent focus of research attention, due both to geographical sampling and corpus size considerations.

2 Data and methods

Lists of councils, shires, and other administrative units were obtained from state, territorial and national government websites in Australia and New Zealand: 157 from New South Wales, 78 from Victoria, 69 from South Australia, 178 from Western Australia, 21 from Northern Territory, 77 from Queensland, 29 from Tasmania, and 9 from the Australian Capital Territory. A list of 78 councils was retrieved for New Zealand.

Of these 696 local government entities, 578 had web pages, which were were then scraped for links to YouTube channels. The procedure returned 515 YouTube channels, of which 482 contained video content. Channels were manually checked to ensure they corresponded to the linked municipality. Latitude-longitude coordinates were retrieved by inputting the street address listed on the corresponding web page to a geo-coding script. Locations of the sampled channels are shown in Figure 1.

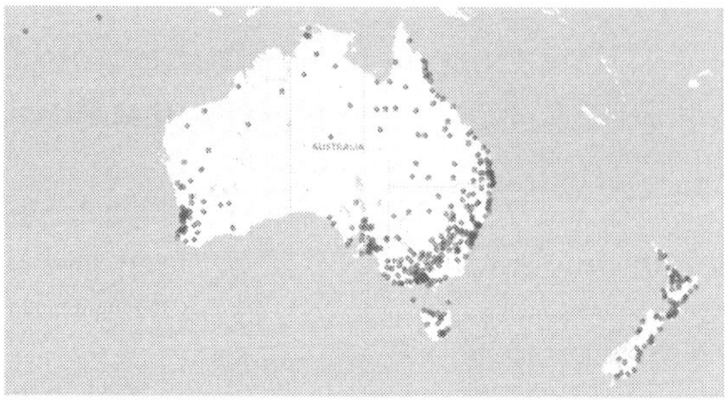

Figure 1: CoANZSE channel locations

All available ASR transcripts were retrieved from the targeted channels with a Python script, using functions in the yt-dlp[2] library. A custom script parsed transcripts and appended word-timing information; part-of-speech tagging was undertaken using SpaCy's en_core_web_sm model.[3] Table 1 shows corpus size by state/territory in terms of channel, transcript, and word count as well as the corresponding aggregate video length.

Many of the transcripts in CoANZSE record meetings, but the transcripts in the corpus are from many other video types as well, such as interviews, informational and public service videos, vlogs, public readings, and other content types.

3 Exploratory analyses

CoANZSE may be useful for many kinds of linguistic analysis, including regional analyses of grammar and syntax and discourse studies of the content of (for example) public meetings. Because the underlying video and audio data are available, scripting pipelines can be set up that extract targeted content for acoustic or multi-modal analysis. Two preliminary, exploratory analyses are noted below.

3.1 Double modals

The syntactic feature of double modals (e.g., *I might could help you with that*; cf. standard English *I could help you with that* or *I might help you with that*), traditionally held to be restricted to speech in the Southern US and the Northern British Isles, is attested as absent for Australian English (Kortmann and Lunkenheimer, 2013). Recent work using naturalistic data, however, shows that the feature has a broader geographical extent than previously thought (Coats, 2022, In review). A preliminary search for double modals in CoANZSE resulted in 3,119 hits; the first approximately 400 of these were examined in their original videos in order to remove false positives. This exploratory query showed a large number of Australian double modals to be authentic naturalistic usages (Fig. 2).

[2] `https://github.com/yt-dlp/yt-dlp.`

[3] `https://spacy.io/usage/models.`

Table 1: Corpus Size by Country Location

Location	Channels	Videos	Words	Length (h)
Australian Capital Territory	8	650	915,542	111.79
New South Wales	114	9,741	27,580,773	3,428.87
Northern Territory	11	289	315,300	48.72
New Zealand	74	18,029	84,058,661	10,175.80
Queensland	58	7,356	19,988,051	2,642.75
South Australia	50	3,537	13,856,275	1,716.72
Tasmania	21	1,260	5,086,867	636.99
Victoria	78	12,138	35,304,943	4,205.40
Western Australia	68	3,815	8,422,484	1,063.78
Total	482	56,815	195,528,896	24,030.82

CoANZSE data may therefore be able to provide researchers with a more realistic starting point for analyses of the geographical distribution of grammatical and syntactic features in spoken English in Australia and New Zealand. From a theoretical perspective, instead of a model in which a given feature is held to be categorically present (or absent) for a pre-defined language variety, CoANZSE data may show that syntactic features of English can be found in naturalistic speech in many locations: the question of their use is "in many cases a matter of statistical frequency rather than the presence or absence of a feature" (Kortmann, 2010, p. 843).

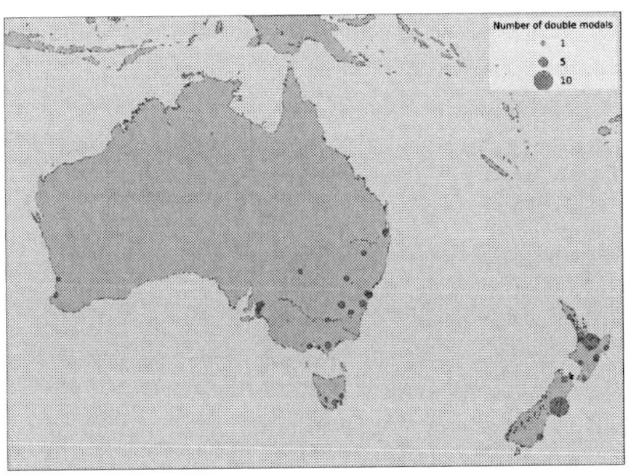

Figure 2: Verified double modal locations

3.2 Lexical distinctiveness

In order to test the hypothesis that Australian and New Zealand varieties of spoken English can be distinguished in CoANZSE, a simple machine learning model was created using Scikit-learn (Pedregosa et al., 2011). A sample of 10,000 randomly-selected CoANZSE transcripts was converted to term frequency-inverse document frequency (tf-idf) matrices using the 500 most common words in these transcripts, then trained using a linear support vector machine (Joachims, 1998) with 80% of the Australian and New Zealand transcripts, using parameters optimized with the GridSearchCV method in Scikit and balanced class weights. The model then predicted the country labels for the test data (1,359 Australian and 641 New Zealand transcripts). Model accuracy is summarized in Table 2.

The overall model accuracy of 0.80 suggests that there may be different usage patterns for common lexical items in discourse in Australian and New Zealand spoken English varieties. This preliminary finding, however, needs more thorough linguistic investigation. One approach would be to undertake a multi-dimensional analysis, using regular expressions to explore the frequencies of a number of grammatical and syntactic phenomena.

4 Caveats

Although the accuracy of ASR transcription systems continues to increase, transcripts of naturalistic speech contain errors due to factors such as audio recording quality, speech fluency or lack thereof, use of out-of-vocabulary words, slang, or dialect words, strong regional accent, or prosodic features (Aksënova et al., 2021). For a subset of CoANZSE videos, both ASR and manually-uploaded transcript files can be retrieved from YouTube; calculating the word error rate (WER) on the basis of these shared transcripts resulted in a value of 0.14, after careful filtering. YouTube transcripts are not diarized (i.e. have no indication of speaker turns), so they are not suitable "out-of-the-box" for analyses of language phenomena on the basis of social or demographic speaker traits. Two

Table 2: Binary classification results

Label	Precision	Recall	F1	Support	Accuracy
Australia	0.82	0.90	0.86	1359	0.80
New Zealand	0.74	0.59	0.66	641	

basic approaches for use of CoANZSE and similar data can be taken: First, the method of manual verification of targeted linguistic phenomena, utilized for the preliminary analysis of double modals noted above, can be done quickly because the transcripts are word-timed and linked to videos. This approach allows the analyst to identify and filter out transcript errors, as well as annotate additional features that may be of interest (for example, some speaker demographic traits). In a large-scale approach, a focus on relatively frequent features and broad geographical granularity will help to mitigate the effects of transcript errors, which would be outweighed by the greater frequency of correct transcriptions (Agarwal et al., 2007).

5 Summary and Outlook

CoANZSE is a large corpus of spoken English from Australia and New Zealand comprising ASR transcripts of YouTube videos uploaded by local councils and other local government entities. Two exploratory analyses using CoANZSE data attest use of double modals in naturalistic speech and show that Australian and New Zealand transcripts can be distinguished on the basis of their different rates of use of common words.

There are many possibilities for future work with CoANZSE data. Because the underlying video and audio recordings of CoANZSE transcripts are available, a script pipeline can be set up to retrieve video or audio excerpts for features of interest, which can then be analyzed using common tools such as ffmpeg and Praat. Such an approach permits, for example, the semi-automatic analysis of acoustic and prosodic properties of speech such as formant frequencies or pitch contours; video data retrieved using a scripting pipeline approach could be used for corpus-based analysis of multi-modal aspects of communication.

A tantalizing possibility for CoANZSE data is to shed light on the possible development of regional varieties of English within Australia and New Zealand in terms of pronunciation (Cox and Palethorpe, 2019), lexis, and grammar. For Australia, previous studies have mostly maintained that little regional variation is evident, at least in grammar or syntax, a situation usually held to result from the relatively young age of the variety (Murray and Manns, 2020). As noted by Burridge, however, the necessary components for regional diversification, namely "time, physical/social distance and the processes of linguistic change" (2020, p. 185), are in place in the broader Australian English speech community.

Finally, because CoANZSE contains transcripts of public meetings and content broadcast by local government entities, its content may prove to be useful for discourse analyses of a broad range of contemporary political and cultural phenomena such as environmental issues, migration, elections, or other topics.

Widespread use of video streaming and sharing sites and ASR transcription have in recent years opened up new sources of data for the empirical study of language. It is hoped that the CoANZSE resource will allow researchers to gain new insights into the current status of English in Australia and New Zealand and thus further our understanding of ongoing the development and diversification of the language.

References

Sumeet Agarwal, Shantanu Godbole, Diwakar Punjani, and Shourya Roy. 2007. How much noise is too much: A study in automatic text classification. In *Seventh IEEE International Conference on Data Mining (ICDM 2007)*, pages 3–12.

Alëna Aksënova, Daan van Esch, James Flynn, and Pavel Golik. 2021. How might we create better benchmarks for speech recognition? In *Proceedings of the 1st Workshop on Benchmarking: Past, Present and Future*, pages 22–34, Online. Association for Computational Linguistics.

Liselotte Anderwald and Suzanne Wagner. 2007. The Freiburg English Dialect Corpus: Applying corpus-linguistic research tools to the analysis of dialect data. In Joan C. Beal, Karen P. Corrigan, and Hermann Moisl, editors, *Creating and digitizing language corpora volume 1: Synchronic databases*, pages 35–53. Palgrave Macmillan, Houndmills, Basingstoke.

Julie Bradshaw, Kate Burridge, and Michael Clyne.

2010. The Monash Corpus of Spoken Australian English. In *Proceedings of the 2008 Conference of the Australian Linguistics Society*. Australian Linguistic Society.

Kate Burridge. 2020. History of Australian English. In Louisa Willoughby and Howard Manns, editors, *Australian English reimagined: Structure, features and developments*, pages 175–192. Routledge.

Steve Cassidy, Michael Haugh, Pam Peters, and Mark Fallu. 2012. The Australian national corpus: National infrastructure for language resources. In *Proceedings of the Eighth International Conference on Language Resources and Evaluation (LREC'12)*, pages 3295–3299, Istanbul, Turkey. European Language Resources Association (ELRA).

Steven Coats. 2022. *Naturalistic double modals in North America*. American Speech.

Steven Coats. In review. Double Modals in contemporary British and Irish Speech.

Karen P. Corrigan, Isabelle Buchstaller, Adam Mearns, and Hermann Moisl. 2012. The Diachronic Electronic Corpus of Tyneside English.

Felicity Cox and Sallyanne Palethorpe. 2019. Vowel variation in a standard context across four major Australian cities. In *Proceedings of the 19th International Congress of Phonetic Sciences, Melbourne, Australia 2019*, pages 577–581. Australasian Speech Science and Technology Association.

John W. Du Bois, Wallace L. Chafe, Charles Meyer, Sandra A. Thompson, Robert Englebretson, and Nii Martey. 2000-2005. Santa Barbara Corpus of Spoken American English.

Jonathan Dunn. 2019. *Global syntactic variation in seven languages: Toward a computational dialectology*. Frontiers in Artificial Intelligence, Section Language and Computation.

Elizabeth Gordon, Margaret Maclagan, and Jennifer Hay. 2007. The ONZE corpus. In Joan C. Beal, Karen P. Corrigan, and Hermann Moisl, editors, *Creating and digitizing language corpora volume 2: Diachronic databases*, pages 82–104. Palgrave Macmillan, Houndmills, Basingstoke.

Sidney Greenbaum, editor. 1996. *Comparing English worldwide: The International Corpus of English*. Clarendon Press.

Sidney Greenbaum. 1998. A proposal for an international computerized corpus of english. *World Englishes*, 7(3):315.

Jack Grieve, Chris Montgomery, Andrea Nini, Akira Murakami, and Diansheng Guo. 2019. Mapping lexical dialect variation in British English using Twitter. *Frontiers in Artificial Intelligence*, 2.

Michael Haugh and Wei-Lin Melody Chang. 2013. Collaborative creation of spoken language corpora. In Tim Greer, Yuriko Kite, and Donna Tatsuki, editors, *Pragmatics and Language Learning, Volume 13*, pages 133–159. National Foreign Language Resource Center, University of Hawaii.

Janet Holmes, Bernadette Vine, and Gary Johnson. 1998. Guide to the Wellington Corpus of Spoken New Zealand English.

Dirk Hovy and Christoph Purschke. 2018. Capturing regional variation with distributed place representations and geographic retrofitting. In *Proceedings of the 2018 Conference on Empirical Methods in Natural Language Processing*, pages 4383–4394.

Thorsten Joachims. 1998. *Text categorization with support vector machines: Learning with many relevant features*. Springer.

Bernd Kortmann. 2010. Areal variation in syntax. In Peter Auer and Jürgen E. Schmidt, editors, *Language and space: An international handbook of linguistic variation, volume 1, theories and methods*, pages 837–64. de Gruyter Mouton.

Bernd Kortmann and Kerstin Lunkenheimer, editors. 2013. *The Electronic World Atlas of Varieties of English (eWAVE)*. Max Planck Institute for Evolutionary Anthropology, Leipzig.

Lee Murray and Howard Manns. 2020. Lexical and morphosyntactic variation in australian english. In Louisa Willoughby and Howard Manns, editors, *Australian English reimagined: Structure, features and developments*, pages 120–133. Routledge.

John Nerbonne. 2009. Data-driven dialectology. *Language and Linguistics Compass*, 3:175–198.

F. Pedregosa, G. Varoquaux, A. Gramfort, V. Michel, B. Thirion, O. Grisel, M. Blondel, P. Prettenhofer, R. Weiss, V. Dubourg, J. Vanderplas, A. Passos, D. Cournapeau, M. Brucher, M. Perrot, and E. Duchesnay. 2011. Scikit-learn: Machine learning in Python. *Journal of Machine Learning Research*, 12:2825–2830.

Benedikt Szmrecsanyi. 2011. Corpus-based dialectometry: A methodological sketch. *Corpora*, 6(1):45–76.

Using public domain resources and off-the-shelf tools to produce high-quality multimedia texts

Manny Rayner
FTI/TIM
University of Geneva, Switzerland
Emmanuel.Rayner@unige.ch

Belinda Chiera
The University of South Australia
Adelaide, Australia
Belinda.Chiera@unisa.edu.au

Cathy Chua
Independent scholar
Adelaide, Australia
cathyc@pioneerbooks.com.au

Abstract

In the turbulent world of 2022, where mass population movements due to war and disaster are becoming increasingly common, language skills are more relevant than ever. People who wish to achieve a high level of proficiency when learning a new language benefit from reading literary texts, but many learners find this a challenging hurdle. Annotating texts with integrated audio and translations is a popular way to try and make them easier to approach. However, doing this automatically with TTS and machine translation engines produces unengaging results, while human annotation is slow and expensive. Here, we present a method that uses simple scripts and readily available computational resources for speech recognition and sentence alignment to combine public-domain resources from sites like Gutenberg and LibriVox into high-quality annotated multimedia versions of literary texts. Initial results with French texts of up to 80K words in length are promising, with audio/text word error rates under 0.25% and audio/translation word error rates around 1%, producing results that are usable after only minimal postediting.

1 Introduction and motivation

In Anthony Powell's semi-autobiographical WW II novel *The Soldier's Art*, the narrator mentions to his division commander that he can read Balzac in the original French, and is surprised by the response: General Liddament immediately tells him to apply for a job in Military Intelligence. Since 1943, there have of course been some important changes. English has firmly established itself as the world language, and language technology has made enormous progress, but the fundamentals are the same. People with strong language skills are still prized by the security services, who see little prospect of replacing them with Google Translate and related AI/ML-based technologies. Large-scale movements of linguistic communities, driven by war, climate change, and economic disaster, are making these skills increasingly relevant, not just to Intelligence but to many related sectors including immigration, law enforcement and social services. Learning to read complex texts is an essential component in acquiring high level language skills. Duolingo and similar gamified platforms are a popular way to get started with a new language and reach low intermediate level, but they will not give the large vocabulary and grasp of idiom that comes from extensive reading.

Benchmarks for language skills are competency in reading, writing, listening and speaking. A simple but effective technology for supporting the development of reading skills, widely used at least since the days of the Roman Empire (Dickey, 2016), is the bilingual text: the text is divided into segments, each one paired with a gloss/translation in the annotation language. More recently, Reading While Listening (RWL; Woodall, 2010; Isozaki, 2014; Chang and Millett, 2014; Friedland et al., 2017; Pellicer-Sánchez et al., 2018; Schwieter and Benati, 2019) simultaneously supports the development of reading and listening skills. As put forward in Krashen's seminal Input Hypothesis and Reading Hypothesis (e.g. Krashen, 1982, 1989, 2004), reading as a language acquisition technique works best where the learner is presented with comprehensible text in a low-stress situation. This is the basic rationale behind both bilingual texts and RWL.

Although RWL studies support the idea that enjoyment is key and that literature is an answer (Woodall, Chang, Isozaki), there are major obstacles to the implementation. Expense — Woodall's study involved copies of hard copy book and audio for the class; lack of resources — Chang could only reference short news items of video plus transcript online; and variety — anecdotally, Lee (2019) gives a detailed example of what we all know intuitively; it is offputting to have to read something we do not enjoy. Added to this, the process is an often less than ideal user experience, for example, constant rewinding of audio.

Online learning environments are an obvious way to resolve the sorts of problems we see in such studies. There are now many platforms that provide functionality which includes bilingual texts, RWL, and additional features: we will call these "multimodal documents". Examples include the Microsoft Azure Immersive Reader[1], LingQ[2], Learning With Texts[3], the Perseus Digital Library's Scaife viewer[4] and Clilstore[5]. The most common strategy for providing audio is to create it using a Text To Speech (TTS) engine; the most common strategy for including translations or glosses is to integrate machine translation engines and/or electronic dictionaries.

A striking example of this approach is the Azure Immersive Reader. The upside of the platform is immediately apparent. For a large number of reading languages and annotation languages, the learner only has to point the tool to the text they wish to read, and they are immediately presented with a version containing TTS audio and machine-translation generated glosses in the annotation language. Unfortunately, after even an hour of using the tool, the downside is equally apparent; the quality of the annotations is quite low. Many learners will find it fatiguing to listen to TTS audio or read MT-engine generated glosses for more than a short time. A couple of recent studies have systematically compared TTS-generated and human-recorded audio for this kind of document (Akhlaghi et al., 2021, 2022a). For the languages where TTS does best, teachers and native speakers rate it as comparable with non-professional human audio from the point of view of pedagogical adequacy; but even non-professional human voices are rated as much more natural and much pleasanter to listen to. However, though human-created annotations produce multimodal texts of substantially higher quality, the time and effort required to create them is considerable.

In this paper, we explore a possible compromise between the competing alternatives of creating multimodal documents by automatic and human annotation. There is a great deal of high-quality public domain literary content available for free download, in both text and audio form; well known sites include Gutenberg[6] and LibriVox[7]. Given a source-language text, source-language audio, and a target-language text, it is in principle possible to perform automatic or semi-automatic alignment to create an annotated multimedia document.

The question is how well the idea works in practice: what tools are needed, how high the error rates are, and how much manual cleaning up has to be be done afterwards. When we started the work described here, we were in fact fairly pessimistic. In particular, descriptions of the process used to generate the widely used LibriSpeech corpus (Panayotov et al., 2015) suggested to us that the error rates for audio alignment of literary texts would be quite high, maybe between 3 and 5 percent. Another moderately recent paper (Xu et al., 2015) suggested to us that the task of performing translation alignment on literary texts was also challenging. It seemed reasonable to assume that performing both tasks at once would be harder than performing either one separately.

The experiments we present here, carried out using the open source LARA platform[8], suggest that the task is much more tractable than we had originally believed. Work is still at an early stage, but we now think it reasonable to hope that, for many literary texts, error rates of 1 percent or lower can be achieved using readily available off-the-shelf tools to perform speech recognition and translation alignment, with the outputs from these tools combined using straightforward methods.

The rest of the paper is organised as follows. Section 2 briefly presents LARA. Section 3 describes the alignment method, and Section 4 our initial experiments. The final section concludes and suggests further directions.

[1] https://azure.microsoft.com/en-us/services/immersive-reader/

[2] https://www.lingq.com/

[3] https://sourceforge.net/projects/learning-with-texts/

[4] https://scaife.perseus.org/

[5] http://multidict.net/clilstore/

[6] https://www.gutenberg.org/

[7] https://librivox.org/

[8] https://www.unige.ch/callector/lara

2 LARA

LARA (Akhlaghi et al., 2019; Bédi et al., 2020; Zuckerman et al., 2021; Akhlaghi et al., 2022b) is a platform for producing annotated multimodal texts, under development by an international consortium since 2018. Texts can include a variety of annotations, including audio, translations, concordances, interactive images and video; links to many such texts can be found on the LARA examples page[9]. For the purposes of the current paper, the only features that will be of interest are audio and translation annotations attached to text segments.

LARA is a good platform for doing this kind of experiment, since it is open source, supports many languages, and produces attractive results which can immediately be posted on the web. In § 4, we provide links to several examples of LARA documents created using the methods described here.

3 Multimedia documents by alignment

We describe a simple method that combines data produced by readily available online resources to add annotations to a text document. The methods were implemented in Python inside LARA but use no special properties of the framework. We assume that the input consists of a) a text in the reading language, b) a translation of the text in the annotation language, and c) an audio version of the text in the reading language. The desired output is a version of the text in the reading language, segmented into units (typically sentence-length or a bit larger) each of which is associated with a translation in the annotation language and an audio file. Table 1 in the next section includes links to examples.

We assume the existence of the following third-party resources:

Splitting on silences A tool that can take an audio file and split it into segments separated by silences of a designed minimum length and loudness contrast.

Speech recognition A tool that can take an audio file and return a (generally more or less inaccurate) text transcription.

Translation alignment A tool that can take a large text and a translation, and convert them into an ordered sequence of aligned units typically of around sentence size.

For these experiments, we used ffmpeg[10] for splitting on silences, Google Cloud Speech-to-Text[11] for speech recognition, and YouAlign[12] for sentence alignment. The processing steps are as follows:[13]

1. **Resources:** Start with a) source-language text, b) annotation-language text, c) source-language audio.

2. **Translation alignment:** Send the source-language and annotation-language text files to the sentence aligner, to create two parallel sentence-segmented corpora.

3. **Source segmented by translation alignment:** Add markings to the source corpus showing the breaks corresponding to the translation alignment.

4. **Split on silences:** Use the split-on-silences tool to divide up the audio corpus, choosing thresholds that make typical pieces a bit smaller than sentences. In practice it is quick to find such thresholds.

5. **Speech recognition:** Send the pieces of audio generated by the previous step to the speech recogniser.

6. **Make double-aligned text:** Use a beam search to align the sequence of recognition results against the text.[14] Add markings to the source corpus showing the breaks corresponding to the audio alignment. The result is a text that is segmented both by translation alignment and by audio alignment.

7. **Post-process double-aligned text:** Post-process the source corpus, iteratively applying a small set of transformations that reduce differences between the translation alignment and the audio alignment. Most importantly, if a translation alignment marker and an audio alignment marker are separated

[9] `https://www.unige.ch/callector/lara-content`

[10] `https://www.ffmpeg.org/`

[11] `https://cloud.google.com/speech-to-text`

[12] `https://youalign.com/`

[13] The appendix to this paper gives details on how to obtain and use the code.

[14] In these experiments, the beam width used was 80 tokens.

by text which does not include a word, move this text to the other side of the earlier marker.

8. **Make joint aligned text:** Segment the source text by breaking at the points where the two types of segmentation markers agree. In each segment of the jointly segmented corpus produced by the previous step, concatenate the component audio segments from the audio segmentation and the component translation segments from the translation segmentation.

The result of the above series of operations gives the final annotated corpus. Obviously there is no guarantee of success: in the worst case, there will only be one segment. In practice, however, we have found that the joint segmentation is fine-grained enough that it appears quite useful.

In the next section, we will give examples of what happens with substantial texts. Figure 1 illustrates the processing flow for a passage taken from one of these.

4 Initial experiments

Table 1 summarises the results of initial experiments. We present the texts used, the metrics, and the results, and discuss their significance.

4.1 Texts

We used four French texts with accompanying audio and English translations: Rimbaud's *Les poètes de sept ans* (long poem), Maupassant's *La parure* (short story), Flaubert's *Un cœur simple* (novella), and Proust's *Combray* (novel). All four are well known pieces of French literature. The first three often appear as course reading in advanced French courses; the fourth is generally regarded as difficult even at this level. Our rationale for choosing it was curiosity to try a worst case scenario. If the method gave credible results on something as challenging as Proust (very long text, very long sentences, very complex grammatical structure, very large vocabulary), we postulated that it would probably work on many other texts too. Audio was in all cases taken from the LitteratureAudio site[15], and text from Gutenberg.

4.2 Metrics

The specific task we study in this paper is not well known in the literature, though it has points of contact with well known tasks. We adapt standard metrics in as conservative a way as possible.

We take the hopefully uncontroversial point of view that the quality of a triple alignment of the kind we are interested in here, simultaneous alignment of audio, text and translation, depends on three things: a) the quality of the audio/source-text alignment, b) the quality of the audio/translation alignment, and c) the quality of the segmentation. (a) and (b) are obvious. (c) is slightly less obvious, but a moment's reflection shows that it is essential. In the trivial alignment where the whole text becomes one segment, the error rates for (a) and (b) are zero, but this is clearly a very bad alignment. We need some measure of the extent to which the segmentation divides the text into appropriate pieces.

For (a), audio/source-text alignment, our metric is simple word error rate (WER). For each segment, we compare the aligned text with the reference text and compute WER in the usual way. For (b), audio/translation alignment, we decided that WER was in this case also the most appropriate metric. It is not a common metric for translation quality, but the specific properties of the task suggested to us that metrics like BLEU, METEOR etc (Papineni et al., 2002; Banerjee and Lavie, 2005) would work much less well as error rates are very low, and we are producing translations by the unusual method of extracting segments of an existing translation. It seemed logical to use a metric which measures how many of the correct words had been extracted: in practice, we found that it was virtually always the case that the correct match could be identified.

The least obvious metric is the one for (c). After reviewing the relevant literature, we decided to use the *boundary similarity* metric of (Fournier, 2013), which returns a number between 0 and 1 measuring the similarity of a given segmentation to a gold standard segmentation. As described in the 2013 paper, boundary similarity is the result of substantial work correcting and improving previous segmentation metrics. It has been used by several studies since then (e.g. Özmen et al., 2014; Shaw, 2015; dos Reis Mota, 2019), and is implemented in a readily available Python package.[16]

For the texts used, we created reference segmentations by comparing the text and translation, dividing them into minimal units where there was intuitively a clear text/translation alignment. In

[15] https://www.litteratureaudio.com/

[16] https://pypi.org/project/segeval/

1 (a). SOURCE LANGUAGE TEXT

```
Une porte s'ouvrait sur le soir; à la lampe
On le voyait, là-haut qui râlait sur la rampe,
Sous un golfe de jour pendant du toit.  L'été
Surtout, vaincu, stupide, il était entêté
À se renfermer dans la fraîcheur des latrines:
Il pensait là, tranquille et livrant ses narines.
```

1 (b). ANNOTATION LANGUAGE TEXT

```
A doorway open to evening:  by the light
You'd see him, high up, groaning on the railing
Under a void of light hung from the roof.  In summer,
Especially, vanquished, stupefied, stubborn,
He'd shut himself in the toilet's coolness:
He could think in peace there, sacrificing his nostrils.
```

2. TRANSLATION ALIGNMENT

```
Une porte s'ouvrait sur le soir; à la lampe ->
A doorway open to evening:  by the light

On le voyait, là-haut qui râlait sur la rampe, ->
You'd see him, high up, groaning on the railing

Sous un golfe de jour pendant du toit.  ->
Under a void of light hung from the roof.

L'été -> In summer,

Surtout, vaincu, stupide, il était entêté ->
Especially, vanquished, stupefied, stubborn,

À se renfermer dans la fraîcheur des latrines:  ->
He'd shut himself in the toilet's coolness:

Il pensait là, tranquille et livrant ses narines.  ->
He could think in peace there, sacrificing his nostrils.
```

3. SOURCE TEXT SEGMENTED BY TRANSLATION ALIGNMENT

```
//Une porte s'ouvrait sur le soir; à la lampe//
On le voyait, là-haut qui râlait sur la rampe,
//Sous un golfe de jour pendant du toit.  //L'été//
Surtout, vaincu, stupide, il était entêté//
À se renfermer dans la fraîcheur des latrines:
//Il pensait là, tranquille et livrant ses narines.//
```

Figure 1: Example of processing (passage from *Les poètes de sept ans*). Source text in black, translated text in blue, LARA markup in red. Double slashes (//) mark segments in the translation alignment. [Continued on next page]

5. RECOGNITION RESULTS FOR SPLIT AUDIO FILES

```
"une porte s'ouvrait sur le soir", "à la lampe on le voyait là au
pire aller sur la rampe sous un golf 2 jours pendant du toit", "l'été
surtout", "vaincu stupide", "il était temps tu étais à se renfermer
dans la fraîcheur des latrines", "il pensa est là tranquille", "et
livrant ses narines"
```

6. DOUBLE-ALIGNED TEXT (BEFORE POSTPROCESSING)

```
//||Une porte s'ouvrait sur le soir; ||à la lampe//
On le voyait, là-haut qui râlait sur la rampe,
//Sous un golfe de jour pendant du toit.  //||L'été//
Surtout, ||vaincu, stupide, ||il était entêté//
À se renfermer dans la fraîcheur des latrines:
//||Il pensait là, tranquille ||et livrant ses narines.
//||
```

7. DOUBLE-ALIGNED TEXT (AFTER POSTPROCESSING)

```
Une porte s'ouvrait sur le soir;|| à la lampe//
On le voyait, là-haut qui râlait sur la rampe,
//Sous un golfe de jour pendant du toit.||// L'été||//
Surtout, vaincu, stupide,|| il était entêté//
À se renfermer dans la fraîcheur des latrines:||//
Il pensait là, tranquille|| et livrant ses narines.||//
```

8. JOINT ALIGNED TEXT

```
Une porte s'ouvrait sur le soir; à la lampe
On le voyait, là-haut qui râlait sur la rampe,
Sous un golfe de jour pendant du toit.|| L'été||
Surtout, vaincu, stupide, il était entêté
À se renfermer dans la fraîcheur des latrines:||
Il pensait là, tranquille et livrant ses narines.||
```

Figure 1: [Continued from previous page] Example of processing (passage from *Les poètes de sept ans*). Source text in black, translated text in blue, LARA markup in red. Double slashes (//) mark segments in the translation alignment. Double vertical bars (||) mark segments in the audio alignment and the reconciled alignment.

Text	Text length		Seg lengths (Wds)				Error rates (%)				Links	
	Wds	Hrs	Splt	Tr-Al	J-Al	Ref	Rec	Seg	Txt	Tr	Raw	Ed
Rimbaud	535	0:04	8.6	7.4	12.6	11.7	27.5	7.1	0.8	0.8	☞	☞
Maupassant	2853	0:17	12.7	12.1	15.7	12.8	16.8	18.3	0.2	0.2	☞	☞
Flaubert	11730	1:37	8.7	17.9	18.6	14.0	18.1	24.9	0.0	1.1	☞	☞
Proust	78283	7:52	19.9	45.5	53.7	34.0	23.5	36.7	0.0	0.9	☞	☞

Table 1: Examples of annotated texts produced. “Rimbaud” = *Les poètes de sept ans*, “Maupassant” = *La parure*, “Flaubert” = *Un cœur simple*, “Proust” = *Combray*, **Text length/Wds** = length of source text in words, **Text length/Hrs** = length of source audio in hours, **Seg lengths/Splt** = average lengths of segments produced by splitting on silences, **Seg lengths/Tr-Al** = average lengths of segments produced by translation alignment, **Seg lengths/J-Al** = average lengths of segments produced by joint alignment, **Seg lengths/Ref** = average lengths of segments in gold standard segmentation, **Error rates/Rec** = speech recognition word error rate, **Error rates/Seg** = 1 − `segeval` boundary similarity score, **Error rates/Txt** = joint alignment word error rate for source text, **Error rates/Tr** = joint alignment word error rate for translations, **Link/Raw** = link to final LARA document without postediting, **Link/Ed** = link to final LARA document with postediting. LARA documents should be viewed in Chrome or Firefox.

practice, reference segments are almost always either sentences or parts of sentences delimited by punctuation marks like semi-colons, colons, dashes or parentheses.

To summarise, the quality of a given alignment is given by a triple of numbers between 0 and 1: the WER for audio/text and audio/translation alignment, and the boundary similarity score for the segmentation. It would ideally be good to reduce this to a single number, but as yet it is not clear to us how to do so effectively.

4.3 Results

We processed all four texts through the pipeline described in §3 and manually annotated the results.[17] Annotation on each text was performed as follows. A script converted the final aligned version into a form where each segment was presented in an editable form where the source text and translation appeared under an audio control. The annotator, a native English speaker with a good knowledge of French, listened to the audio and then corrected the audio and translations if they failed to match[18]. For over 90% of the segments, no correction was needed. For nearly all of the remainder, the correction was to move text either to the preceding or the following segment. The annotator also added the gold standard segmentation information. When annotation was complete, a second script was used to calculate error rates and other statistics:

Seg length/Splt: Average length, in words, of segments produced by splitting on silences.

Seg length/Tr-Al: Average length, in words, of segments produced by translation alignment.

Seg length/J-Al: Average length, in words, of segments produced by reconciliation of translation alignment and audio alignment.

Error rate/Rec: Speech recognition word error rate.

Error rate/Seg: Segmentation word error rate, defined as 1.0 minus the boundary similarity score produced by the `segeval` package.

Error rate/Txt: Word error rate for source text segments produced by reconciliation of translation alignment and audio alignment.

Error rate/Tr Word error rate for translation text segments produced by reconciliation of translation alignment and audio alignment.

Finally, we post-edited the resulting multimodal texts as follows. First, we ran each text through a script which applied the corrections to text and translations given by the manual annotations described at the beginning of this section. Second, we made a small number of layout changes to break out titles as separate segments (this allows LARA to add a table of contents in the longer texts), and to divide the text into pages. The last two columns of Table 1 contrast raw and post-edited versions.

4.4 Discussion

Table 1 gives an impression of how well the alignment method works on representative texts ranging in length from a few hundred words to nearly a hundred thousand words. We look at the three components of the metric in turn.

First, audio alignment has worked very well. Looking at the column **Error rates/Txt**, we see that WER is under 1% for all four texts, and under 0.25% for the three longest ones. It is noteworthy that the good result comes despite quite high word error rates, typically on the order of 20%, in the speech recognition (column **Error rates/Rec**). The recognition WER may be misleading, since French has many silent letters, resulting in an abnormally high proportion of homophones; thus the recogniser may for example recognise *grands* ("large", plural) when the reference word is *grand* ("large", singular). Since the matching algorithm is character-based rather than word-based, this usually makes no difference; however, changing to word-based matching only degraded performance very slightly. We need to investigate the issues further using a larger sample of texts.

Looking at the column **Error rates/Tr**, we see that translation alignment has also worked quite well, though substantially less well than audio alignment; error rates are around 1%. Examination of translation errors shows that they always result from errors in the third-party translation alignment software. Our impression is that this commercial tool has been optimised for speed rather than accuracy, and that lower error rates are possible.

[17]We have also processed other texts, including a second Proust novel. We will present the results when we have finished annotating the data. Anecdotally, the quality is similar to that obtained in the examples given.

[18]We had hoped to use two annotators, in order to obtain inter-rater reliability figures, but were unable to find a second person willing to take on this demanding task at short notice. We will address the issue in future work.

```
Je me demandais quelle heure il pouvait être; || j'entendais le
sifflement des trains qui, plus ou moins éloigné, comme le chant
d'un oiseau dans une forêt, relevant les distances, me décrivait
l'étendue de la campagne déserte où le voyageur se hâte vers la
station prochaine; || et le petit chemin qu'il suit va être gravé
dans son souvenir par l'excitation qu'il doit à des lieux nouveaux,
à des actes inaccoutumés, à la causerie récente et aux adieux sous
la lampe étrangère qui le suivent encore dans le silence de la nuit,
à la douceur prochaine du retour. || J'appuyais tendrement mes joues
contre les belles joues de l'oreiller qui, pleines et fraîches, sont
comme les joues de notre enfance.
```

Figure 2: Passage from *Combray* illustrating problems with segmentation, LARA markup in red. Double bars (||) show segment boundaries from the gold standard segmentation. Only the one in bold (**||**) is found by the alignment pipeline.

By far the least satisfactory result is the segmentation (column **Error rates/Seg**). The error rate, defined as 1 minus the boundary similarity score, varies considerably across the texts, increasing as the texts become more complex and reaching 36% for the very challenging Proust text. This corresponds to quite often feeling that the segments produced are too long: most commonly, a suboptimal segment consists of two sentences which the aligner has failed to split apart, or a long sentence which has not been divided at semi-colons. Figure 2 illustrates. Comparing the columns **Segment lengths/Tr-Al** and **Segment lengths/Ref** makes it clear that, with the translation aligner used in these experiments, it is impossible to attain a good segmentation score, since the segments produced by the translation aligner are already substantially longer than the gold standard segments.

5 Summary and further directions

The decreasing stability of the world means advanced language skills are of correspondingly greater importance. Acquisition of these skills, in particular large vocabularies, requires extensive reading of complex texts. Many learners find this a difficult step; multimodal texts, which include integrated audio and translation, both smooth the transition and help keep the learner's reading and listening skills in sync. We have described an implemented method for creating high-quality multimodal texts from existing online resources and presented encouraging initial results on representative French texts.

When we started, we were far from certain that automatic alignment methods would do well for this task. Based on the results of the LibriSpeech project (Panayotov et al., 2015) and the literary sentence alignment studies from (Xu et al., 2015) and other work cited there, we expected that a good deal of post-editing would be needed. However, for texts we have tried so far, the error rates are much lower than we had anticipated, and the results appear usable with very light post-editing.

It is not clear to us why our results are so much better than expected. The processing pipeline from §3 is an almost minimal recipe for producing a joint alignment using a beam search; the only non-obvious step is (7), post-processing of the double-aligned corpus. Removing it degrades the **Seg** score by a few percent and has almost no effect on the other two metrics, so this is not the explanation.

A more plausible hypothesis is that the LibriSpeech team were simply trying to solve a different problem, producing a large corpus of reliably aligned sentences, and paid no attention to the question, uninteresting to them, of how accurately they could align a complete literary text. Another is that the quality of readily available speech recognition engines and sentence aligners has substantially improved since 2015. We are impressed with the robustness of Google Cloud Speech-to-Text. For example, we discovered that litteratureaudio include background music in some of their offerings, using it at the starts and ends of sections and to underline key passages; also, the voice talents interpret the material in an imaginative way, rendering direct speech dramatically in different voices. We were concerned that both of these aspects might cause problems for speech recognition performance, but in fact there were none. The bottom line is that the task of automatically creating audio- and translation-annotated texts out of public domain corpus resources appears considerably more tractable than we had thought. Our main purpose in the current paper is to communicate this discovery to other members of the community who may also find it interesting and useful.

The data presented here suggests three priorities for continued investigation. First, the method should be tested on more texts, in several languages; second, we require user feedback for the resulting multimedia versions; third, we need to further systematise the post-editing process. We have already begun work on all of these. We briefly outline two specific threads of work initiated during the period Oct–Nov 2022 in collaboration with other LARA partners.

First, together with Ivana Horváthová of the Constantine the Philosopher University, Nitra, Slovakia, we are using the alignment methods to construct a LARA version of A.A. Milne's *Winnie-the-Pooh* with Slovak glosses. As an initial proof-of-concept experiment, we processed the first few pages and obtained excellent results; we are now negotiating with the copyright-holders to obtain the permissions needed to use the Slovak translation of the whole book. If we are able to do this, our plan is to perform an experiment, probably starting in Q1 2023, where we would contrast user perceptions of the resulting LARA document with a version of the same text run on the Azure Immersive Reader.

Second, we are working together with Neasa Ní Chiaráin and Harald Berthelsen of Trinity College Dublin, Ireland, to investigate the idea of performing alignment with a different recogniser, specifically the Kaldi-based ASR platform for Irish developed by the Trinity College group (ABAIR-ÉIST; `https://www.abair.ie/`; Lonergan et al. 2022). We have again only got as far as a proof-of-concept experiment, where we aligned a short Irish text corresponding to about five minutes of audio. Results were encouraging, with error rates similar to those we obtained on the French texts from §4. We hope to be able to progress this work further in the near future.

Ethics Statement

Methods like those described here naturally raise issues involving copyright. To the best of our knowledge, we have appropriate copyright permissions for all the text and audio materials used in the experiments.

Acknowledgements

We would very much like to thank Lieve Macken for pointing us to the YouAlign tool. Many people in the LARA community have directly or indirectly contributed to the development of the alignment method. We would particularly like to thank Branislav Bédi, Harald Berthelsen, Catia Cucchiarini, Ivana Horváthová, Christèle Maizonniaux, Neasa Ní Chiaráin, Chadi Raheb and Rina Zviel-Girshin.

A Appendix: using the scripts

People interested in using the Python scripts we refer to here should consult the online LARA documentation (Rayner et al., 2019–2022), which describes how to download, install and invoke the relevant software. Details can be found in the sections headed "Using the Python code: prerequisites" and "Automatic cutting-up and alignment with audio and translation".

References

Elham Akhlaghi, Ingibjörg Iða Auðunardóttir, Anna Baczkowska, Branislav Bédi, Hakeem Beedar, Harald Berthelsen, Cathy Chua, Catia Cucchiarini, Hanieh Habibi, Ivana Horváthová, Junta Ikeda, Christèle Maizonniaux, Neasa Ní Chiaráin, Chadi Raheb, Manny Rayner, John Sloan, Nikos Tsourakis, and Chunlin Yao. 2022a. Using the LARA Little Prince to compare human and TTS audio quality. In *Language Resources and Evaluation Conference*, pages 2967–2975. European Language Resources Association.

Elham Akhlaghi, Ingibjörg Iða Auðunardóttir, Branislav Bédi, Hakeem Beedar, Harald Berthelsen, Cathy Chua, Catia Cucchiarini, Brynjarr Eyjólfsson, Nedelina Ivanova, Christèle Maizonniaux, Neasa Ní Chiaráin, Manny Rayner, John Sloan, Sigurður Vigfússon, and Ghil'ad Zuckermann. 2022b. Reading assistance through LARA, the learning and reading assistant. In *2nd Workshop on Tools and Resources for REAding DIfficulties (READI)*, page 1.

Elham Akhlaghi, Branislav Bédi, Matthias Butterweck, Cathy Chua, Johanna Gerlach, Hanieh Habibi, Junta Ikeda, Manny Rayner, Sabina Sestigiani, and Ghil'ad Zuckermann. 2019. Overview of LARA: A learning and reading assistant. In *Proc. SLaTE 2019: 8th ISCA Workshop on Speech and Language Technology in Education*, pages 99–103.

Elham Akhlaghi, Anna Bączkowska, Harald Berthelsen, Branislav Bédi, Cathy Chua, Catia Cuchiarini, Hanieh Habibi, Ivana Horváthová, Pernille Hvalsøe, Roy Lotz, Christèle Maizonniaux, Neasa Ní Chiaráin, Manny Rayner, Nikos Tsourakis, and Chunlin Yao.

2021. Assessing the quality of TTS audio in the LARA learning-by-reading platform. In *CALL and professionalisation: short papers from EUROCALL 2021*, pages 1–5.

Satanjeev Banerjee and Alon Lavie. 2005. METEOR: An automatic metric for MT evaluation with improved correlation with human judgments. In *Proceedings of the ACL workshop on intrinsic and extrinsic evaluation measures for machine translation and/or summarization*, pages 65–72.

Branislav Bédi, Matt Butterweck, Cathy Chua, Johanna Gerlach, Birgitta Björg Guðmarsdóttir, Hanieh Habibi, Bjartur Örn Jónsson, Manny Rayner, and Sigurður Vigfússon. 2020. LARA: An extensible open source platform for learning languages by reading. In *Proc. EUROCALL 2020*.

Anna C.S. Chang and Sonia Millett. 2014. The effect of extensive listening on developing L2 listening fluency: Some hard evidence. *ELT journal*, 68(1):31–40.

Eleanor Dickey. 2016. *Learning Latin the ancient way: Latin textbooks from the ancient world*. Cambridge University Press.

Chris Fournier. 2013. Evaluating Text Segmentation using Boundary Edit Distance. In *Proceedings of 51st Annual Meeting of the Association for Computational Linguistics*, Stroudsburg, PA, USA. Association for Computational Linguistics.

Aaron Friedland, Michelle Gilman, Michael Johnson, and Abera Demeke. 2017. Does reading-while-listening enhance students' reading fluency? preliminary results from school experiments in rural uganda. *Journal of Education and Practice*, 8(7):82–95.

Anna Husson Isozaki. 2014. Flowing toward solutions: literature listening and L2 literacy. *The Journal of Literature in Language Teaching*, 3(2):6–20.

Stephen Krashen. 1982. *Principles and practice in second language acquisition*. Pergamon Press.

Stephen Krashen. 1989. We acquire vocabulary and spelling by reading: Additional evidence for the input hypothesis. *The modern language journal*, 73(4):440–464.

Stephen Krashen. 2004. *The power of reading: Insights from the research*. Greenwood Publishing Group.

Sy-Ying Lee. 2019. A fulfilling journey of language acquisition via story listening and reading: A case of an adult scholar. *Language Learning and Teaching*, 8(1):1–9.

Liam Lonergan, Mengjie Qian, Harald Berthelsen, Andy Murphy, Christoph Wendler, Neasa Ní Chiaráin, Christer Gobl, and Ailbhe Ní Chasaide. 2022. Automatic speech recognition for irish: the abair-éist system. In *Proceedings of the 4th Celtic Language Technology Workshop within LREC2022*, pages 47–51.

Can Özmen, Alexander Streicher, and Andrea Zielinski. 2014. Using text segmentation algorithms for the automatic generation of e-learning courses. In *Proceedings of the Third Joint Conference on Lexical and Computational Semantics (* SEM 2014)*, pages 132–140.

Vassil Panayotov, Guoguo Chen, Daniel Povey, and Sanjeev Khudanpur. 2015. Librispeech: an ASR corpus based on public domain audio books. In *2015 IEEE international conference on acoustics, speech and signal processing (ICASSP)*, pages 5206–5210. IEEE.

Kishore Papineni, Salim Roukos, Todd Ward, and Wei-Jing Zhu. 2002. Bleu: a method for automatic evaluation of machine translation. In *Proceedings of the 40th annual meeting of the Association for Computational Linguistics*, pages 311–318.

Ana Pellicer-Sánchez, Elsa Tragant, Kathy Conklin, M Rodgers, A Llanes, and R Serrano. 2018. L2 reading and reading-while-listening in multimodal learning conditions: An eye-tracking study. *ELT Research Papers*, 18(01):1–28.

Manny Rayner, Hanieh Habibi, Cathy Chua, and Matt Butterweck. 2019–2022. *Constructing LARA content*. `https://www.issco.unige.ch/en/research/projects/callector/LARADoc/build/html/index.html`. Online documentation.

Pedro José dos Reis Mota. 2019. *BeamSeg: a Joint Model for Multi-Document Segmentation and Topic Identification*. Ph.D. thesis, Carnegie Mellon University.

John W. Schwieter and Alessandro Benati. 2019. *The Cambridge Handbook of Language Learning*. Cambridge University Press.

Ryan Shaw. 2015. Segmenting oral history transcripts. In *International Conference on Theory and Practice of Digital Libraries*, pages 326–329. Springer.

Billy Woodall. 2010. Simultaneous listening and reading in ESL: Helping second language learners read (and enjoy reading) more efficiently. *TESOL journal*, 1(2):186–205.

Yong Xu, Aurélien Max, and François Yvon. 2015. Sentence alignment for literary texts: The state-of-the-art and beyond. In *Linguistic Issues in Language Technology, Volume 12, 2015-Literature Lifts up Computational Linguistics*.

Ghil'ad Zuckerman, Sigurður Vigfússon, Manny Rayner, Neasa Ní Chiaráin, Nedelina Ivanova, Hanieh Habibi, and Branislav Bédi. 2021. LARA in the service of revivalistics and documentary linguistics: Community engagement and endangered languages. In *Proceedings of the Workshop on Computational Methods for Endangered Languages*, volume 1, pages 13–23.

The Role of Context in Vaccine Stance Prediction for Twitter Users

Aleney Khoo[1,2] **Maciej Rybinski**[1] **Sarvnaz Karimi**[1] **Adam Dunn**[2]
[1]CSIRO Data61, Sydney, Australia
[2]The University of Sydney, Sydney Australia
{firstname.lastname}@csiro.au
adam.dunn@sydney.edu.au

Abstract

Public expression of vaccine related sentiment on social media platforms can be used in information surveillance applications to gain insight into vaccine hesitancy and its spread. Effective identification of vaccine-negative content constitutes one of the most fundamental building blocks in such applications.

Here, we investigate the role of users' previous vaccine-related posts, in the capacity of stance text classifiers to detect vaccine-negative content. We conduct experiments on a dataset of over 7K tweets manually labeled for vaccination stance captured between 2017 and 2019, with unlabeled historical data.

Our results indicate that incorporating user-generated-context improves stance detection. It also bridges the effectiveness gap between simple linear models and state-of-the art text classifiers, highlighting the importance of data capture strategy to the downstream task.

1 Introduction

Vaccine hesitancy is defined as delayed acceptance or refusal of vaccines despite their availability. It is believed that vaccine hesitancy and refusal may be amplified by the spread of vaccine-negative content on social media (Raballo et al., 2022).

Stance detection is a process of identification of speaker's judgment or standpoint towards a given proposition (Biber and Finegan, 1988; Mohammad et al., 2017). It is often modelled as a classification task of assigning an *against*, *for* or *neural* label to a text for a given *target*. In the context of social media, detecting anti-vaccine content can be seen as a building block fundamental to implementation of mitigation and monitoring strategies, understanding fears and concerns expressed in the public discourse (Mitra et al., 2021). In this problem, vaccine hesitancy is considered the target for stance detection.

In this paper we simplify the problem of stance detection by modelling it as a binary text classification task. In this set-up we investigate the impact of including users' historic tweets in detecting vaccine-negative utterances. We conduct experiments on a dataset of over 7K tweets manually labelled for vaccine stance captured between 2017 and 2019, which contains unlabelled historical data from the authors of the labelled tweets. Our work focuses on the impact of the availability of historic user-generated content on effectiveness on the downstream text classification task. We compare Transformer-based models, which allow for modelling the historical context in a cross-encoder, with traditional linear models incorporating these historical tweets in a Bag-of-Words (BoW) representation encompassing the labelled utterance.

2 Related Work

Our study relates to the literature on using social media for public health and, in particular, for detection of vaccination hesitancy. It also relates to Twitter, and other social media, text classification, sentiment and stance detection.

Social Media for Public Health Natural Language Processing (NLP) techniques for social media have been leveraged in different public health applications (Paul and Dredze, 2017; Conway et al., 2019), including for mental health (Calvo et al., 2017), syndromic surveillance (Jimeno Yepes et al., 2015; Ofoghi et al., 2016; Huang et al., 2016) of acute diseases (Joshi et al., 2020b) or infectious diseases (Joshi et al., 2019, 2020a), detecting user behaviour towards vaccination (Joshi et al., 2018), and personal health mention detection (Iyer et al., 2019). A survey of different social media platforms utilised for public health is presented by (Conway et al., 2019), showing a range of different platforms such as Twitter, Whatsapp, Facebook, and Reddit, as well as applications and methods.

Vaccination hesitancy detection Social media, in particular, Twitter have been a data source for gauging the public opinions on vaccines. Morante et al. (2020) present the Vaccination Corpus which annotated a corpus of 294 online debates published in news, blogs, editorial, governmental reports, science articles for their stance towards measles vaccines. Lanyi et al. (2022) analysed Twitter for COVID-19 vaccine hesitancy in order to identify barriers to vaccination in the UK. They approached this as a sentiment analysis and then mapped the tweets to predefined set of potential barriers such as safety or mistrust.

Mitra et al. (2021) studied Twitter data for a four-year period to understand anti-Vaccination attitudes. They used tweets of different users as their context to identify whether they are anti-vaccination. For their analysis they used topic modelling.

Stance Detection in social media Stance and sentiment detection on social media text, especially tweets, pose difficulties. Tweets are short and it can be difficult to identify the user's view either in terms on sentiment (positive, negative, neural) or stance (pro, anti, neutral) on a specific topic (Mohammad et al., 2017).

Medford et al. (2020) emphasise on the importance of Twitter data sentiment analysis during an outbreak of an infectious disease. They processed a large set of tweets using sentiment analysis and topic modelling in the early stages of the COVID-19 pandemic to help understand the effect of the outbreak on the public's emotions and beliefs.

Conforti et al. (2020) annotated a large corpus of tweets (over 51 thousand) for stance detection. The dataset represents public expressions of opinion on mergers and acquisition operations between companies. They also benchmark a number of different stance detection methods, including traditional ones such as SVM and those based on neural networks, such as CrossNet (Zheng et al., 2018). Conforti et al. (2021) uses this dataset to investigate cross-domain learning for stance detection when annotated data does not exist for a given target.

Stance detection using neural network-based methods is also investigated by Xu et al. (2018). They experimented with two different datasets from Twitter and showed promising results for cross-target stance detection using three methods based on BiLSTM (Zhou et al., 2016), MITRE (Augenstein et al., 2016).

Stance detection for opinions towards vaccination is studied by Skeppstedt et al. (2017). They annotated data from the British parental website Mumsnet for three labels of 'against', 'for', and 'undecided' and trained linear SVMs for stance detection.

Tweet Classification using Context Literature has long investigated the potential of context in classification of microblogs (or tweets) as a method to include more information to an otherwise short text. Historical tweets have been used in stance detection on Twitter, namely in fake news and sarcasm detection. Dou et al. (2021) used historical tweets to create a fake news detection framework that fuses historical tweets, news reports and engagement across user networks. Historical tweets can be incorporated in multiple way. Most commonly, they are bundled per user into one *document*. Chaudhry and Lease (2022) assess the impact of adding historical tweets in groups on a LSTM classifier, where the output is then fed into a Gradient Boosted Decision Tree classifier. They choose to retrieve up to 20 historical tweets per user, and separate groups of five. They highlighted the importance of context in these classification tasks, finding qualitatively that tweets were labelled often incorrectly on their own, but with context of a users historical tweets it could correctly label the tweet.

3 Dataset and Experimental Setup

The original dataset We conduct our experiments on a Twitter-based dataset by Dunn et al. (2020). The dataset consists of 10,080 vaccine-related Twitter posts (tweets) manually labelled for vaccine stance (anti-vaccine, pro-vaccine, other/neutral). The tweets were collected with vaccine-specific Twitter queries between January 12, 2017, and December 3, 2019 from U.S. based Twitter users with then-active accounts. The dataset also contains unlabelled historical vaccine-related (i.e., collected with the same queries) tweets from the authors of the labelled tweets. Each tweet in the dataset is represented with a user handle, timestamp, and the tweet content.

The task We frame the stance detection task in our experiments as a binary text classification problem with the focus on detecting the anti-vaccine content. The binarisation is, therefore, straightforward: we treat both the vaccine-positive and neutral classes as a new (binary) negative class, with the tweets labelled as vaccine-negative becoming the new positive class.

Filtering The dataset comes with retweets filtered out (from both labelled and unlabelled data). Additionally, we filter the labelled data based on the availability of historical tweets – we only use tweets from users that have at least four historical tweets in the unlabelled portion of the dataset.

Preprocessing Since the focus of our experiments is on text-content-based stance detection in tweets, we set out to minimise the impact of network-specific features creeping into this textual content. We, therefore, normalise all user mentions with a 'USERNAME' placeholder.

Data at a glance Our dataset after filtering consists of 7,194 labelled tweets from 7,194 unique users (794 positive class/vaccine-negative and 6400 negative class/vaccine-positive-or-neutral), with every user in this dataset having at least 4 unlabelled historical tweets.

Experiments and setup We split the data into training and testing sets, with an 80–20 proportion. The training tweets were posted prior to the test tweets. In experiments where the historical tweets are incorporated, they are incorporated both at training and testing time. For traditional baselines (logistic regression–LR–and SVM) we incorporate the historical tweets by simply appending their text to the text of the labelled tweet (so, the historical context is modelled in the same BOW representation as the labelled tweet). For transformer-based models (RoBERTa variants) the historical tweets are appended after a SEP token (so, the labelled tweet becomes Sentence A of the BERT input, while the historical tweets are concatenated and fed as Sentence B part of the input). The hyperparameter tuning for LR and SVM was done with 3-fold cross-validation with grid search. For BERT-based models the hyperparameters for fine-tuning (batch size, number of epochs, learning rate) were tuned manually on a validation set (25% of the training data). This manual tuning was performed once for RoBERTa-base model with no historical tweets and its results (batch size of 16, learning rate of 2e-5, and 1 epoch of training) were applied directly to all other experiments with BERT derivatives. For each of the models we report results with no historical tweets, and with 1, 2, 3, and 4 historical tweets included in the training and inference.

We experiment with RoBERTa-base (henceforth referred to as 'plain RoBERTa') model as a domain agnostic BERT variant. We use a model trained for sentiment detection on Twitter[1] as a Twitter-optimised initial checkpoint. We chose RoBERTa variants over BERT due to more stable training and higher effectiveness in our initial experiments.

For the more successful of the two RoBERTa variants we run an additional experiment, where the predictions are produced only with the 4 historical context (so, the text of the actual training/test tweet is not used), to illustrate the predictive power behind the historical tweets. All RoBERTa results are averaged across 5 runs.

Where comparison are made between the results, we use approximate paired randomisation test to test for statistical significance of our findings. For transformer-based models we use the predictions resulting in median F1 score for significance testing, where not stated otherwise.

Dealing with imbalance While imbalanced classification adds a layer of complexity to our task, dealing with class imbalance is not our core focus. We therefore deal with the skew in our training dataset using standard approaches. In SVM and logistic regression we use regularisation inversely proportional to class size. In RoBERTa models we oversample the minority (vaccine-negative) class (10-fold). Both approaches yielded improvements of effectiveness on a validation set in our exploratory experiments, so we decided to incorporate them across the board.

4 Results

Our experiments on comparing different methods and different levels of context are presented in Table 1. We report precision, recall and F1-Score on the minority class (vaccine-negative). We observe the best results for plain RoBERTa with user-context incorporated by appending 4 historical tweets. Improvements in classification effectiveness can be seen across the board with incorporation of historical tweets, with linear models improving more, when compared to respective runs with no user-context.

5 Discussion

Our results demonstrate that adding historical tweets improves vaccine-negative stance detection

[1]cardiffnlp/twitter-roberta-base-sentiment-latest

Method	Precision	Recall	F1-Score
LogReg no HT	0.56	0.45	0.50
LogReg 1 HT	0.66	0.54	0.59
LogReg 2 HT	0.69	0.58	0.63
LogReg 3 HT	0.72	0.57	0.64
LogReg 4 HT	0.73	0.58	0.65
Lin. SVM no HT	0.58	0.31	0.40
Lin. SVM 1 HT	0.55	0.6	0.57
Lin. SVM 2 HT	0.64	0.58	0.61
Lin. SVM 3 HT	0.64	0.58	0.61
Lin. SVM 4 HT	0.69	0.61	0.65
RoBERTa no HT	0.67 ± 0.028	0.51 ± 0.027	0.58 ± 0.009
RoBERTa 1 HT	0.69 ± 0.024	0.56 ± 0.028	0.62 ± 0.019
RoBERTa 2 HT	0.72 ± 0.021	0.61 ± 0.034	0.66 ± 0.024
RoBERTa 3 HT	0.71 ± 0.015	0.66 ± 0.028	0.68 ± 0.010
RoBERTa 4 HT	0.74 ± 0.021	0.66 ± 0.038	0.69 ± 0.020
Twitter RoBERTa no HT	0.62 ± 0.027	0.51 ± 0.025	0.56 ± 0.007
Twitter RoBERTa 1 HT	0.68 ± 0.026	0.56 ± 0.009	0.61 ± 0.006
Twitter RoBERTa 2 HT	0.71 ± 0.014	0.57 ± 0.020	0.63 ± 0.016
Twitter RoBERTa 3 HT	0.71 ± 0.016	0.60 ± 0.022	0.65 ± 0.017
Twitter RoBERTa 4 HT	0.72 ± 0.026	0.63 ± 0.025	0.67 ± 0.008
RoBERTa only HT	0.49 ± 0.034	0.71 ± 0.021	0.58 ± 0.022

Table 1: Comparison of different classification methods. HT stands for Historical Tweets.

in tweets, both for transformer-based and traditional ML models. Importantly, in our study the benefits of incorporating user-context clearly outweigh the benefits of using domain-specific intermediate training (compare, e.g., 'RoBERTa no HT' vs 'RoBERTa 2 HT' – with statistically significant F1 improvement with p=0.004 – and 'RoBERTa no HT' vs 'Twitter RoBERTa no HT', resulting in a statistically insignificant decline in F1).

Interestingly, including the historical tweets levels the field between linear models and Transformers. Differences between either RoBERTa 4 HT and logistic regression 4 HT are not statistically significant for the RoBERTa models with median F1 (although the plain RoBERTa model with the highest F1 yields a 'statistically significant' improvement in an uncorrected test). We believe this can be explained by the transformer-based models being better at dealing with very sparse utterances of single tweets (both RoBERTa models with no HT are significantly more effective in terms of F1 than logistic regression without historical tweets; p=0.01 and p=0.05, respectively). The presence of additional contexts yields the dense representations used by RoBERTa to 'fill in the blanks' less useful.

Improvements in effectiveness comparable are in magnitude (although not directly comparable[2]) to improvements attained using more specialised models and user metadata on a super-set of the same data by Naseem et al. (2021). Harnessing topic-specific historical tweets can be seen as an alternative mechanism of user profiling, which arguably carries lower risk of re-identification than combining network feature, user metadata, and textual features.

The last row of Table1 reports an experiment with a model exposed to historical context only, both at training and testing. I.e., the task here can be represented as predicting the stance of the next tweet from a specific user, given their posting history on a specific topic (here, vaccines). Interestingly, it seems to be the only recall-biased model in our experiments, which indicates that the models are more likely to mistake vaccine-positive/neutral contexts for vaccine-negative contexts than they are to mistake a vaccine-positive-or-neutral tweet for a vaccine-negative one.

6 Limitations

The presented work constitutes an initial, exploratory step towards incorporating user-produced context (historic posts) into a vaccine stance surveillance pipeline. We only explore an artificial version of the problem, where we look at artificial user groups with 1 to 5 posts specific to the topic of interest.

Another limitation of our work is relates to limitations of current transformer-based classification models, which can only be applied to texts of limited length. Our exploratory study does not offer solutions towards incorporating broader historical context in training and inference.

7 Conclusions and Future Work

We investigated the problem of vaccination stance detection in Twitter using historical tweets by different Twitter users. We compared different text classification methods to identify stance of users. Our results point to a methodology to improve detection effectiveness through improved data collection pipeline for health-related social media *infoveillance*. We hypothesise that our strategy is especially applicable in scenarios where the public is highly polarised.

As future work, we will explore opportunities, and difficulties, around the use of user-generated context in experimental setup more similar to real-world applications.

[2]The authors of the cited work evaluated their methodology in a multi-class setup, and without filtering for historical tweet availability (thus, with more training data).

Acknowledgements

This work has CSIRO's ethics committee aproval (2021_115_LR). This work is supported by the CSIRO's Precision Health Future Science Platform.

References

Isabelle Augenstein, Tim Rocktäschel, Andreas Vlachos, and Kalina Bontcheva. 2016. Stance detection with bidirectional conditional encoding. In *Proceedings of the 2016 Conference on Empirical Methods in Natural Language Processing*, pages 876–885, Austin, Texas. Association for Computational Linguistics.

Douglas Biber and Edward Finegan. 1988. Adverbial stance types in english. *Discourse Processes*, 11(1):1–34.

Rafael A Calvo, David N Milne, M Sazzad Hussain, and Helen Christensen. 2017. Natural language processing in mental health applications using non-clinical texts. *Natural Language Engineering*, 23(5):649–685.

Prateek Chaudhry and Matthew Lease. 2022. You are what you tweet: Profiling users by past tweets to improve hate speech detection. In *Information for a Better World: Shaping the Global Future*, pages 195–203. Springer International Publishing.

Costanza Conforti, Jakob Berndt, Mohammad Taher Pilehvar, Chryssi Giannitsarou, Flavio Toxvaerd, and Nigel Collier. 2020. Will-they-won't-they: A very large dataset for stance detection on Twitter. In *Proceedings of the 58th Annual Meeting of the Association for Computational Linguistics*, pages 1715–1724.

Costanza Conforti, Jakob Berndt, Mohammad Taher Pilehvar, Chryssi Giannitsarou, Flavio Toxvaerd, and Nigel Collier. 2021. Synthetic examples improve cross-target generalization: A study on stance detection on a Twitter corpus. In *Proceedings of the Eleventh Workshop on Computational Approaches to Subjectivity, Sentiment and Social Media Analysis*, pages 181–187.

Mike Conway, Mengke Hu, and Wendy W. Chapman. 2019. Recent advances in using natural language processing to address public health research questions using social media and consumer generated data. 28(1):208–217.

Yingtong Dou, Kai Shu, Congying Xia, Philip S. Yu, and Lichao Sun. 2021. User preference-aware fake news detection. In *Proceedings of the 44th International ACM SIGIR Conference on Research and Development in Information Retrieval*, page 2051–2055.

Adam G. Dunn, Didi Surian, Jason Dalmazzo, Dana Rezazadegan, Maryke Steffens, Amalie Dyda, Julie Leask, Enrico Coiera, Aditi Dey, and Kenneth D. Mandl. 2020. Limited role of bots in spreading vaccine-critical information among active Twitter users in the United States: 2017–2019. *American Journal of Public Health*, pages 319–325.

Pin Huang, Andrew MacKinlay, and Antonio Jimeno Yepes. 2016. Syndromic surveillance using generic medical entities on Twitter. In *Proceedings of the Australasian Language Technology Association Workshop*, pages 35–44, Melbourne, Australia.

Adith Iyer, Aditya Joshi, Sarvnaz Karimi, Ross Sparks, and Cecile Paris. 2019. Figurative usage detection of symptom words to improve personal health mention detection. In *Proceedings of the 57th Annual Meeting of the Association for Computational Linguistics*, pages 1142–1147, Florence, Italy. Association for Computational Linguistics.

Antonio Jimeno Yepes, Andrew MacKinlay, and Bo Han. 2015. Investigating public health surveillance using Twitter. In *Proceedings of BioNLP 15*, pages 164–170, Beijing, China.

Aditya Joshi, Xiang Dai, Sarvnaz Karimi, Ross Sparks, Cécile Paris, and C Raina MacIntyre. 2018. Shot or not: Comparison of NLP approaches for vaccination behaviour detection. In *Proceedings of the 2018 EMNLP Workshop SMM4H: The 3rd Social Media Mining for Health Applications Workshop & Shared Task*, pages 43–47, Brussels, Belgium. Association for Computational Linguistics.

Aditya Joshi, Sarvnaz Karimi, Ross Sparks, Cécile Paris, and C. Raina Macintyre. 2019. Survey of text-based epidemic intelligence: A computational linguistics perspective. 52(6).

Aditya Joshi, Ross Sparks, Sarvnaz Karimi, Sheng-Lun Jason Yan, Abrar Ahmad Chughtai, Cecile Paris, and C. Raina MacIntyre. 2020a. Automated monitoring of tweets for early detection of the 2014 Ebola epidemic. *PLOS One*.

Aditya Joshi, Ross Sparks, James McHugh, Sarvnaz Karimi, Cecile Paris, and C. Raina MacIntyre. 2020b. Harnessing tweets for early detection of an acute disease event. *Epidemiology*, 31(1):90–97.

Katherine Lanyi, Rhiannon Green, Dawn Craig, and Christopher Marshall. 2022. Covid-19 vaccine hesitancy: Analysing twitter to identify barriers to vaccination in a low uptake region of the uk. *Frontiers in digital health*, 3.

S. N. Medford, R. J.and Saleh, A. Sumarsono, T. M. Perl, and C. U. Lehmann. 2020. An Infodemic: Leveraging high-volume Twitter data to understand early public sentiment for the Coronavirus disease 2019 outbreak. *Open forum infectious diseases*, 7(7).

Tanushree Mitra, Scott Counts, and James Pennebaker. 2021. Understanding anti-vaccination attitudes in social media. In *Proceedings of the International AAAI Conference on Web and Social Media*, pages 269–278.

Saif M. Mohammad, Parinaz Sobhani, and Svetlana Kiritchenko. 2017. Stance and sentiment in tweets. *ACM Transactions on Internet Technology*, 17(3):1–23.

Roser Morante, Chantal van Son, Isa Maks, and Piek Vossen. 2020. Annotating perspectives on vaccination. In *Proceedings of the Twelfth Language Resources and Evaluation Conference*, pages 4964–4973, Marseille, France.

Usman Naseem, Matloob Khushi, Jinman Kim, and Adam G. Dunn. 2021. Classifying vaccine sentiment tweets by modelling domain-specific representation and commonsense knowledge into context-aware attentive gru.

Bahadorreza Ofoghi, Meghan Mann, and Karin Verspoor. 2016. Towards early discovery of salient health threats: a social media emotion classification technique. In *Pacific Symposium on Biocomputing. Pacific Symposium on Biocomputing*, pages 504–515.

Michael J Paul and Mark Dredze. 2017. Social monitoring for public health. *Synthesis Lectures on Information Concepts, Retrieval, and Services*, 9(5):1–183.

Andrea Raballo, Michele Poletti, and Antonio Preti. 2022. Vaccine hesitancy, anti-vax, covid-conspirationism: From subcultural convergence to public health and bioethical problems. *Frontiers in Public Health*, 10.

Maria Skeppstedt, Andreas Kerren, and Manfred Stede. 2017. Automatic detection of stance towards vaccination in online discussion forums. In *Proceedings of the International Workshop on Digital Disease Detection using Social Media*, pages 1–8, Taipei, Taiwan.

Chang Xu, Cécile Paris, Surya Nepal, and Ross Sparks. 2018. Cross-target stance classification with self-attention networks. In *Proceedings of the 56th Annual Meeting of the Association for Computational Linguistics*, pages 778–783.

Haitian Zheng, Mengqi Ji, Haoqian Wang, Yebin Liu, and Lu Fang. 2018. Crossnet: An end-to-end reference-based super resolution network using cross-scale warping. In *European Conference on Computer Vision*, pages 87–104.

Peng Zhou, Zhenyu Qi, Suncong Zheng, Jiaming Xu, Hongyun Bao, and Bo Xu. 2016. Text classification improved by integrating bidirectional LSTM with two-dimensional max pooling. In *The 26th International Conference on Computational Linguistics*, page 3485–3495.

TCG-Event: Effective Task Conditioning for Generation-based Event Extraction

Fatemeh Shiri, Tongtong Wu, Yuan-Fang Li, Gholamreza Haffari
Department of DS&AI, Faculty of Information Technology, Monash University, Melbourne, Australia
fatemeh.shiri, tongtong.wu, YuanFang.Li, Gholamreza.Haffari@monash.edu

Abstract

Event extraction is an important but challenging task. Many existing techniques decompose it into subtasks of event and argument detection/classification, which are themselves complex structured prediction problems. Generation-based extraction techniques lessen the complexity of the problem formulation and are able to leverage the reasoning capabilities of large pre-trained language models. However, the large diversity of available event types makes it hard for generative models to effectively select the correct corresponding templates to predict the structured sequence. In this paper, we propose a task-conditioned generation-based event extraction model, TCG-Event, that addresses these challenges. A key contribution of TCG-Event is a novel task conditioning technique that injects event name information as prefixes into each layer of an encoder-decoder-based language model, thus enabling effective supervised learning. Our experiments on two benchmark datasets demonstrate the strong performance of our TCG-Event model.

1 Introduction

Event extraction (Li et al., 2021a) aims at extracting structured event records from unstructured text. For example, as shown in Figure 1, event extraction aims to map the sentence "Two homemade pressure-cooker bombs are detonated remotely, killing three and injuring some 260 others" to four predefined event types, e.g., <*event type*: explosion, *trigger word*: detonated, *role:bomber*: Tsarnaevs, ..., *role:bomb*: homemade pressure-cooker bombs, *role:place*: Boston Marathon>, as well as other events that are triggered by words *killing*, *injuring* and *lost limbs*.

Event extraction is challenging because of the diversity of natural language expressions and the complexity of event structures. These challenges become even more severe in sentences in which the text generally contains more events. Currently, most event extraction methods employ a decomposition-based approach (Xu et al., 2021), i.e., decomposing the structured prediction problem of a complex event into classification over substructures, such as trigger detection, entity recognition, and argument classification. Many of these methods tackle the subproblems separately, which requires additional annotations for each stage (Paolini et al., 2021). Furthermore, designing an optimal composition architecture of different subtasks is very challenging.

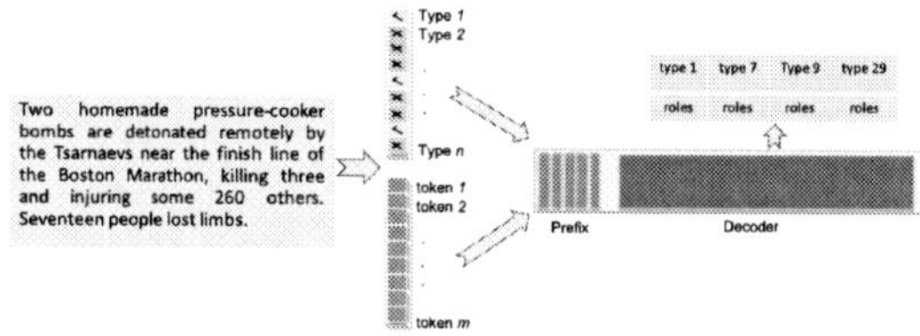

Figure 1: An illustration of the event extraction as a structured generation, with introducing the event type as the task-conditioning to prefix, the decoder can selectively generate sequentialized event representation, which is mentioned in the input text.

Natural language generation techniques have been successfully applied to several NLP tasks (Raffel et al., 2020; Li et al., 2021b; Hsu et al., 2022). They have inspired the use of controlled event generation to tackle event extraction. These approaches use manually designed templates to wrap input sentences and train a model for cloze-style filling. The study by Lu et al. (2021) proposes to generate linearised event records via a pretrained encoder-decoder architecture combined with a constrained decoding mechanism that alleviates the complexity associated with template combination when extracting multiple events. The advantage of the approach of extraction-as-generation is the removal of the need for fine-grained token-level annotations, which are typically utilised in previous event extraction approaches (Nguyen and Nguyen,

2019), thus enjoying greater feasibility.

Structured prediction problems such as event extraction usually assume an external schema to format the output. In contrast, natural language generation problems do not make this assumption. Motivated by this distinction, we propose a novel *task conditioning* technique that injects event type information as *prefixes* on layers of the underlying pretrained language model.

Our main contributions are as follows.

- We propose a novel task conditioning technique that dynamically injects event-type information to both the encoder and decoder of a pretrained language model.
- We carefully design a prefix-based injection mechanism that incorporates cross-attention to improve event extraction.
- We conducted extensive experiments in the fully supervised setting on two benchmark datasets. Our evaluation consistently shows strong performance.

2 Related Work

Event extraction is the task of extracting structured event records from unstructured text (Li et al., 2021b; Shiri et al., 2021). Many approaches have been proposed for sentence-level event extraction (Christopher Walker and Maeda, 2006), varies from hand-designed features (Shen et al., 2021) and neural-learned features (Zhang et al., 2021; Huang and Peng, 2021). Yet many real-world applications need event extraction (Frisoni et al., 2021; He et al., 2021; Verspoor et al., 2016; Nguyen and Verspoor, 2019; Yang et al., 2021; Zhang et al., 2021; Huang and Peng, 2021), in which the information of an event may be mentioned in multi-sentences (Ebner et al., 2019; Li et al., 2021c). Moreover, most of works adopt decomposition strategies in event extraction (Xu et al., 2021), which employ trigger detection (Shen et al., 2021), entity recognition (Lison et al., 2020; Du et al., 2021), and argument classification (Zhang et al., 2020). These decomposition strategies showed high performance while introducing more detailed annotation to model training (Lu et al., 2021; Li et al., 2021b). Inspired by the success of pretrained language models and the corresponding natural language generation-based paradigm for various NLP tasks (Raffel et al., 2020; Li et al., 2021b; Hsu et al., 2022) tackle event

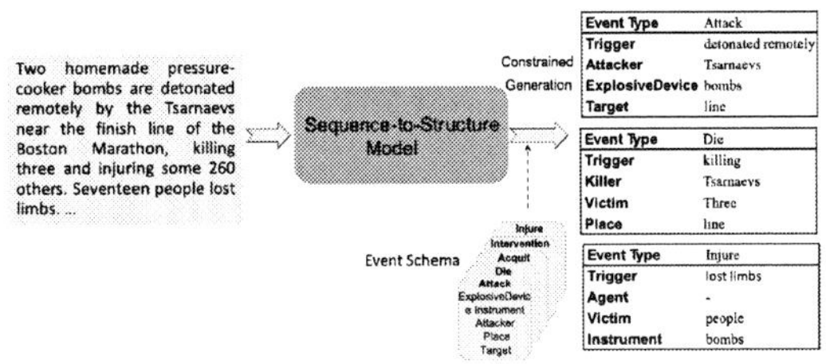

Figure 2: The event extraction task.

extraction as controlled event generation. (Hsu et al., 2022) is an end-to-end conditional generation method with manually designed discrete prompts for each event type, which needs more human effort to find the optimal prompt. To remove the complexity of template combination in extracting multiple events, Lu et al. (2021) proposed to generate the event records directly with a pretrained encoder-decoder architecture and a constrained decoding mechanism. This extraction-as-generation approach does not require fine-grained token-level annotations that are typically needed by previous event extraction methods (Huang et al., 2021; Li et al., 2021b). Liu et al. (2022) proposed a generative template-based event extraction method with dynamic prefixes by integrating context information with type-specific prefixes only to the encoder to learn a context-specific prefix for each context. In contrast, we inject event-type information into both the encoder and the decoder. Particularly, we use interactions between the event type information and the context and inject it into the decoder.

3 Generation-based Event Extraction

Problem Definition. We denote $\mathcal{E}$ and $\mathcal{R}$ as the set of predefined event types and role categories, respectively. An input sequence $\boldsymbol{x} := \{x_1, \ldots, x_{|\boldsymbol{x}|}\}$ comprises tokens x_i, where $|x|$ denotes the sequence length. Given an input sequence, an event extraction model aims to extract one or more structured events, where each event is specified by (i) the event type $e \in \mathcal{E}$ filled with the trigger word t from the sequence, and (ii) the roles $\mathcal{R}_e \subseteq \mathcal{R}$ filled with the corresponding arguments from the sequence (see Figure 2).

Event Extraction as Generation. Given $\mathcal{E}$ and $\mathcal{R}$ in the predefined event schema, generation-based event extraction models generate a structured sequence based on an input sequence constrained by the schema (Lu et al., 2021).

The generated sequence is a linearised representation of events mentioned in the sequence. Specifically, given a text with token sequence $\boldsymbol{x}$ as input, a generation-based extraction model such as TCG-Event outputs the linearised events representations $\boldsymbol{y} = \langle y_1, y_2, \ldots, y_{|\boldsymbol{y}|} \rangle$, where each event y_i is denoted by $\langle e_i, t_i, \langle r_{i,1}, a_{i,1} \rangle, \ldots, \langle r_{i,|r|}, a_{i,|r|} \rangle \rangle$. The angled brackets $\langle \cdot \rangle$ are special tokens indicating the sequence structure. The $e \in \mathcal{E}$ and t are the event type and the trigger words (a subspan of the sequence $\boldsymbol{x}$); furthermore, $r_i \in \mathcal{R}$ and a_i denote roles and arguments (subspans of the sequence $\boldsymbol{x}$).

Architecture. Our TCG-Event model adopts a Transformer-based encoder-decoder architecture for event structure generation. TCG-Event outputs the linearised event representation $\boldsymbol{y}$ for an input sequence $\boldsymbol{x}$. It first computes the hidden representation $\mathbf{H}_{\boldsymbol{x}} = (\boldsymbol{h}_1, \boldsymbol{h}_2, \ldots, \boldsymbol{h}_{|\boldsymbol{x}|}) \in \mathbb{R}^{|\boldsymbol{x}| \times d}$ for each token in the sequence via a multi-layer Transformer encoder:

$$\mathbf{H}_{\boldsymbol{x}} = \text{Encoder}(\boldsymbol{x}), \tag{1}$$

where each layer of Encoder$(\cdot)$ is a Transformer block (Vaswani et al., 2017) with the multi-head self-attention mechanism.

Given the encoding $\mathbf{H}_{\boldsymbol{x}}$, the decoder generates each token sequentially to produce the sequence of events. At step t, the Transformer-based decoder generates the token y_t and hidden state $\boldsymbol{h}_t$ as:

$$y_t, \boldsymbol{h}_t = \text{Decoder}(y_{t-1}; \mathbf{H}_{\boldsymbol{y}_{<t}}, \mathbf{H}_{\boldsymbol{x}}), \tag{2}$$

where each layer of Decoder$(\cdot)$ is a Transformer block, with both the self-attention to past hidden states $\mathbf{H}_{\boldsymbol{y}_{<t}} \in \mathbb{R}^{(t-1) \times d}$ during decoding and the cross-attention to the encoding $\mathbf{H}_{\boldsymbol{x}}$. The conditional probability of the output sequence $p(\boldsymbol{y}|\boldsymbol{x})$ is then,

$$p_\theta(\boldsymbol{y}|\boldsymbol{x}) = \prod_{t=1}^{|\boldsymbol{y}|} p_\theta(y_t | \boldsymbol{y}_{<t}, \boldsymbol{x}), \tag{3}$$

where θ denotes the parameters of the Transformer-based encoder-decoder model.

4 Task Conditioning in Event Generation

In this paper, we investigate how to best leverage pre-trained large language models (LLMs) as the backbone encoder-decoder model for event extraction.[1] Using LLMs is nowadays part of standard practice in NLP, as they lead to strong performance.

Given a labeled training dataset $\mathcal{D}$, we investigate how to best specialise the pre-trained LLM to the event extraction task via prefix-tuning (Li and Liang, 2021). In this section, we show how to effectively *condition* the generation process on the event extraction task as well as the given sequence. One may specialise the underlying LLM to the event extraction task through other methods as well, e.g. fine-tuning of the LLM parameters or adapters injected to the encoder and/or decoder of the LLM (see Figure 3). We show in our experiments that prefix-tuning is more effective than those methods.

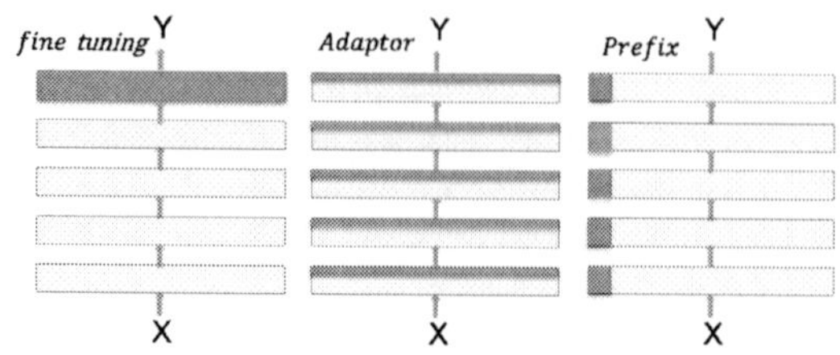

Figure 3: A high-level illustration of three candidate task-conditioning injection paradigm for encoder-decoder models: fine-tuning, adapter-tuning, and prefix-tuning. For each tuning type, each block represents a transformer block in the pretrained language model, and the blue blocks indicate the new-added parameters in the pretrained model.

Our desiderata for prefix-conditioning of a pre-trained LLM for event extraction are as follows. It should enable the model to be aware of (i) the candidate event schemas in the task, (ii) the specific input sequence, and (iii) flexible schema modifications that may happen after the model is trained in the real-world settings. In what follows, we explain how we achieve these desiderata by producing prefixes for the encoder and the decoder based on the events of the task and the input sequence. See Figure 4 for an overview of the framework.

Encoder Conditioning. We condition the encoder on the event types of the underlying event extraction task. Given the event types $\boldsymbol{e} = \{e_1, e_2, \ldots, e_{|\boldsymbol{e}|}\} \subseteq \mathcal{E}$ for a task, we use the encoder to get the encoding representation for the event types $\mathbf{H}_{\boldsymbol{e}} \in \mathbb{R}^{|\boldsymbol{e}| \times d}$. We then combine these events representations through a function $f_{enc} : \mathbb{R}^{|\boldsymbol{k}| \times d} \mapsto \mathbb{R}^{d'}$ to create the events conditioning context, i.e.

$$\mathbf{H}_{\boldsymbol{e}} = \text{Encoder}(\boldsymbol{e}); \; \boldsymbol{h}_{\boldsymbol{e},enc} = f_{enc}(\mathbf{H}_{\boldsymbol{e}}) \tag{4}$$

Since we assume each event type is equally probable *a priori*, we use the pooling average operator as f_{enc}. The vector $\boldsymbol{h}_{\boldsymbol{e},enc}$ is used by a prefix generation network g_{enc} to produce the prefix. As shown in Figure 4, by $\pm$ in $f_enc(.)$, we

[1] In our experiments, we make use of T5 (Raffel et al., 2020), but our methods are applicable to other large pre-trained encoder-decoder models as well.

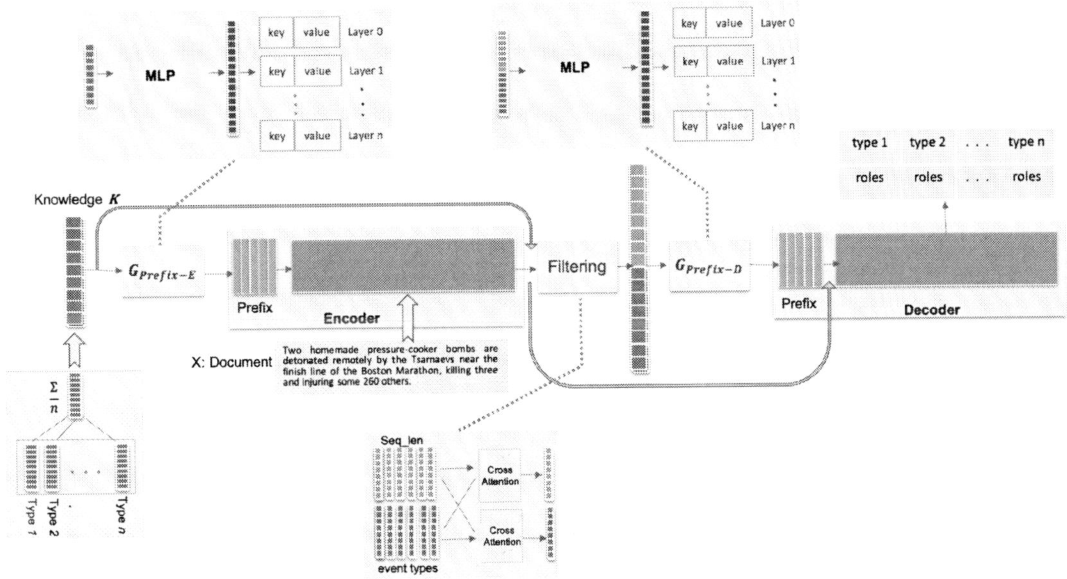

Figure 4: An illustration of our end-to-end framework TCG-Event, where the main architecture in the central is a transformer-based encoder-decoder, the lower blocks represent the task-conditioning construction modules for encoder and decoder respectively and the upper blocks represent the task-conditioning injection modules for encoder and decoder respectively.

suggest that it is flexible to add or remove an event type representation from task conditioning.

Decoder Conditioning. It is expected that the representation of the instance could help the downstream generation in the decoder. Hence we use the representation of both the task and the input sequence to create a prefix for the decoder.

Specifically, let $\mathbf{H}_{\boldsymbol{x}}$ denote the representation of the tokens of the input sequence $\boldsymbol{x}$. We combine the sequence representation $\mathbf{H}_{\boldsymbol{x}}$ and the task representation $\mathbf{H}_{\boldsymbol{e}}$ through the function $f_{dec}:\mathbb{R}^{|\mathbf{e}|\times d}\times\mathbb{R}^{|\mathbf{e}|\times d}\mapsto\mathbb{R}^{d'}\times\mathbb{R}^{d'}$ as follows,

$$\boldsymbol{h}_{\boldsymbol{e},dec},\boldsymbol{h}_{\boldsymbol{x},dec}=f_{dec}(\mathbf{H}_{\boldsymbol{e}},\mathbf{H}_{\boldsymbol{x}}) \tag{5}$$

where f_{dec} is based on dot product-based cross-attention, and $\boldsymbol{h}_{\boldsymbol{e},dec}\in\mathbb{R}^{d'}$, $\boldsymbol{h}_{\boldsymbol{x},dec}\in\mathbb{R}^{d'}$ are the resulting fixed-dimensional vector summaries for decoder conditioning.

Prefix Generation. We create the encoder prefix $\mathbf{Z}_{enc}$ and decoder prefix $\mathbf{Z}_{dec}$ as follows,

$$\begin{aligned}\mathbf{Z}_{enc}&=g_{enc}(\boldsymbol{h}_{\boldsymbol{e},enc})\\ \mathbf{Z}_{dec}&=g_{dec}([\boldsymbol{h}_{\boldsymbol{x},dec};\boldsymbol{h}_{\boldsymbol{x},dec}])\end{aligned} \tag{6}$$

where g_{enc} and g_{dec} are both mapping function $g:\mathbb{R}^{2\times d'}\mapsto\mathbb{R}^{k\times|\mathbf{H}_i|}$, where k is the length of injected prefix and $|\mathbf{H}_i|$ is the number of parameters of the ith injected prefix maintained in the Transformer architecture. With the injection of $\mathbf{Z}_{enc}$ and $\mathbf{Z}_{dec}$, the encoder and the decoder in Equations 1 and 2 are modified as follows:

$$\mathbf{H}_{\boldsymbol{x}}=Encoder(\boldsymbol{x};\mathbf{Z}_{enc}) \tag{7}$$

$$y_t,\boldsymbol{h}_t=\text{Decoder}(y_{t-1};\mathbf{H}_{\boldsymbol{y}_{<t}},\mathbf{Z}_{dec},\mathbf{H}_{\boldsymbol{x}}), \tag{8}$$

where $\mathbf{Z}_{enc}$ and $\mathbf{Z}_{dec}$ can be thought as pseudo-prefix tokens impacting the generation process (Li and Liang, 2021).

Training and Inference We train the model by minimising the negative log-likelihood loss:

$$\theta^*=\underset{\theta}{\operatorname{argmin}}\sum_{(\boldsymbol{x},\boldsymbol{y})\in\mathcal{D}}\log p_\theta(\boldsymbol{y}|\boldsymbol{x},\boldsymbol{e}) \tag{9}$$

where $\mathcal{D}$ is the training set, and

$$p_\theta(\boldsymbol{y}|\boldsymbol{x},\boldsymbol{e})=\prod_{t=1}^{|\boldsymbol{y}|}p_\theta(y_t|\boldsymbol{y}_{<t},\boldsymbol{x},\boldsymbol{e}). \tag{10}$$

For inference, we use constrained decoding (Lu et al., 2021).

5 Experiments

We evaluate our TCG-Event model against a number of recent strong models. In particular, we

Dataset	Event Type	Argument Type	Train	Dev	Test	Instance	Events per Instance
ACE05-EN	33	22	17,172	923	832	1-sent.	Single/Multiple
RAMS	38	65	7,329	924	871	5-sent.	Single

Table 1: Statistics of the event extraction datasets used in the paper, including the numbers of event types, argument types, the type of instances, events per instance and number of instances in different splits.

evaluate it in the supervised learning setting for both sentence-level and paragraph-level extraction tasks to demonstrate the greater effectiveness of our model in these challenging scenarios.

5.1 Evaluation setup

Datasets. We carry out experiments on two event extraction datasets, including the sentence-level dataset Automatic Content Extraction 2005 (ACE05-EN) (Christopher Walker and Maeda, 2006); as well as a paragraph-level dataset: Roles Across Multiple Sentences (RAMS) (Ebner et al., 2019). Statistics of the two datasets can be found in Table 1. Note that we use the official splits of the two datasets for better reproducibility. It is worth noting that these datasets are challenging due to three factors. (1) ***Context length***: each instance in ACE05-EN contains only one sentence, while in RAMS, instances are paragraphs (five sentences). (2) ***Event density***: each instance in RAMS contains only one event, while multiple events could be present in one instance in ACE05-EN. (3) ***Data scarcity***: the amount of training data in ACE05-EN is more than two times that in RAMS.

Evaluation Metrics. We employ the same evaluation metrics used in previous work (Lu et al., 2021; Lin et al., 2020), i.e. F1, precision and recall, for both trigger extraction (Trig-C) and arguments extraction (Arg-C).

Since TCG-Event is a text generation model, to reconstruct the offset of predicted trigger mentions, we consider the input sequence one by one to find the matched utterance. Moreover, in the case of argument mentions, we identify the trigger offset as the nearest matched utterance to the predicted trigger mention.

Baselines. We evaluate TCG-Event against three groups of baselines which use different levels of annotations of decreasing granularity: *Both token-level and entity-level annotation*, *Token-level annotation*, and *Parallel text-record annotation*.

Some methods utilize token annotations, in which each token in an instance is annotated with event labels, along with golden entity annotation to facilitate event extraction. Joint3EE (Lin et al., 2020) is a multi-task model that jointly performs entity, trigger, and argument extraction by shared Bi-GRU hidden representations. DYGIE++ (Nguyen and Nguyen, 2019) is a BERT-based extraction framework that models text spans and captures within-sentence and cross-sentence context. GAIL (Zhang et al., 2019) is an ELMo-based model that proposes a joint entity and event extraction framework based on generative adversarial imitation learning, which is an inverse reinforcement learning method. OneIE (Lin et al., 2020) introduces a classification-based information extraction system that employs global features and beam search to extract event structures.

Some other methods use token-level annotation. TANL (Paolini et al., 2021), a sequence generation-based method, tackles event extraction in a trigger-argument pipeline. Multi-task TANL is the extended version of TANL which transfers structure knowledge from other tasks. BERT-QA (Du and Cardie, 2020) and MQAEE (Li et al., 2020) consider event extraction as a sequence of extractive question answering problems.

Similar to Text2Event (Lu et al., 2021), we use *Parallel text-record annotation*, which only requires (instance, event) pairs without expensive, fine-grained token-level or entity-level annotations. As can be seen in an instance of such an annotation, ⟨"His two brothers were executed.", {Type: Injure, Trigger: tortured, ...}⟩, parallel text-record annotation is the least demanding and thus more practical annotation level. We compare our method with Text2Event (Lu et al., 2021), which introduces a sequence-to-structure generation model that addresses the missing event structure issue via constrained decoding.

Implementation Details We build our TCG-Event method on the T5-base pretraind language model and train it for 120 epochs with a learning rate of 1e-4 and batch size of 8 for the supervised setting. We also optimized TCG-Event using label smoothing Szegedy et al. (2016) and AdamW Loshchilov and Hutter (2017). The prefix length is set to 20 for all experiments in Section 5.2.

Models	Annotation	Arg-C			Trig-C			PLM
		F1	P	R	F1	P	R	
Joint3EE (Nguyen and Nguyen, 2019)	Token+Entity	52.1	52.1	52.1	69.8	68	71.8	-
DYGIE++ (Wadden et al., 2019)	Token+Entity	48.8	-	-	69.7	-	-	BERT-large
GAIL(Zhang et al., 2019)	Token+Entity	52.4	61.6	45.7	72.0	74.8	69.4	ELMo
OneIE (Lin et al., 2020)	Token+Entity	56.8	-	-	74.7	-	-	BERT-large
BERT-QA (Du and Cardie, 2020)	Token	53.3	56.8	50.2	72.4	71.1	73.7	2 x BERT-base
MQAEE (Li et al., 2020)	Token	53.4	-	-	71.7	-	-	3 x BERT-large
TANL (Paolini et al., 2021)	Token	47.6	-	-	68.4	-	-	T5-base
Multi-Task TANL (Paolini et al., 2021)	Token	48.5	-	-	68.5	-	-	T5-base
Text2Event (Lu et al., 2021)	Text-record	49.8	46.7	53.4	69.2	67.5	71.2	T5-base
TCG-Event$_{\text{Fine tuning+Prefix}}$	Text-record	49.0	47.3	50.7	69.3	**69.1**	69.5	T5-base
TCG-Event$_{\text{Full}}$	Text-record	**51.5**	**48.1**	**55.6**	**70.1**	66.7	**73.9**	T5-base

Table 2: Experiment results for the fully supervised event extraction on ACE05-EN. PLM represents the pre-trained language model used by each model. We use *text-record* annotation, which only provides (instance, event) pairs without expensive, fine-grained token-level or entity-level annotations.

5.2 Main Results

We compare our TCG-Event model in the fully supervised setting. The model evaluation is organised by dataset characteristics: sentence-level (ACE05-EN) and paragraph-level (RAMS).

Supervised Setting. In this setting, each model is trained on the full training data of the respective dataset. Table 2 presents the sentence-level event extraction results on ACE05-EN. Note that except for the last block, performance numbers of all baselines are taken directly from Text2Event (Lu et al., 2021).

It can be observed from the table that our TCG-Event model outperforms Text2Event on F1 for both argument extraction and trigger extraction. Moreover, our model surpasses the generation-based baselines using token annotation and achieves competitive performance with SOTA.

Sentence-level performance. As discussed above, among all compared models, our TCG-Event model, together with Text2Event (Lu et al., 2021), is trained on parallel text-record annotations, the weakest form of supervision. In contrast, the other baseline models require token-level annotations and entity annotations, which are more fine-grained and expensive to collect. As expected, more extensive training data induces stronger model performance. The last column also shows that the better-performing models make use of larger pretrained language models (PLMs), such as BERT-large. The larger capacity of these PLMs also contributes to model performance.

Paragraph-level performance. Table 3 shows the performance of the baseline (Text2Event), our model TCG-Event and its different variants for paragraph-level event extraction on the RAMS dataset. The other models in Table 2 are sentence-level and do not support this task. The majority of baselines focus only on event argument extraction from RAMS dataset, which did not handle triggers (Li et al., 2021c; Liu et al., 2021; Lin et al., 2021). Our model supports the joint extraction of both event triggers and arguments from the RAMS dataset.

We can observe from the table that our full model achieves the best F1 values for both argument extraction (Arg-C) and trigger detection (Trig-C) on RAMS. It is especially noteworthy that TCG-Event achieves better performance advantages over Text2Event.

The superiority can be attributed to a model design. Our cross-attention mechanism filters event-type tokens and argument tokens, allowing the model to better handle long context. Detailed analysis on the contributions of each model component will be presented below.

5.3 Ablation Study

This section analyzes the effects of prefix encoder conditioning, prefix decoder conditioning, prefix cross-attention, and constrained decoding in TCG-Event. We designed five ablated variants based on T5-base:

- "w/o$_{\text{_encoder conditioning}}$": indicates TCG-Event without prefix encoder conditioning.
- "w/o$_{\text{_decoder conditioning}}$" indicates TCG-Event without prefix decoder conditioning.
- "w/o$_{\text{_both conditioning}}$" indicates TCG-Event without both prefix encoder and prefix decoder

Models	Arg-C			Trig-C		
	F1	**P**	**R**	**F1**	**P**	**R**
Text2Event (Lu et al., 2021)	29.81	28.98	30.69	67.13	67.09	67.16
TCG-Event$_{\text{Full}}$	**30.88**	**31.07**	30.70	**68.42**	**68.31**	**68.54**
TCG-Event$_{\text{Adapter}}$	23.11	21.34	25.21	62.28	62.10	62.46
TCG-Event$_{\text{Fine tuning+Adapter}}$	30.00	29.95	30.05	67.62	67.27	67.97
TCG-Event$_{\text{Prefix}}$	9.60	18.18	6.53	24.51	20.73	29.97
TCG-Event$_{\text{Fine tuning+Prefix}}$	30.53	30.19	**30.89**	65.87	65.17	66.59

Table 3: Results for supervised learning on the paragraph-level event extraction dataset RAMS.

Models	Arg-C			Trig-C		
	F1	P	R	F1	P	R
w/o$_{\text{_encoder conditioning}}$	46.91	44.60	49.48	68.80	65.91	71.96
w/o$_{\text{_decoder conditioning}}$	45.59	42.02	49.83	68.79	65.89	71.94
w/o$_{\text{_both conditioning}}$	49.41	47.44	51.56	68.35	66.35	70.47
w/o$_{\text{_constraint decoding}}$	48.06	45.83	50.52	67.92	64.72	71.46
w/o$_{\text{_cross attention}}$	49.10	45.01	53.99	68.77	64.84	73.20
TCG-Event-full	**51.5**	**48.1**	**55.6**	**70.1**	**66.7**	**73.9**

Table 4: The ablation study in the supervised learning setting on the ACE05-EN dataset based on T5-base.

conditioning.

- "w/o$_{\text{_constraint decoding}}$" discards the constrained decoding during inference and generates event structures as an unconstrained generation model.
- "w/o$_{\text{_cross attention}}$" indicates TCG-Event without prefix cross-attention.

Table 4 shows the results of the test set of ACE05-EN for the supervised learning setting. We observe that:

- constrained decoding helps, but not too much;
- prefix encoder and decoder conditioning are the most effective module id we use both of them together.

Furthermore, as constraint decoding limits the argument and trigger words generated by the model, our method does not suffer from hallucination problems.

5.4 Analysis

In this section, we conduct comprehensive studies to analyze the design of our method from prefix length perspectives.

Longer prefixes provide more task-conditioning information to the model. Table 5 summarizes the result of model performance of different prefix lengths on the ACE05-EN dataset. As can be seen, longer prefixes improve model performance on Arg-C, while performance on Trig-C improves with increases in prefix length until 20, after which F1 value plateaus. As longer prefixes demand more model parameters, we set the prefix length to 20 as a trade-off between model performance and computational efficiency.

Prefix	Arg-C			Trig-C		
length	**F1**	**P**	**R**	**F1**	**P**	**R**
5	45.67	41.79	50.35	68.74	66.21	71.46
10	46.58	42.96	50.87	69.50	66.37	72.95
20	51.51	48.08	55.55	70.12	66.71	73.89
50	51.50	48.00	55.56	70.19	66.94	73.77
100	51.80	48.31	55.83	68.64	66.2	72.95

Table 5: Results for supervised learning on ACE05-EN with different prefix lengths.

6 Conclusion

In this paper, we formulate the problem of event extraction as a natural-language generation task. We propose TCG-Event, a generation-based event extraction technique that leverages large pre-trained language models. A key component in TCG-Event is a novel task conditioning technique that injects event-type information into the model as prefixes. The cross-attention mechanism in the prefix generator also facilitates effective long-text handling. Extensive experiments on two benchmark datasets demonstrate the effectiveness of TCG-Event, which achieves state-of-the-art performance in event extraction. On the challenging RAMS dataset, TCG-Event outperforms the current best model. For future work, we plan to further investigate new mechanisms of injecting task-specific information.

References

Julie Medero Christopher Walker, Stephanie Strassel and Kazuaki Maeda. 2006. Ace 2005 multilingual training corpus. `https://catalog.ldc.upenn.edu/LDC2006T06`.

Xinya Du and Claire Cardie. 2020. Event extraction by

answering (almost) natural questions. *arXiv preprint arXiv:2004.13625*.

Xinya Du, Alexander M. Rush, and Claire Cardie. 2021. GRIT: generative role-filler transformers for document-level event entity extraction. In *Proceedings of EACL*, pages 634–644.

Seth Ebner, Patrick Xia, Ryan Culkin, Kyle Rawlins, and Benjamin Van Durme. 2019. Multi-sentence argument linking. *arXiv preprint arXiv:1911.03766*.

Giacomo Frisoni, Gianluca Moro, and Antonella Carbonaro. 2021. A survey on event extraction for natural language understanding: Riding the biomedical literature wave. *IEEE Access*, 9:160721–160757.

Jiayuan He, Dat Quoc Nguyen, Saber A Akhondi, Christian Druckenbrodt, Camilo Thorne, Ralph Hoessel, Zubair Afzal, Zenan Zhai, Biaoyan Fang, Hiyori Yoshikawa, et al. 2021. Chemu 2020: Natural language processing methods are effective for information extraction from chemical patents. *Frontiers in Research Metrics and Analytics*, 6:654438.

I-Hung Hsu, Kuan-Hao Huang, Elizabeth Boschee, Scott Miller, Premkumar Natarajan, Kai-Wei Chang, and Nanyun Peng. 2022. Degree: A data-efficient generation-based event extraction model.

Kung-Hsiang Huang and Nanyun Peng. 2021. Document-level event extraction with efficient end-to-end learning of cross-event dependencies. In *Proceedings of NUSE-NAACL*, pages 36–47.

Kung-Hsiang Huang, Sam Tang, and Nanyun Peng. 2021. Document-level entity-based extraction as template generation. *CoRR*, abs/2109.04901.

Fayuan Li, Weihua Peng, Yuguang Chen, Quan Wang, Lu Pan, Yajuan Lyu, and Yong Zhu. 2020. Event extraction as multi-turn question answering. In *Proceedings of the 2020 Conference on Empirical Methods in Natural Language Processing: Findings*, pages 829–838.

Qian Li, Hao Peng, Jianxin Li, Yiming Hei, Rui Sun, Jiawei Sheng, Shu Guo, Lihong Wang, and Philip S. Yu. 2021a. Deep learning schema-based event extraction: Literature review and current trends. *CoRR*, abs/2107.02126.

Sha Li, Heng Ji, and Jiawei Han. 2021b. Document-level event argument extraction by conditional generation. In *Proceedings of NAACL*, pages 894–908.

Sha Li, Heng Ji, and Jiawei Han. 2021c. Document-level event argument extraction by conditional generation. *arXiv preprint arXiv:2104.05919*.

Xiang Lisa Li and Percy Liang. 2021. Prefix-tuning: Optimizing continuous prompts for generation. *CoRR*, abs/2101.00190.

Jiaju Lin, Jin Jian, and Qin Chen. 2021. Eliciting knowledge from language models for event extraction. *arXiv preprint arXiv:2109.05190*.

Ying Lin, Heng Ji, Fei Huang, and Lingfei Wu. 2020. A joint neural model for information extraction with global features. In *Proceedings of the 58th Annual Meeting of the Association for Computational Linguistics*, pages 7999–8009.

Pierre Lison, Jeremy Barnes, Aliaksandr Hubin, and Samia Touileb. 2020. Named entity recognition without labelled data: A weak supervision approach. In *Proceedings of the 58th Annual Meeting of the Association for Computational Linguistics*, pages 1518–1533, Online. Association for Computational Linguistics.

Jian Liu, Yufeng Chen, and Jinan Xu. 2021. Machine reading comprehension as data augmentation: A case study on implicit event argument extraction. In *Proceedings of the 2021 Conference on Empirical Methods in Natural Language Processing*, pages 2716–2725.

Xiao Liu, Heyan Huang, Ge Shi, and Bo Wang. 2022. Dynamic prefix-tuning for generative template-based event extraction. *Proceedings of the 60th Annual Meeting of the Association for Computational Linguistics*.

Ilya Loshchilov and Frank Hutter. 2017. Decoupled weight decay regularization. *arXiv preprint arXiv:1711.05101*.

Yaojie Lu, Hongyu Lin, Jin Xu, Xianpei Han, Jialong Tang, Annan Li, Le Sun, Meng Liao, and Shaoyi Chen. 2021. Text2Event: Controllable sequence-to-structure generation for end-to-end event extraction. In *Proceedings of ACL*, pages 2795–2806.

Dat Quoc Nguyen and Karin Verspoor. 2019. End-to-end neural relation extraction using deep biaffine attention. In *European conference on information retrieval*, pages 729–738. Springer.

Trung Minh Nguyen and Thien Huu Nguyen. 2019. One for all: Neural joint modeling of entities and events. In *Proceedings of the AAAI Conference on Artificial Intelligence*, volume 33, pages 6851–6858.

Giovanni Paolini, Ben Athiwaratkun, Jason Krone, Jie Ma, Alessandro Achille, Rishita Anubhai, Cicero Nogueira dos Santos, Bing Xiang, and Stefano Soatto. 2021. Structured prediction as translation between augmented natural languages. *arXiv preprint arXiv:2101.05779*.

Colin Raffel, Noam Shazeer, Adam Roberts, Katherine Lee, Sharan Narang, Michael Matena, Yanqi Zhou, Wei Li, and Peter J. Liu. 2020. Exploring the limits of transfer learning with a unified text-to-text transformer. *Journal of Machine Learning Research*, 21(140):1–67.

Shirong Shen, Tongtong Wu, Guilin Qi, Yuan-Fang Li, Gholamreza Haffari, and Sheng Bi. 2021. Adaptive knowledge-enhanced bayesian meta-learning for few-shot event detection. In *ACL Findings*, pages 2417–2429.

Fatemeh Shiri, Teresa Wang, Shirui Pan, Xiaojun Chang, Yuan-Fang Li, Reza Haffari, Van Nguyen, and Shuang Yu. 2021. Toward the automated construction of probabilistic knowledge graphs for the maritime domain. In *2021 IEEE 24th International Conference on Information Fusion (FUSION)*, pages 1–8. IEEE.

Christian Szegedy, Vincent Vanhoucke, Sergey Ioffe, Jon Shlens, and Zbigniew Wojna. 2016. Rethinking the inception architecture for computer vision. In *Proceedings of the IEEE conference on computer vision and pattern recognition*, pages 2818–2826.

Ashish Vaswani, Noam Shazeer, Niki Parmar, Jakob Uszkoreit, Llion Jones, Aidan N. Gomez, Lukasz Kaiser, and Illia Polosukhin. 2017. Attention is all you need. In *Advances in Neural Information Processing Systems 30: Annual Conference on Neural Information Processing Systems 2017, December 4-9, 2017, Long Beach, CA, USA*, pages 5998–6008.

Karin M Verspoor, Go Eun Heo, Keun Young Kang, and Min Song. 2016. Establishing a baseline for literature mining human genetic variants and their relationships to disease cohorts. *BMC medical informatics and decision making*, 16(1):37–47.

David Wadden, Ulme Wennberg, Yi Luan, and Hannaneh Hajishirzi. 2019. Entity, relation, and event extraction with contextualized span representations. *arXiv preprint arXiv:1909.03546*.

Runxin Xu, Tianyu Liu, Lei Li, and Baobao Chang. 2021. Document-level event extraction via heterogeneous graph-based interaction model with a tracker. In *Proceedings of ACL*, pages 3533–3546.

Hang Yang, Dianbo Sui, Yubo Chen, Kang Liu, Jun Zhao, and Taifeng Wang. 2021. Document-level event extraction via parallel prediction networks. In *Proceedings of ACL*, pages 6298–6308, Online. Association for Computational Linguistics.

Ningyu Zhang, Xiang Chen, Xin Xie, Shumin Deng, Chuanqi Tan, Mosha Chen, Fei Huang, Luo Si, and Huajun Chen. 2021. Document-level relation extraction as semantic segmentation. In *Proceedings of IJCAI*, pages 3999–4006.

Tongtao Zhang, Heng Ji, and Avirup Sil. 2019. Joint entity and event extraction with generative adversarial imitation learning. *Data Intelligence*, 1(2):99–120.

Zhisong Zhang, Xiang Kong, Zhengzhong Liu, Xuezhe Ma, and Eduard H. Hovy. 2020. A two-step approach for implicit event argument detection. In *Proceedings of ACL*, pages 7479–7485.

Complex Reading Comprehension Through Question Decomposition

Xiao-Yu Guo , Yuan-Fang Li , and Gholamreza Haffari

Faculty of Information Technology, Monash University, Melbourne, Australia

{xiaoyu.guo,yuanfang.li,gholamreza.haffari}@monash.edu

Abstract

Multi-hop reading comprehension requires not only the ability to reason over raw text but also the ability to combine multiple evidence. We propose a novel learning approach that helps language models better understand difficult multi-hop questions and perform "complex, compositional" reasoning. Our model first learns to decompose each multi-hop question into several sub-questions by a trainable *question decomposer*. Instead of answering these sub-questions, we directly concatenate them with the original question and context, and leverage a *reading comprehension* model to predict the answer in a sequence-to-sequence manner. By using the same language model for these two components, our best *seperate/unified* t5-base variants outperform the baseline by 7.2/6.1 absolute F1 points on a hard subset of DROP dataset.

1 Introduction

Multi-hop Reading Comprehension (RC) is a challenging problem that requires compositional, symbolic and arithmetic reasoning capabilities. Facing a difficult question, humans tend to first decompose it into several sub-questions whose answers can be more easily identified. The final answer to the overall question can then be concluded from the aggregation of all sub-questions' answers. For instance, for the question in Table 1, we can naturally decompose it into three simpler sub-questions (1) "return the touchdown yards", (2) "return the fewest of #1", and (3) "return who caught #2". The tokens #1 and #2 are the answers to the first and second sub-questions respectively. Finally, the player with the touchdown of #2 is returned as the final answer.

State-of-the-art RC techniques employ large-scale pre-trained language models (LMs) such as GPT-3 (Brown et al., 2020) for their superior representation and reasoning capablities. Chain of thought prompting (Wei et al., 2022) elicits strong reasoning capability of LMs by providing intermediate reasoning steps. Least-to-most prompting (Zhou et al., 2022) further shows the feasibility of conducting decomposition and multi-hop reasoning, which happen on the decoder side together with the answer prediction procedure. However, compared to supervised learning models, both of these methods rely on extremely large LMs with tens and hundreds of **billions** of parameters to achieve competitive performance, thus requiring expensive hardware and incurring a large computation footprint.

C	First, Detroit's Calvin Johnson caught a 1-yard pass in the third quarter. The game's final points came when Mike Williams of Tampa Bay caught a 5-yard.
Q	Who caught the touchdown for the fewest yards?
$\mathbf{Q_1}$	return the touchdown yards
$\mathbf{Q_2}$	return the fewest of #1
$\mathbf{Q_3}$	return who caught #2
A	Calvin Johnson

Table 1: An example for reading comprehension. **C** is the context, **Q** is a hard multi-hop question, and $\mathbf{Q_1}$, $\mathbf{Q_2}$, $\mathbf{Q_3}$ are sub-questions annotated in BREAK dataset. **A** is the answer to **Q**.

Despite significant research on RC (Dua et al., 2019; Perez et al., 2020), those questions that require strong compositional generalisability and numerical reasoning abilities are still challenging to even the state-of-the-art models (Ran et al., 2019; Chen et al., 2020a,b; Wei et al., 2022; Zhou et al., 2022). While decomposition is a natural approach to tackle this problem, the lack of sufficient ground-truth sub-questions limits our ability to train RC models based on large LMs.

In this paper, we propose a novel low-budget

(only 1‰ parameters of GPT-3) learning approach to improve LMs' performance on hard multi-hop RC such as the Break subset of DROP (Dua et al., 2019). Our model consists of two main modules: (1) an encoder-decoder LM as a *question decomposer* and (2) another encoder-decoder LM as the *reading comprehension* model. First, we train the question decomposer to decompose a difficult multi-hop question to sub-questions from a limited amount of annotated data. Next, instead of solving these sub-questions, we train the reading comprehension model to predict the final answer by directly concatenating the sub-questions with the original question. We further propose a *unified* model that utilizes the same LM for both question decomposition and reading comprehension with task-specific prompts. With 9× weakly supervised data, we design a Hard EM-style algorithm to iteratively optimise the *unified* model.

To prove the effectiveness of our approach, we leverage two different types of LMs: T5 (Raffel et al., 2020) and Bart (Lewis et al., 2020) to build baselines and our variants. The experimental results show that without changing the model structure, our proposed variant outperforms the end-to-end baseline. By adding ground-truth sub-questions, gains on the F1 metric are 1.7 and 0.7 using T5 and Bart separately. Introducing weakly supervised training data can help improve the performance of both *separate* and *unified* variants by at least 4.4 point on F1. And our method beats the state-of-the-art model GPT-3 by a large margin.

2 Related Work

Multi-hop Reading Comprehension mentioned in this paper requires more than one reasoning or inference step to answer a question. For example, multi-hop RC in DROP (Dua et al., 2019) requires numerical reasoning such as addition, subtraction. To address this problem, Dua et al. proposed a number-aware model NAQANet that can deal with such questions for which the answer cannot be directly extracted. NumNet (Ran et al., 2019) leveraged Graph Neural Network to design a number-aware deep learning model. QDGAT (Chen et al., 2020a) distinguished number types more precisely by adding the connection with entities and obtained better performance. Nerd (Chen et al., 2020b) searched possible programs exhaustively based on the ground-truth and employed these programs as weak supervision to train the whole model.

Question Decomposition is the approach that given a complex question, break it into several simple sub-questions. These sub-questions can also be Question Decomposition Meaning Representation (QDMR) (Wolfson et al., 2020) for complex questions. Many researchers (Perez et al., 2020; Geva et al., 2021) have been trying to solve the problem by incorporating decomposition procedures. For example, Perez et al. (2020) propose a model that can break hard questions into easier sub-questions. Then, simple QA systems provide answers of these sub-questions for downstream complex QA systems to produce the final answer corresponding to the original complex question. Fu et al. (2021) propose a three-stage framework called Relation Extractor Reader and Comparator (RERC), based on complex question decomposition. Different from these approaches, we aim to improve the multi-hop capability of current encoder-decoder models without dedicated pre-designing the architecture.

Language Models like BERT (Devlin et al., 2019), GPT families (Radford et al., 2018, 2019; Brown et al., 2020), BART (Lewis et al., 2020) and T5 (Raffel et al., 2020) are demonstrated to be effective on many NLP tasks, base on either fine-tuning or few-shot learning (Wei et al., 2022; Zhou et al., 2022), even zero-shot learning. However, LMs suffer a lot from solving multi-hop questions and logic reasoning and numerical reasoning problems. Although some research (Nye et al., 2021; Wei et al., 2022) has conducted experiments on either simple or synthetic datasets and shown the effectiveness, Razeghi et al. (2022) indicates that the model reasoning is not robust enough.

Recently, Dohan et al. (2022) points out that prompted models can be regarded as employing a unified framework a *language model cascade*. From the perspective view of probabilistic programming, several recent literature (Wei et al., 2022; Zhou et al., 2022) are formalized. In this paper, we also treat our whole process as a probabilistic model that is consistent to Dohan et al. (2022).

3 Complex Question Answering Through Decomposition

Our focus in this work is on complex questions requiring multi-hop reasoning. As such, our approach consists of the following two steps:

1. The complex question is decomposed to a sequence of sub-questions. The decomposition

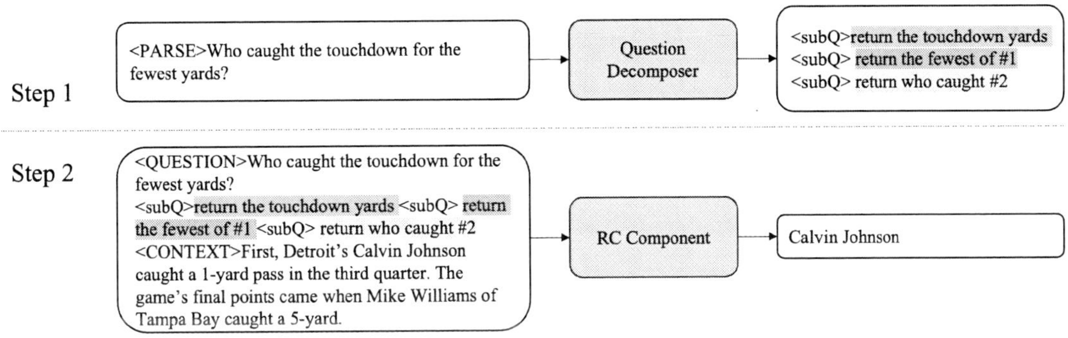

Figure 1: Our model structure on complex reading comprehension through question decomposition. Step 1: Question Decomposer generates a sequence of sub-questions; Step 2: RC component predicts the answer based on question, sub-questions and the given context. The context of this given example is truncated.

of the question is performed by the *question decomposer* component of our system.

2. The model produces the answer to the complex question leveraging the generated sub-questions to provide guidance to the reasoning of the system. This is performed by the *reading comprehension* component.

We use LMs such as T5 and Bart as the backbone[1] for both question decomposer and the reading comprehension (Figure 1). We present several variants of our model, depending whether the models for the above two steps are either separate or unified using multitask learning. As we have the ground truth question decomposition for only a subset of the training data, we treat the missing decompositions as latent variables. We then propose an algorithm based on Hard-EM (Neal and Hinton, 1998) for learning the model. The rest of this section provides more details.

Probabilistic Model. Given a question Q and a C context pair, our system generates the answer A according to the following probabilistic model:

$$P_\theta(A|Q,C) = \sum_Z P_\theta(A,Z|Q,C) \quad (1)$$

$$= \sum_Z P^{\text{dc}}_{\text{LM}}(Z|Q) \times P^{\text{rc}}_{\text{LM}}(A|Q,C,Z) \quad (2)$$

where Z denotes the unobserved decomposition of the question, $P^{\text{dc}}_{\text{LM}}(Z|Q)$ [2] denotes the question decomposer (operationalised based on one specific LM), and $P^{\text{rc}}_{\text{LM}}(A|Q,C,Z)$ denotes the reading comprehension component. In principle, the $P^{\text{dc}}_{\text{LM}}$ and $P^{\text{rc}}_{\text{LM}}$ components can be constructed using different models, so the parameters θ of the whole probabilistic model consists of those for these two models. This is denoted by the *separate* variant.

We further investigate using the same LM for both the question decomposer and reading comprehension component, which we denote by the *unified* variant in the experiments. In this case, the probabilistic model parameter θ consists of only one set of parameters corresponding to the underlying model.

Question Decomposer. To obtain high-quality sub-questions, we first train a question decomposer $P^{\text{dc}}_{\text{LM}}$ to break down difficult multi-hop questions, i.e., the first term in Equation 2. It learns the decomposition based on QDMRs (Wolfson et al., 2020). We only use the specific partition on the DROP dataset (Dua et al., 2019) and treat QDMRs as sub-questions. These sub-questions only cover around 10% QA pairs in DROP. Therefore, we need to predict decompositions for the rest of the dataset. More details will be revealed in Section 4.

Formally, given a multi-hop question Q, the question decomposer $P^{\text{dc}}_{\text{LM}}$ generates the sub-questions $Z := \{Q^1, Q^2, ..., Q^s\}$. Intuitively, We treat it as a seq2seq learning problem: our input to the encoder is "<PARSE>Q", where <PARSE> is a special token. The decoder then generates tokens of the sub-questions in auto-regressive way "<subQ>Q^1<subQ>Q^2<subQ>... Q^s", where <subQ> is a special token [3].

[1] Our approach is general, and it can be used with other pre-trained seq2seq models and language models as well.

[2] We have made the following independence assumption: $P^{\text{dc}}_{\text{LM}}(Z|Q) \approx P^{\text{dc}}_{\text{LM}}(Z|Q,C)$.

[3] We employ the greedy search algorithm to generate the sub-questions Z. However, one can leverage other strategies like beam search to make more than one predictions.

Algorithm 1 Learning with Hard-EM

Require: an initial pre-trained LM M; the full reading comprehesion dataset $\mathcal{D}_1$; the subset with sub-question annotations $\mathcal{D}_2$.

Train M on $\mathcal{D}_2$ to get M^0
for iter **in** N_iters **do**
  For all $\mathcal{D} = \mathcal{D}_1 \setminus \mathcal{D}_2$ employ M^{iter-1} to predict sub-questions and get $\mathcal{D}^{iter}$
  Retrain M^{iter-1} on all examples: $\mathcal{D}_2 \cup \mathcal{D}^{iter}$, get updated model M^{iter}
end for

Reading Comprehension Component. To further obtain answers based on the question and generated sub-questions, the reading comprehension component $P_{\text{LM}}^{\text{rc}}$ generates the answer A, i.e., the second term in Equation 2. In stead of directly answering all the sub-questions given by the trained question decomposer, we train our RC component to predict the final answer in a sequence-to-sequence way.

Formally, given a multi-hop complex question Q and the corresponding sub-questions $Z := \{Q1, Q2, ..., Q^s\}$ generated by a trained question decomposer, our input to the RC encoder is "<QUESTION>Q<subQ>Q^1...<subQ>Q^s<CONTEXT>C", where <QUESTION> and <CONTEXT> are special tokens. In other words, we concatenate the multi-hop question and all the sub-questions, together with the context as the input to our RC component. The decoder then generates the tokens of the answer autoregressively.

Training and Inference. The training objective of our model is

$$\mathcal{L} = \sum_{(Q,C,A)\in\mathcal{D}_1\setminus\mathcal{D}_2} \log P_\theta(A|Q,C) + \sum_{(Q,C,Z^*,A)\in\mathcal{D}_2} \log P_\theta(A, Z^*|Q,C), \tag{3}$$

where Z^* denotes the ground truth decomposition available only for the subset of the training data referred to by $\mathcal{D}_2$. The first term of the training objective involves enumerating over all possible latent decompositions, which is computationally intractable. Therefore, we resort to Hard-EM for learning the parameters of our model (see Algorithm 1) for the unified variant. We found taking 10 iterations of the Hard-EM algorithm to be mostly

Proportions		1%	5%	10%	50%	100%
BLEU		39.08	44.76	47.74	50.12	**54.69**
Rouge-1		77.49	81.75	83.12	84.76	**85.67**
Rouge-2		57.00	62.83	64.97	66.94	**68.61**
RougeL		67.78	72.65	74.37	76.55	**77.43**
RC	EM	26.0	26.5	27.0	**27.8**	27.2
	F1	31.3	31.3	31.6	**32.2**	32.0

Table 2: Experimental results of the Bart based question decomposer: (1) Row 1-4 show intrinsic metrics for the question decomposition by using different proportions of training instances. (2) Row 5-6 show extrinsic metrics of the RC model by using the corresponding decomposer generated sub-questions.

sufficient for learning model parameters in our experiments.

For the separate variant, i.e., using two different LMs for $P_{\text{LM}}^{\text{dc}}$ and $P_{\text{LM}}^{\text{rc}}$, we train the question decomposer on $\mathcal{D}_2$, and then train the reading comprehension component on $\mathcal{D}_2$ as well as $\mathcal{D}_1 \setminus \mathcal{D}_2$ augmented with the generated decomposition Z. We also compare with training the reading comprehension component on $\mathcal{D}_2$ only, in the experiments. During inference time, we first generate the question decomposition $\tilde{Z}$ according to $P_{\text{LM}}^{\text{dc}}$, and then use $\tilde{Z}$ in $P_{\text{LM}}^{\text{rc}}$ to generate the answer.

4 Experiments

4.1 Dataset

We consistently use the same notations as in Algorithm 1.

- $\mathcal{D}_1$: the DROP dataset (Dua et al., 2019) that contains 77,400/9,536 question (Q) answer (A) training/testing pairs for the reading comprehension component.
- $\mathcal{D}_2$: the BREAK dataset (Wolfson et al., 2020) [5] that contains 7,683/1,268 question (Q) decomposition (Z^*) training/testing pairs for the question decomposer [6].
- $\mathcal{D} = \mathcal{D}_1 \setminus \mathcal{D}_2$: the difference set between $\mathcal{D}_1$ and $\mathcal{D}_2$ that contains only question answer pairs without ground-truth decomposition.
- $\mathcal{D}^{iter}$: $\mathcal{D}$ with decomposition (Z) generated by the trained question decomposer.

[5]The full BREAK dataset Wolfson et al. (2020) annotated is a combination of many datasets including DROP. In this paper, we only use the DROP partition of the original BREAK.

[6]This subset of DROP contains the corresponding answers for each question. Therefore, we also use it to evaluate the RC component in our experiments.

LMs		t5-small					t5-base				
Proportions		1% [4]	5%	10%	50%	100%	1%	5%	10%	50%	100%
BLEU		11.21	44.50	50.44	60.15	<u>62.73</u>	34.86	52.98	57.3	62.18	**64.40**
Rouge-1		43.00	76.93	81.53	87.25	<u>88.59</u>	70.66	84.16	85.77	88.50	**89.27**
Rouge-2		28.18	59.13	64.33	72.60	<u>74.76</u>	50.57	66.86	70.24	74.24	**75.72**
RougeL		39.22	68.92	73.66	79.99	<u>81.57</u>	62.10	75.49	78.07	81.20	**82.53**
RC	EM	-	28.9	<u>29.9</u>	29.0	29.0	33.7	34.3	34.3	34.6	**34.8**
	F1	-	33.0	<u>34.0</u>	33.2	33.1	37.8	38.4	38.5	38.5	**38.6**

Table 3: Results of the T5 based question decomposer (left-half: t5-small, right-half: t5-base): (1) Row 1-4 show all intrinsic metrics to evaluate the question decomposer by using different proportions of training instances. (2) Row 5-6 show extrinsic metrics of the RC component by using the corresponding decomposer generated sub-questions.

Note that every question (Q) is associated with a specific context (C). With all question decomposition labelled, $\mathcal{D}_2$ is actually a subset of $\mathcal{D}_1$ and is more challenging.

4.2 Backbone and Evaluation Metric

There are three LMs of different types and sizes we employ as backbones in this paper: (1) t5-small (60M parameters), (2) t5-base (220M parameters), (3) bart-base (140M parameters). We also employ GPT-3 (175B parameters) as it is the current state-of-the-art language model in a various of natural language processing tasks.

Sub-question Decomposition We train and evaluate our question decomposer using $\mathcal{D}_2$, which was proposed to better understand difficult multi-hop questions. We report BLEU (Papineni et al., 2002) and Rouge (Lin, 2004) scores to show the intrinsic performance of the decomposer.

Reading Comprehension We evaluate our RC model on $\mathcal{D}_2$. For the Hard-EM approach, we have $\mathcal{D}_1 \setminus \mathcal{D}_2$ as weakly supervised data. We report F1 and Exact Match(EM) (Dua et al., 2019) scores in the following experiments.

4.3 Results on Decomposition

Based on Bart and T5, Table 2 and Table 3 respectively show the experimental results of the question decomposers. To comprehensively show their performance, we conducted two aspects of experiments including intrinsic decomposition evaluation and extrinsic RC evaluation.

Intrinsic Evaluation We first evaluate the quality of sub-questions generated by different question decomposers. In this part, intrinsic metrics, BLEU and Rouge scores, are shown in the first four rows of Table 2 and Table 3. And also we show the results of five decomposers trained on different proportions (1%, 5%, 10%, 50%, 100%) of the BREAK dataset $\mathcal{D}_2$'s training data. All these evaluations are conducted on the same validation set of $\mathcal{D}_2$.

Comparing column-by-column, we find that with more training data, both question decomposers achieve a better performance for both BLEU and Rouge. We also note that the rate of improvement of these metrics becomes slower when more data is added (e.g. 1% to 5% and 10% to 50%). Therefore, we posit that with more training data, the performance of the decomposer will not improve due to the capability of the LM model.

Extrinsic Evaluation Since the eventual usage of the generated sub-questions is to improve the RC component, we conduct a RC performance comparison experiments to see how can the quality of these sub-questions influence the downstream RC task. Also like the intrinsic evaluation, we show the results based on decomposers trained on different proportions of $\mathcal{D}_2$ by using two extrinsic metrics: EM and F1. All the evaluations are conducted on the same validation set of $\mathcal{D}_2$.

To clarify our settings in this part, we don't employ the ground-truth sub-questions from $\mathcal{D}_2$. Instead, we employ the sub-questions generated by five question decomposers for the RC component to predict answers. As the last two rows of both Table 2 and Table 3 show, both EM and F1 scores show a gradually increasing trend when more training instances are used to train the question decomposer. With more parameters, t5-base tends to have a better performance than t5-small.

4.4 Results on Reading Comprehension

Table 4 shows the experimental results for the downstream RC task. We show two baselines in the first place: "bart-base" and "t5-base". Without taking sub-questions as input, both are trained on the

Backbone	Variant	Training Set	F1	EM
baselines				
bart-base (Lewis et al., 2020)	-	$\mathcal{D}_2$	30.9	27.1
t5-base (Raffel et al., 2020)	-	$\mathcal{D}_2$	37.9	33.9
our bart-base variants				
w/ predicted sub-questions	*separate*	$\mathcal{D}_2$	32.0	27.2
w/ ground-truth sub-questions	*separate*	$\mathcal{D}_2$	33.2	29.0
w/ ground-truth sub-questions	*separate*	$\mathcal{D}_2, \mathcal{D}^1$	**45.0**	**40.5**
w/o Hard-EM	*unified*	$\mathcal{D}_2, \mathcal{D}^1$	44.2	39.9
w/ Hard-EM	*unified*	$\mathcal{D}_2, \mathcal{D}^{iter}$	<u>44.3</u>	<u>40.0</u>
our t5-base variants				
w/ predicted sub-questions	*separate*	$\mathcal{D}_2$	38.6	34.8
w/ ground-truth sub-questions	*separate*	$\mathcal{D}_2$	39.6	35.6
w/ ground-truth sub-questions	*separate*	$\mathcal{D}_2, \mathcal{D}^1$	**45.1**	**40.8**
w/o Hard-EM	*unified*	$\mathcal{D}_2, \mathcal{D}^1$	38.8	34.9
w/ Hard-EM	*unified*	$\mathcal{D}_2, \mathcal{D}^{iter}$	<u>44.0</u>	<u>40.1</u>
GPT-3 (zero-shot)	-	-	15.7	4.6
GPT-3 (few-shot)	-	-	34.9	27.0

Table 4: Overall results for baselines, our separate and unified variants. All models are evaluated on the same test set from $\mathcal{D}_2$.

BREAK dataset $\mathcal{D}_2$. Based on these vanilla models, we show our *separate* and *unified* approaches that use "bart-base" and "t5-base" as backbones separately in Table 4.

4.4.1 Separate Variant

Our *separate* variants are base on the architecture in Figure 1. In Table 4, we have three *separate* variants based on each backbone for comparison. Taking t5-base as one example, comparing to the t5-base, using predicted sub-questions achieves a 0.7-point gain of F1 score. Meanwhile using ground-truth sub-questions, our model outperforms the t5-base by 1.7 points of F1 score. The same improvement can be also concluded from the bart-base model. They employ $\mathcal{D}_2$ for training but their testing sets are different: predicted one use generated sub-questions while ground-truth one use sub-questions from D_2. The reason why our approach is more effective than the baseline model is that concatenating sub-questions can give LMs hints on the reasoning procedure, which helps LMs produce step-by-step thoughts implicitly.

Furthermore, we add $\mathcal{D}^1$ as the training set to train our seperate model. As it shows in Table 4, this kind of *separate* variants show the overall best performance since we have two sets of parameters separately learning question decomposition and reading comprehension. Compared to t5-base, the bart-base variant shows a higher performance gain that proves the effectiveness of our method.

4.4.2 Unified Variant

Our *unified* variants are base on the architecture in Figure 1 and one single model is used to train on both steps. In Table 4, the last two rows of each variants show the performance of our *unified* variant. Without the Hard-EM algorithm, performing multi-task learning achieves a 0.9 point improve over the T5 baseline. However, it shows a performance drop when compared to the *separate* variant with ground-truth sub-questions. This can be caused by the enlarged dataset and the additional decomposition work the *unified* variant need to handle.

When more training data is provided (i.e. $\mathcal{D}^1$ and $\mathcal{D}^{iter}$), though without ground-truth sub-questions, the *unified* variants substantially outperforms the baselines by 10.1 and 6.1 points over bart-base and t5-base model. Furthermore, when compared with the best *separate* variants, our *unified* models also show comparable performance on both F1 and EM metrics. Based on the observations of the last three rows of each backbone, it can be concluded that introducing more weakly-supervised training data can significantly help our model address the original difficult multi-hop RC task.

We also include another evaluation of employ-

Context	Question	GPT-3 (few-shot)	bart-base *separate* (best)	ground-truth answer
... notably striking out Julio Franco, at the time the oldest player in the MLB at 47 years old; Clemens was himself 43. In the bottom of the eighteenth inning, Clemens came to bat again...	Which player playing in the 2005 National League Division Series was older, Julio Franco or Roger Clemens?	Julio Franco (✓)	Julio Franco (✓)	Julio Franco
... Nyaungyan then systematically reacquired nearer Shan states. He captured Nyaungshwe in February 1601, and the large strategic Shan state of Mone in July 1603, bringing his realm to the border of Siamese Lan Na. In response, Naresuan of Siam marched in early 1605 to ...	How many years after capturing Nyaungshwe did Nyaungyan capture the large strategic Shan state of Mone?	3 years (✗)	2 (✓)	2
Kannada language is the official language of Karnataka and spoken as a native language by about 66.54% of the people as of 2011. Other linguistic minorities in the state were Urdu (10.83%), Telugu language (5.84%), Tamil language (3.45%), ...	How many in percent of people for Karnataka don't speak Telugu?	66.54% (✗)	94.04% (✗)	94.16%
A 2013 analysis of the National Assessment of Educational Progress found that from 1971 to 2008, the size of the black-white IQ gap in the United States decreased from 16.33 to 9.94 IQ points. It has also concluded however that, ...	How many IQ points did the black-white IQ gap decrease between 1971 and 2008?	16.33 (✗)	0.9 (✗)	6.39

Table 5: Correct and incorrect outputs from GPT-3 and our *separate* variant. Correct and Wrong supporting facts are annotated in the context using the corresponding color. Correct and wrong answer predictions are also marked with ✓and ✗ (the table is best seen in colours).

ing GPT-3, which is the state-of-the-art language model on many tasks and also in a large parameter scale (175B). The results are shown by last two rows in Table 4. Based on the experimental results, GPT-3 cannot even beat two baseline models under the zero-shot learning paradigm, which again shows the complexity and challenging of the task. When provided with several exemplars, it can easily outperform the bart-base model by 2.4 points on F1 score. However, even with $\times$1000 parameters, GPT-3 is still far behind to our best variants by 10.2 F1 points.

5 Analysis and Discussions

5.1 Qualitative Analysis

In this section, we will further discuss some real-life cases generated by our proposed variants from the dataset. In Table 5, the first row shows a comparison question and both GPT-3 and our bart-base *separate* model can produce the correct answer. However, when the question requires some arithmetic operations, such as addition or subtraction, the GPT-3 model would fail to answer correctly. Our model can handle this as shown by the second row.

There are two types of failures from our variants: one is that our model cannot handle unseen numbers, and the other is arithmetic between float numbers. The unseen number case happens in the third row of Table 5. Asking for the number of a complement set, though the number 94.04% is wrongly predicted by our model, it is more close to the ground-truth (94.16%) when compared to the GPT-3, which directly predict an wrong evidence annotated with red color. Furthermore, the last row shows a subtraction question between two

overlaps		0 ∼ 25%	25% ∼ 50%	50% ∼ 75%	75% ∼ 100%
uni-grams	bart-base	-	0	25.7	27.4
	unified	-	0	32.9	40.2
	separate	-	0	**35.7**	**41.3**
	GPT-3	-	**100.0**	**35.7**	26.4
bi-grams	bart-base	-	16.7	23.6	28.2
	unified	-	33.3	**29.1**	41.9
	separate	-	**50.0**	28.6	**43.2**
	GPT-3	-	44.4	**29.1**	26.2
tri-grams	bart-base	22.2	20.5	25.5	29.3
	unified	38.9	26.2	32.3	45.1
	separate	**50.0**	**30.0**	**33.4**	**45.9**
	GPT-3	**50.0**	28.0	25.8	26.8

Table 6: EM scores separately computed based on overlaps of sub-questions n-grams between training set and testing set on $\mathcal{D}_2$. Four models listed in this table are: the bart-base baseline, the best performed *separate* model, the best performed *unified* model

float numbers. Different from integer number subtraction in the second row, it is much harder to compute this arithmetic for language models. Traditionally, some symbolic methods can handle this problem very well. Tackling these problems can be interesting future work directions.

5.2 Quantitative Analysis

We look into details of $\mathcal{D}_2$ from the perspective of sub-question n-grams for both training and testing data. Intuitively, given one instance from the test set, more n-grams overlap it shows with the training set, higher the EM and F1 scores. Therefore, we further conducted the analysis and list all the statistics in Table 6.

We calculate for uni-grams, bi-grams and tri-grams for four models: bart-base baseline, the best-performed *separate* and *unified* variants proposed in Section 3 and GPT-3 with few-shot learning. The overlaps we choose is four intervals using percentages to represent. For example, $0 \sim 25\%$ overlapping on bi-grams means that the test instance have this proportion of bi-grams overlaps with all the training instances. Note that there is no overlapping for uni-grams and bi-grams in $0 \sim 25\%$.

In Table 6, we report the EM score (F1 score shows the similar results). The bart-base model show a tendency that with more overlaps across all n-grams, the performance will increase, which is consistent with our assumption. However, on the contrary, GPT-3 model show a reverse tendency that is probably due to the pre-trained corpus that shares far less n-grams with the test set. This characteristic improves the compositional generalisation ability as it outperforms the baseline model on the low-overlapping part of test set. Both of our *separate* and *unified* variants show overall improvements over the bart-base baseline. In particular, the first and second columns also show our model can better handle the low-overlapping questions, even without performance drop on the high-overlapping questions ($50\% \sim 100\%$). This experiment can further prove the compositional generalisation of our method is comparable to GPT-3.

6 Conclusion

We propose a two-step process for multi-hop reading comprehension task. The first step involves a question decomposer that maps a difficult multi-hop question into several sub-questions. The second step is to train a reading comprehension model based on (question, sub-questions, paragraph, answer) tuples. With the addition of sub-questions, our bart-/t5-base variants outperform the baseline model by 2.3/1.7 using ground truth sub-questions and 1.1/0.7 using generated ones on F1 score. Based on the hard-EM paradigm, large positive gains of another 11.1/4.4 point on F1 by the unified multi-task learning bart-/t5-base models shows the effectiveness of introducing weakly supervised training data. By further analysing the predicted examples and dataset, we also found our model can make a more comprehensive improvement compared with the SOTA GPT-3 model. But some problems like handling unseen numbers still exist and will be our future research directions.

Acknowledgements

This material is based on research sponsored by DARPA under agreement number HR001122C0029. The U.S. Government is authorized to reproduce and distribute reprints for Governmental purposes notwithstanding any copyright notation thereon.

References

Tom B. Brown, Benjamin Mann, Nick Ryder, Melanie Subbiah, Jared Kaplan, Prafulla Dhariwal, Arvind Neelakantan, Pranav Shyam, Girish Sastry, Amanda Askell, Sandhini Agarwal, Ariel Herbert-Voss, Gretchen Krueger, Tom Henighan, Rewon Child, Aditya Ramesh, Daniel M. Ziegler, Jeffrey Wu, Clemens Winter, Christopher Hesse, Mark Chen, Eric Sigler, Mateusz Litwin, Scott Gray, Benjamin Chess, Jack Clark, Christopher Berner, Sam McCandlish, Alec Radford, Ilya Sutskever, and Dario Amodei. 2020. Language models are few-shot learners. In *Advances in Neural Information Processing Systems 33: Annual Conference on Neural Information Processing Systems 2020, NeurIPS 2020, December 6-12, 2020, virtual.*

Kunlong Chen, Weidi Xu, Xingyi Cheng, Zou Xiaochuan, Yuyu Zhang, Le Song, Taifeng Wang, Yuan Qi, and Wei Chu. 2020a. Question directed graph attention network for numerical reasoning over text. In *Proceedings of EMNLP*, pages 6759–6768.

Xinyun Chen, Chen Liang, Adams Wei Yu, Denny Zhou, Dawn Song, and Quoc V. Le. 2020b. Neural symbolic reader: Scalable integration of distributed and symbolic representations for reading comprehension. In *Proceedings of ICLR*.

Jacob Devlin, Ming-Wei Chang, Kenton Lee, and Kristina Toutanova. 2019. BERT: pre-training of deep bidirectional transformers for language understanding. In *Proceedings of the NAACL HLT 2019*, pages 4171–4186.

David Dohan, Winnie Xu, Aitor Lewkowycz, Jacob Austin, David Bieber, Raphael Gontijo Lopes, Yuhuai Wu, Henryk Michalewski, Rif A. Saurous, Jascha Sohl-Dickstein, Kevin Murphy, and Charles Sutton. 2022. Language model cascades. *CoRR*, abs/2207.10342.

Dheeru Dua, Yizhong Wang, Pradeep Dasigi, Gabriel Stanovsky, Sameer Singh, and Matt Gardner. 2019. DROP: A reading comprehension benchmark requiring discrete reasoning over paragraphs. In *Proceedings of the NAACL HLT 2019*, pages 2368–2378.

Ruiliu Fu, Han Wang, Xuejun Zhang, Jun Zhou, and Yonghong Yan. 2021. Decomposing complex questions makes multi-hop QA easier and more interpretable. In *Findings of the Association for Computational Linguistics: EMNLP 2021*, pages 169–180, Punta Cana, Dominican Republic. Association for Computational Linguistics.

Mor Geva, Tomer Wolfson, and Jonathan Berant. 2021. Break, perturb, build: Automatic perturbation of reasoning paths through question decomposition. *CoRR*, abs/2107.13935.

Mike Lewis, Yinhan Liu, Naman Goyal, Marjan Ghazvininejad, Abdelrahman Mohamed, Omer Levy, Veselin Stoyanov, and Luke Zettlemoyer. 2020. BART: denoising sequence-to-sequence pre-training for natural language generation, translation, and comprehension. In *Proceedings of the 58th Annual Meeting of the Association for Computational Linguistics, ACL 2020, Online, July 5-10, 2020*, pages 7871–7880. Association for Computational Linguistics.

Chin-Yew Lin. 2004. ROUGE: A package for automatic evaluation of summaries. In *Text Summarization Branches Out*, pages 74–81, Barcelona, Spain. Association for Computational Linguistics.

Radford Neal and Geoffrey E. Hinton. 1998. A view of the em algorithm that justifies incremental, sparse, and other variants. In *Learning in Graphical Models*, pages 355–368. Kluwer Academic Publishers.

Maxwell Nye, Anders Johan Andreassen, Guy Gur-Ari, Henryk Michalewski, Jacob Austin, David Bieber, David Dohan, Aitor Lewkowycz, Maarten Bosma, David Luan, Charles Sutton, and Augustus Odena. 2021. Show your work: Scratchpads for intermediate computation with language models. *CoRR*, abs/2112.00114.

Kishore Papineni, Salim Roukos, Todd Ward, and Wei jing Zhu. 2002. Bleu: a method for automatic evaluation of machine translation. pages 311–318.

Ethan Perez, Patrick Lewis, Wen-tau Yih, Kyunghyun Cho, and Douwe Kiela. 2020. Unsupervised question decomposition for question answering. *CoRR*, abs/2002.09758.

Alec Radford, Karthik Narasimhan, Tim Salimans, and Ilya Sutskever. 2018. Improving language understanding by generative pre-training.

Alec Radford, Jeffrey Wu, Rewon Child, David Luan, Dario Amodei, Ilya Sutskever, et al. 2019. Language models are unsupervised multitask learners. *OpenAI blog*, 1(8):9.

Colin Raffel, Noam Shazeer, Adam Roberts, Katherine Lee, Sharan Narang, Michael Matena, Yanqi Zhou, Wei Li, and Peter J. Liu. 2020. Exploring the limits of transfer learning with a unified text-to-text transformer. *J. Mach. Learn. Res.*, 21:140:1–140:67.

Qiu Ran, Yankai Lin, Peng Li, Jie Zhou, and Zhiyuan Liu. 2019. NumNet: Machine reading comprehension with numerical reasoning. In *Proceedings of EMNLP-IJCNLP*, pages 2474–2484.

Yasaman Razeghi, Robert L. Logan IV, Matt Gardner, and Sameer Singh. 2022. Impact of pretraining term frequencies on few-shot reasoning. *CoRR*, abs/2202.07206.

Jason Wei, Xuezhi Wang, Dale Schuurmans, Maarten Bosma, Ed Chi, Quoc Le, and Denny Zhou. 2022. Chain of thought prompting elicits reasoning in large language models. *CoRR*, abs/2201.11903.

Tomer Wolfson, Mor Geva, Ankit Gupta, Yoav Goldberg, Matt Gardner, Daniel Deutch, and Jonathan Berant. 2020. Break it down: A question understanding benchmark. *Trans. Assoc. Comput. Linguistics*, 8:183–198.

Denny Zhou, Nathanael Schärli, Le Hou, Jason Wei, Nathan Scales, Xuezhi Wang, Dale Schuurmans, Olivier Bousquet, Quoc Le, and Ed Chi. 2022. Least-to-most prompting enables complex reasoning in large language models. *CoRR*, abs/2205.10625.

Using Aspect-Based Sentiment Analysis to Classify ATTITUDE-bearing Words

Pradeesh Parameswaran, Andrew Trotman, Veronica Liesaputra, David Eyers
Department of Computer Science
University of Otago
New Zealand
[pradeesh,andrew,veronica,dme]@cs.otago.ac.nz

Abstract

APPRAISAL is widely used by linguists to study how people judge things or people. Automating APPRAISAL could be beneficial for use cases such as moderating online comments. In 2020, the Australasian Language Technology Association (ALTA) organised a shared task to classify a branch APPRAISAL, which involves how humans judge other humans (JUDGEMENT). It proved to be a difficult task as the best performing system obtained an $F_1 = 0.155$. In this work, we hypothesise that JUDGEMENT and APPRECIATION branches in APPRAISAL are similar to opinion in Aspect-Based Sentiment Analysis (ABSA) tasks, as such we can leverage on ABSA opinion extraction techniques to further improve the performance of automated approaches for identifying JUDGEMENT and APPRECIATION. We evaluated the performance of six different ABSA models on two publicly available APPRAISAL data sets (biographies and psychological evaluation) by training them on existing ABSA SemEval data sets. Our results show that there is an overlap between opinion-extraction and APPRAISAL task, as we obtained $F_1 = 0.623$ on biographies data set and 0.414 on psychological evaluation data set. However, we cannot be certain if our findings can be extended across other APPRAISAL data sets due to the challenges in annotating and the availability of these data sets.

1 Introduction

In 2020, ALTA organised a shared task challenge aimed to classify how humans judge other humans using a well-known linguistic taxonomy known as APPRAISAL (Martin and White, 2005) automatically. APPRAISAL allows linguists to evaluate language in a social context such as identifying and understanding how people make judgements about people and objects (ATTITUDE) (Martin and White, 2005). The taxonomy is commonly used by Systemic Functional linguists to analyse the language choices and attitudes used by writers and speakers (Chen, 2022) in various mediums (Starfield et al., 2015; Ross and Caldwell, 2020; Su and Hunston, 2019).

Identifying ATTITUDE-bearing words can help to reduce the workload of moderators such as in online forums and Facebook by analysing the language that is being used and flagging it to moderators to be reviewed if there are any legal implications based on the APPRAISAL taxonomy (Steiger et al., 2021).

Although, there were two winners declared for the ALTA 2020 Shared Task challenge, the task proved to be difficult as the best-performing team only obtained an F_1 score of 0.155 (Mollá, 2020). The main reason for poor scores was the size of data set ($N = 300$): too small for automated methods to generalise from properly. A lot of the larger APPRAISAL data set is not publicly released, thus making it difficult for automated approaches to be be built.

However, there might be a solution for us to tackle this problem without the need of a large data set. Recently, Su and Hunston (2019), proposed that JUDGEMENT and APPRECIATION should be treated as opinions and AFFECT as emotions. Su and Hunston (2019), then provided qualitative examples to illustrate how JUDGEMENT and APPRECIATION can be viewed as opinions. Inspired by the findings of Su and Hunston (2019), we are interested in investigating this area, particularly if we can apply existing aspect-based opinion techniques to tackle this problem.

We argue that if the combination of the JUDGEMENT and APPRECIATION branches is the same as opinion, then the current ABSA opinion extraction techniques and models are applicable and therefore can be applied. BARTABSA is the current state of the art for ABSA's triplet extraction task.

BARTABSA has achieved the highest F_1 score in the triplet extraction task, which is 0.7246 on the laptop data set.[1] Thus, we are interested if we can use these existing models to identify JUDGEMENT and APPRECIATION-bearing words.

Our experimental results suggest that there is an overlap between JUDGEMENT and APPRECIATION words with the ABSA task. Existing ABSA models, that were trained on SemEval data sets, does perform reasonably well on JUDGEMENT data sets (F_1 = 0.623 on biographies, F_1 = 0.414 on psychological evaluation).

2 Related Work

The APPRAISAL taxonomy consists of three main branches: ATTITUDE, ENGAGEMENT and GRADUATION. ATTITUDE expresses the current state of the person who wrote the text or uttered it—it consists of three subcategories: AFFECT (which represents the feeling of the author), JUDGEMENT (which describes the author's opinion of another person or object) and APPRECIATION (which represents the author's opinion on the quality of an object). ENGAGEMENT reflects probability or possibility (i.e., *perhaps*, *seems*). GRADUATION expresses the meaning of a term gradated by an adjective. These APPRAISAL attributes are often expressed with polarity and orientation. Polarity describes the tone of the sentence (i.e., negative, positive or neutral) whereas orientation explores how a sentence is weakened or strengthened (i.e., *very/few/a lot*).

To illustrate, consider the appraisal analysis of the sentence 'Robin Hood gave a sly grin'. It describes the appraiser (i.e., the person who wrote it), their attitude, what it is being appraised, and their polarity.

Appraiser	: *Writer*
Appraised	: *Robin Hood*
Attitude	: *sly* (JUDGEMENT)
Polarity	: *Negative*

Extracting this detail of information can be challenging, but some tasks (such as polarity extraction) have already been tackled in sentiment analysis (Kanayama and Nasukawa, 2006). Here, we narrow our focus to extracting ATTITUDE-bearing words, as we are interested in quantifying the changes proposed by Su and Hunston (2019), to determine if we could use opinion-extraction from ABSA to extract the opinion. From Figure 1, we can see that JUDGEMENT and APPRECIATION are seen as opinions and AFFECT is seen as emotions. This is the key difference from the original taxonomy of Martin and White (2005). ATTITUDE$_{\text{Su}}$ will be used to represent the new change proposed by Su and Hunston (2019) and we are narrowing our focus to the opinion branch of ATTITUDE$_{\text{Su}}$. Although numerous works have attempted to automatically categorise APPRAISAL (Argamon et al., 2007; Bloom and Argamon, 2010; Whitelaw et al., 2005; Neviarouskaya et al., 2010; Taboada et al., 2011), including the 2020 ALTA Shared Task, most of the previous work has focused on identification at the sentence level rather than at the word level (Argamon et al., 2007; Bloom and Argamon, 2010).

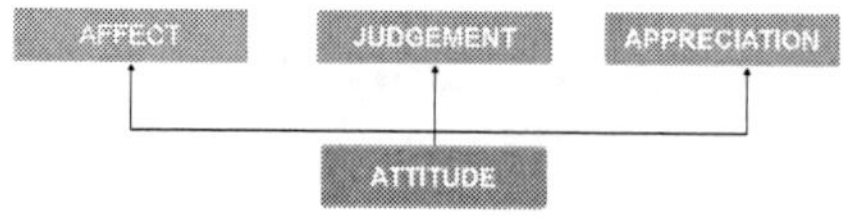

(a) ATTITUDE branch of APPRAISAL taxonomy by (Martin and White, 2005).

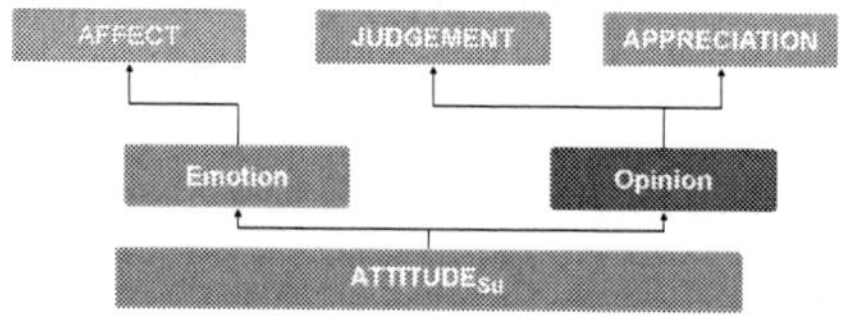

(b) Proposed change in ATTITUDE branch by (Su and Hunston, 2019).

Figure 1: The proposed change in ATTITUDE branch of APPRAISAL taxonomy (ATTITUDE$_{\text{Su}}$) by (Su and Hunston, 2019) and its comparison with the original ATTITUDE by (Martin and White, 2005).

As ABSA is used to identify aspects, opinions, and polarity. It would be interesting to explore if ABSA can be used in our case. We hypothesise that it may be possible to use triplet extraction for JUDGEMENT and APPRECIATION. However, the current sets of publicly available APPRAISAL data sets (Su and Hunston, 2019; Mollá, 2021) only label the ATTITUDE and not the APPRAISED (aspect). Annotating APPRAISAL is not straightforward as experts with a linguistic background are likely to be needed to do so (Parameswaran et al., 2022)—and so crowdsourcing (Standing and Standing, 2018) is likely to yield unusable results. Doing this is beyond the scope of this paper.

For ABSA tasks, transformers are the current state-of-the-art (Do et al., 2019). Transformers such as BERT (Devlin et al., 2019), BART

[1] `https://paperswithcode.com/paper/a-unified-generative-framework-for-aspect`

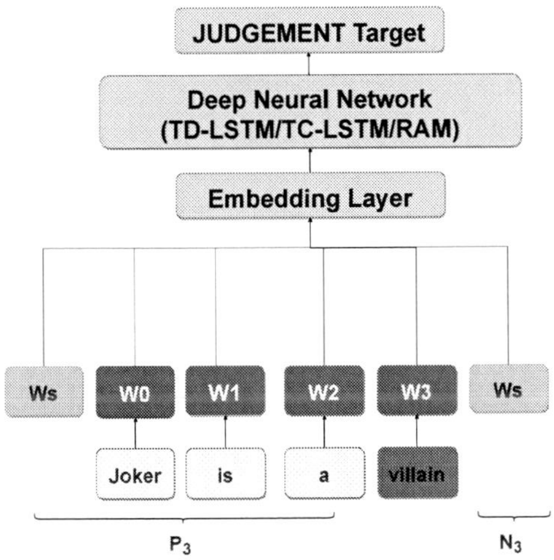

Figure 2: System architecture for LSTM-based models. Here, w_3 is the word to be classified as JUDGEMENT or not.

(Lewis et al., 2020), and GPT-2 (Radford et al., 2019) have consistently shown promising results in many NLP tasks (Adhikari et al., 2020). The current best for ABSA, BARTABSA (Yan et al., 2021), uses a sequence-to-sequence model to solve the triplet extraction problem. BARTABSA achieved an average F_1 score of 0.85 on opinion extraction and 0.58 on triplet extraction using the SemEval ABSA data set.

Prior neural approaches to ABSA such as TC-LSTM (Tang et al., 2016), TD-LSTM (Tang et al., 2016), and BERT-AEN (Song et al., 2019) have been used outside of ABSA. Their use in tasks such as the prediction of the sea temperature (Liu et al., 2018), the optimisation of virtual network demand optimisation (Kim et al., 2019), and sarcasm target identification and extraction of sarcasm targets (Patro et al., 2019) leads us to explore these models for JUDGEMENT extraction.

3 Data Sets Used in this Research

We use three data sets to evaluate our approaches, as summarised below. Two are already publicly available, and the third is a subset of the second, constructed in order to perform a like-to-like comparison with the first.[2]

Bio This is the data used by (Su and Hunston, 2019). It comprises 360 sentences taken from snippets of 100 biographies. The data set contains four fields: the sentence, the words that bear APPRECIATION, JUDGEMENT, and AFFECT in each sentence.

There are 80 sentences in the AFFECT category, 125 in the JUDGEMENT category, and 161 sentences in APPRECIATION. There are overlaps in these sentences because a sentence can contain AFFECT, JUDGEMENT, and APPRECIATION. Only adjectives are annotated in this data set, so nonadjective JUDGEMENT words are not known.

Psyc We crawled the psychological evaluation texts from the APPRAISAL website[3]. Although this data has not been used in the literature on APPRAISAL for analysis, the intended purpose of this data set was to train linguistic students on how to perform APPRAISAL analysis.

This data set contains 50 sentences along with the words that imply AFFECT, JUDGEMENT, and APPRECIATION. Of the 50 sentences, 38 sentences belong to the JUDGEMENT category, 42 in the APPRECIATION category, and 34 in the AFFECT category. Unlike *Bio*, all words (including *adverbs* and *adjectives*) were classified as JUDGEMENT or non-JUDGEMENT.

$Psyc_a$ The previous two data sets differ in their coverage of parts of speech. To make it possible to compare the performance of our models in *Bio* and *Psyc*, we created $Psyc_a$ from *Psyc* by removing all non-adjectives.

In our experiments using *Bio*, *Psyc* and $Psyc_a$ we perform a three-fold cross-validation because there is not a sufficiently large amount of data to divide into training, validation, and test sets.

4 Methodology

We briefly describe our methodology for carrying out our experimentation. We employ LSTM-based and transformer-based approaches.

4.1 Task Definition

We formulated our task as a sequence labelling problem similar to the way it was used for the opinion extraction task (Wang et al., 2016). A sentence S is defined as a sequence of words, $[w_1, w_2, w_3, \ldots, w_n]$. Our aim is to extract a set of phrases $X = \{o_1, o_2, o_3, \ldots, o_m\}$, where each $o \in X$ is either an opinion-ATTITUDE$_{Su}$ word or

[2]We will share the link to the data sets after the peer-review process

[3]http://www.grammatics.com/appraisal/pangesti/pangesti-psy-texts.pdf

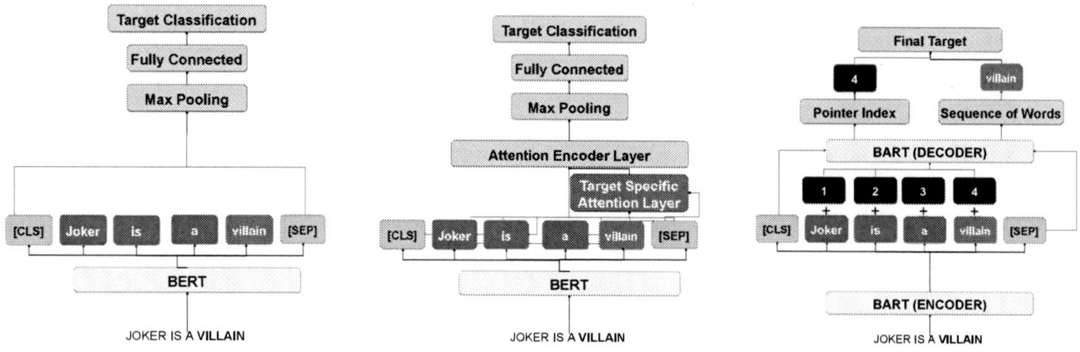

(a) TD-BERT (b) BERT-AEN (c) BARTABSA

Figure 3: System architectures for the transformer-based models.

not and $|X| \leq n$. When a sentence does not contain any ATTITUDES$_{\text{Su}}$ word $|X| = 0$.

4.2 LSTM-based Models

Figure 2 shows the overall architecture of our LSTM-based models (TC-LSTM, TD-LSTM and RAM). For brevity, we summarise the mechanism of our LSTM-based models as shown in Figure 2 below:

- **TD-LSTM** (Tang et al., 2016)—The idea of this model is to use the preceding and the following context surrounding the target word as a feature. Two LSTM networks are used for this; the left LSTM neural network consists of the preceding sentence along with the potential opinion-ATTITUDES$_{\text{Su}}$ word, and the right LSTM neural network consists of the remaining context along with the potential target. The left LSTM network runs from left to right, and the right LSTM network runs from right to left. These LSTM networks are capable of learning the semantics of the sentence (Tang et al., 2016).

- **TC-LSTM** (Tang et al., 2016)—This is a modification of TD-LSTM. The key difference between TC-LSTM and TD-LSTM is that, in TD-LSTM the input at each position includes the embedding of the current word, whereas TC-LSTM contains the concatenation of the set of words preceding and following the opinion-ATTITUDES$_{\text{Su}}$ word. We expect that the concatenation of the words will result in a higher accuracy than that of TD-LSTM.

- **RAM** (Chen et al., 2017)—This uses a bidirectional LSTM to produce a memory slice. The memory slice is used to address the shortcomings of the TC-LSTM model (not being able to capture the target word if it is far away from the target). These memory slices are weighted according to the position of the target. The input of RAM is the entire sentence and the distance of potential opinion-ATTITUDES$_{\text{Su}}$. Then, to classify the target of the results are combined non-linearly with a Gated Recurrent Unit (GRU).

Given the sentence *'Joker is a villain'* and *'villain'* as the current potential opinion-ATTITUDES$_{\text{Su}}$ word, we start by computing the embedding of each word of each sequence. We use the BERT embedding to perform a fair comparison between all LSTM-based models. Once the embeddings are computed, they are then averaged and passed to the deep neural network layer to determine the probability that villain is an ATTITUDES$_{\text{Su}}$-bearing word.

4.3 Transformer-based Models

Figure 3 shows the architecture of the transformers that we used for our experimentation, which are TD-BERT (Gao et al., 2019), BERT-AEN (Yan et al., 2021), and BARTABSA (Yan et al., 2021). We briefly describe the functionality below:

- **TD-BERT** (Gao et al., 2019)—TD-BERT's architecture closely resembles that of BERT. The key difference is that TD-BERT incorporates the potential target information into its classification input, as described above.

- **BERT-AEN** (Song et al., 2019)—This model uses an attention encoder network to model the semantic interaction between the whole sentence and the potential opinion-ATTITUDE$_{Su}$ word. The Target Specific Attention Layer is introduced so that it can compute the hidden states of the input embedding. Moreover, BERT-AEN uses label smoothing regularisation (LSR) in the loss function. LSR reduces overfitting by replacing the 0 and 1 targets for the classifier with smoothed values (such as 0.1 and 0.9, respectively). This works well in our situation, where we have a limited amount of data.

- **BARTABSA** (Yan et al., 2021)— (Yan et al., 2021) formulate ABSA as a sequence-to-sequence generation task. Specifically, they use a pre-trained BART model (Lewis et al., 2020) to extract a sentence's opinion, aspect, and polarity. BART brings together the strength of the GPT-2 model (decoder) and BERT (encoder) for text understanding and generation. Therefore, the researchers were able to exploit the '*student-teacher*' (Malik et al., 2021) concept, in which the network consists of an encoder (the teacher) and a decoder (the student). We are only interested in the opinion phrase, so we modify the model so that the decoder extracts only opinion-ATTITUDE$_{Su}$ words.

First, we feed a sentence S to our transformer-based models, which is a sequence of words $[w_1, w_2, \ldots, w_N]$. We then transform the given sentence (S) into `[CLS]` $+\!\!+$ S $+\!\!+$ `[SEP]` and `[CLS]` $+\!\!+$ w_k $+\!\!+$ `[SEP]` together with the label w_k, where $k \in \{1 \ldots N\}$. Here within is where all the similarities of all the transformer models stop; for BARTABSA—we include positional input which are $P = (p_s, p_1, ...p_k)$, where p_k is the positional encoding for w_k. Positional encoding is introduced to keep in mind the sequence of words that appear in the given S. We did not use these information for our other two models as it was not required.

For TD-BERT and BERT-AEN, we use pre-trained BERT$_{\text{Base}}$ uncased (Devlin et al., 2019) and for BARTABSA, we use BART$_{\text{Base}}$ as the pre-trained model (Lewis et al., 2020). For TD-BERT and BERT-AEN, there are not any positional encoding.

Data Set:	*Lap14*	*Res14*	*Res15*
Number of sentences	3848	3844	2000
Number of opinion terms	3178	4492	1720
Average number of opinion words	0.82	1.16	0.86

Table 1: Details of the SemEval data sets used as part of sanity checks for the models we have described in Section 4.

5 SemEval Data Set and Sanity Check

We use three SemEval data sets: *Lap14*, *Res14* and *Res15* (Pontiki et al., 2015, 2016) to check our implementations. Initially, these data sets contained only aspects and sentiments, but Wang et al. (2016) annotated the data to contain opinion terms. Table 1 describes the distribution of items in the data sets. Wang et al. (2016) used crowdsourcing workers to annotate this data set. However, they did not provide the agreement level between the annotators. We hypothesise that the level of agreement between the annotators is high because models such as BARTABSA were able to obtain high F_1 scores. Therefore, we hypothesise that if the opinion identification task in ABSA is trivial, it would also mean that automated approaches can perform well in identifying JUDGEMENT and APPRECIATION.

These data have already been divided into training and test sets. We maintain those splits in our experiments. The purpose of using the SemEval data set is to validate our implementation to ensure that the scores we obtained are within the range of the scores reported in the literature (Zhang et al., 2022). By verifying if our implementation is correct, we can then evaluate the performance of these models in our data sets.

6 Experimental Setup

For our experiments, we used pyTorch-ABSA[4]. The framework is implemented in PyTorch[5] 1.71, spaCy[6] 1.9 and huggingface 3.4.0. We ran our experiments on Google Cloud Platform with 16 vCPUs (Intel Xeon E5 CPU @ 2.50Ghz), 16 GiB of RAM and an NVIDIA Tesla P100.

We use two baselines. First, we use the Naive Bayes (NB) classifier as our baseline. We trained the NB classifier on the three SemEval data sets

[4] https://github.com/songyouwei/ABSA-PyTorch

[5] https://www.tensorflow.org/

[6] https://pypi.org/project/spacy/

Model	Original implementation (Acc)	Ours (Acc)	Diff
TD-LSTM	0.764 (Tang et al., 2016)	0.746	-2.42%
TC-LSTM	0.760 (Tang et al., 2016)	0.721	-5.14%
Model	Original implementation (F_1)	Ours (F_1)	Diff
RAM	0.708 (Chen et al., 2017)	0.659	-6.86%
TD-BERT	0.769 (Gao et al., 2019)	0.780	1.35%
BERT-AEN	0.737 (Song et al., 2019)	0.712	-3.42%
BARTABSA	0.870 (Yan et al., 2021)	0.828	-4.88%

Table 2: Performance of our implementation compared with the authors' original performance on the *Res14* data set. TD-LSTM and TC-LSTM models comparisons are using accuracy score (Acc) and the others are using F_1 because those are the metrics reported by the original authors.

using the same split. We use SO-CAL (Taboada et al., 2011) as our second baseline because it is the only publicly available APPRAISAL classifier. SO-CAL produces a probability score for each category of the APPRAISAL taxonomy, but we are only interested in JUDGEMENT and APPRECIATION. So we only consider the word to be JUDGEMENT or APPRECIATION if either one of the labels is the highest of the probabilities and if the probability of JUDGEMENT or APPRECIATION is greater than a given threshold.[7]

For LSTM-based models, we set the dropout to 0.2 to avoid overfitting, and the number of hidden LSTM units was set to 300. We use Adam Optimizer with a learning rate of 10^{-5} for 30 epochs. The batch size was 64. We used our validation F_1 score as an early stopping criterion. Training stopped if we reached the maximum number of epochs or if the score did not increase for 20 epochs.

For our transformer-based models, the best parameters we found were with a batch size of 32, a maximum sequence length of 128, the maximum predictions per sequence of 20, and a learning rate of 10^{-5} using the Adam Optimizer.

We performed our experiments five times (using five different random seeds) and reported average performance except when we validated the SemEval scores, as we were interested in validating the correctness of our implementation.

7 Results

First, we reran our models on the SemEval data set to ensure that our implementation was correct. We then evaluated our models in our data sets. Finally, we present our findings of the similarities between opinion-ATTITUDE$_{Su}$ words in APPRAISAL and opinion words in ABSA tasks.

7.1 Validating SemEval Scores

Here, we performed a sanity check on the correctness of our implementation. We applied the six models to the aspect extraction task on the SemEval data. We chose aspect extraction because these were the scores that all of the papers reported, making it a fair basis on which to perform our comparisons. Validating for all data sets requires tremendous computing resources; therefore, we scoped our sanity check on the *Res14* data set. The results are reported in Table 2.

We compared the performance of the LSTM-based models using accuracy, since that was the metric that the original authors used. However, we compared the other models using F_1 because that was the metrics used by the original authors of these models. In all cases, except for TD-BERT, our performance is slightly lower than the performance published by the original authors.

This is not unexpected, as the implementations we use come from the pyTorch library, so they might be slightly different from those of the original authors who would have implemented the systems themselves. This difference in implementation may introduce subtle differences in performance that could easily account for a few percent of the final score. Furthermore, we do not have the same hardware setup as the original authors, which is also known to affect the final performance of machine learning (Crane, 2018). Although we are using transfer learning in transformer networks, the order of operations, the GPU, and the accuracy of the numerical representation all play a role in the final performance. We expect that this might explain a few percent differ-

[7]We set the threshold to 0.5, noting that the probabilities do not need to add to 1.0

ence in the final results.

Nevertheless, from the results in Table 2, it is reasonable to believe that our implementations are sound because the performance is close to that reported in the original papers. Our paired t-test did not show statistically significant differences at the $p < 0.05$ level, so we are confident that our implementations are valid.

7.2 Effectiveness on extracting JUDGEMENT and APPRECIATION words

We evaluated the effectiveness of our LSTM-based models and transformer-based models in identifying ATTITUDE$_{Su}$ words from *Bio*, *Psyc* and *Psyc$_a$*. We present our scores in Table 3.

Across the three data sets that we evaluated, we have observed that the data set on which our models were trained played an essential role in terms of the F_1 scores we obtained. For example, across the six models, we can observe that using a trained *Lap14* results in poor performance in the *Psyc* and *Psyc$_a$* data sets. The poor performance could be explained by the fact that the vocabularies used in *Psyc$_a$* differ from *Lap14*. On the other hand, we can see that our models perform reasonably well in *Bio* as shown by the F_1 scores on the *Res14*-trained models and *Res15*-trained models. Our visual inspection of the *Res14* and *Res15* data sets found that they contain a mixture of APPRECIATION and JUDGEMENT words which is similar to *Bio*. Therefore, our six models could take advantage of these similarities and perform well in the *Bio* data set.

The baseline, SO-CAL, does not perform well compared to machine learning models. This could be due to the use of a lexicon. By their very nature, lexicons are domain-specific, and if the source domain does not match the domain of the data set, then performance can be expected to be impacted. Closer inspection shows that about 39% of the opinion-ATTITUDE$_{Su}$ phrases used in the *Bio* data set is in the SO-CAL lexicon, and about 21% of the opinion-ATTITUDE$_{Su}$ phrases in the *Psyc* data set are in the lexicon.

We find that lexicon based are more susceptible to ambiguity. For example, in the sentence from *Bio*, *'It was lovely of them to help me'*, and for the word *'lovely'*, SO-CAL gave an AFFECT score of 0.60 and a JUDGEMENT score of 0.48; and so incorrectly classified the word. In this case, the context of the sentence is essential for a correct classification. All LSTM and transformer models correctly identified this context and correctly classified the word. We have also observed that the NB Classifier's performance is comparable to SO-CAL. We hypothesise that if we further expand the vocabularies in SO-CAL from our training data set, the performance of SO-CAL could be further improved.

RAM was the best of the LSTM-based models. Although we did not find statistically significant differences between the LSTM-based models when we performed a one-way ANOVA ($p < 0.05$), we believe that incorporating the potential opinion-ATTITUDE$_{Su}$ word in its memory slices allowed the RAM model to understand the nuances of sentences, even if the potential words are far away. In TC-LSTM, the incorporation of target information in each step during training further reduces the scores compared to not using it in TD-LSTM. TD-LSTM, on the other hand, was a little chaotic. The chaotic behaviour could be due to how the opinion-ATTITUDE$_{Su}$ words are located further away in the sentence. We cannot be sure, as the data set on which we evaluated our models was small.

Regarding the transformer-based approach, the best-performing model is BARTABSA: *Bio* (F_1 = 0.623), *Psyc* (F_1 = 0.414) and *Psyc$_a$* data set (F_1 = 0.436), suggesting that the sequence-to-sequence paradigm and the use of BART are an accurate way of extracting opinion-ATTITUDE$_{Su}$ phrases. BARTABSA substantially outperformed our baseline, SO-CAL, scoring more than double on all metrics we used. As for the other transformer models (TD-BERT and BERT-AEN), we find that the performance of these models is similar; in particular, we were impressed by TD-BERT's performance, as the performance is comparable to a more complex transformer-based approach (BERT-AEN). We then performed a paired t-test, which did not show statistically significant differences at the $p < 0.05$ level between these two models.

Our results suggest that positional information helps BARTABSA achieve strong performance. Further improvements in BARTABSA might be possible by incorporating Part-of-Speech (PoS) information. Su and Hunston (2019) demonstrated that JUDGEMENT and APPRECIATION could be identified by their adjective patterns, including the prepositions or clauses that follow after the word

Model	*Bio* (*Lap14*)	*Psyc* (*Lap14*)	$Psyc_a$ (*Lap14*)	*Bio* (*Res14*)	*Psyc* (*Res14*)	$Psyc_a$ (*Res14*)	*Bio* (*Res15*)	*Psyc* (*Res15*)	$Psyc_a$ (*Res15*)
NB	0.101 ± 0.000	0.084 ± 0.000	0.095 ± 0.000	0.188 ± 0.000	0.104 ± 0.000	0.110 ± 0.000	0.164 ± 0.000	0.124 ± 0.000	0.116 ± 0.000
SO-CAL	0.143 ± 0.000	0.122 ± 0.000	0.145 ± 0.000	0.224 ± 0.000	0.148 ± 0.000	0.160 ± 0.000	0.228 ± 0.000	0.144 ± 0.000	0.155 ± 0.000
TD-LSTM	0.428 ± 0.144	0.244 ± 0.112	0.210 ± 0.123	0.528 ± 0.132	0.410 ± 0.135	0.402 ± 0.118	0.468 ± 0.152	0.344 ± 0.153	0.360 ± 0.145
TC-LSTM	0.401 ± 0.202	0.232 ± 0.310	0.298 ± 0.225	0.501 ± 0.199	0.406 ± 0.194	0.398 ± 0.205	0.456 ± 0.188	0.332 ± 0.198	0.358 ± 0.205
RAM	0.450 ± 0.168	0.291 ± 0.197	0.197 ± 0.188	0.548 ± 0.158	0.461 ± 0.174	0.397 ± 0.181	0.492 ± 0.155	0.365 ± 0.158	0.367 ± 0.176
TD-BERT	0.487 ± 0.144	0.315 ± 0.157	0.341 ± 0.169	0.617 ± 0.135	0.412 ± 0.124	0.422 ± 0.143	0.547 ± 0.142	0.399 ± 0.149	0.382 ± 0.140
BERT-AEN	0.504 ± 0.153	0.323 ± 0.170	0.359 ± 0.221	0.618 ± 0.161	0.408 ± 0.175	0.416 ± 0.152	0.564 ± 0.173	0.381 ± 0.162	0.378 ± 0.146
BARTABSA	**0.598 ± 0.185**	**0.364 ± 0.189**	**0.386 ± 0.198**	**0.623 ± 0.196**	**0.414 ± 0.182**	**0.436 ± 0.185**	**0.588 ± 0.185**	**0.403 ± 0.199**	**0.394 ± 0.181**

Table 3: F_1 scores (with standard deviation) of the models evaluated on *Bio* and *Psyc* when trained on *Lap14*, *Res14* and *Res15* data set. BARTABSA is the best-performing model across all three data sets (highlighted in **bold**).

Model	Bio_{opi} (*Lap14*)	$Psyc_{opi}$ (*Lap14*)	Bio_{opi} (*Res14*)	$Psyc_{opi}$ (*Res14*)	Bio_{opi} (*Res15*)	$Psyc_{opi}$ (*Res15*)
RAM	0.446 ± 0.215	0.297 ± 0.198	0.562 ± 0.232	0.487 ± 0.224	0.506 ± 0.000	0.388 ± 0.000
BARTABSA	**0.582 ± 0.153**	**0.384 ± 0.146**	**0.663 ± 0.145**	**0.448± 0.138**	**0.592 ± 0.000**	**0.457 ± 0.000**

Table 4: F_1 scores of the best-performing models (with standard deviation) evaluated on Bio_{opi} and $Psyc_{opi}$ when trained on *Lap14*, *Res14* and *Res15* data sets. The best-performing model is highlighted in **bold**.

(for example, if an adjective is followed by a *that* clause, it is likely to be JUDGEMENT). We leave the investigation of PoS in BARTABSA for future work.

7.3 Are ATTITUDE$_{Su}$ and Opinion similar?

Our above findings do not yet provide a clear indicator of whether opinion-ATTITUDE$_{Su}$ in APPRAISAL tasks and opinions in ABSA tasks are the same. To accurately determine whether they are similar, we then asked three annotators (two undergraduates and a postgraduate) to re-annotate the *Bio* and *Psyc* data set by following ABSA Opinion extraction guidelines. We will refer to these newly annotated data sets of *Bio* and *Psyc* data sets as Bio_{opi} and $Psyc_{opi}$. As a guideline, we provide samples from SemEval tasks with randomly selected examples from the training portion of the SemEval data set. These were the same samples that Wang et al. (2016) used to annotate the SemEval data set.

We present our findings in Table 4. It is noticeable here that the scores we obtained are similar to the scores we reported in Table 3. Observing only the scores would make it difficult to quantify opinion-ATTITUDE$_{Su}$, so we needed to perform a statistical analysis to determine whether opinion-ATTITUDE$_{Su}$ and opinion in ABSA are the same. We first performed a pair chi-square test by comparing the performance of BARTABSA, that is trained on the *Res14* data set, at identifying opinion words in *Bio* and Bio_{opi}. We then proceeded to rerun the same test on the different models (i.e., BARTABSA trained on the *Res15* data set) but evaluated on the same pair of data sets (i.e., Bio and Bio_{opi}). We then repeated the same test on different combinations of models and with *Psyc* and $Psyc_{opi}$.

The analysis did not show statistically significant differences between opinion-ATTITUDE$_{Su}$ and opinion-ABSA in all combinations at the $p < 0.05$ level. Although our finding of no statistical significance supports the argument of Su and Hunston (2019) that opinion bearing words are a combination of JUDGEMENT and APPRECIATION, we cannot be sure that this would always be the case. This is because our data set is too small to draw a solid conclusion, so we cannot be certain that our findings are applicable on other APPRAISAL data sets.

Annotating a large APPRAISAL data set from scratch can be challenging due to the costs of linguists needed for the process (Snow et al., 2008; Lease, 2011). We suggest that this problem can be addressed by using the SemEval data set as a base and annotate the opinions following the APPRAISAL taxonomy.

8 Conclusion & Limitations

In this work, we investigated whether JUDGEMENT and APPRECIATION branches of the APPRAISAL taxonomy and opinion in Aspect-Based Sentiment Analysis (ABSA) tasks are similar. We use existing ABSA data sets and models to evaluate on two publicly available APPRAISAL data sets. Our empirical results show that there are similarities between the two tasks. Our proposed methodology needs to be carefully tested when reapplied: we were only able to perform experiments on small data sets. Secondly, we focus on the JUDGEMENT and APPRECIATION branches of APPRAISAL, although it would be interesting to see if we could use triplet-extraction task from ABSA. We hope that our work here could motivate Systemic Functional linguists community and NLP community to work together.

References

Surabhi Adhikari et al. 2020. NLP Based Machine Learning Approaches for Text Summarization. In *2020 Fourth International Conference on Computing Methodologies and Communication (ICCMC)*, pages 535–538. IEEE.

Shlomo Argamon, Kenneth Bloom, Andrea Esuli, and Fabrizio Sebastiani. 2007. Automatically Determining Attitude Type and Force for Sentiment Analysis. In *Human Language Technology. Challenges of the Information Society, Third Language and Technology Conference, LTC 2007, Poznan, Poland, October 5-7, 2007, Revised Selected Papers*, volume 5603 of *Lecture Notes in Computer Science*, pages 218–231. Springer.

Kenneth Bloom and Shlomo Argamon. 2010. Unsupervised Extraction of Appraisal Expressions. In *Advances in Artificial Intelligence, 23rd Canadian Conference on Artificial Intelligence, Canadian, AI 2010, Ottawa, Canada, May 31 - June 2, 2010. Proceedings*, volume 6085 of *Lecture Notes in Computer Science*, pages 290–294. Springer.

Muxuan Chen. 2022. An Appraisal Analysis of Sina Weibo Texts about Reforms of Undergraduate Education. *Scientific and Social Research*, 4(1):1–16.

Peng Chen, Zhongqian Sun, Lidong Bing, and Wei Yang. 2017. Recurrent Attention Network on Memory for Aspect Sentiment Analysis. In *Proceedings of the 2017 Conference on Empirical Methods in Natural Language Processing, EMNLP 2017, Copenhagen, Denmark, September 9-11, 2017*, pages 452–461. Association for Computational Linguistics.

Matt Crane. 2018. Questionable Answers in Question Answering Research: Reproducibility and Variability of Published Results. *Trans. Assoc. Comput. Linguistics*, 6:241–252.

Jacob Devlin, Ming-Wei Chang, Kenton Lee, and Kristina Toutanova. 2019. BERT: Pre-training of Deep Bidirectional Transformers for Language Understanding. In *Proceedings of the 2019 Conference of the North American Chapter of the Association for Computational Linguistics: Human Language Technologies, NAACL-HLT 2019, Minneapolis, MN, USA, June 2-7, 2019, Volume 1 (Long and Short Papers)*, pages 4171–4186. Association for Computational Linguistics.

Hai Ha Do, P. W. C. Prasad, Angelika Maag, and Abeer Alsadoon. 2019. Deep Learning for Aspect-Based Sentiment Analysis: A Comparative Review. *Expert Syst. Appl.*, 118:272–299.

Zhengjie Gao, Ao Feng, Xinyu Song, and Xi Wu. 2019. Target-Dependent Sentiment Classification With BERT. *IEEE Access*, 7:154290–154299.

Hiroshi Kanayama and Tetsuya Nasukawa. 2006. Fully Automatic Lexicon Expansion for Domain-oriented Sentiment Analysis. In *EMNLP 2006, Proceedings of the 2006 Conference on Empirical Methods in Natural Language Processing, 22-23 July 2006, Sydney, Australia*, pages 355–363. ACL.

Hee-Gon Kim, Do-Young Lee, Se-Yeon Jeong, Heeyoul Choi, Jae-Hyung Yoo, and James Won-Ki Hong. 2019. Machine Learning-Based Method for Prediction of Virtual Network Function Resource Demands. In *2019 IEEE Conference on Network Softwarization (NetSoft)*, pages 405–413. IEEE.

Matthew Lease. 2011. On Quality Control and Machine Learning in Crowdsourcing. In *Human Computation, Papers from the 2011 AAAI Workshop, San Francisco, California, USA, August 8, 2011*, volume WS-11-11 of *AAAI Technical Report*. AAAI.

Mike Lewis, Yinhan Liu, Naman Goyal, Marjan Ghazvininejad, Abdelrahman Mohamed, Omer Levy, Veselin Stoyanov, and Luke Zettlemoyer. 2020. BART: Denoising Sequence-to-Sequence Pre-training for Natural Language Generation, Translation, and Comprehension. In *Proceedings of the 58th Annual Meeting of the Association for Computational Linguistics, ACL 2020, Online, July 5-10, 2020*, pages 7871–7880. Association for Computational Linguistics.

Jun Liu, Tong Zhang, Guangjie Han, and Yu Gou. 2018. TD-LSTM: Temporal Dependence-Based LSTM Networks for Marine Temperature Prediction. *Sensors*, 18(11):3797.

Shaiq Munir Malik, Fnu Mohbat, Muhammad Umair Haider, Muhammad Musab Rasheed, and Murtaza Taj. 2021. Teacher-Class Network: A Neural Network Compression Mechanism. In *32nd British Machine Vision Conference 2021, BMVC 2021, Online, November 22-25, 2021*, page 58. BMVA Press.

J. R. Martin and P. R.R. White. 2005. *The Language of Evaluation*. Palgrave/Macmillan.

Diego Mollá. 2020. Overview of the 2020 ALTA Shared Task: Assess Human Behaviour. *ALTA 2020*, page 127.

Diego Mollá. 2021. Overview of the 2021 ALTA Shared Task: Automatic Grading of Evidence, 10 years later. In *Proceedings of the The 19th Annual Workshop of the Australasian Language Technology Association*, pages 201–204.

Alena Neviarouskaya, Helmut Prendinger, and Mitsuru Ishizuka. 2010. Recognition of Affect, Judgment, and Appreciation in Text. In *COLING 2010, 23rd International Conference on Computational Linguistics, Proceedings of the Conference, 23-27 August 2010, Beijing, China*, pages 806–814. Tsinghua University Press.

Pradeesh Parameswaran, Andrew Trotman, Veronica Liesaputra, and David Eyers. 2022. Reproducibility and automation of the appraisal taxonomy. *Proceedings of the 29th International Conference on Computational Linguistics*.

Jasabanta Patro, Srijan Bansal, and Animesh Mukherjee. 2019. A Deep-Learning Framework to Detect Sarcasm Targets. In *Proceedings of the 2019 Conference on Empirical Methods in Natural Language Processing and the 9th International Joint Conference on Natural Language Processing, EMNLP-IJCNLP 2019, Hong Kong, China, November 3-7, 2019*, pages 6335–6341. Association for Computational Linguistics.

Maria Pontiki, Dimitris Galanis, Haris Papageorgiou, Ion Androutsopoulos, Suresh Manandhar, Mohammad Al-Smadi, Mahmoud Al-Ayyoub, Yanyan Zhao, Bing Qin, Orphée De Clercq, Véronique Hoste, Marianna Apidianaki, Xavier Tannier, Natalia V. Loukachevitch, Evgeniy V. Kotelnikov, Núria Bel, Salud María Jiménez Zafra, and Gülsen Eryigit. 2016. SemEval-2016 Task 5: Aspect Based Sentiment Analysis. In *Proceedings of the 10th International Workshop on Semantic Evaluation, SemEval@NAACL-HLT 2016, San Diego, CA, USA, June 16-17, 2016*, pages 19–30. The Association for Computer Linguistics.

Maria Pontiki, Dimitris Galanis, Haris Papageorgiou, Suresh Manandhar, and Ion Androutsopoulos. 2015. SemEval-2015 Task 12: Aspect Based Sentiment Analysis. In *Proceedings of the 9th International Workshop on Semantic Evaluation, SemEval@NAACL-HLT 2015, Denver, Colorado, USA, June 4-5, 2015*, pages 486–495. The Association for Computer Linguistics.

Alec Radford, Jeffrey Wu, Rewon Child, David Luan, Dario Amodei, and Ilya Sutskever. 2019. Language Models are Unsupervised Multitask Learners.

Andrew S. Ross and David Caldwell. 2020. 'Going negative': An APPRAISAL analysis of the rhetoric of Donald Trump on Twitter. *Lang. Commun.*, 70:13–27.

Rion Snow, Brendan O'Connor, Daniel Jurafsky, and Andrew Y. Ng. 2008. Cheap and Fast - But is it Good? Evaluating Non-Expert Annotations for Natural Language Tasks. In *2008 Conference on Empirical Methods in Natural Language Processing, EMNLP 2008, Proceedings of the Conference, 25-27 October 2008, Honolulu, Hawaii, USA, A meeting of SIGDAT, a Special Interest Group of the ACL*, pages 254–263. ACL.

Youwei Song, Jiahai Wang, Tao Jiang, Zhiyue Liu, and Yanghui Rao. 2019. Attentional Encoder Network for Targeted Sentiment Classification. *CoRR*, abs/1902.09314.

Susan Standing and Craig Standing. 2018. The Ethical Use of Crowdsourcing. *Business Ethics: A European Review*, 27(1):72–80.

Sue Starfield, Brian Paltridge, Robert McMurtrie, Allyson Holbrook, Sid Bourke, Hedy Fairbairn, Margaret Kiley, and Terry Lovat. 2015. Understanding the Language of Evaluation in Examiners' Reports on Doctoral Theses. *Linguist. Educ.*, 31:130–144.

Miriah Steiger, Timir J. Bharucha, Sukrit Venkatagiri, Martin J. Riedl, and Matthew Lease. 2021. The Psychological Well-Being of Content Moderators: The Emotional Labor of Commercial Moderation and Avenues for Improving Support. In *CHI '21: CHI Conference on Human Factors in Computing Systems, Virtual Event / Yokohama, Japan, May 8-13, 2021*, pages 341:1–341:14. ACM.

Hang Su and Susan Hunston. 2019. Language patterns and attitude revisited: Adjective patterns, Attitude and Appraisal. *Functions of Language*, 26(3):343–371.

Maite Taboada, Julian Brooke, Milan Tofiloski, Kimberly D. Voll, and Manfred Stede. 2011. Lexicon-Based Methods for Sentiment Analysis. *Comput. Linguistics*, 37(2):267–307.

Duyu Tang, Bing Qin, Xiaocheng Feng, and Ting Liu. 2016. Effective LSTMs for Target-Dependent Sentiment Classification. In *COLING 2016, 26th International Conference on Computational Linguistics, Proceedings of the Conference: Technical Papers, December 11-16, 2016, Osaka, Japan*, pages 3298–3307. ACL.

Yequan Wang, Minlie Huang, Xiaoyan Zhu, and Li Zhao. 2016. Attention-based LSTM for Aspect-level Sentiment Classification. In *Proceedings of the 2016 Conference on Empirical Methods in Natural Language Processing, EMNLP 2016, Austin, Texas, USA, November 1-4, 2016*, pages 606–615. The Association for Computational Linguistics.

Casey Whitelaw, Navendu Garg, and Shlomo Argamon. 2005. Using Appraisal Groups for Sentiment Analysis. In *Proceedings of the 2005 ACM CIKM International Conference on Information and Knowledge Management, Bremen, Germany, October 31 - November 5, 2005*, pages 625–631. ACM.

Hang Yan, Junqi Dai, Tuo Ji, Xipeng Qiu, and Zheng Zhang. 2021. A Unified Generative Framework for Aspect-based Sentiment Analysis. In *Proceedings of the 59th Annual Meeting of the Association for Computational Linguistics and the 11th International Joint Conference on Natural Language Processing, ACL/IJCNLP 2021, (Volume 1: Long Papers), Virtual Event, August 1-6, 2021*, pages 2416–2429. Association for Computational Linguistics.

Wenxuan Zhang, Xin Li, Yang Deng, Lidong Bing, and Wai Lam. 2022. A Survey on Aspect-Based Sentiment Analysis: Tasks, Methods, and Challenges. *CoRR*, abs/2203.01054.

Fine-tuning a Subtle Parsing Distinction Using a Probabilistic Decision Tree: the Case of Postnominal *"that"* in Noun Complement Clauses vs. Relative Clauses

Zineddine Tighidet
Université Paris Cité
F-75013 Paris, France
tighidet.zineddine@gmail.com

Nicolas Ballier
CLILLAC-ARP and LLF, Université Paris Cité
& CNRS F-75013 Paris France
nicolas.ballier@u-paris.fr

Abstract

In this paper we investigated two different methods to parse relative and noun complement clauses in English and resorted to distinct tags for their corresponding *that* as a relative pronoun and as a complementizer. We used an algorithm to relabel a corpus parsed with the GUM Treebank using Universal Dependency. Our second experiment consisted in using TreeTagger, a Probabilistic Decision Tree, to learn the distinction between the two complement and relative uses of postnominal *"that"*. We investigated the effect of the training set size on TreeTagger accuracy and how representative the GUM Treebank files are for the two structures under scrutiny. We discussed some of the linguistic and structural tenets of the learnability of this distinction.

1 Introduction

English has relative clauses (*the man that I saw*) and noun complement clauses (*the fact that I saw a man*) that may have similar surface representations (often the definite article, a noun, often immediately followed by *that*) but different structural properties (Ballier, 2004). For POS-tagging systems based on trigrams, the distinction between these constructions can be challenging, not to mention the case of ambiguous sentences such as "the suggestion that he was advancing was ridiculous" (Huddleston, 1984).This is an issue for information retrieval, as conceptual argumentation makes heavy uses of noun complement clauses (Ballier, 2007), the governors of these noun complement clauses being "shell nouns" (Schmid, 2000). Complement taking nouns (Bowen, 2005) are crucial for the expression of stance (Charles, 2007) in documents, which is why this distinction may matter more than is usually assumed.

The Penn Treebank (Marcus et al., 1993) tagset (Santorini, 1990) does not make strict distinctions between the part-of-speech (POS) tag of *"that"* when used as a relative pronoun (WDT) or when used as a conjunction when complementizing nouns: it uses IN when complementizing verbs or nouns. Even though the CLAWS8 [1]. (University Centre for Computer Corpus Research on Language, 1995-2004) tagset encodes this distinction with the *CST*[2] and *WPR*[3] tags, this tagger is not free and remains the property of the University Centre for Computer Corpus Research on Language (UCREL). To the best of our knowledge, the precision and recall of these two tags (and their corresponding syntactic structures) have not been reported.

Admitting POS-tagging systems have reached an overall satisfactory precision rate for standard English tagsets, we claim that this is not necessarily the case for tags that reflect such a subtle distinction which may have very similar surface representations. Discussing such POS-tags involves parsing issues of the *that*-clause that follows the noun. Our research question is mostly based on the ability of a system to identify noun complement clauses as apposed to (restrictive) relative clauses, but this can be addressed by analysing dependency relation labels (parsing) or distinct tags that encode this syntactic distinction (POS-tagging). We present the two strategies in two experiments, exploring whether such specific Universal Dependency labels can be learnt. In this paper, we only investigate overt complementizers as we are also investigating how that is tagged and do take into account noun complement clauses with zero complementizer, like in the example *Plus the fact I'm a coward* from the British National Corpus (Consortium et al., 2007).

The rest of the paper is structured as follows. Section 2 details the data we used for our exper-

[1] CLAWS, the Constituent Likelihood Automatic Word-tagging System, is the name of the tagset and of the POS-tagging software for English text, CLAWS (Garside, 1987)

[2] *"that"* as a conjunction

[3] *"that"* as a relative pronoun

iments. Section 3 analyses the Universal Dependency (UD) GUM Treebank for English in terms of precision for the dependency labels of these two structures as well as their distribution across the training, testing and development sets. We describe an experiment replicating one of the specific features of the GUM Treebank. Section 4 details an experiment based on algorithm adapting the UD annotation generated with GUM. Section 5 explains how Treetagger can be used to learn distinct tags for that used as a relative pronoun (WPR) or as a complementizer (CST). Section 6 discusses our results and section 7 outlines our future research.

2 Material and Methods

2.1 Test Sets

For our validation procedure, we used two test sets NCCtest and RCtest, one including 194 noun complement clauses (NCC), the other one included 189 relative clauses (RC). As language is complex, some sentences included other syntactic realisations, and a couple of "distractors" representative of the alternate structure were therefore included in our two test sets. We specify in Table 3 the expected (gold) label counts for each test set. Two annotators agreed on these gold labels of these two test sets ($\kappa = 1$).

2.2 Brown Corpus

We used the Brown corpus (Kucera et al., 1967), which is rather small with its 1 M tokens by contemporary standards, but well-balanced and freely available. Its current distribution in the NLTK python library (Bird, 2006) has been POS-tagged with the Penn Treebank, this is the substrate we used for our re-annotation experiment with TreeTagger. Treetagger is a probabilistic tagger which uses decision trees for probability transitions, which is robust for its retraining and claims accuracy above 96 % (Schmid, 1994).

2.3 Universal Dependency Annotation with UDPipe

UDPipe (Straka, 2018) is a pipeline that takes as input a text file and renders a CoNLL-U[4] file which contains the language-specific part-of-speech tag (*XPOS*), lemma or stem, the *DEPREL* (universal dependency relation) etc.
A file annotated in Universal Dependency contains among other columns the *XPOS* (part of speech) for each token and the dependency relation, *acl:relcl* for relative clauses and (just) *acl* for noun complement clauses, though this more general category (*acl* corresponds to clausal modifier of noun, adnominal clause) also includes non-finite clause.

Clausal modifier of noun (*acl*)
acl stands for finite and non-finite clauses that modify a noun. The governor (head) of the *acl* dependency relation is the noun that is modified, and the dependent is the predicate of the clause that modifies the noun. In Figure 1 the finite clause "as he sees them" modifies the noun "the issues".

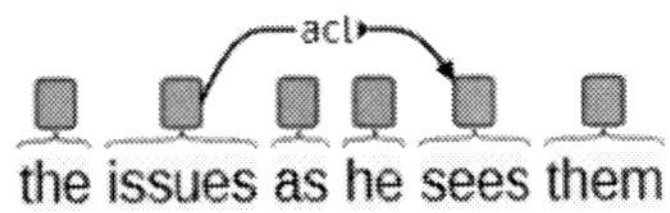

Figure 1: Example of clause modifier of noun (*acl*).

As evidenced by this example taken from the UD documentation, acl is a label that encompasses more than *that* noun complement clauses.

Relative clause modifier (*acl:relcl*)
A relative clause modifier of a noun is a clause that modifies the antecedent. The *acl:relcl* relation points from the governor (the antecedent) head of the modified nominal to the dependent (verb) of the relative clause. In Figure 2 the relative clause "which you bought" modifies the nominal "the book".

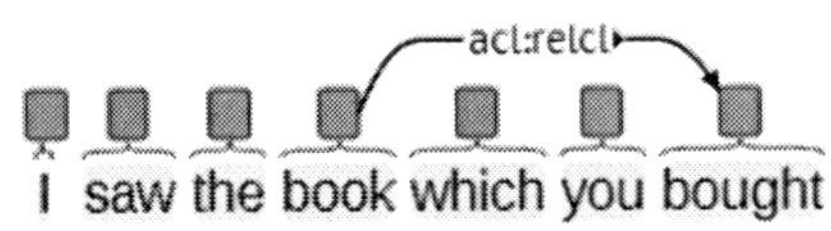

Figure 2: Example of relative clause modifier (*acl:relcl*).

Several treebanks for English are available [5] for the Universal dependency annotation (McDonald et al., 2013). We focused on the GUM Treebank (Zeldes, 2017), based on the Georgetown University Multilayer (GUM) Corpus [6] as its CoNLL-U format [7] contains a specific column that reports the dependency relation and the governor. Our next section analyses the accuracy of these two tags when labelling noun complement clauses and rel-

[4]https://universaldependencies.org/format.html

[5]https://universaldependencies.org/treebanks/en-comparison.html

[6]https://gucorpling.org/gum/

[7]an adaptation of the CoNLL-X format, (Buchholz and Marsi, 2006), https://universaldependencies.org/format.html

deprel	Train	Dev	Test
acl:that	65 (0.513)	13 (0.65)	14 (0.69)
acl:relcl	1419 (11.21)	258 (12.92)	216 (10.70)

Table 1: Frequency of "acl:relcl" and "acl:that" in the GUM Treebank files raw (normalized per 1000 tokens)
.

ative clauses in the development (DEV), training (TRAIN) and testing (TEST) sets of the GUM Treebank based on the GUM corpus (Levine, Lauren and Zeldes, Amir, 2017).

3 Revisiting the GUM Treebank

We noticed some debatable annotations for some cases where ellipsed *such* and *so* led some *that*-clauses expressing consequence to be labelled as acl as in *"As a result, wikiHow is still at the size that every editor eventually gets to know other editors"*. We computed the proportion of Relative Clauses (RC) in relation to noun complement clauses (NCC).

3.1 Frequency of RC and NCC in the GUM Treebank

As can be seen in Table 1, there are at least 15 times more relative clauses (RC) than noun complement clauses (NCC) in the GUM Treebank.

One of the benefits of the GUM Treebank is that it contains extra information, the ninth column conflates the dependency relation (acl) and *that* for noun complement clauses, we have tried to exploit this `acl:that` tag by building a UDPipe model based on this treebank and by trying to recapture this information by an algorithm.

3.2 Replicating the GUM Ninth Column

In the ninth column of the GUM corpus, we were specifically interested in the *"acl:relcl"* and *"acl:that"* annotations to improve the detection of noun complement clauses, since the standard deprel (dependency relation) column only provides the *"acl"* label and does not distinguish between finite and non finite uses of adnominal clauses. We trained a UDPipe model using the training, development and test sets of the GUM Treebank on Github[8]. However, once we applied the model on the same unannotated corpus, the ninth column was empty. It seems that UDPipe only captures the standard columns of the treebanks.

3.3 Emulating the Ninth column

We were therefore interested in reconstructing this column by implementing a heuristic. Once the acl:relcl have been copied from the deprel column, the algorithm consists in exploiting the seventh (Head of the current word) and eighth (Universal dependency relation to the HEAD) columns such that:

Algorithm 1 : Heuristic to emulate acl:that labels in the ninth column

for each $sentence \in corpus$ **do**
  for each $token \in sentence$ **do**

1. Combine the seventh and eighth columns of the $token$ that were generated by the previously trained UDPipe model.
2. If *"that"* is right after the word to which the seventh column of the $token$ points to, then add *"that"* to the ninth column.

4 Learning to tag with TreeTagger

This retagging experiment (Gaillat et al., 2014) relies on the ability of TreeTagger (Schmid, 1994) to be used not only as a POS-tagger but as a tool which can be trained to learn how to tag, provided a specific tagset and sample data are provided. We used samples from the Brown corpus in its NLTK distribution and modified the Penn Treebank tagset to distinguish *that* as WPR (relative pronoun) and *that* as CST (complementizer). In the learning phase, TreeTagger sees a vocabulary file and tokens associated to their tags and generates a .par model file to be used for POS-tagging. This section describes how we modified the tags to train the system [9]. After the annotation of the Brown corpus by UDPipe, a heuristic was applied on the results in order to introduce the *WPR* and *CST* tags which are not previously used in the tagset. To do that, the *DEPREL* label was used, so our method assumes that the UDPipe trained with the English GUM corpus provides a sufficiently correct *DEPREL* label for noun complement clauses:

The aim of this experiment is to see how the TreeTagger accuracy increases as a function of the

[8] https://github.com/UniversalDependencies/UD_English-GUM

[9] The Python implementation is available in this GitHub repository: https://github.com/Zineddine-Tighidet/Relative-Complement-That-Annotator

Algorithm 2 : Heuristic for Brown re-annotation

for each $sentence \in corpus$ **do**
  for each $token \in sentence$ **do**
- If the $token$ is a verb (i.e. XPOS = VB) and is a clausal modifier of noun (i.e. DEPREL = acl) then go steps before that $token$ to see if there is any *"that"*, if so, label it as *CST*.
- If the $token$ is a verb (i.e. XPOS = VB) and is part of a relative clause (i.e. DEPREL = acl:relcl) then go steps before that $token$ to see if there is any *"that"*, if so, label it as *WPR*.

deps column	Train	Dev	Test
acl:that	0.78	0.76	0.71
acl:relcl	0.92	0.92	0.94

Table 2: Accuracy of acl:relcl and acl:that annotations in the "deps" column recreated by combining the "head" and "deprel" columns for each of the GUM Treebank files.

training set size. To do this, the TreeTagger received different proportions of a training set as input. To be more specific, there are 500 training files representing the annotated Brown corpus, for the first training the first 10 files were used, and then the 30, 100, 200, 300, 400 and finally the 500 training files. For each training a *.par* file that corresponds to the model was returned.

5 Results

5.1 Emulating the Ninth column

To assess this algorithm that selects only *that*- (finite) clauses among the acl clauses, we tested it with the GUM treebank, comparing our results in our reconstructed column with the original data. The heuristic gave good results for the annotations of relative clauses "acl:relcl" with an accuracy that exceeds 90% (see table 2).

Nevertheless, the algorithm works less well for "acl:that", this is partly due to some coordinated NCC clauses and to multi-word-units (like *quid pro quo*).

5.2 Re-annotating with TreeTagger

We used our specifically designed testing files that contain respectively 189 *"that"* as *WPR* and 194 *"that"* as *CST*. The first one named RCtest (Relative Clause) was used to compute the accuracy for *WPR* and the second one named NCCtest (Noun Complement Clause) for *CST* (see Figure 3 and 4). We used these specific files because they are manually annotated and each one of them contains a majority of the two tags we are interested in, which makes it convenient for our experiments.

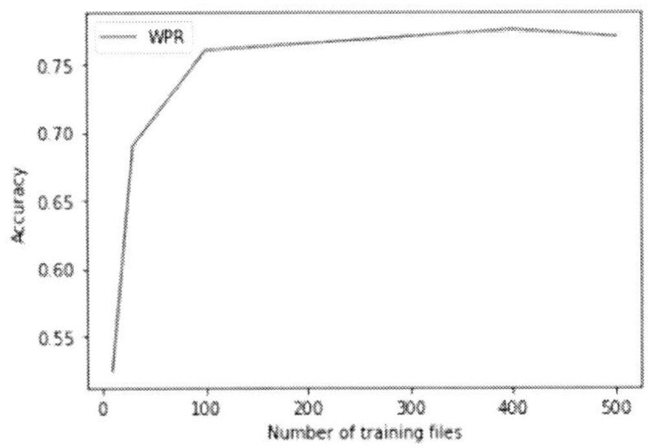

Figure 3: TreeTagger accuracy curve for *WPR* tag (computed using the RCtest data).

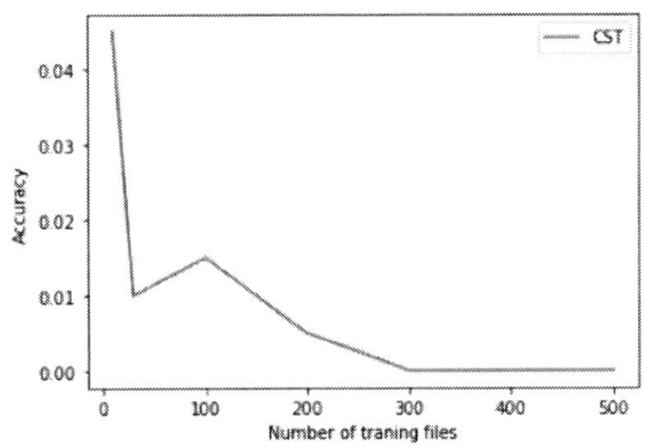

Figure 4: TreeTagger accuracy curve for *CST* tag (computed on the NCCtest data).

As shown in Figures 3 and 4 the TreeTagger accuracy increases with the number of training files for the RCtest data. This is a natural behaviour from a probabilistic model such as the TreeTagger, the probability increases as the weight of Relative clauses increases in the data it has. However, there is a drastic decrease in the *CST* curve around 100 training files, and the TreeTagger did not perform very well annotating the *"that"* with *CST* tag, as shown with Figure 4 the accuracy is very low, and as the number of training files increases, the accuracy goes down. Whatever technique is used, the detection of noun complement clauses is more challenging than for relative clauses.

6 Discussion

Two approaches for explaining the results obtained for the CST tag can be either statistically or linguistically motivated. Starting with the first approach, as shown in Table 3, as the number of training files goes up, the number of other tags increases, especially for the IN tag, which in this case represents a confusion by the TreeTagger to annotate with the right tag, in fact IN is not a specific tag but rather a generic tag as it also corresponds to verbal *that*-clauses, therefore, this shows that the TreeTagger generated noise due to a confusion on the annotation of "that" (this is better illustrated in the figure 9 especially for the graph that represents the IN tag in blue.) The second approach consists in analysing the competing labels for *that*.

6.1 Accuracy in relation to other categories

The Penn Treebank tagset (Santorini, 1990), even though it does not acknowledge the whole complex range of functional realisations of *that*, e.g. adverbial, proform vs deictic uses, see (Ballier et al., 2022) can help visualise the complex interaction of the learning process of the identification of the different functional uses of *that*. As the training data increases, the variable proportions of the different functional realisations of *that* probably changes, so that a probabilistic tagger generates models variable in their results for this tagging task. The tagger has to learn the different competing tags for *that*. Our two test datasets allow us to monitor the evolution of the training phase as the size of the training data increases. Whereas we tried to train Treetagger to learn CST for NCC *that* and WPR for relative pronouns, we also computed the distribution of other tags that "*that*" may take, such as "WDT" (*that* when used as a relative pronoun, but also "WH"-determiners such as *which*), "DT" (Determiners), and "IN" (Subordinating conjunction, whether for nouns or for verbs) for each of the RC and NCC corpus. Table 3 recaps the changes observed when we evaluated the labels with our two testing sets (RCtest and NCCtest). For each testing set, we indicate the expected count of each label in the columns RCtest GOLD and NCCtest GOLD.

Here is an example of these potential mishaps in the POS-tagging: "that meeting that|IN [vs DT]

	RCtest	RCtest GOLD	NCCtest	NCCtest GOLD
10 training files				
WPR	107	189	20	17
CST	22	26	10	194
IN	95	0	183	0
DT	7	15	16	14
30 training files				
WPR	146	189	28	17
CST	5	26	3	194
IN	72	0	189	0
DT	8	15	9	14
100 training files				
WPR	158	189	25	17
CST	2	26	3	194
IN	65	0	194	0
DT	6	15	7	14
200 training files				
WPR	156	189	27	17
CST	1	26	1	194
IN	66	0	196	0
DT	8	15	0	14
300 training files				
WPR	157	189	22	17
CST	2	26	0	194
IN	67	0	202	0
DT	5	15	5	14
400 training files				
WPR	159	189	21	17
CST	2	26	0	194
IN	64	0	199	0
DT	6	15	7	14
500 training files				
WPR	158	189	23	17
CST	1	26	4	194
IN	65	0	188	0
DT	7	15	7	14

Table 3: Statistics about *WPR*, *CST*, *IN* and *DT* tags obtained for each of the 7 models (i.e. trained with 10, 30, 100, 200, 300, 400 and 500 files).

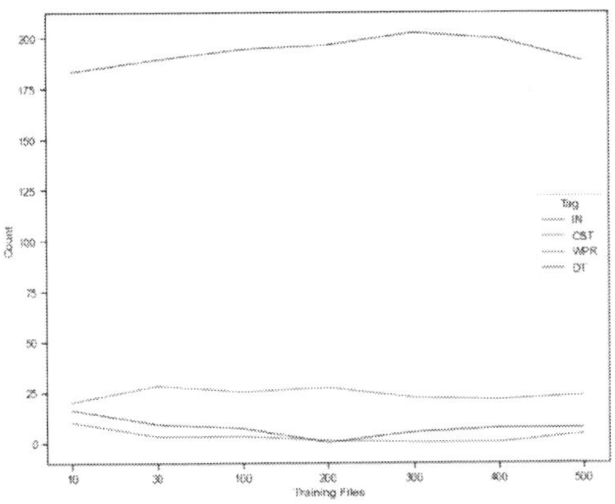

Figure 5: Evolution of IN, CST, WPR and DT tags with training files in the NCCtest corpus.

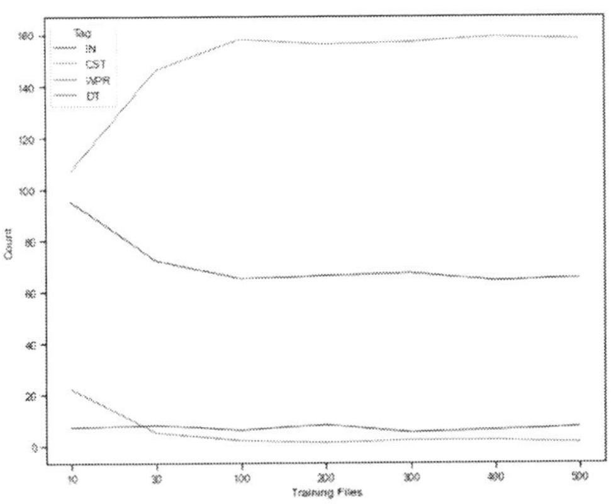

Figure 6: Evolution of IN, CST, WPR and DT tags with training files in the RCtest corpus.

morning was about a public case that|IN [vs WPR] we might make". The first deictic *that* was properly labelled, the second one was erroneously labelled as a subordinating conjunction and for the third occurrence, the relative pronoun was tagged as a subordinating conjunction (see additional examples in the Appendix).

6.2 Weakness of the TreeTagger-based heuristic

We re-annotated a corpus initially tagged with the Penn Treebank, which means that we modified some IN tags to CST and some IN tags to WPR for relative pronouns but the Brown corpus data retained some WDT labels. As shown in Table 3, there are many *WDT* tags, this is simply because the *WDT* tag is both an older and more general version of the *WPR* tag, and seemingly the TreeTagger kept the older version. So the *WDT* and *WPR* tags are likely labels for relative pronouns considered as equivalent in the computing of the metrics, even though strictly speaking some WDT tokens in the Brown corpus may correspond to WH-determiners such as *which*. The main objection to our method is that we only relabelled a portion of the IN tags, so that the system has to learn a WPR versus CST distinction while still being fed with some examples of IN. In this sense, we can only partially monitor the behaviour of Treetagger when subjected to more examples. Figure 5 and Figure 6 plot the evolution of the tagging of the NCCtest and RCtest sets (respectively) as the corpus size increases. We expect the system to learn to relabel IN as either WPR or CST but this is hardly the case for CST. It should be noted that we did not control the input of the respective number of examples with CST and with WPR when increasing the data size of the training data. We only report the total counts of the tags assigned to *that*, we did monitor the individual behaviour of the tagging system for each occurrence of *that*.

6.3 Long-Distance Dependencies

As already pointed out, noun complement clauses can follow a relative clause for the same noun (but not the other way round). *That*-relative clauses tend to be adjacent to their antecedents (and are often restrictive relative clauses) whereas (*that-*) noun complement clauses can be separated from their governor. So we explored a simple metric which is the distance (i.e. number of tokens) separating a *"that"* (annotated either with *CST* or *WPR*) and the last noun before it. As shown in the boxplots in Figure 7 there is a tendency showing that the *"that"* tagged with *CST* using a verb with a *DEPREL = acl* have a higher distance separating them from the last noun before them. This can probably cause some ambiguity due to the higher distance. However, as we can see for the *"that"* tagged with *WPR* using a verb with a *DEPREL = acl:relcl* the distance with the last noun is smaller, and there are less misclassifications (i.e. less noise) for the *"that"* used as *WPR*. This is just a statistical approach to see if there is any bias that can explain why the heuristic produces a lot of noise.

Our metric is rather crude but head nouns of NCCs need not be adjacent to the *that*-clauses, so that an inventory of structures in-between could be taken into account. The distance between the governor and the *that*-clause of these long-distance

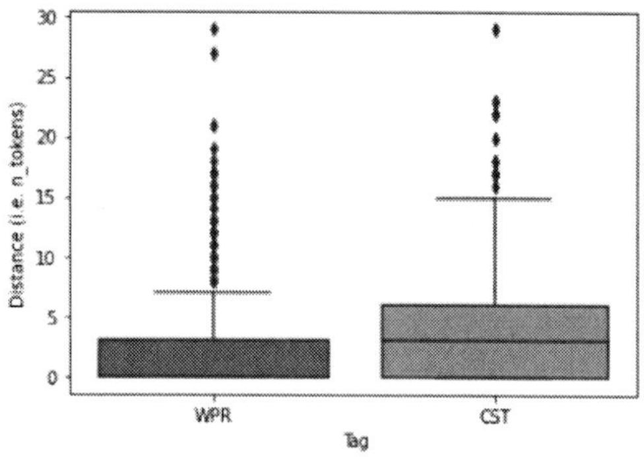

Figure 7: Distribution of the distance (number of tokens) separating a *"that"* and the last noun before it for each of the *WPR* and *CST "that"*.

dependencies (Osborne, 2019) could be more systematically investigated.

6.4 Relevance of UD Deprel Labels for NCC?

It should be noted that UD changed the dependency label for noun complement clauses, as explained on the UD website: "In earlier versions of SD/USD, complement clauses with nouns like fact or report were also analyzed as ccomp [clausal complement]. However, we now analyze them as acl. Hence, ccomp does not appear in nominals. This makes sense, since nominals normally do not take core arguments." We may challenge this view since ccomp implies a "clausal complement" and nouns may require a "core argument", even more so than for adjectives.[10] One of the unfortunate consequences is that adverbs like *now* in the sentence "Now that the world is in the age where lighting seems to be a daily necessity" are labelled as a governor of the "adnominal" clause. It maybe the case that acl is a debatable label, also used after verbs as for that verbal complement clauses ("if this seems incredibly far-fetched, comfort yourself that double chute failure in modern times is also extremely unlikely, and that you have already beaten worse odds"). Consequently, the (SUD) Surface-Syntactic Universal Dependencies (Gerdes et al., 2018) has suggested alternative labels for acl. Another approach might be to restrict noun complement clauses to a subcategory of acl specific to noun complement clauses (possibly labelled as acl:ncl).

[10]For a similar argumentation see (Osborne and Gerdes, 2019).

7 Further Research

7.1 Quality Monitoring of the Training Phase

We have only estimated the accuracy of the annotation on our testing sets but we have not monitored the qualitative aspect of the annotation. Are some sentences systematically mislabelled or can we observe some changes during the training phase? For example, this NCC gets to be interpreted as a relative clause: *"O'Neill had an emotional reaction that [tagged as WPR] the level of corruption was too high to do serious projects in Russia," Deripaska recalls.* Some configurations seem to remain challenging for parsing, and qualitative monitoring of the accuracy should take into account these sentences for which labelling improves or not. Controlling for frequency of exposure in the training data should prove to be very fruitful to maybe detect thresholds in frequency (or proportions) in the training data for accurate tagging. For example, an example in our appendix seems to suggest that a trigram sequence no/N/that (and corresponding identification of noun complement clauses) seems to be learned after exposure to the 100 training files (36 occurrences). As some of the examples of mislabellings in the Appendix also suggest, it is likely that our relabelling algorithm for WPR is too greedy, and a more elaborate version should filter out alternative relative pronouns that should inhibit the relabelling process. We should also apply stricter conditions on the type of *that* which can be re-tagged. Assuming the DT label is correct, only IN labels should be re-tagged.

7.2 More data?

More training files from the Brown corpus have been manually annotated and given to the TreeTagger, and an improvement in the *CST* accuracy was observed (see Figure 8). Though a plateau seems to be observed for the tag CST (*that* for NCC complementizer), one may wonder if more examples of NCCs in the training data would alter this curve. We have only analysed the GUM Treebank for the UD analysis, but no less than six treebanks are available on github for the Universal Dependency analysis of English.

7.3 Learnability and Dispersion

Our monitoring of the learning curve of the tag distinction in our TreeTagger experiment could be finer-grained: we did not control for genre types within the Brown corpus and the relative distribu-

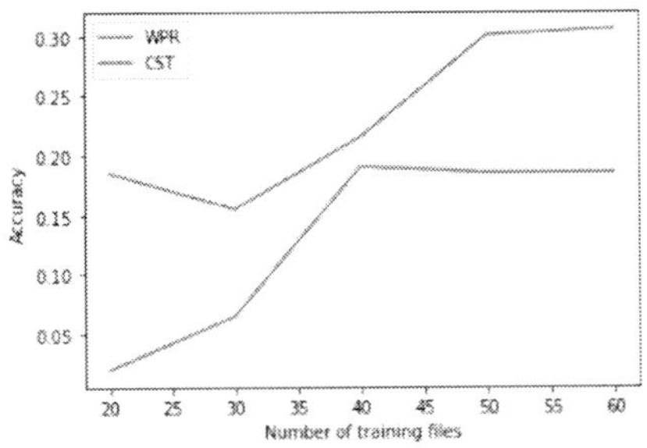

Figure 8: TreeTagger accuracy for *"that"* annotated with *CST* in red and *WPR* in green with more training files.

tions of the two structures. If relative clauses seem to be more frequent than NCCs in the GUM Treebank, NCCs are more likely to be more frequent in argumentative texts (Ballier, 2007). Our experiment only reported the effect of the number of the Brown files in the training data, not the specific distribution of the two structures across the different registers of the Brown corpus. The dispersion of these linguistic structures in the training data could be monitored across the corpus subparts using adequate dispersion measures (Gries, 2020) or by comparing the vocabulary growth curves (Evert and Baroni, 2007) of the two constructions across the Brown corpus files. Our Figure 9 crudely plots the distribution of the different tags in the training data as the size of the corpus increases (measured in number of files, but not with the corresponding text genres). Increasing the size of the corpus may require more attention to a frequency/textual diversity trade off.

8 Conclusion

In this study, we have experimented two methods to detect noun complement clauses, either by using the universal dependency GUM treebank or by retagging the Brown corpus with specific *WPR* and *CST* tags. We also explored an automated way to do this annotation using a specific heuristic. We have evidenced the longer distance between the noun and the *that*-clause for noun complement clauses. The detection of relative clauses does seem to be much more robust than for noun complement clauses, which remains a problem for information retrieval as text genres could be interestingly classified with this criterion. The difference in frequency and in adjacency may account for such a discrepancy in the accuracy of the identification of the clause type. We have only begun to explore the parameters of the learnability of these tags corresponding to such a subtle linguistic distinction.

Acknowledgements

We thank the three reviewers for their careful comments on a preliminary version of this paper. Thanks are due to Université Paris Cité MSc in Machine Learning for Data Science, which triggered this joint paper. Part of this research was carrried out on a CNRS research leave at the Laboratoire de Linguistique Formelle CNRS research lab, for which grateful thanks are acknowledged. We thank Issa Kanté for his collection of examples for the test datasets, partially reflecting his PhD data (Kanté, 2017).

Appendix

8.1 Example of a noun complement clause where that gets properly tagged after 100 files in the training data (containing 36 occurrences of the *no N that* sequence)

"However, there is no guarantee ***that****[tagged as CST] only the genuine repentant will produce works of value to the society."*

8.2 Examples of remaining errors in our test sets

We include examples of persistent mislabelling in our test data. After 500 training files, 6 sentences with that in noun complement clauses are still tagged as if they were relative pronouns (with WPR).

- *The statement that|WPR the tribunal has made an "error of law" means no more or less than that|CST the construction placed upon the term by the court is preferred to that|DT of the tribunal.*
- *There was no dispute that|WPR Bunn throughout acted with the authority of the bank.*
- *This included a commitment that|WPR "if one of the two states should become the target of aggression, then the other side will give the aggressor no military aid or other support".*
- *We have received information that|WPR today, between 1400 and 1500, there was an explosion at the residence of Seyed Ali Khamenei.*
- *Recently there was the illusion that|WPR Hamas, while not a perfect partner, was at*

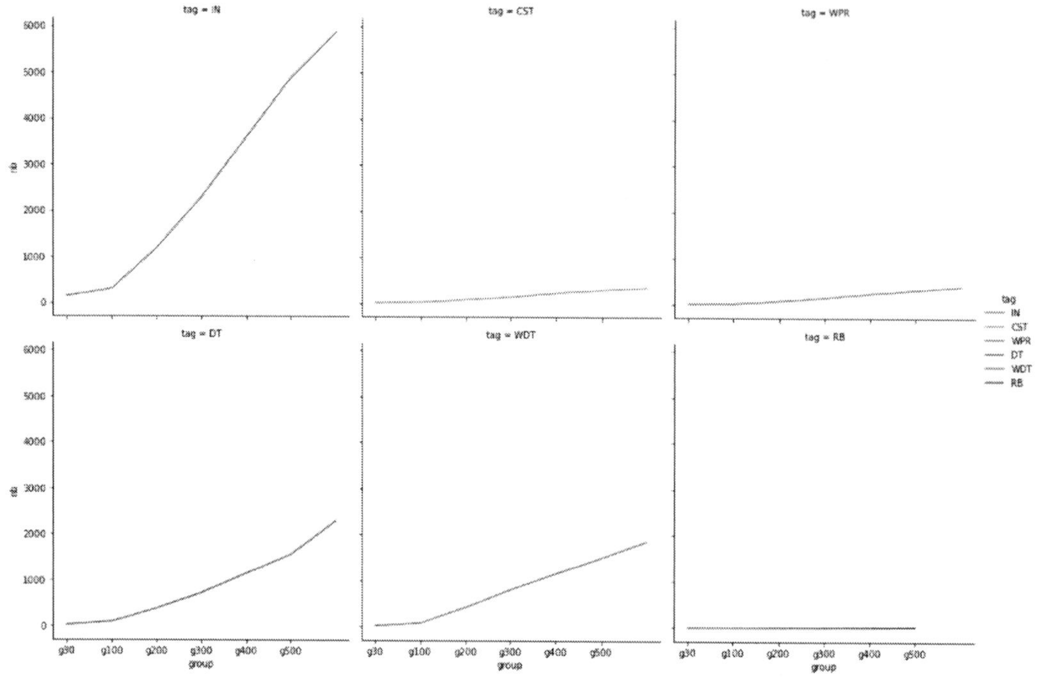

Figure 9: Evolution of the number of different tags for the re-annotated Brown corpus file groups (10, 30, 100, 200, 300, 400, 500 files.)

least a group that could implement decisions," he said.

- *Where there is a contract for the sale of goods by description, there is an implied condition* ***that***|*WPR the goods shall correspond with the description.*

8.2.1 Example from our test sets that has been annotated with DT rather than with CST

We illustrate the complexity of the polyfunctionality of *"that"* by showing an example of overfitting for the deictic/pronominal uses of *"that"*.

"A high-ranking official in the Clinton administration expressed shock ***that****[tagged as DT rather than CST] "the kids" in the White House "did not stand up when the president entered the room."*

8.2.2 Examples from the RC test set that have been annotated with IN rather than with WPR

- *High death rates among children reduce the value* ***that*** *|IN parents place on education; and so on.*
- *The distinction* ***that*** *|IN matters is from that of 'patronage', which itself, as we shall see, is highly varied.*

8.2.3 Examples from the NCCtest set that have been annotated with IN rather than with CST

- *They're living proof* ***that*** *asthma can be passed from generation to generation.*
- *Where there is a contract for the sale of goods by description, there is an implied condition* ***that*** *the goods shall correspond with the description.*

8.3 An example of false positives for the Brown relabelling heuristic

- *"... But one does not have to affirm the existence of an evil order irredeemable in* ***that****[tagged as WPR] sense, or a static order in which no changes will take place in time, to be able truthfully to affirm the following fact: there has never been justitia imprinted in social institutions and social relationships except in the context of some pax-ordo preserved by clothed or naked force ... "* (it should be *DT* rather than *WPR*). The relative clause is with WHICH, not with THAT.

References

Nicolas Ballier. 2004. *Praxis métalinguistiques et ontologie des catégories*. Habilitation thesis in linguistics, Université de Paris X-Nanterre.

Nicolas Ballier. 2007. La complétive du nom dans le discours des linguistes. *D. Banks, La coordination et la subordination dans le texte de spécialité, Paris, L'Harmattan*, pages 55–76.

Nicolas Ballier, Antonio Balvet, Taylor Arnold, and Thomas Gaillat. 2022. *Some metalinguistic assumptions behind tagsets for English: evidence from that in different versions of the Brown corpus*, pages 27–81. Peter Lang, Bern.

Steven Bird. 2006. NLTK: the natural language toolkit. In *Proceedings of the COLING/ACL 2006 Interactive Presentation Sessions*, pages 69–72.

Rhonwen Bowen. 2005. Noun complementation in english : a corpus-based study of structural types and patterns.

Sabine Buchholz and Erwin Marsi. 2006. CoNLL-X shared task on multilingual dependency parsing. In *Proceedings of the tenth conference on computational natural language learning (CoNLL-X)*, pages 149–164.

Maggie Charles. 2007. Argument or evidence? disciplinary variation in the use of the noun that pattern in stance construction. *English for Specific Purposes*, 26(2):203–218.

BNC Consortium et al. 2007. British National Corpus XML edition. *Oxford Text Archive. http://hdl.handle.net/20.500*, 12024:2554.

Stefan Evert and Marco Baroni. 2007. zipfR: Word frequency distributions in R. In *Proceedings of the 45th annual meeting of the ACL on interactive poster and demonstration sessions*, pages 29–32.

Thomas Gaillat, Pascale Sébillot, and Nicolas Ballier. 2014. Automated classification of unexpected uses of *this* and *that* in a learner corpus of english. *Language and Computers*, 78:309–324.

Roger Garside. 1987. The CLAWS word-tagging system. *The Computational analysis of English: A corpus-based approach. London: Longman*, pages 30–41.

Kim Gerdes, Bruno Guillaume, Sylvain Kahane, and Guy Perrier. 2018. SUD or Surface-Syntactic Universal Dependencies: An annotation scheme near-isomorphic to UD. In *Universal dependencies workshop 2018*.

Stefan Th. Gries. 2020. Analyzing Dispersion. In *A Practical Handbook of Corpus Linguistics*, pages 99–118, Cham. Springer International Publishing.

Rodney Huddleston. 1984. *Introduction to the Grammar of English*. Cambridge University Press.

Issa M Kanté. 2017. Étude sémantico-syntaxique de la complétive nominale en anglais et en français. *Étude sémantico-syntaxique de la complétive nominale en anglais et en français*.

Henry Kucera, Henry Kučera, and Winthrop Nelson Francis. 1967. *Computational analysis of present-day American English*. Brown University Press.

Levine, Lauren and Zeldes, Amir. 2017. GUM: The Georgetown University multilayer corpus.

Mitchell P. Marcus, Beatrice Santorini, and Mary Ann Marcinkiewicz. 1993. Building a large annotated corpus of English: The Penn Treebank. *Computational Linguistics*, 19(2):313–330.

Ryan McDonald, Joakim Nivre, Yvonne Quirmbach-Brundage, Yoav Goldberg, Dipanjan Das, Kuzman Ganchev, Keith Hall, Slav Petrov, Hao Zhang, Oscar Täckström, et al. 2013. Universal dependency annotation for multilingual parsing. In *Proceedings of the 51st Annual Meeting of the Association for Computational Linguistics (Volume 2: Short Papers)*, pages 92–97.

Timothy Osborne. 2019. *A dependency grammar of English: An introduction and beyond*. John Benjamins Publishing Company.

Timothy Osborne and Kim Gerdes. 2019. The status of function words in dependency grammar: A critique of Universal Dependencies (UD). *Glossa: a journal of general linguistics*, 4(1):1–28.

Beatrice Santorini. 1990. Part-of-speech tagging guidelines for the penn treebank project (3rd revision). *Technical Reports (CIS)*, page 570.

Hans-Jörg Schmid. 2000. *English abstract nouns as conceptual shells*. De Gruyter Mouton, Berlin.

Helmut Schmid. 1994. TreeTagger-a language independent part-of-speech tagger. *http://www.ims.uni-stuttgart.de/projekte/corplex/TreeTagger/*.

Milan Straka. 2018. UDPipe 2.0 prototype at CoNLL 2018 UD Shared Task. In *Proceedings of the CoNLL 2018 Shared Task: Multilingual Parsing from Raw Text to Universal Dependencies*, pages 197–207, Brussels, Belgium. Association for Computational Linguistics.

University Centre for Computer Corpus Research on Language. 1995-2004. Constituent likelihood automatic word-tagging system 8.

Amir Zeldes. 2017. The GUM corpus: Creating multilayer resources in the classroom. *Language Resources and Evaluation*, 51(3):581–612.

Robustness of Hybrid Models in Cross-domain Readability Assessment

Ho Hung Lim, Tianyuan Cai, John S. Y. Lee, Meichun Liu
Department of Linguistics and Translation
City University of Hong Kong
{hhlim3,jsylee,meichliu}@cityu.edu.hk, tianycai-c@my.cityu.edu.hk

Abstract

Recent studies in automatic readability assessment have shown that hybrid models — models that leverage both linguistically motivated features and neural models — can outperform neural models. However, most evaluations on hybrid models have been based on in-domain data in English. This paper provides further evidence on the contribution of linguistic features by reporting the first direct comparison between hybrid, neural and linguistic models on cross-domain data. In experiments on a Chinese dataset, the hybrid model outperforms the neural model on both in-domain and cross-domain data. Importantly, the hybrid model exhibits much smaller performance degradation in the cross-domain setting, suggesting that the linguistic features are more robust and can better capture salient indicators of text difficulty.

1 Introduction

Automatic Readability Assessment (ARA) predicts how difficult it is for the reader to understand a text. Traditional machine learning approaches for ARA typically train statistical classifiers with hand-crafted features (Pitler and Nenkova, 2008; Sung et al., 2015). Similar to other NLP tasks, neural approaches have recently achieved superior performance (Tseng et al., 2019; Azpiazu and Pera, 2019; Martinc et al., 2021). Combining linguistic features and neural models has been found to benefit a variety of NLP tasks (Lei et al., 2018; Strubell et al., 2018). While these 'hybrid' models have also been applied in ARA, there have been varying results ranging from no effect (Deutsch et al., 2020), marginal improvement (Filighera et al., 2019), to significant improvement (Lee et al., 2021).

Past studies comparing hybrid and neural models have mostly been conducted in an in-domain setting, with the training and test data drawn from the same source. However, real-word applications of ARA models are often targeted at cross-domain or cross-corpus data. Consider the task of retrieving extra-curricular reading materials for language learning from web texts, which likely diverge in style and content from the training data. In-domain evaluation therefore may not accurately reflect the actual performance on such tasks.

This paper focuses on the task of predicting the grade level of an input text. We present the first comparison between hybrid, neural and linguistic models on this task in the cross-domain setting. Our contribution is two-fold. First, we show that the hybrid model outperforms the neural model both in-domain and cross-domain in Chinese datasets, providing further evidence on the contribution of linguistic features. Second, the hybrid model exhibits much smaller performance degradation on cross-domain data, suggesting their robustness and ability to capture more salient indicators of text difficulty.[1]

After a review of previous work (Section 2), we present our datasets (Section 3). We then outline our approach (Section 4) and report experimental results (Section 5).

2 Background

2.1 Hybrid model design

Statistical classifiers can be trained on a variety of features, capturing lexical, syntactic and semantic characteristics of a text, to determine its readability or grade level (Dell'Orletta et al., 2011; François and Fairon, 2012; Sung et al., 2015). While these classifiers lend themselves to more explainable and linguistically-motivated results, neural models can achieve superior performance and do not require feature engineering (Tseng et al., 2019; Martinc et al., 2021).

Various methods for combining these approaches have been investigated. For example,

[1] Our implementation is available at https://github.com/hhlim333/ALTA2022Readability

a Bi-LSTM can incorporate part-of-speech information (Azpiazu and Pera, 2019). A statistical classifier can directly use sentence embeddings as features (2021). It can also incorporate the decision of the neural model as a single numeric feature (Deutsch et al., 2020), or 'soft' labels expressing the probabilities of each grade as predicted by the neural model (Lee et al., 2021). Our experiments will directly compare the performance of these three approaches.

2.2 In-domain vs. cross-domain evaluation

There can be a mismatch between ARA training datasets and the texts on which the ARA model is deployed. Domain adaptation techniques can be applied to address differences between native and non-native texts. For example, scores from an ARA ranking model trained on graded texts for native speakers can help estimate the CEFR level of a text for non-native learners (Xia et al., 2016).

Another type of mismatch is caused by cross-domain or cross-corpus data, which has been investigated in the ranking task in ARA. When ranking models are trained on Newsela, they suffered a performance degradation when tested on OneStopEnglish and Vikidia (Lee and Vajjala, 2020). For the grade prediction task, however, cross-domain evaluation has been reported mainly in terms of correlation (Chen and Meurers, 2016). This may be due to the fact that different grade scales are adopted in the major benchmarks, such as Newsela, OneStopEnglish and WeeBit. In this work we leverage two comparable datasets in Chinese (Section 3) to conduct cross-domain evaluation on hybrid models to assess the contribution of linguistic features in the grade prediction task.

3 Data

Since the benchmark ARA corpora adopt different grade scales (Section 2.2), we utilize two datasets of Chinese-language textbook materials, graded under comparable scales but drawn from different sources.

Mainland China texts (in-domain): Drawn from textbooks for Chinese language used in Mainland China (Lee et al., 2020), this dataset consists of 7.15M characters distributed in 4,831 passages in 12 grades (Cheng et al., 2020).

Hong Kong texts (cross-domain): Chinese-language textbooks in Hong Kong follow similar language proficiency standards as those in the Mainland. They are however compiled independently from different sources and use traditional rather than simplified characters, thus providing a challenging cross-domain scenario. We constructed a corpus of 298K characters distributed in 502 passages in 12 grades, all taken from current textbooks in Hong Kong.

Grade	# text	# char
1	50	4793
2	50	9042
3	50	15107
4	50	22191
5	50	28345
6	50	32776
7	50	35957
8	42	32859
9	46	44906
10	35	31179
11	13	22703
12	16	18686

Table 1: Statistics on the corpus of Hong Kong texts

4 Approach

We compared the following ARA models for predicting the grade (1-12) of an input text.

4.1 Baseline: Neural Model

We fine-tuned[2] MacBERT (Cui et al., 2020), RoBERTa (Cui et al., 2020), BERT (Devlin et al., 2019) and BERT-wwm (Cui et al., 2020) on the Mainland dataset for grade prediction.[3]

4.2 Baseline: Linguistic Model

We trained a statistical classifier on the 221 linguistic features provided by ChiLingFeat [4], an open-source toolkit that extracts most features used in previous Chinese ARA studies (Sung et al., 2015; Lu et al., 2020). We evaluated SVM, Random Forest (RF), and XGBoost (XGB) using the implementation in scikit-learn (Pedregosa et al., 2011).

[2] We used the code by Lee et al. (2021) in default parameters for fine-tuning, accessed from https://github.com/yjang43/pushingonreadability_transformers

[3] We used macbert-large, chinese-roberta-wwm-ext, bert-base-chinese, and chinese-bert-wwm, respectively.

[4] https://github.com/ffliu6/ChiLingFeat

Trans-former	Hybrid model type	In-domain	Cross-domain
BERT	Hard labels	0.312	0.288
	Soft labels	**0.342**	**0.290**
	Sent. Embed.	0.322	0.269
BERT-wwm	Hard labels	0.295	**0.283**
	Soft labels	**0.341**	0.278
	Sent Embed.	0.318	**0.283**
RoBERTa	Hard labels	0.301	0.285
	Soft labels	**0.341**	**0.301**
	Sent Embed.	0.318	0.287
MacBERT	Hard labels	0.305	0.283
	Soft labels	**0.353**	**0.309**
	Sent. Embed.	0.329	0.269

Table 2: Accuracy of the three hybrid model types (Section 4.3)

We applied Variance Threshold algorithm in scikit-learn for feature selection, but obtained the best result with the full feature set.

4.3 Hybrid Model

Following Lee et al. (2021), we adopted the simple approach of wrapping linguistic features and neural model output in a non-neural, statistical classifier. We evaluated three types of hybrid models:

Hard labels (Deutsch et al., 2020): The grade of the input text, as predicted by the neural model (Section 4.1) serves as an additional feature in the classifier.

Soft labels (Lee et al., 2021): The probabilities of each grade, as predicted by the neural model (Section 4.1), serve as additional features.

Sentence Embeddings (Imperial, 2021): The sentence vectors, produced by SBERT (Reimers and Gurevych, 2019) from the sentences in the input text, serve as additional features.

5 Experiments

In-domain evaluation used stratified 5-fold cross-validation on the Mainland Chinese dataset, based on a train:dev:test split of 8:1:1. Cross-domain evaluation used the entire Mainland China corpus as training data, and the entire Hong Kong corpus as test data. Among the three classifiers, RF outperformed SVM and XGB in most settings and metrics. The rest of the paper will refer to results based on RF.

5.1 Metrics

We use accuracy, F1, adjacent accuracy and quadratic weighted kappa (QWK) as our metric for the experiment. For adjacent accuracy, the system is considered correct if the predicted label is within one grade higher or lower than the gold grade. QWK also helps capture the distance between gold and predicted grades. These metrics give a comprehensive evaluation of model performance from different perspectives.

5.2 Hybrid model types

Table 2 reports the performance of the three hybrid model types (Section 4.3). For in-domain evaluation, hybrid models with soft labels outperformed those with hard labels and sentence embeddings, regardless of the transformer. For cross-domain evaluation, that was also the case for BERT, RoBERTa and MacBERT. The only exception was BERT-wwm, for which hard labels and embeddings performed slightly better (0.283), but still less accurate than the other transformers. The results presented below will be based on soft labels.

5.3 In-domain evaluation

Baselines. As shown in Table 3, the Linguistic Model yielded 0.276 accuracy in the in-domain setting. It was outperformed by the Neural Model regardless of the transformer used. MacBERT achieved the best performance for the Neural Model on accuracy (0.333) and all other metrics.

Hybrid Model. The Hybrid Model trained on MacBERT attained the highest accuracy (0.353) and F1, while RoBERTa led to the best adjacency accuracy and QWK (tied with BERT). Regardless of the choice of transformer or metric, the Hybrid Model outperformed both baselines. The absolute accuracy gains over the Neural Model ranged from 2.0% (MacBERT) to 4.8% (RoBERTa).[5] Consistent with previous results on English datasets (Lee et al., 2021), linguistic features enhance the performance of neural models on the Chinese datasets.

5.4 Cross-domain evaluation

Baselines. As expected, model performance degraded in the cross-domain setting. MacBERT produced the best-performing Neural Model in terms of all four metrics. Unlike the in-domain evaluation, the Linguistic Model outperformed the Neural

[5]The improvement is statistically significant for all four models at $p < 0.01$ according to McNemar's Test with continuity correction.

Metric	Linguistic Model (RF)		Neural Model			Hybrid Model	
	In-domain	Cross-domain	Transformer	In-domain	Cross-domain	In-domain	Cross-domain
Acc.	0.276	0.263	BERT	0.303	0.197 (-0.106)	0.342	0.290 (-0.052)
		(-0.013)	BERT-wwm	0.308	0.196 (-0.112)	0.341	0.278 (-0.063)
			RoBERTa	0.293	0.196 (-0.097)	0.341	0.301 (-0.040)
			MacBERT	0.333	0.239 (-0.094)	**0.353**	**0.309** (-0.044)
Adj. Acc.	0.596	0.561	BERT	0.618	0.504 (-0.114)	0.690	0.656 (-0.034)
		(-0.035)	BERT-wwm	0.627	0.485 (-0.142)	0.688	0.639 (-0.049)
			RoBERTa	0.599	0.488 (-0.111)	**0.699**	**0.683** (-0.016)
			MacBERT	0.644	0.563 (-0.081)	0.685	0.677 (-0.008)
F1	0.259	0.221	BERT	0.273	0.154 (-0.119)	0.338	0.262 (0.076)
		(-0.038)	BERT-wwm	0.280	0.154 (-0.126)	0.337	0.249 (-0.088)
			RoBERTa	0.256	0.147 (-0.109)	0.335	0.273 (-0.062)
			MacBERT	0.307	0.198 (-0.109)	**0.348**	**0.276** (-0.072)
QWK	0.739	0.475	BERT	0.759	0.633 (-0.126)	**0.841**	0.817 (-0.024)
		(-0.264)	BERT-wwm	0.755	0.612 (-0.143)	0.833	0.782 (-0.051)
			RoBERTa	0.731	0.597 (-0.134)	0.841	0.822 (-0.019)
			MacBERT	0.768	0.712 (-0.056)	0.829	**0.832** (+0.003)

Table 3: Performance of the Hybrid Model and the two baselines. The gap between in-domain and cross-domain performance is shown in brackets

Training dataset size	Linguistic Model (RF)		Neural Model		Hybrid Model	
	In-domain	Cross-domain	In-domain	Cross-domain	In-domain	Cross-domain
20%	0.281	0.247 (-0.034)	0.267	0.231 (-0.036)	0.325	0.294 (-0.031)
60%	0.286	0.259 (-0.027)	0.307	0.236 (-0.071)	0.337	0.299 (-0.036)
100%	0.276	0.263 (-0.013)	0.333	0.239 (-0.106)	0.353	0.309 (-0.044)

Table 4: Model accuracy at different training dataset size, expressed in percentage of the full dataset. The gap between in-domain and cross-domain performance is shown in brackets

Model in terms of accuracy (0.263 vs. 0.239) and F1, though worse in terms of adjacent accuracy and QWK. Its competitive performance can be attributed to the robustness of linguistic features in the face of dissimilar materials. While the Linguistic Model degraded only slightly (-0.013) in accuracy on cross-domain data, the Neural Model suffered a much more substantial drop (-0.094).

Hybrid Model. The Hybrid Model outperformed both baselines in all metrics and all transformers.[6] MacBERT again led to the best performance in terms of accuracy (0.309), F1 and QWK, but was slightly worse than RoBERTa in adjacent accuracy.

The superior performance of the Hybrid Model resulted from its smaller degradation on cross-domain data. This can be seen by the gap between in-domain and cross-domain performance, shown in brackets in the "Cross-domain" column in Table 3). For all transformers and all metrics, the gap was substantially smaller with the Hybrid Model. For example, the gap was only 0.044 cross-domain but more than doubled (0.094) in-domain for MacBERT. This suggests that some textual characteristics learned by the Neural Model may be only accidentally correlated with readability in the training corpus, while the Hybrid Model benefits from linguistic features that are more generally relevant to readability and therefore transferable to new domain.

Our hypothesis can be corroborated with the analysis on various dataset sizes in Table 4. When trained on only 20% of the dataset, all three models exhibited a similar gap between in-domain and cross-domain performance. With additional training data, the Neural Model became more accurate

[6]The improvement of the hybrid model over the neural model is statistically significant for BERT, BERT-wwm and RoBERTa at $p < 0.00001$ according to McNemar's Test.

in-domain (0.267 to 0.333). However, the improvement hardly carried over cross-domain, leading to a growing performance gap (-0.036 to -0.106), possibly indicating overfit to corpus-specific textual characteristics. In contrast, the gap shrank for the Linguistic Model, and remained relatively stable for the Hybrid Model, even as it improved steadily in accuracy.

6 Conclusions

We have presented the first cross-domain comparison of hybrid, neural and linguistic models for ARA. Results on a Chinese dataset show that the hybrid model outperforms the neural model both in-domain and cross-domain. Analyses on the gap between in-domain and cross-domain performance further demonstrate the robustness of linguistic features. While the gap grows for the neural model as more training data becomes available, it remained more stable for the hybrid model. These results are expected to inform future ARA research by showing that linguistic features can help neural models capture more generalizable characteristics for text difficulty, especially in the cross-domain context.

Acknowledgements

We thank Prof. Dekuan Xu for providing access to the corpus of textbooks from Mainland China. This work was partly supported by the Language Fund from the Standing Committee on Language Education and Research (project EDB(LE)/P&R/EL/203/14) and by the General Research Fund (project 11207320).

References

Ion Madrazo Azpiazu and Maria Soledad Pera. 2019. Multiattentive recurrent neural network architecture for multilingual readability assessment. *Transactions of the Association for Computational Linguistics*, 7:421–436.

Xiaobin Chen and Detmar Meurers. 2016. Characterizing text difficulty with word frequencies. In *Proceedings of the 11th Workshop on Innovative Use of NLP for Building Educational Applications*, pages 84–94, San Diego, CA. Association for Computational Linguistics.

Yong Cheng, Dekuan Xu, and Jun Dong. 2020. On key factors of text reading difficulty grading and readability formula based on chinese textbook corpus [in chinese] 基于语文教材语料库的文本阅读难度分级关键因素分析与易读性公式研究. *Applied Linguistics* 语言文字应用, 1:132–143.

Yiming Cui, Wanxiang Che, Ting Liu, Bing Qin, Shijin Wang, and Guoping Hu. 2020. Revisiting pre-trained models for chinese natural language processing. In *Findings of EMNLP*. Association for Computational Linguistics.

Felice Dell'Orletta, Simonetta Montemagni, and Giulia Venturi. 2011. Read-it: Assessing Readability of Italian Texts with a View to Text Simplification. In *Proc. 2nd Workshop on Speech and Language Processing for Assistive Technologies*.

Tovly Deutsch, Masoud Jasbi, and Stuart Shieber. 2020. Linguistic Features for Readability Assessment. In *Proceedings of the Fifteenth Workshop on Innovative Use of NLP for Building Educational Applications*.

Jacob Devlin, Ming-Wei Chang, Kenton Lee, and Kristina Toutanova. 2019. BERT: Pretraining of Deep Bidirectional Transformers for Language Understanding. In *Proc. North American Chapter of the Association for Computational Linguistics - Human Language Technologies (NAACL-HLT)*.

Anna Filighera, Tim Steuer, and Christoph Rensing. 2019. Automatic text difficulty estimation using embeddings and neural networks. In *European Conference on Technology Enhanced Learning*, page 335–348. Springer.

Thomas François and Cédric Fairon. 2012. An "AI Readability" Formula for French as a Foreign Language. In *Proc. EMNLP-CONLL*.

Joseph Marvin Imperial. 2021. BERT Embeddings for Automatic Readability Assessment. In *Proc. Recent Advances in Natural Language Processing*, page 611–618.

Bruce W. Lee, Yoo Sung Jang, and Jason Hyung-Jong Lee. 2021. Pushing on Text Readability Assessment: A Transformer Meets Handcrafted Linguistic Features. In *Proceedings of the 2021 Conference on Empirical Methods in Natural Language Processing*.

John Lee, Meichun Liu, and Tianyuan Cai. 2020. Using Verb Frames for Text Difficulty Assessment. In *Proc. International FrameNet Workshop 2020: Towards a Global, Multilingual FrameNet*.

Justin Lee and Sowmya Vajjala. 2020. A Neural Pairwise Ranking Model for Readability Assessment. In *Findings of the Association for Computational Linguistics: ACL 2022*, pages 3802–3813.

Wenqiang Lei, Yuanxin Xiang, YuweiWang, Qian Zhong, Meichun Liu, and Min-Yen Kan. 2018. Linguistic Properties Matter for Implicit Discourse Relation Recognition: Combining Semantic Interaction, Topic Continuity and Attribution. In *Proc. AAAI*, pages 4849–4855.

Dawei Lu, Xinying Qiu, and Yi Cai. 2020. Sentence-level readability assessment for l2 chinese learning. *CLSW 2019, LNAI*, 11831:381–392.

Matej Martinc, Senja Pollak, Marko, and Robnik-Šikonja. 2021. Supervised and Unsupervised Neural Approaches to Text Readability. *Computational Linguistics*, 47(1):141–179.

F. Pedregosa, G. Varoquaux, A. Gramfort, V. Michel, B. Thirion, and O. Grisel. 2011. Scikit-learn: Machine learning in python. *Journal of machine learning research*, 12(Oct):2825–2830.

Emily Pitler and Ani Nenkova. 2008. Revisiting Readability: a Unified Framework for Predicting Text Quality. In *Proc. Conference on Empirical Methods in Natural Language Processing (EMNLP).*

Nils Reimers and Iryna Gurevych. 2019. Sentence-BERT: Sentence Embeddings using Siamese BERT-Networks. In *Proc. EMNLP-IJCNLP.*

Emma Strubell, Patrick Verga, Daniel Andor, David Weiss, and Andrew McCallum. 2018. Linguistically-informed self-attention for semantic role labeling. In *Proceedings of the 2018 Conference on Empirical Methods in Natural Language Processing*, pages 5027–5038, Brussels, Belgium. Association for Computational Linguistics.

Yao-Ting Sung, Wei-Chun Lin, Scott Benjamin Dyson, Kuo-En Chang, and Yu-Chia Chen. 2015. Leveling L2 Texts Through Readability: Combining Multilevel Linguistic Features with the CEFR. *The Modern Language Journal*, 99(2):371–391.

Hou-Chiang Tseng, Hsueh-Chih Chen, Kuo-En Chang, Yao-Ting Sung, and Berlin Chen. 2019. An Innovative BERT-Based Readability Model. In *Lecture Notes in Computer Science, vol 11937.*

Menglin Xia, Ekaterina Kochmar, and Ted Briscoe. 2016. Text readability assessment for second language learners. In *Proc. 11th Workshop on Innovative Use of NLP for Building Educational Applications*, page 12–22.

Specifying Optimisation Problems for Declarative Programs in Precise Natural Language

Rolf Schwitter
School of Computing
Macquarie University
Sydney NSW 2109
Rolf.Schwitter@mq.edu.au

Abstract

We argue that declarative programs can be written in precise natural language and back this claim by using a complex optimisation problem. The problem specification is expressed in natural language and automatically translated into an executable answer set program, and an answer set solver is then used to find (optimal) solutions for natural language questions. Our approach enables subject matter experts to express their knowledge in a natural and truly declarative notation without the need to encode this knowledge in a formal way.

1 Introduction

Declarative programming involves stating *what* is to be computed, but not *how* it is to be computed; it is a programming paradigm that expresses the logic of computation without describing its control flow (Lloyd, 1994). Logic programming languages (Körner et al., 2022) and functional programming languages (Hu et al., 2015) belong to the declarative programming paradigm and result in code that is characterised by a high level of abstraction. One of the main benefits of declarative programming languages is their ability to describe problems with less code than imperative programming languages. Furthermore, declarative languages are known to be elaboration-tolerant, precise, and easier to optimise than imperative languages. In the context of logic programming, the development of the stable model semantics for logic programs (Gelfond and Lifschitz, 1988) has led to answer set programming (Janhunen and Nimelä, 2016), a powerful model-based language for knowledge representation and non-monotonic reasoning with industrial applications (Falkner et al., 2018). Writing an answer set program involves identifying objects and the relations between them and formally encoding this information as facts, rules and constraints. However, the resulting formal notation may be difficult to understand by subject matter experts who have detailed knowledge about the application domain but do not have a background in formal logic. Instead of encoding a problem specification in answer set programming notation, we suggested in previous work to express such a specification in a precise subset of natural language (Schwitter, 2018). Such a precise subset of natural language is also known as a controlled natural language (Kuhn, 2014). It has been shown that the writing of a specification in controlled language can be supported by a predictive authoring tool like the writing of code with the help of a code editor (Schwitter, 2020; Schwitter et al., 2003). That means the authoring tool instructs the user about the language constructs that can be used to construct a textual specification. As in the case of writing code, writing a specification in controlled language is a process that requires careful planning and an understanding of the application domain. In this paper, we focus on an extension of our controlled language PENG^{ASP} and illustrate how this controlled language can be used to specify a complex optimisation problem that goes beyond our previous work but uses similar unification-based techniques for the translation into an answer set program (Guy and Schwitter, 2017). The novelty is the use of choice rules, aggregates, and optimisation statements that can be expressed directly on the level of the controlled language. A state-of-the-art answer set solver like *clingo*[1] can then be used to find the (optimal) solutions to the problem.

2 Answer Set Programming

Answer set programming (ASP) has its roots in the fields of logic programming and non-monotonic reasoning (Lifschitz, 2019; Gelfond and Kahl,

[1]https://potassco.org/clingo/

2014) and has been applied to a wide range of areas in artificial intelligence, among them also to natural language processing tasks (Mitra et al., 2019; Sharma, 2019; Schüller, 2018; Dzifcak et al., 2009). ASP is supported by powerful reasoning tools and offers a rich representation language that allows for recursive definitions, (strong and weak) negation, (strong and weak) constraints, aggregates, optimisation statements, and external functions (Gebser et al., 2019). An ASP program consists of a set of rules of the following form:

```
l1 ;...; lm :-
  lm+1,..., ln, not ln+1,..., not lo.
```

Here each l_i is a literal. A literal is either a positive atom of the form $p(t_1, \ldots, t_k)$ or its strong negation $-p(t_1, \ldots, t_k)$, where p is a predicate name and all t_i are terms that are composed of function symbols and variables. The symbol :- ("if") separates the head of a rule from its body. The symbol ; in the head of a rule stands for an (epistemic) disjunction, and the symbol not in the body for default negation (aka negation as failure). A rule is called a fact if $m = o = 1$, normal if $m = 1$, and an integrity constraint if $m = 0$. Semantically, the rule above states that if $l_{m+1}, \ldots, l_n$ are true and there is no reason to believe that $l_{n+1}, \ldots, l_o$ are true, then at least one of $l_1, \ldots, l_m$ is believed to be true.

To ease the use of ASP for practical applications, several simplifying notations and extensions have been developed (see (Gebser et al., 2019) for details). The most notable ones in our context are: choice rules, aggregates, and objective functions.

A choice rule has the following form:

```
s { e1 ;...; em } t :- body.
```

Here e_i is a choice element of the form $a{:}L_1, \ldots, L_k$, where a is an atom; L_i are possible default-negated literals; and s and t are integers which express lower and upper bounds on the cardinality of elements. Intuitively, a choice rule means that if the body of the rule is true, then an arbitrary number of elements can be chosen as true as long as this number complies with the lower and upper bounds. Note that if $e_i \geq 2$ and $s = t = 1$, then a choice rule implements an exclusive disjunction; similarly, if $s = 1$, $t = nil$, then it implements an inclusive disjunction. Aggregates are functions that apply to sets and can be used to calculate for example the number of elements of a set. For instance, the expression:

```
#count { X, Y : p(X, Y) }
```

represents the number of elements of the set p/2. Expressions like this can be used in the body of an ASP rule as one side of a comparison, with a variable on the other side, for example:

```
number_of_elements(N) :-
  N = #count { X, Y : p(X, Y) }.
```

When an ASP program has several answer sets, we may be interested in finding the best possible one, according to some measure of quality. Objective functions can be used in this case to minimise or maximise the sum of a set of weighted tuples (w_i, t_i) that are subject to some conditions c_i. These objective functions are expressed in ASP as directives of the following form:

```
#minimize { w1@l1, t1 :  c1 ;...;
                 wn@ln, tn :  cn }.
```

Note that w_i is a numerical constant, l_i is an optional (lexicographically ordered) priority level, t_i is a sequence of terms, and c_i is a sequence of possibly default-negated literals. Alternatively, optimisation statements can be implemented as weak constraints. In contrast to integrity constraints that weed out answer sets as solutions, weak constraints rank solutions.

3 Finding an Optimal Accommodation

Let us assume a traveller wants to choose the best one among three different accommodations (Aloe, Metro, Oase); each of them comes with a star rating and a weekly room rent. Furthermore, one of the accommodations is located on the main street and known to be noisy. Considering the available options, the traveller faces the following optimisation problem: (a) minimising noise has the highest priority; (b) minimising the cost per star has the second highest priority; and (c) maximising the number of stars of an accommodation that is otherwise not distinguishable has the lowest priority.[2]

We can start expressing the factual information about these three different accommodations in a precise way in controlled language:

1. *The bedroom apartment Oase is rated three stars and costs 240 dollars.*
2. *The bedroom apartment Aloe is rated two stars and costs 160 dollars.*

[2]This example is inspired by (Gebser et al., 2019).

3. *The studio apartment Metro that is located on the main street is rated three stars and costs 200 dollars.*

Furthermore, we specify ontological statements that are necessary to solve the problem directly in controlled language and describe what counts as an accommodation (4 and 5); as a noisy accommodation (6); as the cost per star of an accommodation (7); and as the star rating of an accommodation (8):

4. *Every studio apartment is an accommodation.*
5. *Every bedroom apartment is an accommodation.*
6. *If an accommodation is located on a main street then the accommodation is noisy.*
7. *If an accommodation costs N dollars and is rated M stars then N / M is the cost per star of the accommodation.*
8. *If an accommodation is rated N stars then N is the start rating of the accommodation.*

Next, we specify that one of the accommodations is the optimal one, using an exclusive disjunction in controlled language:

9. *Either one of Aloe or Metro or Oase is optimal.*

The relevant optimisation statements are expressed with the help of predefined key phrases *Minimise/Maximise with a priority of I* that include a priority level, where a higher integer (*I*) indicates a higher priority:

10. *Minimise with a priority of 3 that an optimal accommodation is noisy.*
11. *Minimise with a priority of 2 that C is the cost per star of an optimal accommodation.*
12. *Maximise with a priority of 1 that S is the star rating of an optimal accommodation.*

Finally, the questions to be answered can be expressed as follows:

13. *How many accommodations are there?*
14. *Which accommodation is optimal?*

This entire specification can be translated automatically into an executable ASP program. The three factual statements (1-3) result in a number of ASP facts. In our case, these facts are based on a reified notation that relies on a small number of predefined predicates. Constants that start with `c` followed by a positive integer `I` are Skolem constants and replace existentially quantified variables.

```
class(c1, bedroom_apartment).          % 1
named(c1, oase).
prop(c1, c2, rated).
data_prop(c2, 3, cardinal).
class(c2, star).
pred(c1, c3, cost).
data_prop(c3, 240, cardinal).
class(c3, dollar).

class(c4, bedroom_apartment).          % 2
named(c4, aloe).
prop(c4, c5, rated).
data_prop(c5, 2, cardinal).
class(c5, star).
pred(c4, c6, cost).
data_prop(c6, 160, cardinal).
class(c6, dollar).

class(c7, studio_apartment).           % 3
named(c7, metro).
prop(c7, c8, located_on).
class(c8, main_street).
prop(c7, c9, rated).
data_prop(c9, 3, cardinal).
class(c9, star).
pred(c7, c10, cost).
data_prop(c10, 200, cardinal).
class(c10, dollar).
```

The ontological statements (4-8) result in five ASP rules that define classes and properties:

```
class(A, accommodation) :-             % 4
  class(A, studio_apartment).

class(B, accommodation) :-             % 5
  class(B, bedroom_apartment).

prop(C, noisy) :-                      % 6
  class(C, accommodation),
  prop(C, D, located_on),
  class(D, main_street).

prop(E/F, G, cost_per_star) :-         % 7
  class(G, accommodation),
  pred(G, H, cost),
  data_prop(H, E, cardinal),
  class(H, dollar),
  prop(G, I, rated),
  data_prop(I, F, cardinal),
  class(I, star).

prop(J, K, star_rating) :-             % 8
  class(K, accommodation),
  prop(K, L, rated),
  data_prop(L, J, cardinal),
  class(L, star).
```

The two rules for the ontological statements 7 and 8 are interesting since both of them contain an atom as rule head that has been derived from a relational noun (*cost per star* and *star rating*) and introduce properties. The property that represents *cost per star* contains an arithmetic function (`E/F`) with two variables as its first argument. This arithmetic function picks up two cardinal numbers and evaluates their ratio during grounding. The property that represents *star rating* picks up a cardinal number (J) as its first argument.

The statement 9 is translated into a choice rule. The integers before and after the expression in the braces express lower and upper bounds on the cardinality. In our case, the lower bound and upper bound is 1, meaning that exactly one accommodation is optimal:

```
1 { prop(M, optimal) :                % 9
    named(M, (aloe ;
              metro ;
              oase)) } 1.
```

The optimisation statements (10-12) are translated into weak constraints with the help of `#minimize` and `#maximize` directives. The first argument `W@l` of these directives consists of a weight (W) and priority level (l), greater levels being more significant than smaller ones. These directives instruct *clingo* to look for the best stable model of the given ASP program.

```
#minimize { 1@3,                        % 10
  N : prop(N, optimal),
      class(N, accommodation),
      prop(N, noisy) }.

#minimize { O@2,                        % 11
  P : prop(O, P, cost_per_star),
      prop(P, optimal),
      class(P, accommodation) }.

#maximize { Q@1,                        % 12
  R : prop(Q, R, star_rating),
      prop(R, optimal),
      class(R, accommodation) }.
```

Questions such as (13 and 14) are translated into an ASP rule with a specific answer literal (`answer/1`) as head. These literals will contain the answer to the question after grounding and will be displayed using the `#show` directive (15):

```
answer(T) :- T = #count {               % 13
  S : class(S, accommodation) }.

answer(V) :-                            % 14
  named(U, V),
  class(U, accommodation),
  prop(U, optimal).

#show answer/1.                         % 15
```

Note that question (13) is not necessary to find the optimal solution but illustrates the use of an aggregate construct.

4 Evaluation

If we submit our ASP program to the answer set solver *clingo*, then the solver will generate and display three answer sets (models), one for each accommodation together with the weights used for finding the optimal solution. These answer sets also contain the answers to the questions (13 and 14) that are displayed with the help of the `#show` directive (15):

```
clingo version 5.6.1
Reading from asp.lp
Solving...
Answer: 1
answer(3) answer(metro)
Optimization: 1 66 -3
Answer: 2
answer(3) answer(aloe)
Optimization: 0 80 -2
Answer: 3
answer(3) answer(oase)
Optimization: 0 80 -3
OPTIMUM FOUND

Models        : 3
  Optimum     : yes
Optimization  : 0 80 -3
Calls         : 1
Time          : 0.037s (...)
CPU Time      : 0.000s
```

We can see in the output that the accommodation Metro is noisy (1) and therefore not optimal with respect to the most important optimisation statement. The accommodations Aloe and Oase are not noisy (0) and are both optimal with respect to the cost per star ratio (80); the second most important optimisation statement. This tie is broken by the least important optimisation statement that looks at the number of stars. Note that since we maximise the number of stars, the values are displayed as negative integers (-2 and -3). In summary, the optimal accommodation is Oase, since it is not noisy, has a cost per star ratio of 80 and is rated three stars.

5 Conclusion

We showed in this paper that complex optimisation statements can be expressed directly in precise natural language. The resulting specification can then be automatically translated into an executable ASP program. The writing of such a specification in controlled language is usually supported by a predictive authoring tool that has similar features as a code editor for a programming language. As in the case of writing declarative code, writing a textual specification in controlled language needs to be carefully planned and will never be a fast process, but our approach has the potential to close the gap between a (seemingly) informal textual specification and a declarative program. In this sense, programming in controlled language is the most extreme form of declarative programming.

References

Juraj Dzifcak, Matthias Scheutz, Chitta Baral, and Paul W. Schermerhorn. 2009. What to do and how to do it: Translating natural language directives into temporal and dynamic logic representation for goal management and action execution. *2009 IEEE International Conference on Robotics and Automation*, pages 4163–4168.

Andreas Falkner, Gerhard Friedrich, Konstantin Schekotihin, Richard Taupe, and Erich C. Teppan. 2018. Industrial applications of answer set programming. *KI - Künstliche Intelligenz*, 32(2):165–176.

Martin Gebser, Roland Kaminski, Benjamin Kaufmann, Marius Lindauer, Max Ostrowski, Javier Romero, Torsten Schaub, Sven Thiele, and Philipp Wanko. 2019. *Potassco User Guide, Version 2.2.0*.

Michael Gelfond and Yulia Kahl. 2014. *Knowledge Representation, Reasoning, and the Design of Intelligent Agents, The Answer-Set Programming Approach*. Cambridge University Press.

Michael Gelfond and Vladimir Lifschitz. 1988. The stable model semantics for logic programming. In *Proceedings of International Logic Programming Conference and Symposium*, pages 1070–1080. MIT Press.

Stephen Guy and Rolf Schwitter. 2017. The PENG^{ASP} system: Architecture, language and authoring tool. *Journal of Language Resources and Evaluation, Controlled Natural Language*, 51:67–92.

Zhenjiang Hu, John Hughes, and Meng Wang. 2015. How functional programming mattered. *National Science Review*, 2(3):349–370.

Tomi Janhunen and Ilkka Nimelä. 2016. The answer set programming paradigm. *AI Magazine*, 37(3):13–24.

Tobias Kuhn. 2014. A survey and classification of controlled natural languages. *Computational Linguistics*, 40(1):121–170.

Philipp Körner, Michael Leuschel, João Barbosa, Vítor Santos Costa, Verónica Dahl, Manuel V. Hermenegildo, Jose F. Morales, Jan Wielemaker, Daniel Diaz, Salvador Abreu, and Giovanni Ciatto. 2022. Fifty years of prolog and beyond. *Theory and Practice of Logic Programming*, page 1–83.

Vladimir Lifschitz. 2019. *Answer Set Programming*. Springer, Cham.

John W. Lloyd. 1994. Practical advantages of declarative programming. In *Proceedings of GULP-PRODE'94*, volume I, pages 3–17, Peñíscola, Spain.

Arindam Mitra, Peter Clark, Oyvind Tafjord, and Chitta Baral. 2019. Declarative question answering over knowledge bases containing natural language text with answer set programming. In *Proceedings of the Thirty-Third AAAI Conference on Artificial Intelligence*, pages 3003–3010, Honolulu, Hawaii, USA. AAAI Press.

Rolf Schwitter. 2018. Specifying and verbalising answer set programs in controlled natural language. *Journal of Theory and Practice of Logic Programming*, 18:691–705.

Rolf Schwitter. 2020. Lossless semantic round-tripping in PENG^{ASP}. In *Proceedings of the Twenty-Ninth International Joint Conference on Artificial Intelligence, IJCAI-20*, pages 5291–5293.

Rolf Schwitter, Anna Ljungberg, and David Hood. 2003. Ecole: A look-ahead editor for a controlled language. In *Controlled Language Translation*, pages 141–150. Dublin University.

Peter Schüller. 2018. Answer set programming in linguistics. *KI - Künstliche Intelligenz*, 32(2):151–155.

Arpit Sharma. 2019. Using answer set programming for commonsense reasoning in the winograd schema challenge. *Theory and Practice of Logic Programming*, 19(5-6):1021–1037.

Improving Text-based Early Prediction by Distillation from Privileged Time-Series Text

Jinghui Liu[a,b] **Daniel Capurro**[a] **Anthony Nguyen**[b] **Karin Verspoor**[c,a]
[a] School of Computing and Information Systems, The University of Melbourne
[b] Australian e-Health Research Centre, CSIRO
[c] School of Computing Technologies, RMIT
jinghui.liu@student.unimelb.edu.au
dcapurro@unimelb.edu.au, anthony.nguyen@csiro.au
karin.verspoor@rmit.edu.au

Abstract

Modeling text-based time-series to make prediction about a future event or outcome is an important task with a wide range of applications. The standard approach is to train and test the model using the same input window, but this approach neglects the data collected in longer input windows between the prediction time and the final outcome, which are often available during training. In this study, we propose to treat this neglected text as privileged information available during training to enhance early prediction modeling through knowledge distillation, presented as **L**earning **u**sing **P**rivileged **tI**me-s**E**ries **T**ext (LuPIET). We evaluate the method on clinical and social media text, with four clinical prediction tasks based on clinical notes and two mental health prediction tasks based on social media posts. Our results show LuPIET is effective in enhancing text-based early predictions, though one may need to consider choosing the appropriate text representation and windows for privileged text to achieve optimal performance. Compared to two other methods using transfer learning and mixed training, LuPIET offers more stable improvements over the baseline, standard training. As far as we are concerned, this is the first study to examine learning using privileged information for time-series in the NLP context.

1 Introduction

Time-series forecasting, or early prediction, is an important machine learning task with a wide range of applications, such as weather prediction (Krasnopolsky and Fox-Rabinovitz, 2006; Espeholt et al., 2022) and stock forecasting (Xu and Cohen, 2018; Sharma et al., 2017). Predicting future events or outcomes would enable timely responses that can bring significant social and economic benefits. Meanwhile, most existing works on forecasting or early prediction use structured measurements or features as input (Steyerberg, 2009), and studies to leverage unstructured text

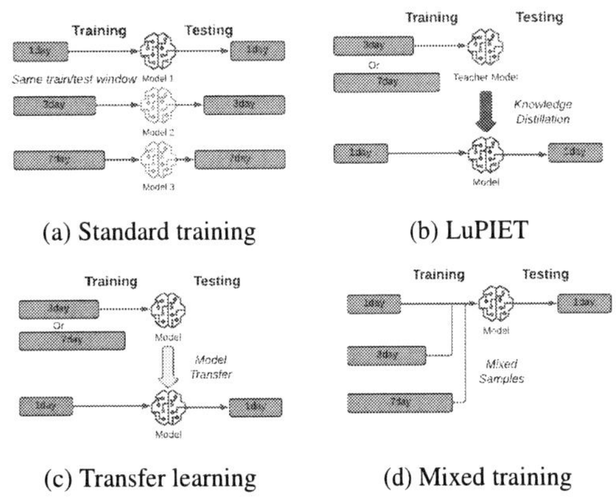

(a) Standard training (b) LuPIET (c) Transfer learning (d) Mixed training

Figure 1: Different methods to leverage later data from the time-series to assist early prediction. LuPIET refers to learning using privileged time-series text in training via knowledge distillation. Here *1-day* is the baseline prediction window at test time. Models may leverage data from the prolonged training windows, e.g., *3-day*, to enhance the performance for the shorter test window.

to explore temporal patterns are still scarce (Assale et al., 2019). Moreover, user-generated, domain-specific textual data, such as clinical and social media texts, can be noisy and complex to model (Baldwin et al., 2013; Huang et al., 2020). This creates challenges in utilizing text for early prediction.

The standard framework for early prediction trains and tests machine learning models using the same input window, depicted in Figure 1a. Though this is the widely adopted approach, it discards data that are outside the prediction window but are collected in practice as part of the training set. Ideally, these data can be utilized to enhance early prediction, such as learning the future trajectory of the time-series to assist modeling. Leveraging data available at training time but not at test time – referred to as *privileged information* – for training has been proposed as Learning using Privileged Information (LuPI) (Vapnik and Vashist, 2009; Vapnik and Izmailov, 2015). Recent studies have shown LuPI can be successfully applied to utilize time-series privileged information for early prediction (Hayashi et al., 2019; K.A. Karlsson et al., 2022). However, these experiments focus on structured features from synthetic data or distributions under certain assumptions. It remains unknown whether the approach applies to text-based early prediction applications, where natural language presents distinct characteristics and variation.

In this study, we adapt the time-series LuPI to textual data, presented as **L**earning **u**sing **P**rivileged t**I**me-s**E**ries **T**ext (LuPIET). We evaluate LuPIET on a range of tasks to evaluate its efficacy. LuPIET trains a more performant model using a longer predictive window that includes data created after the target prediction point as a teacher model. This is applied to guide the training of the early model through knowledge distillation. Figure 1b gives an example where the prediction window is *1-day*, and we aim to guide the training of the early model with the teacher model trained from a *3-day* window. To compare with LuPIET, we also apply two other methods, common in other domains but not well-examined for text-based time-series, to leverage data collected after the prediction time but available for training. These are transfer learning and mixed training, depicted in Figure 1c and Figure 1d, respectively.

We examine LuPIET using two challenging and domain-specific datasets containing clinical and social media text. Specifically, we explore four risk and diagnosis prediction tasks with clinical text and two mental health status prediction tasks with social media. The results show LuPIET can be an effective and stable approach for improving early prediction based on textual input.

In summary, this work examines the usefulness of privileged time-series information in the NLP context to support early prediction. Our main contributions include:

1. Proposing LuPIET to improve time-series modeling for text-based early prediction.

2. Evaluating the performance of LuPIET on two domains using clinical and social media corpora, presenting results on six prediction tasks. We show that when the privileged text is appropriately chosen and represented, LuPIET can improve over the baseline for early prediction by being more sample efficient.

3. Benchmarking the performances of two other competitive methods to support early prediction. We find although they can sometimes outperform LuPIET, they are in certain cases detrimental to modeling. LuPIET offers more consistent and stable improvements over the baseline.

2 Related Work

Early prediction with text Forecasting or early prediction has been widely studied in various domains and applications. For example, Steyerberg (2009) demonstrates the different facets and modeling strategies for clinical prediction modeling. Most initial works in the field focus on structured measurements as input features, with some attempts to extract and include shallow textual features or topics (Suresh et al., 2017; Ghassemi et al., 2015, 2014). More recent studies aim to put more stress on text by applying more powerful models to handle the complexity of language (Matero and Schwartz, 2020; Seinen et al., 2022). They have shown promise in modeling various types of text to support the prediction of mental health issues (Halder et al., 2017), stock market trends (Xu and Cohen, 2018), and clinical outcomes (Hsu et al., 2020).

Learning using privileged information LuPI presents a framework to leverage features only available at the train time but not at test time (Vapnik and Vashist, 2009). It has shown improved results in a range of applications, including recommendation (Xu et al., 2020) and image processing (Lee et al., 2020). Recently, the approach has been applied to improve early prediction using time-series data, which leverages data observed between the prediction time and the future outcome as privileged information. Hayashi et al. (2019) examines this approach on a synthetic dataset and a real-world dataset on air conditions with eight variables. K.A. Karlsson et al. (2022) further formalizes the framework for time-series as Learning using Privileged Time-Series (LuPTS) and proves it is guaranteed to result in more efficient learning when the time-series are drawn from a non-stationary Gaussian-linear dynamic system. However, none of the prior works examines text as input.

Knowledge distillation In knowledge distillation (KD), a more performant teacher model guides a smaller student model to achieve better results by matching the distributions of their predictions or output logits (Hinton et al., 2015). By training with the teacher output, the student model is provided with soft targets that contain more nuanced information about the label distribution compared to the true, hard labels. KD has been widely used for model compression (Sanh et al., 2019; Tung and Mori, 2019; Jiao et al., 2020) and other machine learning applications (Furlanello et al., 2018; Clark et al., 2019) to transfer knowledge across models with different strengths, sizes, or even architectures. In contrast, the classic transfer learning focuses on a single model and transfers knowledge across datasets, often from larger datasets to smaller ones (Devlin et al., 2019). Early works have shown the connection between LuPI and KD, unified them under *generalized distillation* (Lopez-Paz et al., 2016). Distillation has become a standard implementating technique to leverage privileged information (Hayashi et al., 2019; Xu et al., 2020).

3 Methods

Here we present the problem setting for early prediction and then describe how learning using privileged time-series text (LuPIET) works.

3.1 Problem setting

The goal for early prediction is to learn a mapping function $f(\theta)$ between input $X_{t,n} \in \mathcal{R}^{n\times d}$ and future events or outcomes $Y \in \mathcal{R}$, where $t = 1 \dots T$ is a time point of the time-series defined by the prediction window, and $n = 1 \dots N$ is a textual note or post available in the window X_t. Since N can vary across prediction windows, we neglect the notation of n from now on for simplicity. Note that $[X_1, X_2, ..., X_T]$ share the same label Y as they come from the same sample, where X_t is always a subset of X_{t+1}. We assume the *baseline* prediction window by setting $t = 1$, and the baseline model trained in Figure 1a is obtained as

$$\theta_{base} = \arg\min_{\theta\in\Theta} \mathcal{H}(f(X_1), Y) \tag{1}$$

where $\mathcal{H}$ is the cross entropy loss. We then aim to improve θ_{base} by leveraging texts created chronologically after X_1, namely $[X_2, X_3, ...X_T]$.

3.2 Learning with privileged time-series text

LuPIET optimizes a knowledge distillation loss that maps the predictions between the baseline model and the new model trained with privileged text, which can be viewed as a teacher model. We train this teacher model using input from a prolonged prediction window compared to baseline, namely X_t where $t \geq 2$, to obtain

$$\theta_t = \arg\min_{\theta\in\Theta} \mathcal{H}(f(X_t), Y) \tag{2}$$

Then let $p_{base}(x)$ and $p_t(x)$ be the output logits from the base model and teacher model, and we scale them with a temperature τ before taking the softmax, as defined in the original setting of knowledge distillation (Hinton et al., 2015):

$$p^{\tau}_{base}(x_i) = \frac{e^{p_{base}(x_i)/\tau}}{\sum_{j=1}^{K} e^{p_{base}(x_j)/\tau}} \tag{3}$$

$$p^{\tau}_{t}(x_i) = \frac{e^{p_{t}(x_i)/\tau}}{\sum_{j=1}^{K} e^{p_{t}(x_j)/\tau}} \tag{4}$$

where K is the number of labels. We calculate the distillation loss as the KL-divergence between the two scaled logit distributions as

$$\mathcal{L}_{KD} = \mathcal{D}_{KL}(p^{\tau}_{base}(x)||p^{\tau}_{t}(x)) \tag{5}$$

This distillation loss is then added to the cross entropy loss to train the final model that consumes the baseline input X_1, which is obtained by optimizing the following training objective:

$$\mathcal{L} = (1-\alpha)\mathcal{H}(f(X_1), Y) + \alpha\mathcal{L}_{KD} \tag{6}$$

where α is a hyperparameter and $0 \leq \alpha \leq 1$.

3.3 Other options to improve early baseline

Besides LuPIET, we also examine two other simple methods to leverage privileged text to assist early training — transfer learning and mixed training. Transfer learning (Zhuang et al., 2021) refers to further fine-tuning θ_t using X_1 by minimizing the standard cross entropy loss. In other words, we initialize the training in Eq 1 using the model parameters from Eq 2, as shown in Figure 1c.

In the mixed training method, the approach is to mix X_t with X_1 and train the model from scratch. This can be considered as a data augmentation approach (Wen et al., 2021) which enriches the training set and encourages the model to learn from all variations of the same sample. This is depicted in Figure 1d.

4 Experiments

We examine LuPIET using datasets from two challenging textual domains: clinical notes and social media posts. All datasets contain notes or posts that are created chronologically, naturally forming the text-based time series. Here we introduce them in more detail.

4.1 Clinical datasets and tasks

For clinical text, we use the MIMIC-III database (Johnson et al., 2016) to construct the datasets to predict four clinical outcomes and targets, which are in-hospital mortality, in-ICU mortality, length-of-stay (LOS) over 3 days, and diagnostic related groups (DRG). These are popular tasks in the literature for clinical early prediction and we follow previous works to define and extract cohorts for them (Wang et al., 2020; Liu et al., 2021, 2022a). We note that the early DRG prediction is different from the typical medical coding performed post-discharge (Dong et al., 2022; Liu et al., 2022b) as it aims to predict diagnosis and estimate care costs while patients are still in the hospital (Gartner et al., 2015; Islam et al., 2021).

For each patient in the cohort, we extract all clinical notes during the hospital course that are created before the prediction time, sort them chronologically, and remove empty or duplicated notes. The prediction window is defined by the number of days after the patient ICU admission. For example, the *3-day* window would include all clinical notes charted by the end of the third day of ICU admission.

We define the baseline window for the clinical prediction tasks as *1-day*, which would allow timely interventions and resource arrangements to be made for the hospitalized patients. This is also a common choice made in the literature (Wang et al., 2020; Hsu et al., 2020). We then examine two extended prediction windows to train LuPIET, which are *3-day* and *7-day*. Notice there are cases whose time-series lengths are less than *3-day* or *7-day*. We did not distinguish these cases from others in the data extraction process to ensure we can directly compare with baseline results. For example, if a case has a length of 2 days, then the input texts for this case under *3-day* and *7-day* are the same. The numbers of train/validation/test cases are presented in Table 1. Notice the two mortality predictions and LOS prediction share the same cohort.

4.2 Social media datasets and tasks

For social media texts, we focus on the eRisk 2018 datasets (Losada and Crestani, 2016; Losada et al., 2018) to use Reddit posts to predict potential mental health issues, which are depression and anorexia. Predicting mental health status using social media data is an important yet challenging task (Guntuku et al., 2017) that draws much attention in recent years from the NLP community (Benton et al., 2017; Cohan et al., 2018). To parse the datasets, we use both the title and the content as input text for the post. The datasets present the posts in ten chunks, which are evenly split by time and sorted in the chronological order. We follow this format to define the prediction window by the number of chunks used as input, e.g., a *3-chunk* window includes all posts in the first three chunks.

	# train	# validation	# test	# labels
Mortality & LOS	26729	3407	3392	2
DRG	16296	972	1866	570
eRisk Depression	656	82	82	2
eRisk Anorexia	376	47	48	2

Table 1: Number of cases for the train, validation, and test sets of the examined prediction tasks.

Since social media text could present noisier temporal patterns, we examine two baseline windows for the prediction tasks, which are *3-chunk* and *7-chunk*, and only use the full *10-chunk* as prolonged prediction window. We make this choice also because the eRisk datasets are relatively small and the performance can be unstable. We use all samples from the datasets for each task and split them in a 0.8/0.1/0.1 ratio, and the numbers are again presented in Table 1.

4.3 Text representation and modeling

We examine two text representations for the text-based time-series modeling. The first one is to model all input text as a single text string by concatenating all notes or posts together. This allows us to model the input as a sequence of words, which considers the word-level details. This is a standard practice in NLP. The other representation is to encode all notes or posts into document embeddings and model them at the document level. This method, on the other hand, may lose details during the document encoding process, but it helps to maintain the temporal patterns of the texts.

For word-level representation, we use domain-specific pretrained word embeddings for the two datasets. Specifically, we use BioWordVec (Zhang et al., 2019) for clinical text and GloVe-840B (Pennington et al., 2014) for social media. Since the concatenated text string is rather long, we adapt MultiResCNN (Li and Yu, 2020) for modeling, which is a CNN-based model that has shown strong results in long-document classification. The model enhances the vanilla text-CNN model by adding more filters with residual connections. Given space restrictions here, we do not introduce the architecture in detail and refer readers to the original paper for more information.

For document-level modeling, we first encode notes or posts using BERT (Devlin et al., 2019) by extracting the [CLS] token as the final representation. We again try to align BERT with the domains of the text by using ClinicalBERT (Alsentzer et al., 2019) for clinical notes and RoBERTa (Liu et al., 2019) for Reddit posts. We then apply LSTM (Hochreiter and Schmidhuber, 1997) to model the sequence of notes and use the last hidden state for final prediction. We use LSTM due to its power to extract and model temporal patterns.

4.4 Training and evaluation

We tune the hyperparameters for all examined methods based on the validation set and then retrain the model with the best configuration with multiple random seeds. Specifically, we tune the filter number and sizes for the CNN model, hidden size for the LSTM model, and the number of layer, dropout, learning rate, weight decay for both models. Adam (Kingma and Ba, 2014) is used as the optimizer throughout the experiments. After obtaining the best architectural configuration for the baseline model, we fix the setup and tune τ and α for LuPIET. We adopt random search for the clinical datasets and grid search for social media datasets given the former takes much longer to run. We facilitate the hyperparameter searching with asynchronous successive halving algorithm (Li et al., 2020), based on the implementation from Ray Tune (Liaw et al., 2018). We perform all our experiments using pytorch (Paszke et al., 2019) and pytorch-lightning[1] on V100 GPUs.

For evaluation, we use area under the receiver operating characteristics curve (AUROC) and precision-recall curve (AUPR) for the binary classification tasks, and accuracy and macro F1 for multiclass classification. We run the final, tuned model for each task with five random seeds for the clinical datasets and average the results, and run with ten seeds for the social media datasets given the small data size.

[1]https://www.pytorchlightning.ai/

5 Results

5.1 Comparing LuPIET with baseline

We present our main results with the word-level modeling for clinical prediction tasks in Table 2. We observe LuPIET using the extended *3-day* and *7-day* windows improves over the standard baseline window on *1-day* for in-hospital mortality, in-ICU mortality, and DRG predictions. Meanwhile, LuPIET does not provide much benefit for predicting LOS>3days. We believe this is related to the nature of the task as the extended windows are already longer than the target in consideration, so the teacher models can take advantage of this shortcut to make accurate and confident predictions that are close to the true labels and can no longer serve as soft targets (Hinton et al., 2015; Cho and Hariharan, 2019).

The results for social media datasets are presented in Table 3. Here we examine *3-chunk* and *7-chunk* as the baseline windows and apply LuPIET trained using full length, i.e., *10-chunk*. We again observe the benefit of LuPIET over the baseline results, especially under AUROC. However, we note that due to the much smaller dataset size, the variances in the results can be large. In a couple of cases, LuPIET achieves slightly lower AUPR scores than the baseline, but the results are still comparable given the variance.

5.2 Comparing LuPIET with other methods

We focus on the clinical datasets to compare LuPIET with transfer learning and mixed training approaches given they have relatively sufficient data to observe their behavior. In Table 2, we find LuPIET still performs strongly when compared to these two approaches, but other methods may outperform LuPIET, such as mixed training on DRG prediction. In this particular case, we believe this is caused by the DRG dataset being a multiclassification task with 570 labels, thus not having enough samples for training. By mixing different windows of the same sample together serves as a data augmentation strategy, which alleviates the low-resource situation for DRG to achieve better results. Similarly, when modeling at the note level (Table 4), transfer learning may be able to better transfer the temporal relations across windows thus achieving slightly better results.

However, we observe that transfer learning and mixed training do not always improve over the baseline, which is further shown when we examine

	In-hospital Mortality		In-ICU Mortality		LOS>3days		DRG	
	AUROC	AUPR	AUROC	AUPR	AUROC	AUPR	Acc	MacroF1
Baseline								
1-day	0.867 (0.0032)	0.474 (0.0151)	0.862 (0.0110)	0.373 (0.0252)	0.690 (0.0034)	0.625 (0.0047)	0.282 (0.0058)	0.105 (0.0106)
LuPIET								
3-day → 1-day	0.876 (0.0027)	0.491 (0.0039)	**0.880 (0.0020)**	**0.429 (0.0092)**	0.693 (0.0042)	0.626 (0.0058)	0.287 (0.0068)	0.116 (0.0067)
7-day → 1-day	**0.879 (0.0029)**	**0.501 (0.0093)**	0.880 (0.0024)	0.413 (0.0076)	0.692 (0.0035)	**0.627 (0.0041)**	0.290 (0.0097)	0.115 (0.0130)
Transfer								
3-day → 1-day	0.863 (0.0026)	0.466 (0.0063)	0.866 (0.0060)	0.381 (0.0231)	**0.695 (0.0036)**	0.612 (0.0049)	0.293 (0.0033)	0.134 (0.0059)
7-day → 1-day	0.865 (0.0040)	0.482 (0.0073)	0.860 (0.0051)	0.379 (0.0089)	0.691 (0.0046)	0.616 (0.0068)	0.284 (0.0027)	0.113 (0.0072)
7-day → 3-day → 1-day	0.864 (0.0040)	0.482 (0.0110)	0.855 (0.0073)	0.374 (0.0098)	0.683 (0.0031)	0.606 (0.0054)	0.285 (0.0093)	0.112 (0.0081)
Mix-train								
1-day + 3-day + 7-day	0.866 (0.0031)	0.490 (0.0031)	0.860 (0.0079)	0.398 (0.0077)	0.642 (0.0037)	0.561 (0.0057)	**0.298 (0.0025)**	**0.140 (0.0081)**

Table 2: Results of word-level modeling for the four clinical prediction tasks.

	Depression		Anorexia	
	AUROC	AUPR	AUROC	AUPR
Baseline - *3-chunk*	0.819 (0.0636)	**0.458 (0.1606)**	0.796 (0.0742)	0.334 (0.1071)
+ LuPIET	**0.868 (0.0203)**	0.431 (0.1150)	**0.830 (0.0742)**	**0.339 (0.0963)**
Baseline - *7-chunk*	0.836 (0.0303)	0.470 (0.1374)	0.798 (0.0401)	**0.429 (0.1217)**
+ LuPIET	**0.869 (0.0332)**	**0.495 (0.0792)**	**0.807 (0.0239)**	0.423 (0.0705)

Table 3: Results for the two mental health prediction tasks using social media posts.

the note-level modeling results in Table 4. For example, though it could bring benefits to tasks like DRG, mixed training is rather detrimental to the LOS>3days prediction. On the other hand, LuPIET either improves over the baseline or at least maintains the performance under both text representation and modeling strategies.

We also see LOS>3days task does not benefit much from transfer learning and mixed training either, similar to the results with LuPIET. This shows when adopting these methods to improve the time-series modeling, it can be important to consider the nature of the task and to choose proper windows accordingly.

5.3 Comparing text representations

The results presented in Table 2 and Table 4 for word- and note-level modeling are comparable for all the four tasks. Overall, we see modeling at word level performs much better than at note level, demonstrating the need to attend to the fine-grained textual details for these tasks. The LOS>3days is again an exception where the two sets of results are similar, showing the task can be inherently more difficult. Furthermore, modeling at word level tends to benefit more from LuPIET. For example, we see much better mortality prediction scores with LuPIET in Table 2. This indicates that the proper training of LuPIET exploits the nuances in the data and it would benefit more when modeling at a finer granularity.

We do not present the results with document embeddings for the social media tasks as their AUROC results are sub-optimal and barely over 0.5. We suspect this is because the Reddit posts are much noisier and the model needs to sift away much unrelated information, so encoding all posts into embeddings is unhelpful.

6 Discussion

6.1 Sampling efficiency

K.A. Karlsson et al. (2022) shows under certain conditions, such as when the time-series is from linear dynamical systems with Gaussian noise and is in Markov structure, privileged information is guaranteed to improve the learning efficiency of time-series models. Given these conditions do not necessarily hold for the natural language that has distinctive data distribution, here we empirically ex-

	In-hospital Mortality		In-ICU Mortality		LOS>3days		DRG	
	AUROC	AUPR	AUROC	AUPR	AUROC	AUPR	Acc	MacroF1
Baseline								
1-day	0.844 (0.0058)	0.417 (0.0122)	0.860 (0.0049)	0.369 (0.0172)	0.695 (0.0059)	0.629 (0.0061)	0.228 (0.0057)	0.056 (0.0043)
LuPIET								
3-day → 1-day	0.850 (0.0040)	0.428 (0.0108)	0.861 (0.0060)	0.362 (0.0178)	0.696 (0.0034)	0.631 (0.0054)	**0.238 (0.0063)**	0.056 (0.0055)
7-day → 1-day	0.851 (0.0033)	0.430 (0.0125)	0.860 (0.0046)	0.370 (0.0168)	**0.698 (0.0027)**	**0.635 (0.0039)**	0.237 (0.0042)	0.057 (0.0029)
Transfer								
3-day → 1-day	**0.853 (0.0038)**	**0.439 (0.0080)**	0.862 (0.0069)	**0.384 (0.0093)**	0.688 (0.0022)	0.615 (0.0044)	0.232 (0.0067)	0.059 (0.0043)
7-day → 1-day	0.833 (0.0037)	0.415 (0.0086)	0.861 (0.0065)	0.371 (0.0123)	0.686 (0.0056)	0.623 (0.0057)	0.230 (0.0070)	0.064 (0.0039)
7-day → 3-day → 1-day	0.829 (0.0073)	0.405 (0.0108)	0.861 (0.0080)	0.362 (0.0147)	0.688 (0.0029)	0.621 (0.0022)	0.232 (0.0052)	**0.066 (0.0049)**
Mix-train								
1-day + 3-day + 7-day	0.838 (0.0019)	0.416 (0.0113)	**0.866 (0.0055)**	0.382 (0.0125)	0.671 (0.0035)	0.605 (0.0066)	0.236 (0.0073)	0.061 (0.0043)

Table 4: Results of document-level modeling for the four clinical prediction tasks.

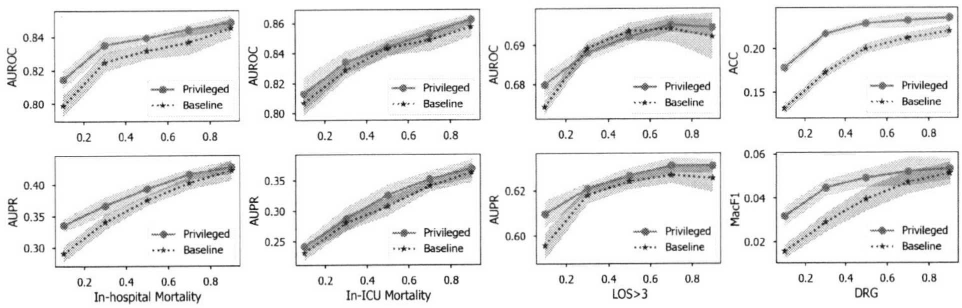

Figure 2: Learning curves for the four clinical prediction tasks under two evaluation metrics. The blue curves depict the results of standard training and the red curves depict those of LuPIET.

amine if privileged text can still benefit NLP modeling efficiency without making other assumptions. Figure 2 shows the learning curves for the four clinical prediction tasks, with x-axis is the ratio of the full dataset used to train the model. We find LuPIET can lead to more sample efficient learning in multiple tasks. For example, when training with only 10% of the whole dataset, privileged learning achieves significant improvements over the baseline on in-hospital mortality, LOS, and DRG. When the model is fed with more samples, we see the difference between LuPIET and the baseline gradually converge. This also happens to the much smaller social media datasets, where we see the larger extent of improvements with LuPIET under AUROC in Table 3. Furthermore, LuPIET could reduce the modeling variance compared to baseline, consistent with findings on structured time-series (K.A. Karlsson et al., 2022).

Meanwhile, in certain scenarios, such as for the in-ICU mortality prediction and for the LOS prediction with sufficient data, we find the benefits of LuPIET are much weaker. This may reflect our observations on LOS in Sec 5.1, where the choice of input windows can be important. Extending input windows in certain scenarios may not necessarily include more data. For instance, in the ICU admissions stays are much shorter compared to hospital stays. This may explain why little benefit is observed for in-ICU mortality prediction.

6.2 Limitations

There are a few limitations with our study. Firstly, we find it is important to apply LuPIET to appropriate task settings but we did not formalize the definition of appropriateness, though we offer some possible intuitions (e.g., on the case of LOS in Sec 5.1). Domain knowledge about the nature of the task may be needed to realize optimal results with LuPIET, which could in some ways correspond to the assumptions about data distribution made for successful LuPI in previous works (Lopez-Paz et al., 2016; K.A. Karlsson et al., 2022). Future works are needed to provide the theoretical explanation for the empirical results and to guide more effective application of LuPIET.

Secondly, we find sometimes the teacher models do not benefit from extending the input window and consuming more time-series data, for example, the shorter *3-chunk* can outperform *7-chunk* for anorexia prediction (Table 3). We did not further investigate this phenomenon and leave it to future work to explore the potential causes. We also focused on the specific time steps for baseline and extended input windows and did not evaluate in more time steps, but in the future we would like to consider various time steps in the time-series for both training and evaluation. Similar evaluation setup has been examined in prior work (Harutyunyan et al., 2019), such as framing patient deterioration assessment as hourly patient mortality predictions. We regard this setup a promising extension of our current experiments to examine LuPIET. Lastly, we do not explore how factors in successful KD applications (Gou et al., 2021), such as creating consistent teacher models (Beyer et al., 2022), affect LuPIET, which we consider as a future direction to better utilize privileged information and to enhance LuPI in general.

7 Conclusion

In this study, we present LuPIET, a framework to incorporate longer-range time-series data available during training to improve text-based early predictions. Though similar ideas have been examined recently for structured time-series (Hayashi et al., 2019; K.A. Karlsson et al., 2022), we are not aware of any previous studies on the use of this privileged information in the context of text-based time-series. We find LuPIET is an effective strategy for enhancing early prediction and for efficient time-series modeling when applied to appropriate task settings.

LuPIET is implemented by simply optimizing a distillation loss. Therefore, future works may extend LuPIET by training with more advanced distillation techniques, e.g., matching hidden state instead of logits (Zhang et al., 2018), or combining with other inputs, e.g., using multi-modal privileged information.

Acknowledgements

We would like to thank the anonymous reviewers for their helpful reviews and comments. This research was undertaken using the LIEF HPC-GPGPU Facility hosted at the University of Melbourne. This Facility was established with the assistance of LIEF Grant LE170100200.

References

Emily Alsentzer, John Murphy, William Boag, Wei-Hung Weng, Di Jindi, Tristan Naumann, and Matthew McDermott. 2019. Publicly available clinical BERT embeddings. In *Proceedings of the 2nd Clinical Natural Language Processing Workshop*, pages 72–78, Minneapolis, Minnesota, USA. Association for Computational Linguistics.

Michela Assale, Linda Greta Dui, Andrea Cina, Andrea Seveso, and Federico Cabitza. 2019. The revival of the notes field: Leveraging the unstructured content in electronic health records. *Frontiers of medicine*, 6:66.

Timothy Baldwin, Paul Cook, Marco Lui, Andrew MacKinlay, and Li Wang. 2013. How noisy social media text, how diffrnt social media sources? In *Proceedings of the Sixth International Joint Conference on Natural Language Processing*, pages 356–364, Nagoya, Japan. Asian Federation of Natural Language Processing.

Adrian Benton, Margaret Mitchell, and Dirk Hovy. 2017. Multitask learning for mental health conditions with limited social media data. In *Proceedings of the 15th Conference of the European Chapter of the Association for Computational Linguistics: Volume 1, Long Papers*, pages 152–162, Valencia, Spain. Association for Computational Linguistics.

Lucas Beyer, Xiaohua Zhai, Amélie Royer, Larisa Markeeva, Rohan Anil, and Alexander Kolesnikov. 2022. Knowledge distillation: A good teacher is patient and consistent. In *2022 IEEE/CVF Conference on Computer Vision and Pattern Recognition (CVPR)*, pages 10915–10924.

Jang Hyun Cho and Bharath Hariharan. 2019. On the efficacy of knowledge distillation. In *Proceedings of the IEEE/CVF International Conference on Computer Vision*, pages 4794–4802.

Kevin Clark, Minh-Thang Luong, Urvashi Khandelwal, Christopher D Manning, and Quoc V Le. 2019. BAM! Born-Again Multi-Task networks for natural language understanding. In *Proceedings of the 57th Annual Meeting of the Association for Computational Linguistics*, pages 5931–5937, Florence, Italy. Association for Computational Linguistics.

Arman Cohan, Bart Desmet, Andrew Yates, Luca Soldaini, Sean MacAvaney, and Nazli Goharian. 2018.

SMHD: a Large-Scale resource for exploring online language usage for multiple mental health conditions. In *Proceedings of the 27th International Conference on Computational Linguistics*, pages 1485–1497, Santa Fe, New Mexico, USA. Association for Computational Linguistics.

Jacob Devlin, Ming-Wei Chang, Kenton Lee, and Kristina Toutanova. 2019. BERT: Pre-training of deep bidirectional transformers for language understanding. In *Proceedings of the 2019 Conference of the North American Chapter of the Association for Computational Linguistics: Human Language Technologies, Volume 1 (Long and Short Papers)*, pages 4171–4186, Minneapolis, Minnesota. Association for Computational Linguistics.

Hang Dong, Matúš Falis, William Whiteley, Beatrice Alex, Joshua Matterson, Shaoxiong Ji, Jiaoyan Chen, and Honghan Wu. 2022. Automated clinical coding: what, why, and where we are? *NPJ digital medicine*, 5(1):159.

Lasse Espeholt, Shreya Agrawal, Casper Sønderby, Manoj Kumar, Jonathan Heek, Carla Bromberg, Cenk Gazen, Rob Carver, Marcin Andrychowicz, Jason Hickey, Aaron Bell, and Nal Kalchbrenner. 2022. Deep learning for twelve hour precipitation forecasts. *Nature communications*, 13(1):5145.

Tommaso Furlanello, Zachary Lipton, Michael Tschannen, Laurent Itti, and Anima Anandkumar. 2018. Born again neural networks. In *Proceedings of the 35th International Conference on Machine Learning*, volume 80 of *Proceedings of Machine Learning Research*, pages 1607–1616. PMLR.

Daniel Gartner, Rainer Kolisch, Daniel B Neill, and Rema Padman. 2015. Machine learning approaches for early DRG classification and resource allocation. *INFORMS journal on computing*, 27(4):718–734.

Marzyeh Ghassemi, Tristan Naumann, Finale Doshi-Velez, Nicole Brimmer, Rohit Joshi, Anna Rumshisky, and Peter Szolovits. 2014. Unfolding physiological state: mortality modelling in intensive care units. In *Proceedings of the 20th ACM SIGKDD international conference on Knowledge discovery and data mining*, KDD '14, pages 75–84, New York, NY, USA. Association for Computing Machinery.

Marzyeh Ghassemi, Marco A F Pimentel, Tristan Naumann, Thomas Brennan, David A Clifton, Peter Szolovits, and Mengling Feng. 2015. A multivariate timeseries modeling approach to severity of illness assessment and forecasting in ICU with sparse, heterogeneous clinical data. *Proceedings of the AAAI Conference on Artificial Intelligence*, 2015:446–453.

Jianping Gou, Baosheng Yu, Stephen J Maybank, and Dacheng Tao. 2021. Knowledge distillation: A survey. *International journal of computer vision*, 129(6):1789–1819.

Sharath Chandra Guntuku, David B Yaden, Margaret L Kern, Lyle H Ungar, and Johannes C Eichstaedt. 2017. Detecting depression and mental illness on social media: an integrative review. *Current Opinion in Behavioral Sciences*, 18:43–49.

Kishaloy Halder, Lahari Poddar, and Min-Yen Kan. 2017. Modeling temporal progression of emotional status in mental health forum: A recurrent neural net approach. In *Proceedings of the 8th Workshop on Computational Approaches to Subjectivity, Sentiment and Social Media Analysis*, pages 127–135, Copenhagen, Denmark. Association for Computational Linguistics.

Hrayr Harutyunyan, Hrant Khachatrian, David C Kale, Greg Ver Steeg, and Aram Galstyan. 2019. Multitask learning and benchmarking with clinical time series data. *Scientific data*, 6(1):96.

Shogo Hayashi, Akira Tanimoto, and Hisashi Kashima. 2019. Long-Term prediction of small Time-Series data using generalized distillation. In *2019 International Joint Conference on Neural Networks (IJCNN)*, pages 1–8.

Geoffrey Hinton, Oriol Vinyals, and Jeff Dean. 2015. Distilling the knowledge in a neural network.

Sepp Hochreiter and Jürgen Schmidhuber. 1997. Long short-term memory. *Neural computation*, 9(8):1735–1780.

Chao-Chun Hsu, Shantanu Karnwal, Sendhil Mullainathan, Ziad Obermeyer, and Chenhao Tan. 2020. Characterizing the value of information in medical notes. In *Findings of the Association for Computational Linguistics: EMNLP 2020*, pages 2062–2072, Online. Association for Computational Linguistics.

Rongtao Huang, Bowei Zou, Yu Hong, Wei Zhang, Aiti Aw, and Guodong Zhou. 2020. NUT-RC: Noisy user-generated text-oriented reading comprehension. In *Proceedings of the 28th International Conference on Computational Linguistics*, pages 2687–2698, Barcelona, Spain (Online). International Committee on Computational Linguistics.

Md Mohaimenul Islam, Guo-Hung Li, Tahmina Nasrin Poly, and Yu-Chuan Jack Li. 2021. Deep-DRG: Performance of artificial intelligence model for Real-Time prediction of Diagnosis-Related groups. *Healthcare (Basel, Switzerland)*, 9(12).

Xiaoqi Jiao, Yichun Yin, Lifeng Shang, Xin Jiang, Xiao Chen, Linlin Li, Fang Wang, and Qun Liu. 2020. TinyBERT: Distilling BERT for natural language understanding. In *Findings of the Association for Computational Linguistics: EMNLP 2020*, pages 4163–4174, Online. Association for Computational Linguistics.

Alistair E W Johnson, Tom J Pollard, Lu Shen, Li-Wei H Lehman, Mengling Feng, Mohammad Ghassemi, Benjamin Moody, Peter Szolovits, Leo Anthony Celi, and Roger G Mark. 2016. MIMIC-III, a freely accessible critical care database. *Scientific data*, 3:160035.

Rickard K.A. Karlsson, Martin Willbo, Zeshan M Hussain, Rahul G Krishnan, David Sontag, and Fredrik Johansson. 2022. Using time-series privileged information for provably efficient learning of prediction models. In *Proceedings of The 25th International Conference on Artificial Intelligence and Statistics*, volume 151 of *Proceedings of Machine Learning Research*, pages 5459–5484. PMLR.

Diederik P Kingma and Jimmy Ba. 2014. Adam: A method for stochastic optimization.

Vladimir M Krasnopolsky and Michael S Fox-Rabinovitz. 2006. Complex hybrid models combining deterministic and machine learning components for numerical climate modeling and weather prediction. *Neural networks: the official journal of the International Neural Network Society*, 19(2):122–134.

Wonkyung Lee, Junghyup Lee, Dohyung Kim, and Bumsub Ham. 2020. Learning with privileged information for efficient image Super-Resolution. In *Computer Vision – ECCV 2020*, pages 465–482. Springer International Publishing.

Fei Li and Hong Yu. 2020. ICD coding from clinical text using Multi-Filter residual convolutional neural network. *Proceedings of the AAAI Conference on Artificial Intelligence*, 34(5):8180–8187.

Liam Li, Kevin Jamieson, Afshin Rostamizadeh, Ekaterina Gonina, Jonathan Ben-tzur, Moritz Hardt, Benjamin Recht, and Ameet Talwalkar. 2020. A system for massively parallel hyperparameter tuning. In *Proceedings of Machine Learning and Systems*, volume 2, pages 230–246.

Richard Liaw, Eric Liang, Robert Nishihara, Philipp Moritz, Joseph E Gonzalez, and Ion Stoica. 2018. Tune: A research platform for distributed model selection and training.

Jinghui Liu, Daniel Capurro, Anthony Nguyen, and Karin Verspoor. 2021. Early prediction of diagnostic-related groups and estimation of hospital cost by processing clinical notes. *NPJ digital medicine*, 4(1):103.

Jinghui Liu, Daniel Capurro, Anthony Nguyen, and Karin Verspoor. 2022a. "Note Bloat" impacts deep learning-based NLP models for clinical prediction tasks. *Journal of biomedical informatics*, 133:104149.

Leibo Liu, Oscar Perez-Concha, Anthony Nguyen, Vicki Bennett, and Louisa Jorm. 2022b. Hierarchical label-wise attention transformer model for explainable ICD coding. *Journal of biomedical informatics*, 133:104161.

Yinhan Liu, Myle Ott, Naman Goyal, Jingfei Du, Mandar Joshi, Danqi Chen, Omer Levy, Mike Lewis, Luke Zettlemoyer, and Veselin Stoyanov. 2019. RoBERTa: A robustly optimized BERT pretraining approach.

David Lopez-Paz, Léon Bottou, Bernhard Schölkopf, and Vladimir Vapnik. 2016. Unifying distillation and privileged information. In *International Conference on Learning Representations*.

David E Losada and Fabio Crestani. 2016. A test collection for research on depression and language use. In *Proc. of Experimental IR Meets Multilinguality, Multimodality, and Interaction, 7th International Conference of the CLEF Association, CLEF 2016*, pages 28–39. Springer International Publishing.

David E Losada, Fabio Crestani, and Javier Parapar. 2018. Overview of erisk: Early risk prediction on the internet. In *Proc. of Experimental IR Meets Multilinguality, Multimodality, and Interaction, International Conference of the CLEF Association, CLEF 2018*, pages 343–361. Springer International Publishing.

Matthew Matero and H Andrew Schwartz. 2020. Autoregressive affective language forecasting: A Self-Supervised task. In *Proceedings of the 28th International Conference on Computational Linguistics*, pages 2913–2923, Barcelona, Spain (Online). International Committee on Computational Linguistics.

Adam Paszke, Sam Gross, Francisco Massa, Adam Lerer, James Bradbury, Gregory Chanan, Trevor Killeen, Zeming Lin, Natalia Gimelshein, Luca Antiga, Alban Desmaison, Andreas Kopf, Edward Yang, Zachary DeVito, Martin Raison, Alykhan Tejani, Sasank Chilamkurthy, Benoit Steiner, Lu Fang, Junjie Bai, and Soumith Chintala. 2019. PyTorch: An imperative style, High-Performance deep learning library. In *Advances in Neural Information Processing Systems 32*, pages 8024–8035. Curran Associates, Inc.

Jeffrey Pennington, Richard Socher, and Christopher Manning. 2014. GloVe: Global vectors for word representation. In *Proceedings of the 2014 Conference on Empirical Methods in Natural Language Processing (EMNLP)*, pages 1532–1543, Doha, Qatar. Association for Computational Linguistics.

Victor Sanh, Lysandre Debut, Julien Chaumond, and Thomas Wolf. 2019. DistilBERT, a distilled version of BERT: smaller, faster, cheaper and lighter.

Tom M Seinen, Egill A Fridgeirsson, Solomon Ioannou, Daniel Jeannetot, Luis H John, Jan A Kors, Aniek F Markus, Victor Pera, Alexandros Rekkas, Ross D Williams, Cynthia Yang, Erik M van Mulligen, and Peter R Rijnbeek. 2022. Use of unstructured text in prognostic clinical prediction models: a systematic review. *Journal of the American Medical Informatics Association: JAMIA*, 29(7):1292–1302.

Ashish Sharma, Dinesh Bhuriya, and Upendra Singh. 2017. Survey of stock market prediction using machine learning approach. In *2017 International conference of Electronics, Communication and*

Aerospace Technology (ICECA), volume 2, pages 506–509. ieeexplore.ieee.org.

E W Steyerberg. 2009. Applications of prediction models. In Ewout W Steyerberg, editor, *Clinical Prediction Models: A Practical Approach to Development, Validation, and Updating*, pages 11–31. Springer New York, New York, NY.

Harini Suresh, Nathan Hunt, Alistair Johnson, Leo Anthony Celi, Peter Szolovits, and Marzyeh Ghassemi. 2017. Clinical intervention prediction and understanding with deep neural networks. In *Proceedings of the 2nd Machine Learning for Healthcare Conference*, volume 68 of *Proceedings of Machine Learning Research*, pages 322–337. PMLR.

Frederick Tung and Greg Mori. 2019. Similarity-preserving knowledge distillation. In *Proceedings of the IEEE/CVF International Conference on Computer Vision*, pages 1365–1374.

Vladimir Vapnik and Rauf Izmailov. 2015. Learning using privileged information: Similarity control and knowledge transfer. *Journal of machine learning research: JMLR*, 16(61):2023–2049.

Vladimir Vapnik and Akshay Vashist. 2009. A new learning paradigm: learning using privileged information. *Neural networks: the official journal of the International Neural Network Society*, 22(5-6):544–557.

Shirly Wang, Matthew B A McDermott, Geeticka Chauhan, Marzyeh Ghassemi, Michael C Hughes, and Tristan Naumann. 2020. MIMIC-Extract: a data extraction, preprocessing, and representation pipeline for MIMIC-III. In *Proceedings of the ACM Conference on Health, Inference, and Learning*, CHIL '20, pages 222–235, New York, NY, USA. Association for Computing Machinery.

Qingsong Wen, Liang Sun, Fan Yang, Xiaomin Song, Jingkun Gao, Xue Wang, and Huan Xu. 2021. Time series data augmentation for deep learning: A survey. In *Proceedings of the Thirtieth International Joint Conference on Artificial Intelligence, IJCAI-21*, pages 4653–4660. International Joint Conferences on Artificial Intelligence Organization.

Chen Xu, Quan Li, Junfeng Ge, Jinyang Gao, Xiaoyong Yang, Changhua Pei, Fei Sun, Jian Wu, Hanxiao Sun, and Wenwu Ou. 2020. Privileged features distillation at taobao recommendations. In *Proceedings of the 26th ACM SIGKDD International Conference on Knowledge Discovery & Data Mining*, KDD '20, pages 2590–2598, New York, NY, USA. Association for Computing Machinery.

Yumo Xu and Shay B Cohen. 2018. Stock movement prediction from tweets and historical prices. In *Proceedings of the 56th Annual Meeting of the Association for Computational Linguistics (Volume 1: Long Papers)*, pages 1970–1979, Melbourne, Australia. Association for Computational Linguistics.

Yijia Zhang, Qingyu Chen, Zhihao Yang, Hongfei Lin, and Zhiyong Lu. 2019. BioWordVec, improving biomedical word embeddings with subword information and MeSH. *Scientific data*, 6(1):52.

Ying Zhang, Tao Xiang, Timothy M Hospedales, and Huchuan Lu. 2018. Deep mutual learning. In *Proceedings of the IEEE Conference on Computer Vision and Pattern Recognition*, pages 4320–4328.

Fuzhen Zhuang, Zhiyuan Qi, Keyu Duan, Dongbo Xi, Yongchun Zhu, Hengshu Zhu, Hui Xiong, and Qing He. 2021. A comprehensive survey on transfer learning. *Proceedings of the IEEE*, 109(1):43–76.

A DistilBERTopic Model for Short Text Documents

Junaid Rashid[1], Jungeun Kim[2], Usman Naseem[3], Amir Hussain[4]
[1]Department of Computer Science and Engineering, Kongju National University, South Korea
[2]Department of Software, Kongju National University, South Korea
[3]School of Computer Science, University of Sydney, Australia
[4]School of Computing, Edinburgh Napier University, UK
[1]junaidrashid062@gmail.com, [2]jekim@kongju.ac.kr
[3]usman.naseem@sydney.edu.au, [4]a.hussain@napier.ac.uk

Abstract

The analysis of short text documents has become a vital and challenging task. Topic models are utilized to extract topics from a large amount of text data. However, these topic models typically suffer from data sparsity problems when applied to short texts because of relatively lower word co-occurrence patterns. As a result, they tend to provide repetitive or trivial topics of poor quality. Therefore, we presented a DistilBERTopic model to remove the sparsity problem and discover quality topics more accurately from short texts. DistilBERTopic model utilized the pre-trained transformer-based language models, reduced the dimensionality effect on embedding, clustered these embeddings, and discovered the topics from short text documents. Experimental results demonstrate that the DistilBERTopic model achieves better classification and topic coherence than other state-of-the-art topic models for real-world datasets.

1 Introduction

Numerous Web applications, including online social networks, recommendation systems, and question and answer systems, have recently grown in popularity. User-generated content has proliferated, particularly the massive increase in short text in various contexts like blogging, text messages, or customer reviews. It has become a crucial and difficult challenge in many applications to automatically discover latent semantic topics from huge amounts of short texts.

Considerable effort has been devoted to tackling the issue of data sparsity in topic modeling for short text documents. In prior work, for instance, a method is developed for aggregation of a few specific sentences that recreate a lengthier pseudo document by employing appropriate strategies like as combining all text messages originating from a single author (Hong and Davison, 2010a) or establishing relation information between hashtags (Wang, Liu, Qu, Huang, Chen, and Feng, 2014). In addition, some brief messages can contain contextual information such as URL, location, or timestamp. A large amount of the world's textual data comes from news sources and web portals, and all these sources often include various descriptions (Ramage, Hall, Nallapati, and Manning, 2009). However, these strategies may fail in the absence of contextual information (Naseem, Razzak, Khan, and Prasad, 2021). Conventional topic modeling techniques like Latent Semantic Analysis (LSA) (Deerwester, Dumais, Furnas, Landauer, and Harshman, 1990), Probabilistic Latent Semantic Analysis (PLSA) (Hofmann, 1999), and Latent Dirichlet Allocation (LDA) (Blei, Ng, and Jordan, 2001) is extensively employed for discovering the topics from documents.

The formation of co-occurring word pairs across the same document is explicitly modeled in the biterm topic model (BTM) (Cheng, Yan, Lan, and Guo, 2014). The technique avoids the sparsity issue at the document level by aggregating the corpora biterms into a big pseudo document from which the topic distribution is inferred. However, the method does not consider word order. LF-DMM (Nguyen, Billingsley, Du, and Johnson, 2015) enriches Dirichlet Multinomial Mix with latent feature word representations by substituting the topics term with a combination of a Dirichlet multinomial and word embedding. In particular, (Weng, Lim, Jiang, and He, 2010) combines all of the shorter texts produced by that particular individual into a trained model before applying a standard LDA model. The two different aggregation strategies for short texts include the authors of the text and each word in the corpus(Hong and Davison, 2010b). The data preprocessing step for LDA (Mehrotra, Sanner, Buntine, and Xie, 2013) presents alternative tweet clustering strategies to build pseudo documents.

A word network topic model is presented that generates pseudo documents based on the network of words used together in the network (Zuo, Zhao, and Xu, 2016c). In (Zuo, Wu, Zhang, Lin, Wang, Xu, and Xiong, 2016a), inferring topic distribution from the high number of hidden pseudo documents with a drastically reduced amount of these documents. WNTM (Zuo, Zhao, and Xu, 2016d) constructs a network based on how often certain words appear, find word groups and distribute across word topics, as opposed to documents. The model makes the conceptual density in a dataset and creates topic inference slightly sensitive to differences in text length and how topics are spread out. Previous studies showed that using fuzzy clustering for extracting topics from documents also improved the performance for classification and clustering tasks (Rashid et al., 2022).

An efficient topic model derived from the Dirichlet Multinomial Mixture (DMM) model is called GPU-DMM (Li, Duan, Wang, Zhang, Sun, and Ma, 2017). They use the extended Polya urn (GPU) model for short texts, which uses auxiliary embeddings to get generic word semantic information (Mahmoud, 2008). PTM (Zuo, Wu, Zhang, Lin, Wang, Xu, and Xiong, 2016b) assumes that a substantial majority of text documents are produced from a small number of frequent texts and that the idea of a "pseudo document" is used to affirmatively group shorter text together in the presence of sparse data without the necessity of further context. TRNMF (Yi, Jiang, and Wu, 2020) topic model utilizing regularized nonnegative matrix factorization for short documents. Some methods (Gruber et al., 2007) attempt to reduce the sparsity problem by presuming that terms in all sentences interact with the same topic. In addition, the findings of these topic models are typically attained at the posterior in topics, which makes the topic model susceptible to overfitting (Blei et al., 2001).

Therefore, in this research, we presented a DistilBERTopic model that discovers the semantically relevant quality topics and removes the sparsity issue for short text, where probabilities of documents and topics are defined. DistilBERTopic model used the pre-trained transformer-based language models, and before Density-based Spatial clustering, the detrimental impact of high dimensionality is minimized by singular value decomposition. DistilBERTopic model is compared with the state-of-the-art short text topic models using real-world short text document datasets. Experimental results show that DistilBERTopic performs better than other models in terms of topic coherence and classification.

2 Methodology

Consider a variety of Z short text containing vocabulary of size V, which are denoted by $X = x_1, x_2, x_3, ..., x_V$ and K is the number of topics. Dirichlet parameters are α and β.

2.1 Pre-processing

The text data probably contain a significant amount of noise, including different word forms, stop words, punctuation, and special characters. The text data is converted to lowercase to eliminate any potential confusion caused by word variances. The text is first broken up into phrases, which are subsequently tokenized into individual words. A document is broken down into tokens. Stop words are eliminated. Words are normalized by deploying Porter's stemmer algorithm (Patil and Sandip, 2013; Porter, 1980), which culminates in eliminating inflectional endings for the words.

2.2 DistilBERT

DistilBERT (Sanh, Debut, Chaumond, and Wolf, 2019) is developed from BERT by applying knowledge distillation (Kenton and Toutanova, 2019). DistilBERT is a compact Bidirectional Encoder Representation of BERT that preserves the BERT comprehension capabilities by adopting a knowledge distillation technique. The model is distilled in very large batches through the use of dynamic masking and with the assistance of the next sentence prediction. In this context, masking and next sentence prediction refer to the procedure in which a word that is to be predicted is transformed to the value ["MASK"] in the Masked Language model, and the entire sequence is trained to predict that specific word. The trained model aids in establishing the context of words by attempting to identify the meaning of a document. The implementation comprises a loss function comprised of a distillation loss and a cosine embedding loss. To build a more compact version of BERT, the architects of DistilBERT eliminated token-type embeddings and the pooler from the architecture and decreased the number of layers by a factor of two. DistillBERT is used to turn the documents into embeddings.

2.3 Singular Value Composition

The documents with related topics are clustered together to discover the topics in these clusters. The embedding dimensionality is reduced because many clustering methods poorly handle high dimensionality. To reduce the negative effects of higher dimensionality, we apply singular value decomposition (SVD), a well-known technique for reducing data dimension before clustering (Fodor, 2002).

2.4 Hierarchical Density-based Spatial Clustering

The HDBSCAN (Hierarchical Density-based Spatial Clustering) (Campello, Moulavi, and Sander, 2013) is used. HDBSCAN clustering technique represents clusters and allows noise to be treated as outliers. When dealing with noise and varied cluster densities, HDBSCAN is used to discover the dense regions of document vectors. The utilization of HDBSCAN is motivated by the fact that it produces only significant clusters and does not cluster noise. Thus, compared to other clustering algorithms, the quality of the clusters is high. The interactive use of cluster selection epsilon, which hierarchically mixes and separates clusters, allows us to control the size of the clusters. This allows us to discover more specific topics within a specific cluster.

2.5 Probability of the Documents

The probability of Z documents j is calculated by equation 1. Where n is the amount of data.

$$P(Z_j) = \frac{\sum_{i=1}^{m}(X_i, Z_j)}{\sum_{i=1}^{m}\sum_{j=1}^{n}(X_i, Z_j)} \quad (1)$$

2.6 Probability of the Documents to Topics

Equation 2 calculates the probability for documents j with topics k.

$$P(Z_j, Y_k) = P(Y_k|Z_j) \times P(Z_j) \quad (2)$$

Then, for each topic, the normalization probability of documents in the topic is defined by equation 3.

$$P(Z_j|Y_k) = \frac{P(Z_j|Y_k)}{\sum_{j=1}^{n} P(Z_j|Y_k)} \quad (3)$$

2.7 Probability of the Words in Documents

Equation 4 finds the probability of words in the documents.

$$P(X_i|Z_j) = \frac{P(X_i|Z_j)}{\sum_{j=1}^{m} P(X_i|Z_j)} \quad (4)$$

Table 1: Dataset statistics

Datasets	Labels	Z	X	V
TMNews	7	32503	4.9	6347
Twitter	4	2520	5.0	1390

3 Experiments and Results

In this section, DistilBERTopic model is compared with other state-of-the-art topics models. The classification and topic coherence results are given for two real-world datasets TMNews and Twitter.

3.1 Datasets

TWNews and Twitter datasets are selected for the experiments due to the diversity between datasets. TWNews dataset is English news articles taken from the RSS feeds of three prominent newspaper websites[1]. The dataset comprises business, sports, health, U.S., science technology, world, and entertainment. We keep news descriptions because it is often comprised of brief sentences.

The Twitter corpus contains categorized tweets[2]. These tweets are assigned to one of four categories: Apple, Google, Microsoft, and Twitter. Table 1 shows the statistics of the datasets.

3.2 Baseline Topic Models

We compared the presented DistilBERTopic model with BTM (Cheng, Yan, Lan, and Guo, 2014),LF-DMM (Nguyen, Billingsley, Du, and Johnson, 2015), WNTM (Zuo, Zhao, and Xu, 2016d), GPU-DMM (Li, Duan, Wang, Zhang, Sun, and Ma, 2017), PTM (Zuo, Wu, Zhang, Lin, Wang, Xu, and Xiong, 2016b) and TRNMF (Yi, Jiang, and Wu, 2020) over short text data. The topic models BTM, WNTM, and GPU-DMM all use the same hyperparameter values of $alpha = 50/K$ and $beta = 0.01$. For WNTM, the sliding window length was set at 10. As indicated by the authors, for LF-DMM, we adjusted the parameters $\lambda = 0.6$, $\alpha = 0.1$ and $\beta = 0.01$. We used the values of $\alpha = 0.1$, $\lambda = 0.1$, and $\beta = 0.01$, respectively, for PTM and TRNMF. Therefore, in the evaluation of experiments, $\alpha = 0.1$, $\beta = 0.01$ and $\lambda = 0.1$ values are set. The Gibbs sampling method is applied to each model for a total of 1,000 iterations, with the

[1](http://acube.di.unipi.it/tmn-dataset/), (nyt.com, usatoday.com, reuters.com),

[2](http://www.sananalytics.com/lab/index.php)

Table 2: Classification accuracy for TMNews and Twitter datasets with 30, 50 and 90 topics

Dataset	Model	K=30	K=50	K=90
	BTM	0.626	0.526	0.395
	LF-DMM	0.635	0.592	0.658
	WNTM	0.705	0.691	0.701
	GPU-DMM	0.424	0.364	0.336
TMNews	PTM	0.443	0.310	0.296
	TRNMF	0.763	0.735	0.646
	DistilBERTopic	**0.785**	**0.757**	**0.668**
	BTM	0.586	0.474	0.272
	LF-DMM	0.183	0.234	0.241
	WNTM	0.810	0.807	0.764
	GPU-DMM	0.683	0.568	0.510
Twitter	PTM	0.340	0.0.248	0.267
	TRNMF	0.821	0.816	0.771
	DistilBERTopic	**0.842**	**0.837**	**0.792**

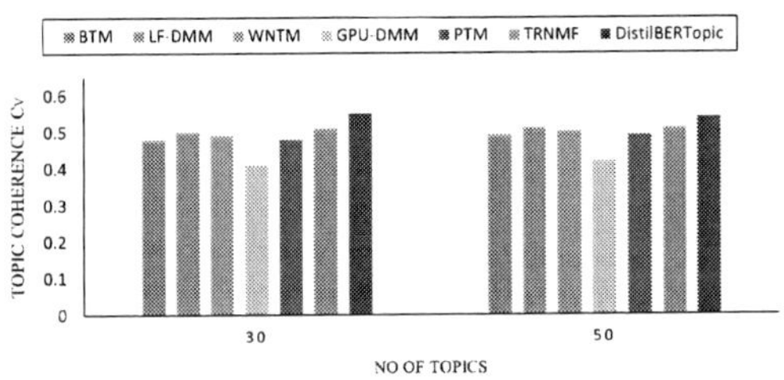

Figure 1: Topic coherence with TMNews dataset with 5 topic words

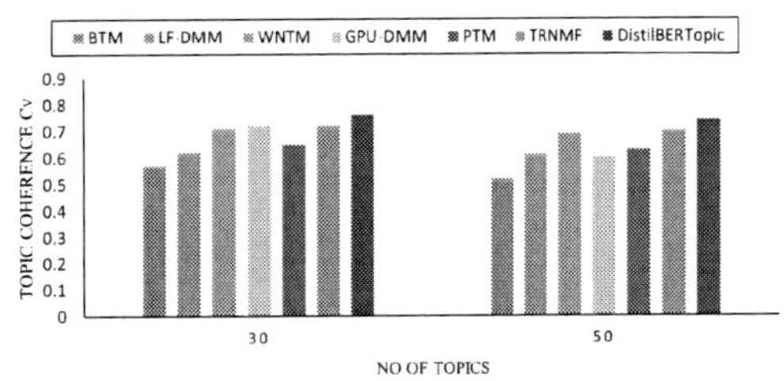

Figure 2: Topic coherence with Twitter dataset with 5 topic words

number of latent topics set to 30, 50, and 90.

3.3 Classification

We represent each document using topic modeling by using P(Y|Z) for topic distribution. P(Y|Z) means the probability of topics with the documents. P(Y|Z) represents the probability of a given topic appearing in a given set of documents. As a result, the topic's quality is efficiently assessed using text classification accuracy. The high classification accuracy shows that the topics are more discriminate and comprehensive. We used Weka for the classification with Naive Bayes. A 5-fold cross-validation method is utilized to assess classification accuracy. The classification accuracy for two datasets with baseline topic models is shown in Table 2. In terms of accuracy of classification across a diverse range of topics, DistilBERTopic model performs significantly better than the other topic models. The classification results showed that DistilBERTopic performs better than several baseline topic models for both datasets with 30, 50, and 90 topics.

3.4 Topic Coherence

Topic coherence is determined by the co-occurrence of words in external corpora. It is revealed that a correlation exists between topic coherence and human judgments and that this correlation has a high degree of generalizability. Topic coherence numerous approaches have been presented for the automatic assessment of individual topics and the automatic evaluation of entire topic models (Newman, Lau, Grieser, and Baldwin, 2010; Lau, Newman, and Baldwin, 2014). We prefer to use the CV approach (Röder, Both, and Hinneburg, 2015). This consistency metric retrieves the co-occurrence value counts of the specified words using a sliding window. The normalized point-wise mutual information calculates co-occurrence counts (NPMI) (Bouma, 2009) between each top word. Equation 5 is used to calculate the NPMI score.Where, $P(w_i)$ probability of encountering the word w_i in any text and $P(w_i, w_j)$ probability of finding the words w_i and w_j together in a randomized documents. The most likely word sequence is x, 1,x, 2, x, 3, ...x, with N as the total.

$$NPMI\,(x_i, x_j) = \sum_{j}^{N-1} \frac{log\frac{P(x_i,x_j)}{P(x_i)P(x_j)}}{-logP(x_i, x_j)} \qquad (5)$$

Figures 1 and 2 demonstrate the TWNews and Twitter topic coherence outcomes of DistilBERTopic model and all comparable topic models. We specifically set T = 5 for the number of top words per topic, K = 30, and 50 as the number of topics.

DistilBERTopic model outperforms and competing others baseline topic models on all two datasets, whereas the WNTM model beats other models on Twitter. Our proposed topic model gives a higher performance in comparison to WNTM and LF-DMM. PTM performs the best among baseline approaches on TWNews datasets, but BTM provides the lowest coherence score. Despite poor prior results, GPU-DMM outperforms LF-DMM in terms of topic coherence. GPU-DMM performs poorly on TMnews, which may indicate that news descriptions frequently encompass multiple topics. On the other hand, GPU-DMM gives a fairly high score of topic coherence for Twitter, which may mean that titles in Twitter data hide rarer topics than news descriptions. Overall, the DistilBERTopic model achieved higher topic coherence results than other baseline topic models.

4 Conclusion

Finding informative content is becoming more challenging as the volume of short texts available increases. In the absence of context information, the short text has sparseness issues. In this paper, we presented the DistilBERTopic model, which extracts semantically coherent topics from short text and ameliorates the sparsity issue. The document embedding is constructed with pre-trained transformer-based language models and clustered using Hierarchical Density-based Spatial Clustering. The singular value composition method reduced the higher dimensionality effect before clustering. We conducted comprehensive experiments on two short corpora of real-world short text data. The experimental outcomes demonstrate that the DistilBERTopic model is more effective and efficient than existing state-of-the-art topic models. DistilBERTopic model achieved better classification and topic coherence results. We will use other word embedding methods with hierarchical and partitioning clustering in the future.

Acknowledgements

This research was partly supported by Basic Science Research Program through the National Research Foundation of Korea (NRF) funded by the Ministry of Education (No.2020R1I1A3069700) and by the National University Development Project by the Ministry of Education in 2022.

References

David Blei, Andrew Ng, and Michael Jordan. 2001. Latent dirichlet allocation. *Advances in neural information processing systems*, 14.

Gerlof Bouma. 2009. Normalized (pointwise) mutual information in collocation extraction. *Proceedings of GSCL*, 30:31–40.

Ricardo JGB Campello, Davoud Moulavi, and Jörg Sander. 2013. Density-based clustering based on hierarchical density estimates. In *Pacific-Asia conference on knowledge discovery and data mining*, pages 160–172. Springer.

Xueqi Cheng, Xiaohui Yan, Yanyan Lan, and Jiafeng Guo. 2014. Btm: Topic modeling over short texts. *IEEE Transactions on Knowledge and Data Engineering*, 26(12):2928–2941.

Scott Deerwester, Susan T Dumais, George W Furnas, Thomas K Landauer, and Richard Harshman. 1990. Indexing by latent semantic analysis. *Journal of the American society for information science*, 41(6):391–407.

Imola K Fodor. 2002. A survey of dimension reduction techniques. Technical report, Lawrence Livermore National Lab., CA (US).

Amit Gruber, Yair Weiss, and Michal Rosen-Zvi. 2007. Hidden topic markov models. In *Artificial intelligence and statistics*, pages 163–170. PMLR.

Thomas Hofmann. 1999. Probabilistic latent semantic indexing. In *Proceedings of the 22nd annual international ACM SIGIR conference on Research and development in information retrieval*, pages 50–57.

Liangjie Hong and Brian D Davison. 2010a. Empirical study of topic modeling in twitter. In *Proceedings of the first workshop on social media analytics*, pages 80–88.

Liangjie Hong and Brian D Davison. 2010b. Empirical study of topic modeling in twitter. In *Proceedings of the first workshop on social media analytics*, pages 80–88.

Jacob Devlin Ming-Wei Chang Kenton and Lee Kristina Toutanova. 2019. Bert: Pre-training of deep bidirectional transformers for language understanding. In *Proceedings of NAACL-HLT*, pages 4171–4186.

Jey Han Lau, David Newman, and Timothy Baldwin. 2014. Machine reading tea leaves: Automatically evaluating topic coherence and topic model quality. In *Proceedings of the 14th Conference of the European Chapter of the Association for Computational Linguistics*, pages 530–539.

Chenliang Li, Yu Duan, Haoran Wang, Zhiqian Zhang, Aixin Sun, and Zongyang Ma. 2017. Enhancing topic modeling for short texts with auxiliary word embeddings. *ACM Transactions on Information Systems (TOIS)*, 36(2):1–30.

Hosam Mahmoud. 2008. *Pólya urn models*. Chapman and Hall/CRC.

Rishabh Mehrotra, Scott Sanner, Wray Buntine, and Lexing Xie. 2013. Improving lda topic models for microblogs via tweet pooling and automatic labeling. In *Proceedings of the 36th international ACM SIGIR conference on Research and development in information retrieval*, pages 889–892.

Usman Naseem, Imran Razzak, Shah Khalid Khan, and Mukesh Prasad. 2021. A comprehensive survey on word representation models: From classical to state-of-the-art word representation language models. *Transactions on Asian and Low-Resource Language Information Processing*, 20(5):1–35.

David Newman, Jey Han Lau, Karl Grieser, and Timothy Baldwin. 2010. Automatic evaluation of topic coherence. In *Human language technologies: The 2010 annual conference of the North American chapter of the association for computational linguistics*, pages 100–108.

Dat Quoc Nguyen, Richard Billingsley, Lan Du, and Mark Johnson. 2015. Improving topic models with latent feature word representations. *Transactions of the Association for Computational Linguistics*, 3:299–313.

Chaitali G Patil and Patil Sandip. 2013. Use of porter stemming algorithm and svm for emotion extraction from news headlines. *International Journal of Electronics, Communication and Soft Computing Science and Engineering (IJECSCSE)*, 2(7):9.

Martin F Porter. 1980. An algorithm for suffix stripping. *Program*.

Daniel Ramage, David Hall, Ramesh Nallapati, and Christopher D Manning. 2009. Labeled lda: A supervised topic model for credit attribution in multi-labeled corpora. In *Proceedings of the 2009 conference on empirical methods in natural language processing*, pages 248–256.

Junaid Rashid, Jungeun Kim, Amir Hussain, Usman Naseem, and Sapna Juneja. 2022. A novel multiple kernel fuzzy topic modeling technique for biomedical data. *BMC bioinformatics*, 23(1):1–19.

Michael Röder, Andreas Both, and Alexander Hinneburg. 2015. Exploring the space of topic coherence measures. In *Proceedings of the eighth ACM international conference on Web search and data mining*, pages 399–408.

Victor Sanh, Lysandre Debut, Julien Chaumond, and Thomas Wolf. 2019. Distilbert, a distilled version of bert: smaller, faster, cheaper and lighter. *arXiv preprint arXiv:1910.01108*.

Yuan Wang, Jie Liu, Jishi Qu, Yalou Huang, Jimeng Chen, and Xia Feng. 2014. Hashtag graph based topic model for tweet mining. In *2014 IEEE International Conference on Data Mining*, pages 1025–1030. IEEE.

Jianshu Weng, Ee-Peng Lim, Jing Jiang, and Qi He. 2010. Twitterrank: finding topic-sensitive influential twitterers. In *Proceedings of the third ACM international conference on Web search and data mining*, pages 261–270.

Feng Yi, Bo Jiang, and Jianjun Wu. 2020. Topic modeling for short texts via word embedding and document correlation. *IEEE Access*, 8:30692–30705.

Yuan Zuo, Junjie Wu, Hui Zhang, Hao Lin, Fei Wang, Ke Xu, and Hui Xiong. 2016a. Topic modeling of short texts: A pseudo-document view. In *Proceedings of the 22nd ACM SIGKDD international conference on knowledge discovery and data mining*, pages 2105–2114.

Yuan Zuo, Junjie Wu, Hui Zhang, Hao Lin, Fei Wang, Ke Xu, and Hui Xiong. 2016b. Topic modeling of short texts: A pseudo-document view. In *Proceedings of the 22nd ACM SIGKDD international conference on knowledge discovery and data mining*, pages 2105–2114.

Yuan Zuo, Jichang Zhao, and Ke Xu. 2016c. Word network topic model: a simple but general solution for short and imbalanced texts. *Knowledge and Information Systems*, 48(2):379–398.

Yuan Zuo, Jichang Zhao, and Ke Xu. 2016d. Word network topic model: a simple but general solution for short and imbalanced texts. *Knowledge and Information Systems*, 48(2):379–398.

Generating Code-Switched Text from Monolingual Text with Dependency Tree

Bryan Gregorius
School of Science and Technology
Kwansei Gakuin University
Hyogo, Japan
contact@selubi.tech

Takeshi Okadome
School of Science and Technology
Kwansei Gakuin University
Hyogo, Japan
tokadome@acm.org

Abstract

Various methods have been proposed to generate code-switched texts. Many of these involve training neural networks and, in turn, require some (albeit small) amounts of code-switched texts or parallel corpora to train the model itself. In this paper, we propose a method to convert monolingual text into a bilingual code-switched sentence using a dependency parser and machine translator. We leverage the characteristics of the dependency tree to identify the switching point and then pass it to machine translation to generate the code-switched sentence. We then surveyed multilingual people of respective language pairs to review the generated sentences and categorize the result. We found that our method is capable of generating natural code-switched text for various language pairs with the same algorithm. Our method does not require training and thus does not require training data. Our implementation of the model uses off-the-shelf components. The implementation is also built with the possibility of using purpose-built components and rapid deployability in mind.

1 Introduction

Code-Switching (CS) is a phenomenon where a speaker alternates between two or more languages in a single conversation. This phenomenon is frequently observed in multilingual communities, with sentences alternating between a base language and one or more inserted languages. One of the reasons for doing CS is to clarify important information that cannot be explained in one language or code.

An example of this can be seen in Table 1. Here, while the English translation appears natural, the concept "内々定" (informal promise of employment) does not exist in English. Therefore, the word "offer" is a good substitute. However, for people who understand Japanese, "内々定" provides more context. In this example, the base language that provides the grammatical structure is English, and the inserted language is Japanese.

CS-related research is integral to Natural Language Processing (NLP) research, as it helps us understand how multilingual people use and understand languages. Most NLP-related corpora are an aggregation of scripts taken from books, movies, and other media. However, those media are primarily targeted at a particular demographic and, thus, mostly monolingual. This makes CS-related corpus scarce and CS corpus generation a research topic of interest. Furthermore, CS corpus generation is but a step in building CS language models. As such, there is a demand for rapidly deployable CS sentence generators.

In this paper, we propose a method to generate CS sentences from monolingual sentences. Our model is designed to work on various language pairs. Our model implementation is easily expandable to other language pairs and is made with the possibility of being used in tandem with custom components in mind. To our knowledge, we are the first to build a highly extensible code-switched generator that only needs monolingual inputs while also supporting the generation of multiple language pairs with the same algorithm.

2 Related Research

Research in CS is being done extensively. An example of a topic in this field is researching the model itself, such as using subword level aspects in addition to word level aspects to rep-

Table 1: Lost in translation code-switching sentence example

CS Sentence	My 内々定承諾期限 is in July.
English Translation	My offer acceptance deadline is in July.

resent CS data (Winata et al., 2019) and measuring the effectiveness of multilingual models, such as mBERT on CS tasks (Winata et al., 2021).

Since the nature of CS is a mix of two or more languages, it takes mastery in all the languages involved to do research and validation. Therefore, it is understandable that most of the work involves only a pair of two languages. Even then, it is hard for a reader that does not understand both languages to tell how well a model performs. There is also always a possibility that a good CS breakthrough might be left undetected because it is written in a language pair that is not well known. To alleviate these issues, there are several benchmarks to measure a model's performance on CS tasks. The LinCE Benchmark (Aguilar et al., 2020) is one example of it. However, the problem persists even with these benchmarks. Ultimately, only multilingual people who understand both languages can rate the models' performance from a human perspective.

Due to extensive research being done on modeling CS, great demand for CS corpora exists. There have been efforts to provide natural CS corpora both in text form, such as in Barik et al. (2019) and in speech form, such as in Nguyen and Bryant (2020). However, the number of CS corpora pales compared to even parallel or multilingual ones. This, in turn, increases the interest in research fields in CS corpora generation.

In regards to CS corpora generation, there has been an effort to implement findings of CS from the linguistics field, namely the equivalence constraint (EC) theory (Poplack, 1980) by Pratapa et al. (2018). Pratapa et al. used a constituency-based parse tree and parallel monolingual sentences (two monolingual sentences of the same meaning) to generate CS sentences. Although simple, this synthetic CS generation method has been proven to be helpful in training neural network models, such as neural networks that generate even higher quality CS texts (Tarunesh et al., 2021).

Pratapa et al. modeled their method on the Spanish-English language pair, which is linguistically close and has some parallel corpora. Our proposed model works on multiple language pairs, even on linguistically distant pairs such as Japanese-English (Chiswick and Miller, 2005). Our model does not need a parallel monolingual sentence to function and provides an alternative to Pratapa et al.'s proposed model.

3 Model and Implementation

3.1 Proposed Method

The dependency-based parse tree is one of two types of parse trees, the other being the constituency-based parsed tree used in (Pratapa et al., 2018). The dependency-based parse tree differs from constituency-based parsed by lacking phrasal categories, thus making the tree more straightforward. In an English constituency-based parse tree, the number of words usually equals the number of leaves. On the other hand, in English dependency-based parse trees, the number of words usually equals the number of vertices. There are several types of dependency-based parse trees, but we will focus on the syntactic dependency tree (we will refer to this as just dependency tree from hereon). The dependency tree is an ordered tree; as such, flattening the tree can be defined as concatenating the vertices of the tree in the order of the original sentence. Figure 1 is an example of a dependency tree.

Our proposed model works by first getting the dependency tree of a monolingual sentence (base sentence or [X]-base from hereon) by passing said sentence into a dependency parser. We then determine the switching point from the dependency tree and translate the switching point in place with a machine translation model. We define the switching point as the part of the sentence that will later be passed to a machine translator and gets trans-

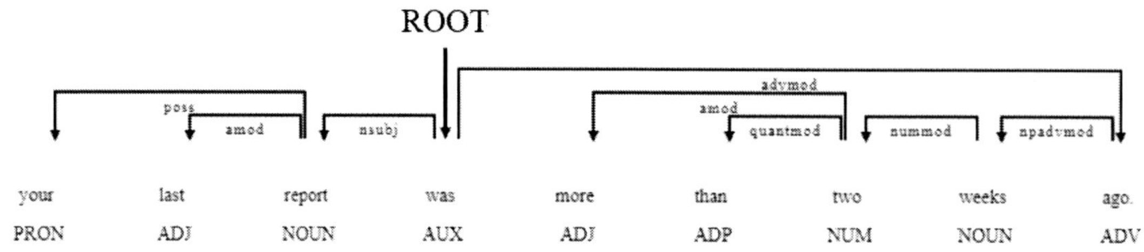

Figure 1: English dependency tree example

lated into the inserted language. We assume access to both a dependency parser and a machine translator. Therefore, to create a [X]-[Y] Code-Switched sentence, we need a dependency parser that can output a dependency tree of [X] and a machine translator that can translate from [X] to [Y]. Here, [X] and [Y] are languages represented by the ISO 639-1 code. For example, EN-JA means a code-switched sentence generated from a monolingual English base sentence (EN-Base) and the switching point translated into Japanese.

3.2 Determining the Switching Point

Given a dependency tree T with root vertex r, let V_i be the set of all vertex at depth i of T. We define the root as the only depth 0 vertex, as such $V_0 = \{r\}$. Here, we define $|v|$ as the number of vertex of a subtree of T with vertex v as the root, given $v \neq r$ and v is a vertex of T. The switching point is the flattened subtree of T with any vertex $s \in S$ as its root. S is given by

$$S = \begin{cases} \text{argmax}_{V_1} f, & \text{if} \max_{V_1} f > 1 \\ \{v \mid v \text{ is noun}, v \in V_1\}, & \text{if} \max_{V_1} f = 1 \end{cases}$$

where

$$f(v) = |v|.$$

In Figure 1, $V_1 = \{\text{report}, \text{ago}\}$ and $f(\text{report}) = 3, f(\text{ago}) = 5$. As such, $S = \{\text{ago}\}$ and the switching point is the flattened subtree with the root "ago", which is "more than two weeks ago."

In other words, we propose the switching point to be the flattened largest subtree with the dependency tree root's direct children as the subtree's root. By choosing the largest subtree, we maximize the chance that the switching point is contextually independent enough to produce a good translation, especially since the machine translator is an independent component and cannot access the whole sentence to infer additional context. In most cases, the largest subtree size should be at least 2. However, in simple sentences such as "I eat meat," we choose to translate nouns only as it has the highest likelihood of being contextually independent.

3.3 Implementation

We implemented our solution with Spacy (Honnibal et al., 2020) as the dependency parser and both DeepL and Google Cloud Translation AI as the machine translators. We use Google Cloud Translation AI for language pairs not supported by DeepL. In our implementation, if there are multiple vertices in S, we choose the leftmost vertex as the switching point root. The repository of our implementation can be found at (Gregorius, 2022).

This implementation is made with rapid deployability in mind; hence adding a language pair is relatively simple. The implementation also features a demo that generates EN-JA and JA-EN sentences from the JESC corpus's (Pryzant et al., 2018) test data using DeepL. There are 2000 lines of English and Japanese sentences in that data. Generating EN-JA sentences took 13 minutes and 24 seconds and JA-EN 15 minutes and 27 seconds, which results in average speeds of 2.49 lines/second and 2.16 lines/second, respectively. For more information about the implementation, we recommend visiting the repository itself.

4 Results

We generated sentences using our implementation and asked multilingual people of respective language pairs for review (the reviewers from hereon). We conducted the review by asking if the sentence was natural and asking for an explanation of the unnatural sentences. From the response, we observed that the code-switched sentence could be categorized into four categories: natural, incorrect grammar with correct context, context changed but natural grammar usage, and incomprehensible. Moving forward, the notation T_n^m to refer the n-th entry in Table m. For example, T_1^2 refers to the pair of EN-Base sentence of "your last report was more than two weeks ago." and its EN-JA generated sentence of "your last report was 二週間以上前."

4.1 Results : Natural Code-Switched Texts

All entries in Table 2 are deemed natural by the reviewers. These texts require no additional grammar correction and lose no context during translation. In testing, we observe more natural results like this, but we will only show one sentence for each directional language pair due to space limitations.

4.2 Results: Incorrect Grammar with Correct Context

All the entries in Table 3 need grammatical correction to varying degrees but have correct context and are understandable.

T_1^3 and T_2^3 require preposition to be added. In T_2^3, "First" should be "At first" for it to be natural. T_3^3 can sound more natural by adding a verb at the end. These required changes are relatively minor.

T_4^3 and T_5^3 have double subjects in its code-switched sentences. In T_4^3 the model generated "저는" and "I" which both mean "I" and in T_5^3 it generated "저는" and "我" which also both means "I".

4.3 Results: Context Changed but Natural Grammar

All the code-switched text entries in Table 4 are grammatically correct. However, compared to the base texts, these texts lost or changed the context from the original.

T_1^4, T_2^4, and T_3^4 context changed due to vocabulary choice. In T_1^4 base text, "忠告" (advice, warning) gets translated to "建议" (suggestion) even though the word "忠告" exists in Chinese. T_2^4 ZH-Base's "商家" (businessman, merchant) gets translated to "加盟店" (member store [of a store association]) where it should be "商人" (businessman, merchant). There are also better word choices to explain "弱者と危機に瀕している" (socially vulnerable and at-risk) than "संवेदनशील और जोखिम वाल" for T_3^4.

T_4^4, T_5^4, and T_6^4 lost context implication during translation. T_4^4 and T_5^4 base sentence translates implies that the writer has not been able to buy a ticket despite waiting for a long time. This context got lost in both sentences. A proper substitute for T_4^4 inserted language part would be "But I haven't been able to buy a ticket yet" and T_5^4 "でも、まだチケット取れてないんです". The Thai part of T_6^4 translates to "might be yours," but by the wording, its closer to "(things) might be yours" compared to the JA-Base sentence which translates to "you may think like that (but I don't)."

4.4 Results: Incomprehensible Code-Switched Texts

All code-switched text in Table 5 is incomprehensible. The reviewers cannot understand the meaning without looking at the base sentence.

The machine translator failed to detect the name "tup" In T_1^5 and tries to translate it, resulting in an incomprehensible sentence. Also, the second sentence's "今がそのとき" translates to "it's now the time," contains an implied subject. Thus the sentence also has a double subject just like T_4^3 and T_5^3. T_2^5's "社会的弱者と危機に瀕しているグループ" (socially vulnerable and at-risk groups) translates to "กลุ่มเสี่ยงและกลุ่มเสี่ยง" (risk group and risk group) which is incomprehensible. In T_3^5, the translator failed to translate "商家的诚信," and the generated Korean is incomprehensible.

5 Discussion

Our model heavily relies on a dependency parser and machine translator. As a result, any errors in those components reflect directly on the performance of our model. The machine translator may output different translation results even with the same machine translator and input. For example, T_{13}^2's JA-ID is a natural result but sometimes the DeepL translator outputs "kelompok rentan dan berisiko"

Table 2: Natural Generated Code-Switched Texts

1	EN-Base	your last report was more than two weeks ago.
	EN-JA	your last report was 二週間以上前.
2	EN-Base	you are a good soldier, tup. it's time to go now.
	EN-ZH	this symbol is you are 一个好的士兵，Tup . it 's 现在是时候走了
3	JA-Base	私の忠告がほとんど重要でないというのか?
	JA-EN	My advice ほとんど重要でないというのか?
4	ZH-Base	商家的诚信和口碑有着密不可分的联系。
	ZH-EN	Merchant's integrity and reputation 有着密不可分的联系。
5	JA-Base	この記号は 昔の 地下鉄トンネル網の地図よ
	JA-ZH	この記号は古老的地下隧道网络地図よ
6	JA-Base	しかし社会的弱者と危機に瀕しているグループに力点を置いています
	JA-KO	しかし사회적 약자와 위기에 처한 그룹力点を置いています
7	KO-Base	저는 어제 약국에 가서 약을 많이 샀어요.
	KO-JA	저는昨日薬局に行って약을많이샀어요.
8	EN-Base	so you quit school and quit looking for work and decided to become a chef.
	EN-TH	so you quit school and quit looking for work and ตัดสินใจเป็นเชฟ
9	EN-Base	you are a good soldier, tup. it's time to go now.
	EN-HI	you are एक अच्छा सैनिक , tup. it's अब जाने का समय .
10	JA-Base	あなたにはそうかもしれないが 私そう思わない
	JA-HI	यह आपके लिए हो सकता है 私そう思わない
11	EN-Base	you are a good soldier, tup. it's time to go now.
	EN-ID	you are prajurit yang baik, tup. it's waktu untuk pergi sekarang.
12	JA-Base	しかし社会的弱者と危機に瀕しているグループに力点を置いています
	JA-ID	しかし untuk kelompok rentan dan berisiko 力点を置いています

Table 3: Incorrect Grammar Generated Code-Switched Texts

1	EN-Base	you are a good soldier, tup. it's time to go now.
	EN-TH	you are ทหารที่ดี tup. it's เวลาไปตอนนี้ .
2	JA-Base	最初はうまく いかなかったんだよ
	JA-EN	First うまくいかなかったんだよ
3	EN-Base	so you quit school and quit looking for work and decided to become a chef
	EN-KO	so you quit school and quit looking for work and 요리사가 되기로 결심.
4	KO-Base	저는 어제 약국에 가서 약을 많이 샀어요.
	KO-EN	저는 I went to the pharmacy yesterday 약을많이샀어요.
5	KO-Base	저는 어제 약국에 가서 약을 많이 샀어요.
	KO-ZH	저는昨天去了药房약을많이샀어요.

Table 4: Context Changed Natural Generated Code-Switched Texts

1	JA-Base	私の忠告がほとんど重要でないというのか?
	JA-ZH	我的建议ほとんど重要でないというのか?
2	ZH-Base	商家的诚信和口碑有着密不可分的联系
	ZH-JA	加盟店の誠実さ、評判有着密不可分的联系。
3	JA-Base	しかし社会的弱者と危機に瀕しているグループに力点を置いています
	JA-HI	しかし संवेदनशील और जोखिम वाले समूह 力点を置いています
4	ZH-Base	尽管我早晨六点到了售票处，但是我还没买到票
	ZH-EN	尽管我早晨六点到了售票处，But I haven't bought a ticket yet
5	ZH-Base	尽管我早晨六点到了售票处，但是我还没买到票
	ZH-JA	尽管我早晨六点到了售票处，でも、まだチケット取ってないんです
6	JA-Base	あなたにはそうかもしれないが 私そう思わない
	JA-TH	อาจเป็นของคุณ 私そう思わない

Table 5: Incomprehensible Code-Switched Texts

1	EN-Base	you are a good soldier, tup. it' s time to go now.
	EN-JA	you are けいぐんたいとう . it 's 今がその時 .
2	JA-Base	しかし社会的弱者と危機に瀕しているグループに力点を置いています
	JA-TH	しかし กลุ่มเสี่ยงและกลุ่มเสี่ยง 力点を置いています
3	ZH-Base	商家的诚信和口碑有着密不可分的联系。
	ZH-KO	비즈니스 무결성 및 평판有着密不可分的联系。

Table 6: Code-Switching Generation Comparison Between DeepL and Google Cloud Translation AI

EN-Base	you are a good soldier, tup. it' s time to go now.
EN-JA (DeepL)	you are けいぐんたいとう . it 's 今がその時 .
EN-JA (Google)	you are 良い兵士、タップ . it ' s 今行く時間 .

(vulnerable and at-risk groups) and truncates "untuk" (for) which gets categorized as incorrect grammar with correct context instead of natural (due to needing preposition).

If we change the machine translator, the result is even more apparent. Table 6 EN-Base and EN-JA (DeepL) is the same entry as T_1^5, which is incomprehensible. In comparison, the Google Cloud Translation AI managed to translate it flawlessly, even localizing the name "tup" into its Japanese version, "タップ." This turns it from being categorized as incomprehensible to being categorized as natural translation, or at worst incorrect grammar with correct context due to a double subject in the second sentence.

When reviewing the code-switched texts, we observe that some language pairs tended to produce more natural texts. EN-ZH and JA-KO are examples of this. Meanwhile, problems that do not occur in other pairs may appear in some language pairs. A good example is the double subject problem we discussed in 4.2, which occurs due to Japanese and Korean having implied subjects built into the language.

6 Conclusion

In this paper, we proposed a model to generate CS text using a dependency tree. We also showed that, albeit heuristic in nature, this model could produce natural CS text in various language pairs, even pairs of languages distant from each other. Our model only needs a single monolingual sentence as the input. Therefore, it is an excellent alternative to existing models using parallel monolingual inputs. Our implementation focuses heavily on rapid deployability and modularity with custom components. We hope that it will be integrated with custom-built components to generate even higher-quality CS texts in the future.

It is impossible to test all combinations of language in one paper. Therefore we would like to invite future readers and researchers to try this model on various language pairs. We also showed that the machine translator significantly affects our model performance. Fortunately, our model is relatively straightforward to implement, and we are excited to see what happens if we integrate it with a custom-built machine translator and dependency parsers. For example, a machine translator that analyzes the base sentences and prevents double subjects for Japanese and Korean may have great potential. Our implementation translates only a single part of the dependency tree to an inserted language, which results in a bilingual code-switched text. Expanding this idea, there is potential for translating multiple parts of the tree in different languages resulting in trilingual or even multilingual code-switched sentences. We hope our research provides progress in understanding code-switching, and we are excited to see future developments in this field.

References

Gustavo Aguilar, Sudipta Kar, and Thamar Solorio. 2020. LinCE: A Centralized Benchmark for Linguistic Code-switching Evaluation. In *Proceedings of The 12th Language Resources and Evaluation Conference*, pages 1803–1813, Marseille, France. European Language Resources Association.

Anab Maulana Barik, Rahmad Mahendra, and Mirna Adriani. 2019. Normalization of Indonesian-English code-mixed Twitter data. In *Proceedings of the 5th Workshop on Noisy User-generated Text (W-NUT 2019)*, pages 417–424, Hong Kong, China. Association for Computational Linguistics.

Barry R. Chiswick and Paul W. Miller. 2005. Linguistic distance: A quantitative measure of the distance between english and other languages. *Journal of Multilingual and Multicultural Development*, 26(1):1–11.

Bryan Gregorius. Selubi/csify: Csify v1.0.6 [online]. 2022.

Matthew Honnibal, Ines Montani, Sofie Van Landeghem, and Adriane Boyd. 2020. spaCy: Industrial-strength Natural Language Processing in Python.

Li Nguyen and Christopher Bryant. 2020. CanVEC - the canberra Vietnamese-English code-switching natural speech corpus. In *Proceedings of the Twelfth Language Resources and Evaluation Conference*, pages 4121–4129, Marseille, France. European Language Resources Association.

Shana Poplack. 1980. Sometimes i' ll start a sentence in spanish y y termino en español: toward a typology of code-switching1. *Linguistics*, 18(7-8):581–618.

Adithya Pratapa, Gayatri Bhat, Monojit Choudhury, Sunayana Sitaram, Sandipan Dandapat, and Kalika Bali. 2018. Language modeling for code-mixing: The role of linguistic theory based synthetic data. In *Proceedings of the 56th Annual Meeting of the Association for Computational Linguistics (Volume 1: Long Papers)*, pages 1543–1553, Melbourne, Australia. Association for Computational Linguistics.

Reid Pryzant, Youngjoo Chung, Dan Jurafsky, and Denny Britz. 2018. JESC: Japanese-English subtitle corpus. In *Proceedings of the Eleventh International Conference on Language Resources and Evaluation (LREC 2018)*, Miyazaki, Japan. European Language Resources Association (ELRA).

Ishan Tarunesh, Syamantak Kumar, and Preethi Jyothi. 2021. From machine translation to code-switching: Generating high-quality code-switched text. In *Proceedings of the 59th Annual Meeting of the Association for Computational Linguistics and the 11th International Joint Conference on Natural Language Processing (Volume 1: Long Papers)*, pages 3154–3169, Online. Association for Computational Linguistics.

Genta Indra Winata, Samuel Cahyawijaya, Zihan Liu, Zhaojiang Lin, Andrea Madotto, and Pascale Fung. 2021. Are multilingual models effective in code-switching? In *Proceedings of the Fifth Workshop on Computational Approaches to Linguistic Code-Switching*, pages 142–153, Online. Association for Computational Linguistics.

Genta Indra Winata, Zhaojiang Lin, Jamin Shin, Zihan Liu, and Pascale Fung. 2019. Hierarchical meta-embeddings for code-switching named entity recognition. In *Proceedings of the 2019 Conference on Empirical Methods in Natural Language Processing and the 9th International Joint Conference on Natural Language Processing (EMNLP-IJCNLP)*, pages 3532–3538, Hong Kong, China. Association for Computational Linguistics.

Stability of Forensic Text Comparison System

Susan Brown[1], Shunichi Ishihara[2]
firstname.lastname@anu.edu.au

[1,2] Speech and Language Laboratory, The Australian National University, Canberra, Australia
[1] College of Arts and Social Science, The Australian National University, Canberra, Australia
[2] College of Asia and the Pacific, The Australian National University, Canberra, Australia

Abstract

This study investigates how the reliability of likelihood ratio (LR)-based forensic text comparison (FTC) systems is affected by the sampling variability regarding author numbers in databases. When 30–40 authors (each contributing two 4 kB documents) are included in each of the test, reference and calibration databases, the experimental results demonstrate: 1) the overall performance (validity) of the FTC system reaches the same level of performance as a system with 720 authors, and 2) the variability of the system performance (reliability) starts to converge. A similar trend can be observed regarding the magnitude of fluctuation in derived LRs. The variability of the overall system performance is mostly due to the large variability in calibration, not discrimination. Furthermore, FTC systems are more prone to instability when the dimension of the feature vector is high.

1 Introduction

Many studies on source-detection systems emphasise improving the system's overall performance or system validity. In data-driven forensic science, empirical testing of the system, demonstrating the system's validity and reliability, is essential for evidence to be accepted in court (President's Council of Advisors on Science and Technology [U.S.], 2016). However, studies of reliability are limited (Wang et al., 2022). The current study analyses the reliability of forensic text comparison (FTC) regarding the effect of sampling variability and sample size. Sample size is a well-known factor affecting the system's validity and reliability (Ishihara, 2016, 2020).

When reporting the system performance in court as an expert witness, an astute lawyer may question whether the system could achieve the same level of performance if it were tested with another set of samples from the same population, particularly when the sample size is small. Thus, forensic scientists must measure reliability to reduce the probability of a miscarriage of justice (Brümmer and Swart, 2014; Morrison, 2011, 2016).

FTC typically involves the analysis of two documents: the source-known (suspect) document and the source-questioned (offender) document. It is widely acknowledged that expert opinions should be expressed as the strength of evidence, quantified as a likelihood ratio (LR) (Robertson et al., 2016). The importance of the LR framework, long argued as the logically and legally correct framework (Aitken, 1995; Aitken and Stoney, 1991), is now recognised for FTC (Grant, 2022). However, FTC studies based on the LR framework are limited (cf. Ishihara, 2021; Ishihara and Carne, 2022).

The current study investigates the reliability and validity of the LR-based FTC system by conducting repeated random sampling (50 iterations) of a given number of authors from a large database. The experiments are conducted with two different dimensions of feature vectors (20 and 500), anticipating some different degrees of reliability. Logistic Regression calibration (Morrison, 2013) was employed to convert the estimated scores with the Dirichlet-Multinomial model (Bolck and Stamouli, 2017) to LRs. See Subsection 2.4 for the details of calibration as it is used in a difference sense from ML/NLP. Word unigrams are used to model each document.

2 Methodology

2.1 Database and Comparisons

The present study assessed a database of 4 kB-sized documents extracted from the dataset prepared by Ishihara (2021). This database is based on the Amazon Product Data Authorship Verification Corpus (Halvani et al., 2017) and includes 4,320 documents (two documents each from 2,160 authors. The average document length is 830.47 words (standard deviation, 33.998 words). Ishihara (2021) provided justification for the use of product review texts for forensic studies.

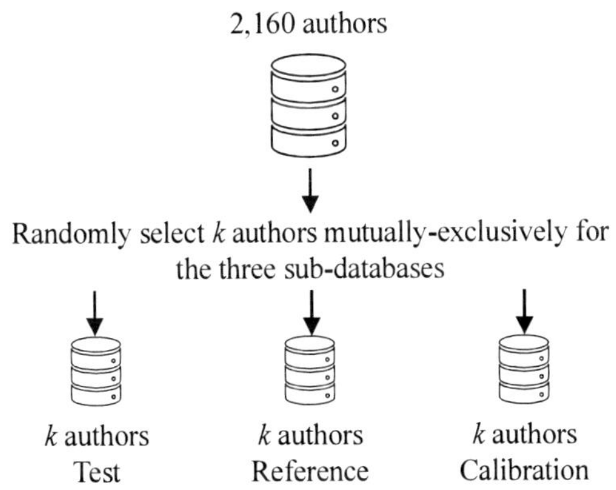

Figure 1: Random selections of authors

In order to test the reliability of the FTC system; in other words, the (in)stability of the system, arising from the sampling variability and the number of authors included in the experiments, k (=$\{5,10,20,30,40,60,80,100,125,150,175,200,225,250\}$) authors were randomly selected for each of the three sub-databases of test, reference and calibration 50 times (see Figure 1). Therefore, 50 random samplings of data for each experiment of k authors were conducted. For a small k, a high level of fluctuation in system performance across the 50 iterations of the experiment is predicted.

From k authors in the test sub-database, k same-author (SA) and $\binom{k}{2}$ different-author (DA) comparisons are possible. Note that more DA than SA comparisons can be made for the same number of authors.

The system is assumed to be unstable if the dimension of a feature vector is high because the amount of data for the statistical model to be appropriately trained exponentially increases as the feature dimension increases (Silverman, 1986). As such, two different feature numbers (20 and 500) are compared to investigate to what extent the feature vector dimension influences system reliability.

2.2 Tokenisation and Word Unigrams

The `tokens()` function of the quanteda R library (Benoit et al., 2018), which recognises punctuation marks and special characters as single words, was used to perform tokenisation. No stemming algorithm was used. Each document was modelled with word unigrams. From the entire database, the 500 most frequent words (term frequency) were identified, and those words, sorted in descending order of frequency, were used as the elements of a feature vector; i.e. a global feature selection was applied.

Figure 2 illustrates the process of calculating LRs. The LRs are calculated for SA and DA comparisons generated from the test sub-database. Estimating LRs is a two-stage process consisting of the score calculation stage, followed by the calibration stage. For the score calculation stage, the same processes are applied to the test and calibration sub-databases. However, the scores of the test sub-database were calibrated to LRs, while the score of the calibration sub-database were used to train the calibration model. The documents stored in the reference database are used to obtain statistical information for the typicality assessment of the documents being compared.

2.3 Score Calculation

When the LR interpretive framework is applied to FTC, textual evidence (E) is assessed under the two competing hypotheses; the SA (H_{SA}) and the DA (H_{DA}). These are generally called the prosecution and defence hypotheses, respectively. The evidence usually includes two types of text samples: the source-known text from the suspect (X) and the source-questioned text from the offender (Y). Thus, the score is expressed as given in Equation (1).

$$Score = \frac{f(E|H_{SA})}{f(E|H_{DA})} = \frac{f((X,Y)|H_{SA})}{f((X,Y)|H_{DA})} \quad (1)$$

Each piece of evidence (X and Y) are modelled with the counts of a given set of unigrams (m; maximum m = 500): $X = \{x_1, x_2, \cdots x_m\}$ and $Y = \{y_1, y_2, \cdots y_m\}$. The similarity between X and Y is assessed as the probability of X against the multinomial model given Y of which the parameter is $\Pi = \{\pi_1, \pi_2, \cdots \pi_m\}$. If a prior is assumed for the model parameter, it can be formulated by a Dirichlet distribution with a hyperparameter ($A = \{a_1, a_2, \cdots a_m\}$). With the multivariate Beta function ($B = (\Gamma(a_1)\cdots\Gamma(a_m))/(\Gamma(a_1 + \cdots a_m))$), Equation (1) can be rewritten as Equation (2).

$$Score = \frac{B(A)B(A+X+Y)}{B(A+X)B(A+Y)} \quad (2)$$

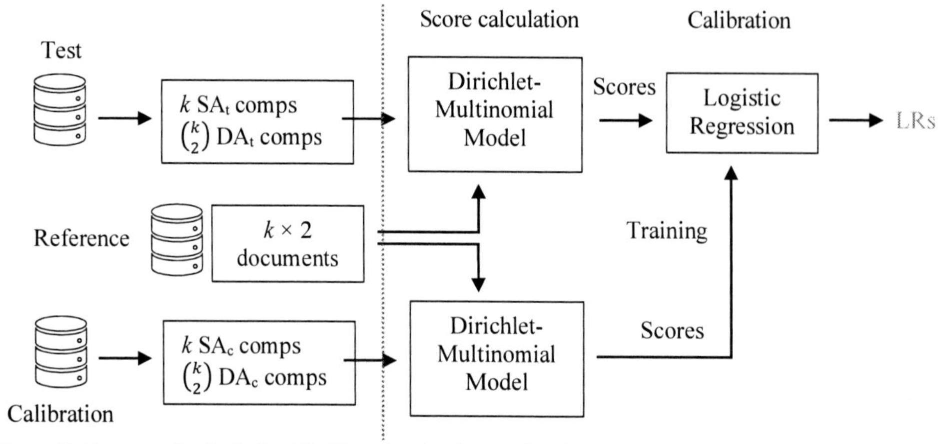

Figure 2: Process of calculating likelihood ratios (LRs). k = the number of authors in sub-database; SA = same-author; DA = different-author; t = test sub-database; comps = comparisons; c = calibration sub-database.

The maximum likelihood estimation was employed to obtain the parameter values of the Dirichlet model using the reference sub-database. Note that although the Dirichlet-Multinomial model follows Bayesian logic, the parameters of the Dirichlet model are fixed in this study instead of random variables. See Section 4 for the application of a Bayesian statistical approach as a future study. Refer to Bolck and Stamouli (2017) for a detailed derivational process from Equation (1) to (2).

2.4 Score to Likelihood Ratio Conversion

The calculated score for each comparison of the test sub-database must be converted to a LR, as the uncalibrated score alone cannot be interpreted as demonstrating the strength of the evidence. Logistic regression is most commonly used to calculate the LR (Morrison, 2013; Ramos and Gonzalez-Rodriguez, 2013). The calculated comparison scores from the calibration sub-database are used to train the logistic regression model.

2.5 System Evaluations

For the evaluation of a forensic system of which the outcome is used to assist the factfinders' legal decision, those evaluation metrics which are based on classification or identification accuracy are not appropriate. This is because 1) the category-based classification accuracy does not properly assess the magnitude of LRs, which is continuous and 2) it implicitly refers to the accuracy of the decision making: guilty vs not guilty; which is only permitted for the factfinders.

The standard evaluation metric for LR-based forensic systems is the log LR cost (C_{llr}), mathematically expressed in Equation (3).

$$C_{llr} = \frac{1}{2}\left(\frac{1}{N_{SA}} \sum_{i}^{N_{SA}} log_2\left(1 + \frac{1}{LR_{SA_i}}\right) + \frac{1}{N_{DA}} \sum_{j}^{N_{DA}} log_2\left(1 + LR_{DA_j}\right) \right) \quad (3)$$

In Equation (3), N_{SA} and N_{DA} are the number of SA and DA comparisons, respectively, and LR_{SA_i} and LR_{DA_j} are the i_{th} SA and j_{th} DA linear LRs, respectively. The C_{llr} is the overall average of the pooled costs calculated for all LRs. A certain amount of cost is computed for each LR, but the cost is greater as the value is further away from unity (LR = 1), and contrary-to-fact LRs give rise to a far greater cost than consistent-with-fact LRs. The closer to C_{llr} = 0, the better the performance. A $C_{llr} \geq 1$ denotes that the evidence is not informative for inference. The C_{llr} can be decomposed into C_{llr}^{min} and C_{llr}^{cal} to assess the discrimination and calibration performance of the system, respectively; thus, $C_{llr} = C_{llr}^{min} + C_{llr}^{cal}$.

The variability or (in)stability of the performance across the 50 random samplings of k authors is quantified by the range of the C_{llr} values observed across the 50 iterations.

3 Results: System Performance

3.1 Reference Performance

The 2,160 authors of the entire database were evenly separated into three sub-databases, with 720 authors in each. With this maximum number of

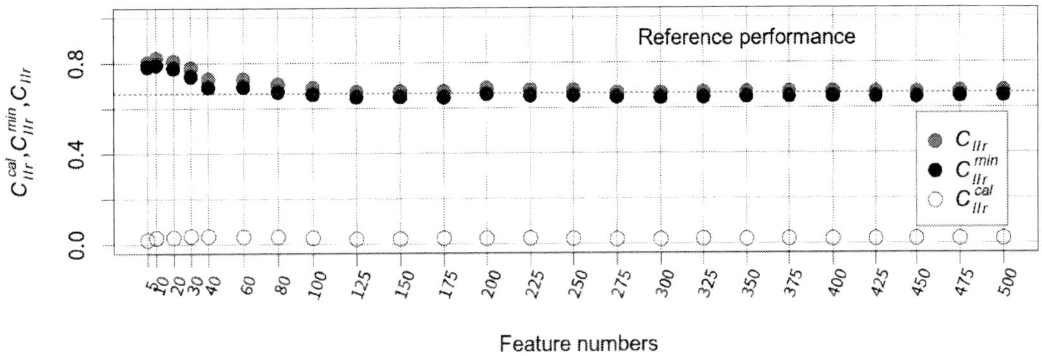

Figure 3: Reference performance of the forensic text comparison system with 720 authors in each sub-database. The red dotted horizontal line indicates the best C_{llr} value (0.66469), attained with 300 features.

authors (720) in each sub-database, a set of experiments was carried out by gradually increasing the number of features = {5,10,20,30,40,60,80,100,125,...500}) to understand how well the FTC system works with the full dataset, but with different feature numbers. The C_{llr}, C_{llr}^{min} and C_{llr}^{cal} were plotted as a function of the number of features in Figure 3.

Regardless of the feature numbers, the C_{llr}^{cal} values were all close to zero, indicating that the resultant LRs are very well calibrated. The overall performance of the system (C_{llr}) improves as the feature number increases to approximately 125 features, after which the C_{llr} value stays more or less unchanged even with the addition of more features. The system achieved the best performance for 300 features (C_{llr} = 0.66469). The C_{llr}^{min} values exhibit a very similar trend to the C_{llr} values.

3.2 Variability in Performance

The reliability and validity of the system caused by the random sampling of given numbers of authors for the sub-databases were analysed. For this, the mean and range of the C_{llr} values of the 50 iterations of experiments were plotted together according to the number of authors in Figure 4; Panel a) shows the data for 20 features, and Panel b) shows the data for 500 features.

For the mean C_{llr} values, the system does not require many authors to achieve the same level of performance as systems with the full number of authors. Figure 4a and 4b demonstrate that regardless of the feature numbers, systems with 10 authors averaged the same level of performance as the systems using the full number of authors. When the feature dimension is low (20 features) (see Figure 4a), the average system performance is similar for any number of authors. However, when the feature dimension is high (500 features) (Figure 4b), analyses using 5 authors substantially worsened the system performance. This indicates that system (in)stability is subject to the feature dimension.

As can be seen from Figure 4b, the range of the C_{llr} values was large for 50 iterations for 5 authors but narrowed with an increasing number of authors. Although the range appeared to converge with the inclusion of 30–40 authors, it continues to decrease in very small increments as the number of authors further increases. With only 5 authors, the range of the C_{llr} values is far wider for 500 features (116.292) than for 20 features (2.53864).

To visually compare the levels of (in)stability caused by the different feature numbers, the ranges of C_{llr} values for 20 and 500 features are plotted together in Figure 4c. A narrower scale (between 0 and 1) is used for the Y-axis of Figure 4c to make visual comparison easier. However, this scale reduction resulted in some C_{llr} range values being out of the plot; thus, the C_{llr} range values are given in Table 1 for 5, 10 and 20 authors.

Author number	Feature number	
	20	**500**
5	2.53864	116.292
10	1.25353	1.80968
20	0.59871	0.83678

Table 1: Ranges of the C_{llr} values with 20 and 500 features.

Figure 4c and Table 1 show that the C_{llr} range values are higher for 500 features than 20 features. However, the ranges are similar for author numbers ≥150. In contrast, for fewer authors (≤20), the

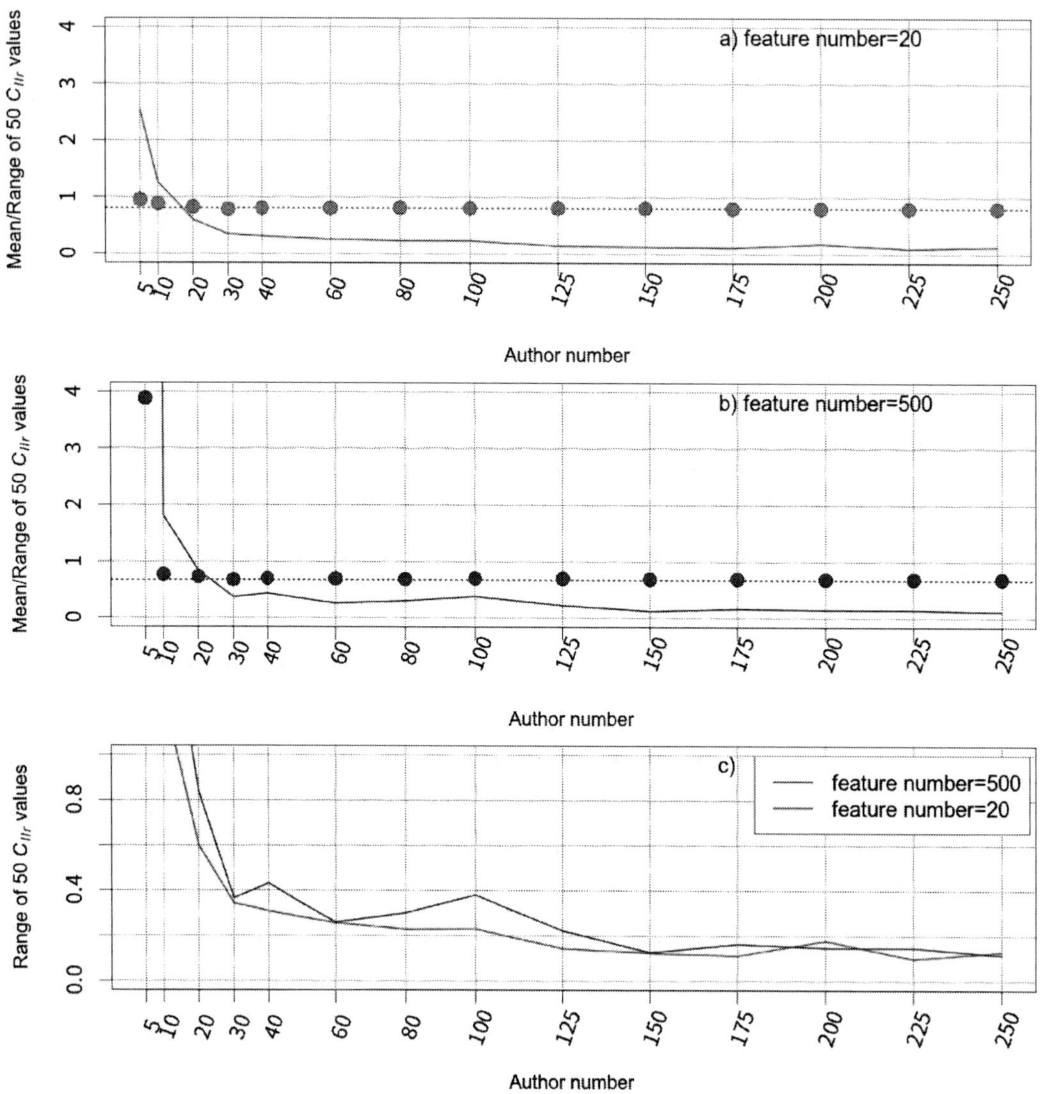

Figure 4: Mean C_{llr}values (circles), plotted as a function of the number of authors with the range of the C_{llr}values (solid curves). Panels a) and b) demonstrate the C_{llr}values for 20 and 500 features, respectively. The ranges of the C_{llr}values are plotted together in Panel c) for better visual comparison. The dotted horizontal lines of Panels a) and b) show the C_{llr}value for the maximum authors (720). Note that some values extend beyond the range of the Y-axis, which is narrower in Panel c).

difference in the C_{llr} range between 20 and 500 features is larger (113.75, 0.55615 and 0.23807, for 5, 10 and 20 authors, respectively) than for author numbers >20.

The experimental results presented in this subsection demonstrate that the performance instability caused by the sampling variability is evident in FTC. When the author number is very small (5 authors), the magnitude of the performance instability, measured in terms of the range of C_{llr}values, is large. Equally, the average performance is low compared to the systems with the full number of authors.

However, performance instability is quickly reduced as more authors are added. For example, with 30–40 authors, the range of C_{llr} values becomes substantially moderate and starts to converge. With 30–40 authors, the average performance of the system is as good as that of a system with the full number of authors.

It appears that the (in)stability of the system is interrelated with the number of features. That is, the system is prone to instability with a higher feature vector dimension. In particular, the instability is more sizeable with a small number of authors, but becomes negligible when many authors (≥150) are

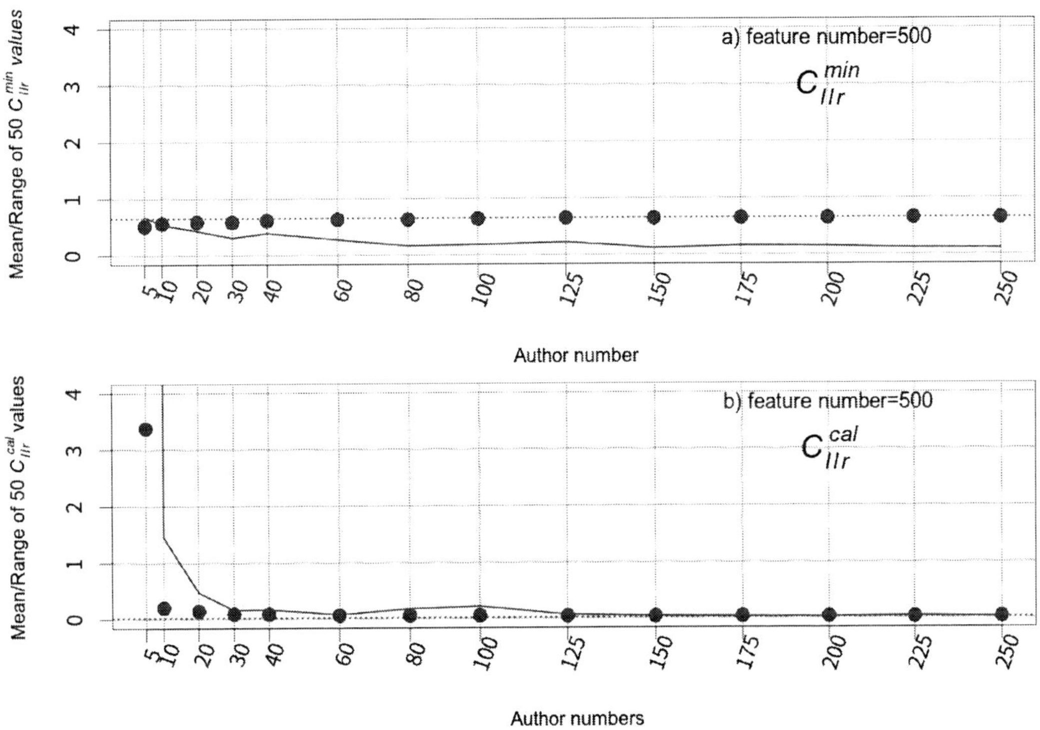

Figure 5: Mean C_{llr}^{min} (a) and C_{llr}^{cal} (b) values (circles), plotted as a function of author numbers, the curves show the range of the C_{llr}^{min} and C_{llr}^{cal} values (curves). The dotted horizontal lines in a) and b) show the best C_{llr}^{min} and C_{llr}^{cal} values, respectively, for the maximum authors (720). Note that some values extend beyond the range of the Y-axis.

included in each sub-database; therefore, there is improved stability when the statistical model is trained with an appropriate amount of data.

3.3 Cause of Variability

Subsection 3.2 investigated to what extent 50 random samplings of a given set of authors affect the reliability and validity of the system by assessing the C_{llr} values. However, as explained in Subsection 2.5, the C_{llr} is an assessment metric for the overall performance of a LR-based system, and consists of two components: discrimination (C_{llr}^{min}) and calibration (C_{llr}^{cal}). In this subsection, the previously observed variability is further investigated from the viewpoints of the discrimination and calibration performance.

Figure 5 shows how the mean and ranges of the C_{llr}^{min} and C_{llr}^{cal} values vary as a function of author numbers. Figure 5 shows this variation for 500 features, and the observation made for 20 features is uniform. As can be observed in Figure 5a, the mean C_{llr}^{min} value stays more or less the same regardless of the author numbers (even for 5 authors). This observation means that, on average, the discrimination ability of the system is not largely influenced by the number of included authors.

The range of discrimination ability, measured using C_{llr}^{min}, displays trifling fluctuations even with the small numbers of authors ($\leq$40 authors), and the degree of fluctuation is far smaller than the ones observed for the C_{llr} (see Figure 4).

In contrast to the discrimination ability of the system, the changes in the mean and range of the C_{llr}^{cal} values display a similar trend as observed for the C_{llr} counterparts presented in Figure 4. Even with as few as 10 authors, a very similar level of mean calibration performance (C_{llr}^{cal} = 0.20338) is found in the case with the maximum number of authors (C_{llr}^{cal} = 0.01955). However, with 5 authors, the mean C_{llr}^{cal} value deviates (C_{llr}^{cal} = 3.37324) far from the calibration performance achieved with the maximum number of authors (C_{llr}^{cal} = 0.01955). Likewise, the range of the C_{llr}^{cal} values is large (116.06) with 5 authors. As can be observed in Figure 5b, the large range observed for 5 authors decreases as the author number increases, and the range becomes as narrow as 0.16045 with 30 authors.

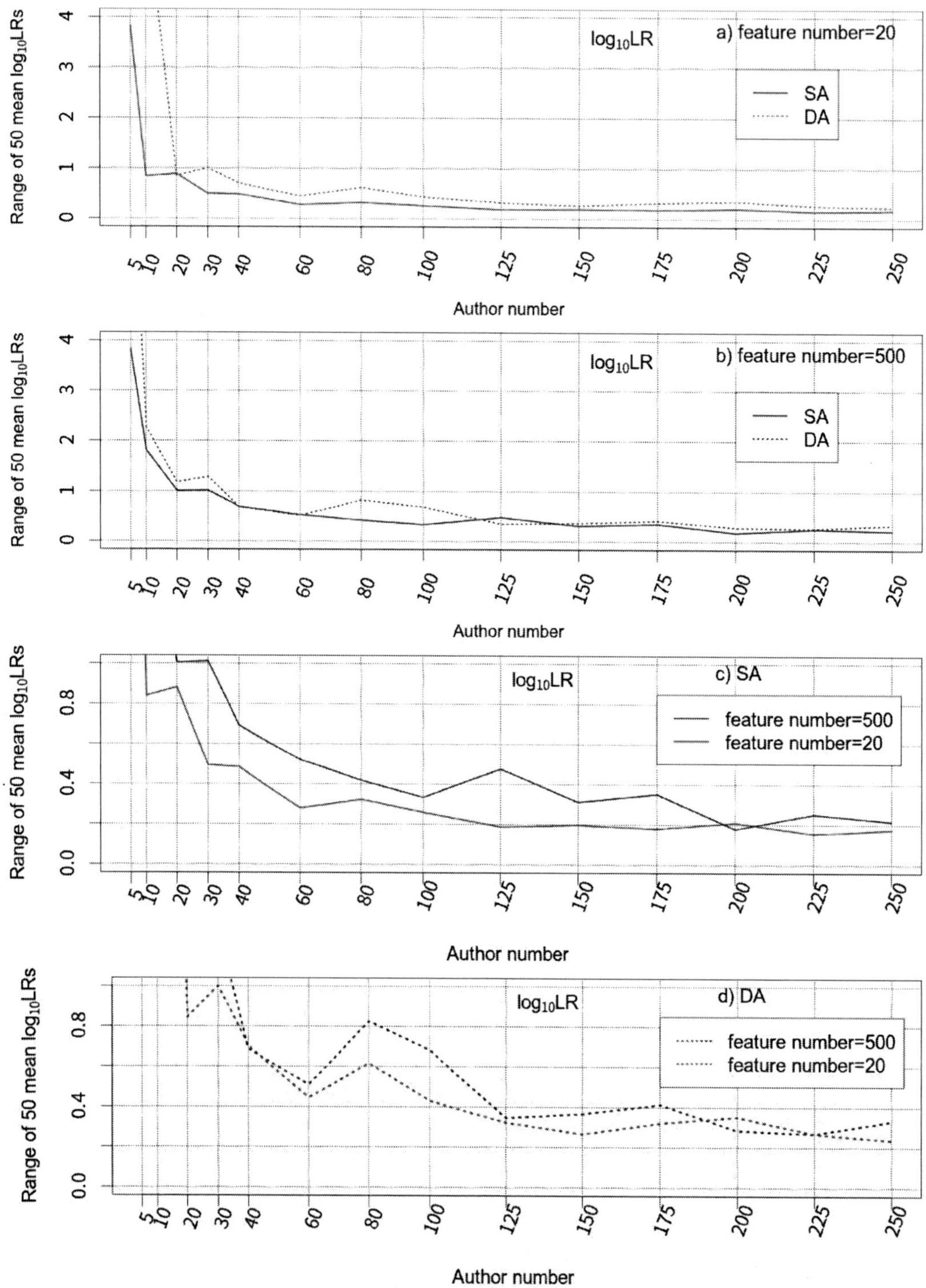

Figure 6: Range of the 50 mean $\log_{10}$LRs plotted separately for (a) 20 features, (b) 500 features, (c) SA LRs and (d) LRs. The Y-axis is narrower for Panels c) and d). Some values are beyond the range of the Y-axis.

The different characteristics displayed between Panels a) and b) of Figure 5 for discrimination ability and calibration, respectively, mean that the deterioration in mean overall performance and wide range of performance fluctuation shown for a small number of authors in Figure 4 are largely due to poor performance in calibration, not discrimination performance.

3.4 Variability in Likelihood Ratios

The variability in performance reported in Subsection 3.2 is fundamentally caused by variability in the derived LRs. Thus, this subsection investigates the characteristics of the derived SA and DS LRs. For each number of k authors, experiments were repeated 50 times by randomly sampling authors from the entire database for each sub-database. Therefore, for the same k, each iteration of the experiment should return k SA LRs and $\binom{k}{2}$ DA LRs. The mean values of the SA and DA LRs were calculated for each iteration. Wide variation in the mean LR was expected for a small k. The range of the mean SA and DA LRs was also calculated for each k to assess the degree of variability observed in LRs.

The ranges of the mean LRs for 20 and 500 features are plotted in Figure 6a and 6b, respectively. As for the variability in overall performance (see Figure 4), the range of the mean LRs observed with 5 authors quickly tapers and starts converging for 30–40 authors, regardless of the number of features and whether SA or DA comparisons are made.

In Figure 6c and 6d, the range of mean $\log_{10}$LR values are plotted against SA or DA LRs, respectively, to visually investigate any influences arising from the different number of features on the (in)stability of the derived LRs. A narrower Y-axis range was used in Figures 6c and 6d; the values beyond the Y-axis range are given in Table 2.

	Author number	Features number	
		20	**500**
SA	**5**	3.81995	3.83104
	10	0.84000	1.81251
	20	0.88233	1.00447
DA	**5**	4.35546	8.46658
	10	6.27607	2.26897
	20	0.84479	1.17478

Table 2: Ranges of the mean $\log_{10}$LR values with 20 and 500 features for 5, 10 and 20 authors.

Although the data in Figure 6c and 6d and Table 2 is not straightforwardly clear for the DA LRs, the derived LRs are susceptible to instability when the dimension of the feature vector is high. However, this difference is negated when 200 or more authors are included.

4 Conclusions

This study investigated the reliability and validity of a LR-based FTC system by varying the sampling number and sample size. When only 5 authors were included in the test, reference and calibration sub-databases (two 4 kB documents from each author), the reliability and validity of the system were considerably compromised. However, adding more authors to the database compensated for this deterioration in reliability and validity. When 30–40 authors were included, the mean performance (validity) of the system was nearly equivalent to that for as many as 720 authors. Likewise, when 30–40 authors were included, the fluctuation (reliability) of the system performance substantially decreases and starts to converge. A similar observation was made for the derived LRs; the wide range of the mean LR values across 50 iterations of experiments with 5 authors greatly diminishes if 30–40 authors are included in each sub-database.

The experimental results also show: 1) a system with a high dimension of feature vector (500 features) is more prone to instability than a system with fewer feature vectors (20 features), and 2) the low reliability and poor validity found when a small number of authors are included (e.g., 5 and 10 authors) are largely due to the poor calibration, not discrimination ability, of the system.

The approach that was employed in this study is rather primitive; e.g. the number and type of features, and there would be considerable potential to improve the model, consequently leading to a better performance. However, this may compromise the stability of the system due to the resultant even higher dimensionality of feature vector. This needs further investigation, while seeking the benefits of feature selection/reduction.

In the current study, the (in)stability and overall performance of the FTC system was measured. However, besides the quantification, the instability of the system ultimately needs to be minimised to prevent the misinterpretation of evidence and miscarriage of justice. As such, it is essential to apply a Bayesian statistical approach that considers the degree of uncertainty to the LRs (Morrison and Poh, 2018) with the outcome being Bayes factors. Obviously, the application of a Bayesian statistical approach to FTC is another step to take as an extension of the current study.

Acknowledgments

The authors thank the reviewers for their valuable comments.

References

Colin G. G. Aitken. 1995. *Statistics and the Evaluation of Evidence for Forensic Scientists*. John Wiley & Sons Ltd, Chichester.

C. G. G. Aitken and D. A. Stoney. 1991. *The Use of Statistics in Forensic Science*. Ellis Horwood, New York, NY.

K. Benoit, K. Watanabe, H. Wang, P. Nulty, A. Obeng, S. Müller, A. and Matsuo. 2018. quanteda: An R package for the quantitative analysis of textual data. *Journal of Open Source Software*, 3(30):774–776. https://doi.org/10.21105/joss.00774

A. Bolck and A. Stamouli. 2017. Likelihood ratios for categorical evidence: Comparison of LR models applied to gunshot residue data. *Law, Probability and Risk*, 16(2–3):71–90. https://dx.doi.org/10.1093/lpr/mgx005

N. Brümmer and A. Swart. 2014. Bayesian calibration for forensic evidence reporting. *Proceedings of Interspeech*, 2014:388–392.

T. Grant. 2022. *The Idea of Progress in Forensic Authorship Analysis*. Cambridge University Press, Cambridge.

O. Halvani, C. Winter and L. Graner. 2017. Authorship verification based on compression-models. *Computing Research Repository*. ArXiv:1706.00516. Version 1.

S. Ishihara. 2016. An effect of background population sample size on the performance of a likelihood ratio-based forensic text comparison system: A Monte Carlo simulation with Gaussian mixture model. In *Proceedings of the Australasian Language Technology Association Workshop 2016*, pages 113–121.

S. Ishihara. 2020. The influence of background data size on the performance of a score-based likelihood ratio system: A case of forensic text comparison. In *Proceedings of the 18th Workshop of the Australasian Language Technology Association*, pages 21–31.

S. Ishihara. 2021. Score-based likelihood ratios for linguistic text evidence with a bag-of-words model. *Forensic Science International*, 327:110980. https://doi.org/10.1016/j.forsciint.2021.110980

S. Ishihara and M. Carne. 2022. Likelihood ratio estimation for authorship text evidence: An empirical comparison of score- and feature-based methods. *Forensic Science International*, 334:111268. https://doi.org/10.1016/j.forsciint.2022.111268

G. S. Morrison. 2011. Measuring the validity and reliability of forensic likelihood-ratio systems. *Science & Justice*, 51(3):91–98. https://dx.doi.org/10.1016/j.scijus.2011.03.002

G. S. Morrison. 2013. Tutorial on logistic-regression calibration and fusion: Converting a score to a likelihood ratio. *Australian Journal of Forensic Sciences*, 45(2):173–197. https://dx.doi.org/10.1080/00450618.2012.733025

G. S. Morrison. 2016. Special issue on measuring and reporting the precision of forensic likelihood ratios: Introduction to the debate. *Science and Justice*, *56*(5):371–373. http://dx.doi.org/10.1016/j.scijus.2016.05.002

G. S. Morrison and N. Poh. 2018. Avoiding overstating the strength of forensic evidence: Shrunk likelihood ratios/Bayes factors. *Science & Justice*, 58(3):200–218. https://doi.org/10.1016/j.scijus.2017.12.005

President's Council of Advisors on Science and Technology (U.S.). 2016. *Forensic Science in Criminal Courts: Ensuring Scientific Validity of Feature-Comparison Methods*. Retrieved on 29 December 2018, from https://obamawhitehouse.archives.gov/sites/default/files/microsites/ostp/PCAST/pcast_forensic_science_report_final.pdf

D. Ramos and J. Gonzalez-Rodriguez. 2013. Reliable support: Measuring calibration of likelihood ratios. *Forensic Science International*, 230(1–3):156–169. https//dx.doi.org/10.1016/j.forsciint.2013.04.014

B. Robertson, G. A. Vignaux and C. E. H. Berger. 2016. *Interpreting Evidence: Evaluating Forensic Science in the Courtroom* (second ed.). John Wiley & sons Ltd, Chichester.

B. W. Silverman. 1986. *Density Estimation for Statistics and Data Analysis*. Chapman and Hall, London, New York.

B. X. Wang, V. Hughes and P. Foulkes. 2022. The effect of sampling variability on systems and individual speakers in likelihood ratio-based forensic voice comparison. *Speech Communication*, 138:38–49. https://doi.org/10.1016/j.specom.2022.01.009

Academic Curriculum Generation using Wikipedia for External Knowledge

Anurag Reddy Muthyala
IIIT Hyderabad
India
anurag.reddy@research.iiit.ac.in
&
Vikram Pudi
IIIT Hyderabad
India
vikram@iiit.ac.in

November 15, 2022

Abstract

In this paper, we address the problem of automatic academic curriculum generation. A curriculum outlines definitive topics with their sub-topics and enables teachers and students to form an overall idea of the course outcomes and goals, and a plan of what to teach and learn to achieve those goals. Automatic curriculum generation is relevant in modern times with the ever increasing, rapidly changing, digitally-available academic content, that is too large for manual processing by human teams. Using Wikipedia as an external knowledge-base, along with a pipeline of standard components, we show that it is possible to generate human-interpretable 2-level topic hierarchies. We show that our approach works on publicly available textbooks, by first removing their title-structure, and then automatically regenerating a 2-level title structure that is on-par.

1 Introduction

We address the problem of automatic academic curriculum generation. We treat a curriculum as one that outlines definitive topics with their sub-topics, in order to enable teachers and students to form an overall idea of the course outcomes and goals, along with a plan of what to teach and learn to achieve those goals.

Automatic curriculum generation is relevant in modern times with the ever increasing, rapidly changing, digitally-available academic content, that is too large for manual processing by human teams. The need for automation is crucially felt in interdisciplinary fields [Jacobi(2014)], and to personalize content and presentation for individual student needs and flow [Katuk and Ryu(2010)].

We formulate the problem as generating a 2-level human-interpretable topic hierarchy consisting of module titles and the topics within those modules. This caters to the most common requirement of most academic curricula. However, we add that this formulation is not restrictive as it is possible, when needed, to devise methods to generate deeper hierarchies using the base method for 2-level hierarchies through recursive application.

We aim to implement a subject-centered generative model that generates topics based on the domain knowledge instead of the learner's ability. This ensures that we generate a uniform structure for all learners, which is the typical goal of a curriculum.

Our model is an unsupervised approach based on the probability distribution of words for topic generation. We incorporate the salient features necessary for generating curriculum from given set of documents.

The primary objective is to generate a 2-level module-topic hierarchy following a data-driven approach that does not depend on the academic domain and discipline. Our model is a simple pipeline of standard components. In order to create a semantic structure (titles) from the candidates that are generated, we use Wikipedia for external knowledge and links to Wikipedia pages as learning objects to enhance learner's curiosity. Employing the previously mentioned approaches, we generate module-topic hierarchies that are on par with human generated ones, by using ideas (described in Section 3) of semantic structure, maximum coverage, relationship sanity and curriculum ambiguity.

2 Related Work

There is very little work that focuses on academic curriculum generation. In [Jacobi(2014)], the authors propose an approach for interdisciplinary fields that is based on how curricula may be designed manually in the real world. For instance, it contains steps to generate a consensus on the topics chosen. Several steps of this method require manual input by domain experts, who may be hard to find for novel interdisciplinary fields. Inputs include a core skill levels list, application skill levels list, etc. Our system aims to overcome this limitation and extend the capability by being entirely data-driven. The area of topic modelling has been widely studied over the years for its extensive applications in diverse fields [J. Boyd-Graber and Mimno(2017)]. Topic models help the reader to understand the general theme of the given document. This is achieved by associating each topic in the document to generated key phrases which best represent them. Although there are several topic modelling algorithms like LDA [David M. Blei and Jordan(2003)] and its variants, they are designed to derive a fixed set of topics from a corpus. The intuition behind LDA is based on reverse-engineering the process of creating a document using keywords occurring in it. LDA generates a set of keywords which are not structured into hierarchies, and hence cannot be directly used for our task. A variant of LDA was implemented in [P. Liu and Wang(2012)] which generates a *hierarchy* of topics. Unfortunately both LDA and this variant produce topics that are mathematical representations suitable for machine-processing but not for human readability. Aside from LDA and its derived methods, graph-based ranking algorithms similar to PageRank Algorithm [Page et al.(1998)Page, Brin, Motwani, and Winograd] have been implemented for the task of topic modelling. The TextRank Algorithm [Mihalcea and Tarau(2004)] was the first one to generate keyphrases pertaining to the topics by creating a graph using the words, and their edge relations were derived based on the offset in the document. However, this algorithm doesn't consider the hierarchical relationships between topics that is necessary for curriculum generation. Similar drawback can be observed in the SingleRank Algorithm [Wan and Xiao(2008)] which considers different documents to enrich the topics generated.

3 Design of Our Approach

In order to generates module-topic hierarchies that are on par with human generated ones, we pay attention to the following factors:

- *Natural Language:* The topics that are generated by our model should be human-readable. This requires that topics are not just machine-readable mathematical representations, but grammatically-sound natural language phrases. We easily achieve this by using titles of Wikipedia articles as topic and module titles.

- *Maximum Coverage:* While generating the curriculum, we need to ensure that all key topics are included. While we filter out some topics on the basis that they are not noun-phrases, we ensure that all the remaining topics are included. As our topics correspond to Wikipedia article titles, we consider them as valid topics to be included in some module of the curriculum.

- *Relationship Sanity:* Understanding the relationship between modules and topics is paramount to the process of curriculum generation. While establishing links, we need to ensure that a module is paired with a topic if they are similar (using standard similarity measures of their word-probability distributions). It is also important to keep a module:topic pair disjoint if they are different. In our current approach, each topic is mapped to exactly one module. However, a topic's assignment to multiple modules may be permitted easily if desired. Existing models like TextRank and SingleRank employ ranks or thresholds to map topics to modules. In contrast, we use a clustering-based approach as we already have topics and their titles using

Wikipedia and only need to cluster them into modules.

- *Curriculum Ambiguity:* The keywords, topics and modules extracted are subjective, and there can be quite a bit of disagreement even among human-teams generating them. Variations in the topic distribution generated by different models are possible, and these can lead to different curricula. Thus, several different possible curricula generated can be considered valid since they each include keywords, topics and modules that describe the text. Hence, the validation of the model's performance cannot be restricted to one structure obtained from the document. We need to apply proper metrics which does not penalize the variations in the curriculum obtained.

For generating the curriculum, we need to generate topics (with human-readable titles) and then aggregate similar topics together to generate and name the modules.

4 Detailed Methodology

We propose an unsupervised, extractive model with a little abstraction offered from the external knowledge base to accomplish the task.

4.1 Candidate Generation

The initial step of the model is to extract keywords from the document. This is achieved by generating n-grams which will act as the candidates set for topics. During the exploration of the Wikipedia data dump; it was observed that 81.25% of the total (near 16 million) Wikipedia titles considered were made up of 1-3 words. The number of n-grams generated can be scaled with the size of processing text. The candidates set which occurs frequently with incorrect semantic structure does not add any importance, hence we eliminate the n-grams which are semantically or grammatically incorrect.
To accomplish the task of removing any semantically incorrect candidates, we consider the candidates which form a noun phrase. While exploring the data dump, it was also observed that more than 94% of the titles consisted of noun phrases. To incorporate this, we devised an approach to find candidate sets for different values of n. For unigrams/uni-grams, verify if the derived monogram is either a singular or plural noun. If the uni gram belongs to any other POS (parts of speech), discard it. The unigrams/uni-grams identified were also filtered based on occurrences for accurate prediction of titles. If the bigrams/bi-grams and trigrams/tri-grams are noun phrases with minor occurences of stopwords, they are added to the candidate set.

4.2 Using Wikipedia as external Knowledge Base

Wikipedia is the largest and most comprehensive knowledge source on the web with the latest information. It is well-structured with each Wiki page providing information on a particular topic and title serves as the main topic and references and links present show related topics. We have used close to 16 million titles in our task for generating titles based on the candidate set. As described previously, the model is developed with the focus to make it robust in its use. Our model can generate the titles from documents structured in different formats like articles, papers, transcribed speeches, scripts, comments etc. This model is also capable of segregating the modules belonging to different domains without compromising the module-topic relations. Wikipedia has information on various domains which expands our field of study into all those domains.

4.3 Search and Similarity Comparison

An efficient search engine was developed for our system for searching relevant titles from the Wikipedia title dump [1]. In the previous sections, we have discussed how the n-grams which constitute the candidate set are generated to find the topics. Each candidate can be considered as an entity adding significance to the document. We use these candidates to search for the appropriate titles from Wikipedia which can be used as the topics. For each candidate set, we retrieve an average of 15 titles which contain most of the keywords in the candidate set. However, all the titles that are retrieved will not be considered during the generation of the curriculum. These topics are used later for the hierarchical modelling which generates the curriculum.

[1] Wikipedia Title Dump

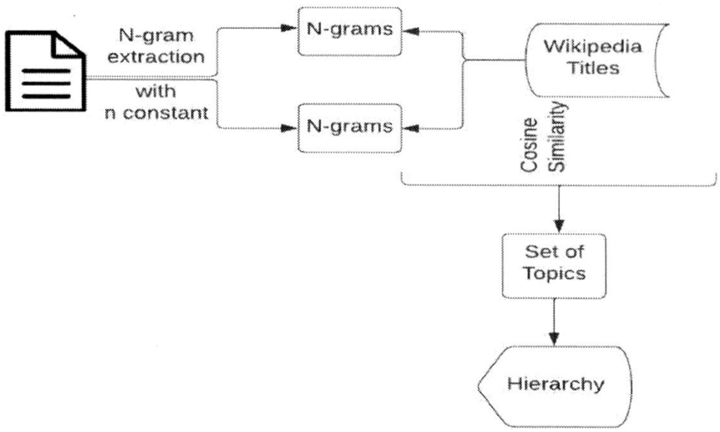

Figure 1: Methodology for leveraging Wikipedia Titles for Module Generation

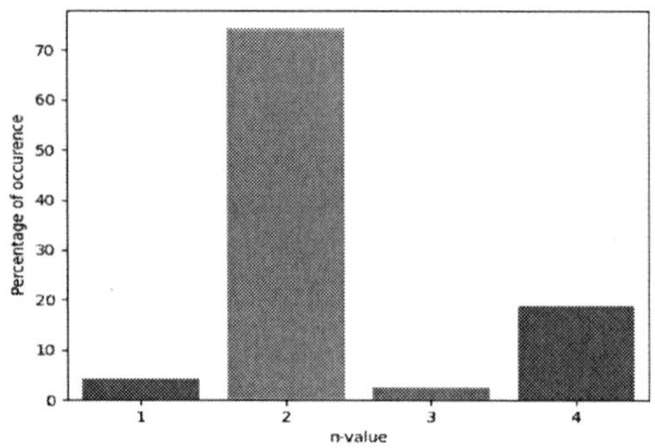

Figure 2: Percentage occurrence of n-grams

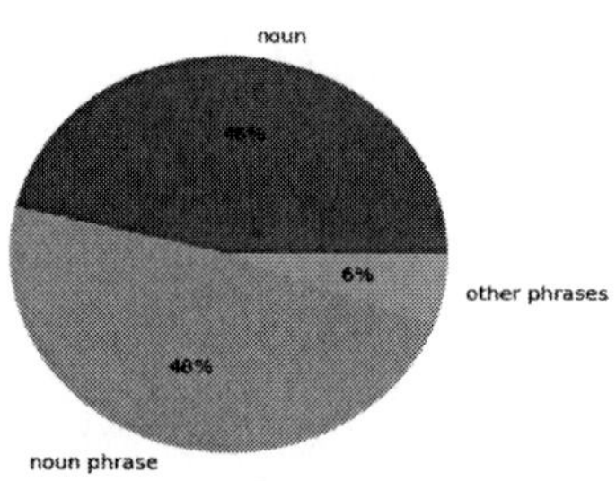

Figure 3: Percentage of occurence for noun phrases

The next step in topic generation is to remove any unwanted topics retrieved and segregate the remaining topics into modules to generate the curriculum. We have performed various experiments like distance metrics (L-norms), similarity metrics like levenshtein distance, cosine similarity etc to remove any unwanted titles. After experimentation, the best approach to get the titles was comparing cosine similarity of n-grams obtained and the Wikipedia titles derived. For any two vectors $v1$ and $v2$,

$$sim(v1, v2) = \frac{v1.v2}{||v1||.||v2||} \tag{1}$$

Before comparing similarity, we obtain a vector representation for the keyphrases and the titles which are to be compared. We achieve this using the unsupervised FastText representation over each keyphrase or title. Since the words can be from any domain, an unsupervised approach is recommended for vector embeddings of the words. Hence, we do not consider supervised representations like GLoVE, CoVE etc. The FastText model is trained on the wikipedia data dump before it is used for generating vector representations of each candidate generated. Cosine similarity is obtained between two sentence vectors obtained from the keyphrase and the title. The Wikipedia titles with high cosine similarity were considered to maintain accuracy in the titles. The result of this step is the topics and sub-topics for the given text document.

4.4 Hierarchical Modeling

A deep understanding of any module can occur if and only if the sub-topics can be clustered and put together to form a concept corresponding to that module. A 2-level hierarchy for a curriculum is the best way to portray the contents. Consider the matrix M where $M_{i,j}$ denotes the similarity between titles t_i, t_j. We use the Indicator function I_c defined as,

$$I_c(i,j) = \begin{cases} 1 & \text{if } M_{i,j} \geq \lambda \\ 0 & \text{if } otherwise \end{cases} \tag{2}$$

The proposed system derives a method wherein modules are formed by connecting all the Wikipedia titles with each other in a matrix based on similarity and classifying them into modules using the Indicator function mentioned above with a threshold(λ) as the clustering factor. Given a cluster of titles $m_i = \{t_1, t_2, t_3, ..., t_{N_i}\}$ where N_i denotes the number of titles in cluster m_i, the title of the module is given by,

$$title(m_i) = LCS(t_1, t_2, ..., t_{N_i}) \tag{3}$$

where, $LCS(.)$ is the longest common subsequence function. In our analysis, we have observed that the module titles are formed from the words that are common to two or more titles and form noun phrases. Hence, we consider this title function after verification using POS tagging.

5 Experiments

5.1 Dataset

To show the results of our curriculum generation system, we used publicly available textbooks, where title structure has been removed, from the Central Board of Secondary Education (CBSE) [2] website from classes 8-12 and for different subjects but not limited to Biology, Physics and Social Sciences, available at National Council of Educational Research and Training (NCERT) [3] website. The curriculum within the books enabled us to compare our results with the curriculum generated with our model.

[2] CBSE official website

[3] NCERT Textbooks Link

5.2 Results

A quantifiable evaluation of the result is difficult due to lack of standard procedures for topic detection and curriculum generation tasks. However, we have showcased results obtained through LDA in Table 1, to compare as the baseline method. It is evident that we are extracting module titles which are monograms. LDA was developed with the intent to generate documents based on the keywords corresponding to them.

Topic Name
ACCELERATION
AXIS
BODY
CENTER
ENERGY
FORCE
LAW
MASS
MOMENTUM
MOTION
OBJECT
PARTICLE
POINT
SPEED
SYSTEM
TIME
VELOCITY

Table 1: LDA keyword extraction performed on 10th grade CBSE Physics Textbook

The results shown in Table 2, has 8 modules in contents whereas our model generated 12 learning objects with precise distinction. On evaluation from faculty and observation, it was noticed that our model has grouped sub-topics based on the right parameters and upon evaluation, it is noticed that all Wikipedia pages in sub-topics are related as references to the title Wikipedia page. The module names with no sub-topics are not grouped together because the model performs an extractive task and recognises words from the input text provided like the module *Kinematics* which would contain *average speed, average velocity, acceleration*.

The 12th grade Biology textbook considered for the model of Table 3 lists only topics in the curriculum page. Our system was able to generate sub-topics and depict a correlation between them. Similar results have been produced for several other textbooks and articles from the Internet. Apart from that, we were able to generate a inter-disciplinary

Module Name	Sub-Topics
GRAVITY	Center of Gravity Force of Gravity
UNITS	SI Units Base Units Derived Units
LAWS	Law of Gravitation Laws of Motion Laws of Nature
MOTION	Uniform Motion Translational Motion Rotational Motion
FRICTION	Static Friction Kinetic Friction Co-efficient of Friction Force of Friction
QUANTITIES	Base Quantities Physical Quantities
MOMENTUM	Total Angular Momentum Change in Momentum Linear Angular Momentum Angular Momentum
MOMENT	Moment of Inertia Moment of Force
AVERAGE SPEED	
KINETIC ENERGY	
ACCELERATION	
AVERAGE VELOCITY	

Table 2: Hierachy obtained on 10th grade CBSE Physics Textbook

curriculum for the given text with several modules formed for different subjects.

Module Name	Sub-Topics
REPRODUCTION	Human Reproduction Asexual Reproduction Sexual Reproduction Reproductive Health
GENETIC	Genetic Evolution Genetic Inheritance
HUMAN WELFARE	Human Biological Welfare
BIOTECHNOLOGY	Principles of Biotechnology Biotechnology Applications
ECOLOGY	

Table 3: Hierachy obtained on 12th grade CBSE Biology Textbook

Though there are no established metrics for quantifying the quality of the modules and subtopics generated, considering the unsupervised learning criterion, we try to quantify it assuming the modules as clusters.

Subject	Intracluster	Intercluster
Biology	0.04	0.3
Physics	0.04	0.2
Physics and Politics	0.04	0.2

Table 4: Similarity metrics for the modules generated

In Table 4, we see the average intercluster and intracluster distances between the modules and the topics within them. We expect the intercluster distances to be high and intracluster distances to be low. By this, we can say that the modules generated are distinct from each other, and the topics within the module are similar to the module they belong to. Upon observing the values in the table, we can see that though the values are very low, relatively, intercluster distances are greater than intracluster distances. This shows that the modules generated are properly structured.

Subject	Min	Max	Avg
Physics	0.238	0.937	0.476
Biology	0.416	0.973	0.742
Physics and Politics	0.377	0.937	0.601

Table 5: METEOR Scores for the modules generated

In Table 5, we see the minimum,maximum and average METEOR[Lavie and Agarwal(2007)] scores for each textbook. We chose this metric over other machine translation outputs metrics because of it's additional feature of stemming and synonymy matching, along with greater co-relation with human judgment than the other metrics like ROUGE, BLEU etc. We have mapped our system-generated topic and module names with ones in our dataset and calculated the metric. As we can observe, the maximum METEOR score for all textbooks is 0.937, almost equal to 1, which demonstrates that generated modules are very close to the original textbook modules. The average score is almost 0.6, which shows that our system-generated topics and modules are analogous to textbook modules and topics.

The results in Table 6 depict the performance and distinguishability of our model when is the input is from two different disciplines but distinct modules with an inter-disciplinary hierarchy has been formed.

Module Name	Sub-Topics
HEAT	Heat and Electricity Heat and Light Conductors of Heat
CELL	Cell Structure Cell Membrane Cell Wall Plant cells Animal cells
FRICTION	Force of Friction Static Friction Sliding Friction Rolling Friction
REFLECTION	Laws of Reflection Angle of Reflection Diffused Reflection
POLLUTION	Noise Pollution Air Pollution
SOLAR SYSTEM	
FORCE	Applied Force Muscular Force Frictional Force
PRESSURE	Atmospheric Pressure
COMBUSTION	
COAL	
PETROLEUM	
DEMOCRACY	Democracy and Equality Development of Democarcy
HEALTH CARE FACILITIES	
GENDER	Gender Equality
MEDIA	
MARKETS	Putting-Out-System
WOMEN	Women Harassment Women Equality Women Empowerment

Table 6: Hierarchy obtained on 8th grade Science and 7th grade Social textbook

6 Conclusion

In this paper, we presented a pipeline of standard components and using Wikipedia as the external Knowledge Base to generate human interpretable 2-level hierarchies.

Based on the concept of candidate item set generation, we are able to create a set of unigrams/unigrams, bigrams/bi-grams and trigrams/tri-grams which are the learning objects and can be mapped to Wikipedia titles. The proposed model is evaluated with the help of general observations and experienced faculty on publicly available data sets. The input is not limited to a single subject textbook and can contain text from the web such as web content, news articles, blogs, etc.

The task of Curriculum Generation is carried out by an extractive model and therefore, titles which do not occur in text cannot be grouped under module names.

We believe that our model can be extended to developing deeper hierarchies beyond 2 levels. For future work, we will further improve our candidate item set generation techniques, taking into context the data they are present in. Moreover, we will utilize the linking structure between Wikipedia pages to develop a deeper hierarchy with better co-relations. Aside from the drawbacks of extractive models, we can also try to pursue the problem using abstractive approaches.

References

[David M. Blei and Jordan(2003)] Andrew Y. Ng David M. Blei and Michael I. Jordan. 2003. Latent dirichlet allocation. *Journal of Machine Learning Research 3*, pages 993–1022. Version 3.

[J. Boyd-Graber and Mimno(2017)] Y. Hu J. Boyd-Graber and D. Mimno. 2017. *Applications of Topic Models. Foundations and Trends 244 in Information Retrieval*, volume 11.

[Jacobi(2014)] Steffen Krawatzeck Robert Dinter Barbara Lorenz Anja. Jacobi, Frieder Jahn. 2014. Towards a design model for interdisciplinary information systems curriculum development, as exemplified by big data analytics education. In *22nd European Conference on Information Systems*.

[Katuk and Ryu(2010)] Norliza Katuk and Hokyoung Ryu. 2010. Finding an optimal learning path in dynamic curriculum sequencing with flow experience.

[Lavie and Agarwal(2007)] Alon Lavie and Abhaya Agarwal. 2007. Meteor: An automatic metric for mt evaluation with high levels of correlation with human judgments. pages 228–231.

[Mihalcea and Tarau(2004)] Rada Mihalcea and Paul Tarau. 2004. TextRank: Bringing order into text. In *Proceedings of the 2004 Conference on Empirical Methods in Natural Language Processing*, pages 404–411, Barcelona,

Spain. Association for Computational Linguistics.

[P. Liu and Wang(2012)] W. Heng P. Liu, L. Li and B. Wang. 2012. Hlda based text clustering. *2012 IEEE 2nd International Conference on Cloud Computing and Intelligence Systems*, pages 1465–1469.

[Page et al.(1998)Page, Brin, Motwani, and Winograd] Larry Page, Sergey Brin, R. Motwani, and T. Winograd. 1998. The pagerank citation ranking: Bringing order to the web.

[Wan and Xiao(2008)] Xiaojun Wan and Jianguo Xiao. 2008. Single document keyphrase extraction using neighborhood knowledge.

Interactive Rationale Extraction for Text Classification

Jiayi Dai[1] and **Mi-Young Kim**[2] and **Randy Goebel**[1,3]
[1]Department of Computing Science
University of Alberta
[2]Department of Science, Augustana Faculty
University of Alberta
[3]Alberta Machine Intelligence Institute
University of Alberta
{dai1, miyoung2, rgoebel}@ualberta.ca

Abstract

Deep neural networks show superior performance in text classification tasks, but their poor interpretability and explainability can cause trust issues. For text classification problems, the identification of textual sub-phrases or "rationales" is one strategy for attempting to find the most influential portions of text, which can be conveyed as critical in making classification decisions. Selective models for rationale extraction faithfully explain a neural classifier's predictions by training a rationale generator and a text classifier jointly: the generator identifies rationales and the classifier predicts a category solely based on the rationales. The selected rationales are then viewed as the explanations for the classifier's predictions. Through exchange of such explanations, humans interact to achieve higher performance in problem solving. To imitate the interactive process of humans, we propose a simple interactive rationale extraction architecture that selects a pair of rationales and then makes predictions from two independently trained selective models. We show how this architecture outperforms both base models for text classification tasks on datasets *IMDB movie reviews* and *20 Newsgroups* in terms of predictive performance.

1 Introduction

Selective (or select-predict) models for rationale extraction in text classification (Lei et al., 2016; Bastings et al., 2019), with the general structure shown in Figure 1, are designed to extract a set of words, namely a *rationale* (Zaidan et al., 2007), from an original text where, for prediction purposes, the rationale is expected to be *sufficient* as the input for the classification model to obtain the same prediction based on the whole text. For the purpose of interpretability, the rationale should be *concise* and *contiguous*. A rationale extraction model is *faithful* (Lipton, 2018) if the extracted rationales are truly the information used for classification (Jain et al., 2020). The problem of extracting rationales that satisfy the criteria above is complex from a machine learning perspective and becomes more difficult with only instance-level supervision (i.e., without token-level annotations) (Jain et al., 2020). One model's identification of rationales can suffer from high variance because of the complex training process. An ensemble of more than one model helps to reduce variance, which leads to the exploration of *how to take use of two rationale extraction models and how to make a choice when the two models make different predictions.*

When two humans have different answers to a problem, they tend to exchange their reasons or explanations, after which there might be a change of mind. To show why this interaction of humans is effective, we use the problem of proving a mathematical conjuncture as an instance: because searching for a correct mathematical proof, which then leads to a correct claim about the conjuncture, is usually much more difficult than verifying a proof (e.g., $\mathcal{P} \subseteq \mathcal{NP}$ in computation theory), often one who is not capable of finding a good proof can tell if a proof is good when the proof is given. Considering the complexity for a generator to search among all possible rationales with only remote instance-level supervision, the work of rationale extraction can be much more difficult than classification.

We may then consider selective models for rationale extraction to be naturally compatible with the interactive pattern of humans by viewing the rationales extracted by a generator as the proofs for the decisions of its classifier, which means the interaction between two base models can be performed by the exchange of their rationales. Subsequently, the problem becomes how to decide if a rationale is good or not so that we know which pairs of rationale and prediction are appropriate choices when

[0]The implementation is provided on https://github.com/JiayiDai/RationaleExtraction.

two base models make different predictions. A *good rationale* here is expected to give a correct prediction when input to a decent classifier.

Intuitively, a good rationale is supposed to contain strong indicators for the correct "gold label" instead of insignificant words which do not contribute to classification, which leads to two simple rules for handling base models' disagreements: first, a good rationale is more likely to produce consistent predictions among classifiers (i.e., a good explanation convinces people); second, a good rationale is more likely to produce a higher *confidence level* (Section 2.2) for the prediction of one classifier (i.e., one with a good reason is often confident). The two rules are created a basis for classification, as opposed to random guessing based on otherwise randomly selected words. Note that the two rules are based on the assumption that the probability that base models extract strong indicators for wrong labels is very low, which should be considered to be true for decent generators and decent classifiers (i.e., better than random guessing).

To imitate the interactive pattern of humans in problem solving, we introduce **Interactive Rationale Extraction for Text Classification** to interactively connect two independently trained selective rationale extraction models. We show the architecture achieves higher predictive performance than either base models with similar performance on *IMDB movie reviews* and *20 Newsgroups*. This is done by selecting pairs of rationale and prediction from the base models using the above simple rules. In addition, because this interactive architecture makes decisions solely based on the base models' rationales, the faithfulness and interpretability of the base models' rationales are not compromised.

2 Background

2.1 Selective Rationale Extraction

The original selective rationale extraction model was proposed by (Lei et al., 2016) with an architecture shown in Figure 1. Their model faithfully explains a neural network-based classifier's predictions by jointly training a generator and a classifier with only instance-level supervision. We summarize their work as follows. The generator g consumes the embedded tokens of the original text, namely $x = [x_1, x_2, ..., x_l]$ where l is the number of the tokens in the text and each token $x_i \in \mathbb{R}^d$ is an d dimensional embedding vector, and outputs a probability distribution $p(z|x)$ over the hard mask $z = [z_1, z_2, ..., z_l]$ where each value $z_i \in \{0, 1\}$ denotes whether the corresponding token is selected. A rationale r is defined as (z, x) representing the hard mask z over the original input x. Subsequently, the classifier f takes (z, x) as input to make a prediction $f(z, x)$. Given gold label y, the loss function used to optimize both generator g and classifier f is defined as

$$loss(z, x, y) =$$
$$||f(z, x) - y||_2^2 + \lambda_1||z|| + \lambda_2 \sum_{i=1}^{l-1} |z_i - z_{i+1}| \quad (1)$$

which consists of three parts: prediction loss, selection loss and contiguity loss. The parameters λ_1 and λ_2 in the loss function are used to tune the constraints on rationales (i.e., conciseness and contiguity). Jain et al. (2020) modified the loss function to apply hard constraints on rationales (i.e., maximum length) by not punishing a model when a given limit on the number of words is not reached.

Because of the absence of token-level supervision and the use of hard masking which is not differentiable, Lei et al. (2016) turned to REINFORCE (Williams, 1992) for gradient estimation, which causes high variance and sensitivity to hyperparameters (Jain et al., 2020). Following the select-predict architecture proposed by Lei et al. (2016), Bastings et al. (2019) explored a reparameterization heuristic called HardKuma for gradient estimation. Furthermore, Guerreiro and Martins (2021) exposed the trade-off between differentiable masking and hard constraints in selective rationale extraction models.

2.2 Confidence Level

Confidence level (CL) indicates how far a neural network's prediction is from being neutral. Given a neural network's non-probabilistic output $k = [k_1, k_2, ..., k_n]$ for a n-class classification, Kumar et al. (2022) defined the CL of the classification with a softmax function

$$CL(k) = \frac{exp(max(k))}{\sum_{i=1}^{n} exp(k_i)} \quad (2)$$

where $max(k)$ is the value of the output node k_i with the highest value (i.e., i is the final prediction).

Guo et al. (2017) stated that a classification network should not only have a high accuracy but also indicate how likely each prediction is correct or

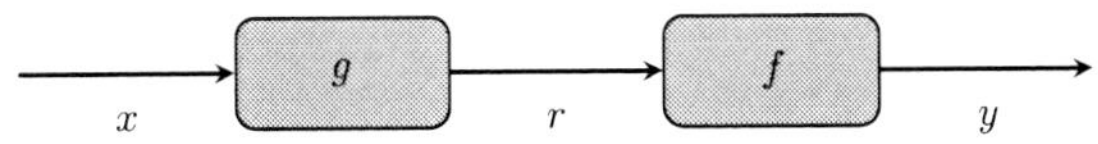

Figure 1: Schematic of selective rationale extraction models where x is an embedded text, g is a generator and f is a classifier. Generator g extracts a rationale r based on which classifier f makes a prediction y.

incorrect for trust purposes. In addition, their study on neural networks' calibration Guo et al. (2017) suggested that accuracy, even if not nearly identical to CL for some neural networks, is generally positively correlated to CL. This means that, when two base models with similar expected performance make different predictions, the prediction with a higher CL is generally more likely to be correct.

3 Algorithm

As demonstrated in Figure 2, after the interaction between two base select-predict models, a total of 4 predictions are generated: $y_1 = f_1(r_1)$, $y_1' = f_1(r_2)$, $y_2' = f_2(r_1)$ and $y_2 = f_2(r_2)$ where y_1 and y_2 are the predictions based on their own rationales and y_1' and y_2' are predictions based on the exchanged rationales, as shown in the table below.

	r_1	r_2
f_1	y_1	y_1'
f_2	y_2'	y_2

Given an input text, when the predictions of two base models are the same, namely $y_1 = y_2$, both rationales r_1, r_2 are good and the final prediction is the shared prediction. When two base models initially show a disagreement, we check if one rationale causes more consistent predictions. If r_1 causes more consistent predictions, in order words, if r_1 changes the prediction of f_2 to y_1 when given as an input rationale (namely, $y_1 = y_2'$), but r_2 does not change the prediction of f_1 to y_2 when given as an input rationale ($y_2 \neq y_1'$), then the pair (r_1, y_1) is chosen as the final rationale and prediction; symmetrically, if r_2 causes more consistent predictions, the pair (r_2, y_2) is chosen. For the cases where no rationale causes more consistent predictions, we rely on confidence levels which are real numbers between 0 and 1 as defined by expression (2). If the confidence level of f_1 on r_1 is higher than that of f_2 on r_2 (say $CL(f_1, r_1) > CL(f_2, r_2)$ with (f_1, r_1) and (f_2, r_2) separately denoting their corresponding non-probabilistic outputs), the pair (r_1, y_1) is chosen; otherwise, the pair (r_2, y_2) is chosen. The process of selecting a pair of rationale and prediction is formalized in Algorithm 1. It's worth mentioning that, in implementation, the exchange of rationales only needs to be performed when base models have a disagreement in prediction (i.e., $y_1 \neq y_2$).

4 Experiments

4.1 Datasets

IMDB movie reviews (Maas et al., 2011) This is a dataset of 50,000 movie reviews collected from the Internet Movie Database (IMDB) with binary labels (i.e., positive and negative). The dataset is originally split into two subsets: 25,000 for training and 25,000 for testing. We randomly split the training data into 20,000 (80%) for training and 5,000 (20%) for development. The numbers of the two labels are perfectly balanced in each subset.

20 Newsgroups It is a publicly available dataset containing a total of 18,846 texts, with 11,314 for training and 7,532 for testing, in 20 distinct categories of news topics. We split the training data randomly into 9,051 (80%) for training and 2,263 (20%) for development. The numbers of the 20 labels are not perfectly balanced and varying from 304 to 490 in the training data, 73 to 131 in the development data and 251 to 399 in the testing data.

4.2 Setup

Training Instead of REINFORCE (Williams, 1992), a reparameterization heuristic Gumbel-Softmax (Jang et al., 2017) is used to simplify gradient estimation. Convolutional neural network (Kim, 2014) is used for both generators and classifiers with filter sizes of [3,4,5], filter number of 100 and dropout rate of 0.5. Hidden dimensions of 100 and 120 are separately used for the first and the second base model, which is the only difference among all parameters for training two base models. Adam is used as the optimizer with a weight decay of 5e-06 and an initial learning rate of 0.001. If no improvement is achieved in loss in development dataset from the previous best model after 5 epochs, the learning rate is halved (i.e., 0.001, 0.0005...) and the training process starts over from

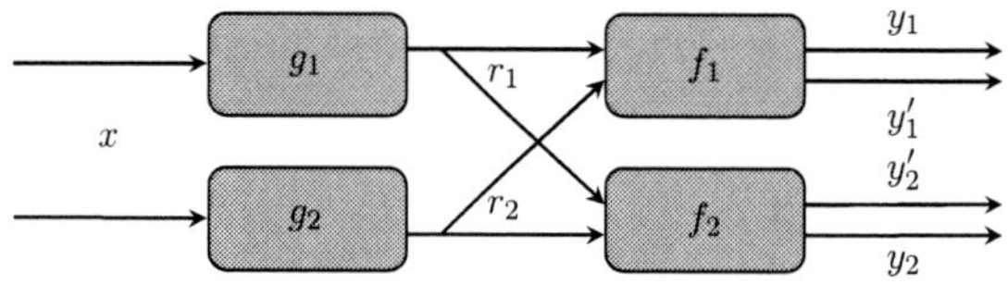

Figure 2: Schematic of our interactive rationale extraction where rationales are exchanged. The notations follow Figure 1.

Algorithm 1 Rationale-prediction Selection after Interaction

```
Require: f1, f2, r1, r2, y1, y'1, y'2, y2 from Figure 2, CL(f, r) for the confidence level of f on r.
if y1 = y2 then                                        ▷ agreement
    return (r1, y1)                                    ▷ or (r2, y2)
else                                                   ▷ disagreement
    if y1 = y'2 and y2 ≠ y'1 then                      ▷ model 2 convinced by model 1
        return (r1, y1)
    else if y1 ≠ y'2 and y2 = y'1 then                 ▷ model 1 convinced by model 2
        return (r2, y2)
    else
        if CL(f1, r1) > CL(f2, r2) then                ▷ model 1 is more confident
            return (r1, y1)
        else                                           ▷ model 2 is more confident
            return (r2, y2)
        end if
    end if
end if
```

the previous best model. In total, 20 epochs are used for training. Cross-entropy is used as the loss objective. Batch size is set to be 128. For Gumbel-Softmax (Jang et al., 2017), the initial temperature is 1 with a decay rate of 1e-5. GloVe (Pennington et al., 2014) of embedding dimension 300 is used for word embedding. The maximum text lengths are separately set to be 80 and 200 words for *20 Newsgroups* and *IMDB movie reviews*.

Testing For each dataset, two base models are independently trained and tested with two settings of hyper-parameters (λ_1, λ_2) from the loss function. $\{(0.005, 0), (0.001, 0.001)\}$ are used for *20 Newsgroups* and $\{(0.001, 0), (0.0002, 0.0002)\}$ are used for *IMDB movie reviews*. The four settings are chosen in a way to show the performance of the algorithm under different rationale length and contiguity (Table 1). For each hyper-parameter setting, both base models are trained and tested with 6 random seeds (i.e., {2022, 2023, 2024, 2025, 2026, 2027}), and the invalid cases where two base models show a significant difference in the performance in development dataset (i.e., > 3% in accuracy) are removed. The numbers of invalid cases are separately 2, 1, 1, 0 out of 6 for the four hyper-parameter settings.

4.3 Quantitative Evaluation

For quantitative evaluation, we report the predictive performance of the classifiers from base models and the interactive model. In Table 2, the interactive model outperforms the better base model by 2% in *IMDB movie reviews* and 2-3% in *20 Newsgroups* and shows a relatively smaller variance in both datasets. The improvement in predictive performance and reduced variance is general for most experiments in addition to the four settings. We found that, in the cases of extreme hyper-parameter settings where rationales contain almost whole texts or no words, there is no improvement. This seems reasonable as, when base models generate rationales of whole texts or no words, the rationales are identical, which makes the exchange of rationales meaningless. Also, in some cases where one base model is trained well and one is not (e.g., 80% and 60% accuracy in *IMDB movie reviews*), the interactive model shows a slightly lower performance than the better base model. The

20 Newsgroups				
(λ_1, λ_2)	(5e-3, 0)		(1e-3, 1e-3)	
Base Model	Model 1	Model 2	Model 1	Model 2
Length	11.33	11.18	21.76	22.68
Contiguity Loss	17.12	16.84	21.92	21.45
Interaction Cases	(331, 363, 1129, 1211.5)		(228.6, 264, 974.2, 1075.8)	
Case Accuracy	(0.41, 0.43, 0.30, 0.26)		(0.38, 0.44, 0.31, 0.27)	
IMDB movie reviews				
(λ_1, λ_2)	(1e-3, 0)		(2e-4, 2e-4)	
Base Model	Model 1	Model 2	Model 1	Model 2
Length	13.99	17.59	29.22	27.37
Contiguity Loss	21.84	26.45	37.14	35.48
Interaction Cases	(855.6, 946.0, 1187.4, 1250.0)		(681.7, 665.2, 1101.8, 1295.7)	
Case Accuracy	(0.66, 0.65, 0.59, 0.59)		(0.66, 0.64, 0.58, 0.60)	

Table 1: Experiment details (average values). We report the rationale length (i.e., number of words) and contiguity loss of each base model and also numbers of interaction cases and each case's accuracy under each hyper-parameter setting. Four values in an interaction case are the average numbers of the cases separately for base model 1 convinced, base model 2 convinced, base model 1 more confident, and base model 2 more confident. These are the four cases from handling disagreements in Algorithm 1.

	20 Newsgroups		IMDB movie reviews	
(λ_1, λ_2)	(5e-3, 0)	(1e-3, 1e-3)	(1e-3, 0)	(2e-4, 2e-4)
Model 1	.55 (.53-.57)	.58 (.56-.59)	.81 (.80-.82)	.82 (.81-.83)
Model 2	.54 (.52-.57)	.57 (.55-.59)	.81 (.80-.82)	.82 (.81-.83)
Interaction	**.58 (.56-.60)**	**.60 (.59-.61)**	**.83 (.82-.84)**	**.84 (.83-.84)**

Table 2: Average performance (accuracy) of maximum six experiments for base (Models 1 and 2) and interactive models under each hyper-parameter setting for each dataset. The (min, max) performance of each model are also reported to demonstrate variances.

reason can be that a relatively better rationale generated by the better model can not convince the classifier of the poor performance model, where the first rule that a good rationale is more likely to produce consistent predictions is not followed. If no rationale is causing consistent predictions, the second rule about confidence level is applied but a poor classifier can sometimes be overconfident, which causes errors.

For a binary classification task, when two base models with similar performance have a disagreement, the expected accuracy of each base model is around 50% and the probability of blindly choosing a prediction turning out to be correct should also be near 50% (i.e., random guessing). However, as shown in Table 1, in *IMDB movie reviews*, the accuracy after interaction is 8-16% higher than random guessing.

In addition, we observed that, when the constraints on rationales are less strict (i.e., allowing more words and more contiguity loss), generally the performance of base models increases but the improvement after interaction deceases. The reason may be that, with weaker rationale constraints, strong indicators are easier to identify causing the rationales generated by two base models to contain more overlapped strong indicators, which increases the accuracy of base models but decreases the number of cases for disagreement. It is also worth mentioning that the performance gain of the interactive algorithm is not achieved by having a tendency of choosing longer rationales as shown in Table 3.

4.4 Human Evaluation

For human or qualitative evaluation, we report human judgements on the rationales from *IMDB movie reviews* to demonstrate how informative the rationales are for humans. For each of the four disagreement cases in Algorithm 1, we randomly collect 10 movie review instances where each instance contains two rationales separately extracted by two base models and one of the two rationales is

	20 Newsgroups		IMDB movie reviews	
(λ_1, λ_2)	(5e-3, 0)	(1e-3, 1e-3)	(1e-3, 0)	(2e-4, 2e-4)
selected r	(9.19, 14.15)	(18.74, 19.42)	(14.90, 23.39)	(27.22, 36.21)
not selected r	(8.85, 13.80)	(19.03, 19.50)	(15.12, 23.71)	(27.47, 36.59)

Table 3: Lengths (numbers of words) and contiguity loss of rationales. We report the average (length, contiguity loss) of rationales that are separately selected and not selected by the interactive algorithm for handling disagreement cases under each hyper-parameter setting.

selected by the algorithm (i.e., $10 * 2 * 4 = 80$ rationales in total). Three human annotators only have access to the extracted rationales (i.e., the original texts are not provided) to ensure the sufficiency of the rationales.

Given two rationales of one instance, for each of the two rationales, we ask each human annotator to make a prediction (i.e., positive or negative) based on the rationale and tell how confident the human annotator is about this prediction on a scale from 0 to 3 (i.e., 0 represents random guessing and 3 represents very confident). The results are shown in Table 4.

annotator #	1	2	3
acc selected	.53	.70	.70
acc not selected	.48	.70	.65
CL selected	1.20	1.38	0.75
CL not selected	1.20	1.40	0.5

Table 4: Human evaluation results. The averaged prediction accuracy (acc) and confidence levels (CL) of each human annotator over 40 rationales selected by our algorithm (acc selected and CL selected) and 40 rationales not selected by the algorithm (acc not selected and CL not selected).

The overall prediction accuracy and confidence levels of human annotators are low which is reasonable as the 80 rationales are extracted from the cases where base models have disagreements and may not be able to extract strong rationales (i.e., difficult cases). Generally, human annotators do slightly better in terms of predictive performance when fed with the rationales selected by the algorithm but the difference of the results for selected and not selected rationales is not significant. Because human annotators are provided with both rationales for each instance, when asked to make a classification based on one rationale, they might also unconsciously use information from another rationale even though they are asked not to, which is a natural flaw of comparing two rationales from one instance and can possibly cause close results for two rationales. In future work, we plan to find an alternative way of survey where humans can better evaluate our algorithm's effectiveness.

5 Conclusion

To handle the high variance of selective rationale extraction models, we proposed the method we call **Interactive Rationale Extraction for Text Classification**, which selects rationales and predictions from base models based on simple rules through imitating the interaction process between humans for handling disagreements. The experimental results show that the interactive process is effective in terms of improving performance, choosing a better rationale, and reducing variance.

Acknowledgements

Adam Yala provided the implementation of base selective rationale extraction models with Gumbel-Softmax in the GitHub repository `https://github.com/yala/text_nn`, which greatly saves the implementation time for our experiments. This research was supported by the Alberta Machine Intelligence Institute (AMII) and the Canadian Natural Sciences and Engineering Research Council (NSERC) [including funding reference numbers RGPIN-2022-03469 and DGECR-2022-00369].

References

Jasmijn Bastings, Wilker Aziz, and Ivan Titov. 2019. Interpretable neural predictions with differentiable binary variables. In *Proceedings of the 57th Annual Meeting of the Association for Computational Linguistics*, pages 2963–2977, Florence, Italy. Association for Computational Linguistics.

Nuno M. Guerreiro and André F. T. Martins. 2021. SPECTRA: Sparse structured text rationalization. In *Proceedings of the 2021 Conference on Empirical Methods in Natural Language Processing*, pages 6534–6550, Online and Punta Cana, Dominican Republic. Association for Computational Linguistics.

Chuan Guo, Geoff Pleiss, Yu Sun, and Kilian Q. Weinberger. 2017. On calibration of modern neural networks. In *Proceedings of the 34th International Conference on Machine Learning*, volume 70 of *Proceedings of Machine Learning Research*, pages 1321–1330. PMLR.

Sarthak Jain, Sarah Wiegreffe, Yuval Pinter, and Byron C. Wallace. 2020. Learning to faithfully rationalize by construction. In *Proceedings of the 58th Annual Meeting of the Association for Computational Linguistics*, pages 4459–4473, Online. Association for Computational Linguistics.

Eric Jang, Shixiang Gu, and Ben Poole. 2017. Categorical reparameterization with gumbel-softmax. In *International Conference on Learning Representations*.

Yoon Kim. 2014. Convolutional neural networks for sentence classification. In *Proceedings of the 2014 Conference on Empirical Methods in Natural Language Processing (EMNLP)*, pages 1746–1751, Doha, Qatar. Association for Computational Linguistics.

Ananya Kumar, Tengyu Ma, Percy Liang, and Aditi Raghunathan. 2022. Calibrated ensembles can mitigate accuracy tradeoffs under distribution shift. In *Proceedings of the Thirty-Eighth Conference on Uncertainty in Artificial Intelligence*, volume 180 of *Proceedings of Machine Learning Research*, pages 1041–1051. PMLR.

Tao Lei, Regina Barzilay, and Tommi Jaakkola. 2016. Rationalizing neural predictions. In *Proceedings of the 2016 Conference on Empirical Methods in Natural Language Processing*, pages 107–117, Austin, Texas. Association for Computational Linguistics.

Zachary C. Lipton. 2018. The mythos of model interpretability. *Commun. ACM*, 61(10):36–43.

Andrew L. Maas, Raymond E. Daly, Peter T. Pham, Dan Huang, Andrew Y. Ng, and Christopher Potts. 2011. Learning word vectors for sentiment analysis. In *Proceedings of the 49th Annual Meeting of the Association for Computational Linguistics: Human Language Technologies*, pages 142–150, Portland, Oregon, USA. Association for Computational Linguistics.

Jeffrey Pennington, Richard Socher, and Christopher Manning. 2014. GloVe: Global vectors for word representation. In *Proceedings of the 2014 Conference on Empirical Methods in Natural Language Processing (EMNLP)*, pages 1532–1543, Doha, Qatar. Association for Computational Linguistics.

Ronald J. Williams. 1992. Simple statistical gradient-following algorithms for connectionist reinforcement learning. *Mach. Learn.*, 8(3–4):229–256.

Omar Zaidan, Jason Eisner, and Christine D. Piatko. 2007. Using “annotator rationales” to improve machine learning for text categorization. In *NAACL*.

Automatic Explanation Generation For Climate Science Claims

Rui Xing[1] **Shraey Bhatia**[1] **Timothy Baldwin**[1,2] **Jey Han Lau**[1]
[1]The University of Melbourne [2]MBZUAI
ruixing@student.unimelb.edu.au, shraeybhatia@gmail.com,
tb@ldwin.net, jeyhan.lau@gmail.com

Abstract

Climate change is an existential threat to humanity, the proliferation of unsubstantiated claims relating to climate science is manipulating public perception, motivating the need for fact-checking in climate science. In this work, we draw on recent work that uses retrieval-augmented generation for veracity prediction and explanation generation, in framing explanation generation as a query-focused multi-document summarization task. We adapt PRIMERA to the climate science domain by adding additional global attention on claims. Through automatic evaluation and qualitative analysis, we demonstrate that our method is effective at generating explanations.

1 Introduction

The rapid dissemination of misinformation and disinformation through social media is a pressing issue, especially in the domain of climate science (Diggelmann et al., 2020; Anderegg et al., 2010) where climate change has become one of the biggest challenges to humankind. Claims such as *97% consensus on human-caused global warming has been disproven* seed scepticism, discredit climate science, and manipulate public perception and interpretation. To alleviate the influence of such potentially false claims, experts have increasingly engaged in science communication, including investigating such claims based on scientific evidence through websites such as climatefeedback.org and skepticalscience.com. This paper concerns the use of external knowledge to semi-automate the process of claim verification, as an assistive technology for contributors to such websites.

Inspired by recent work on retrieval-augmented generation (Lewis et al., 2020) and explainable fact-checking (Atanasova et al., 2020), we aim to (semi-)automate the process of claim veracity classification along with explanation generation. Our work draws on previous work on generating explanations in the climate science domain (Bhatia et al., 2021a) in using claims to retrieve relevant documents from knowledge sources and then generate explanations based on these documents. Unlike prior work, we frame it as a *query-focused summarization* task (Mollá et al., 2020; Sarker et al., 2013), where the query is a claim in our case, and the goal is to summarize information from the retrieved documents that addresses the claim. We evaluate our framework quantitatively and qualitatively, and explore the impact of different variants of attention on explanation generation.[1]

Text	Label
C: Sea-level rise is not accelerating.	REFU
E1: Climate-change driven accelerated sea-level rise detected in the altimeter era.	REFU
E2: Antarctica ice melt has accelerated by 280% in the last 4 decades.	REFU
E3: However scientists have found that ice is being lost, and at an accelerating rate.	REFU
E4: Climate scientists expect the rate to further accelerate during the 21st century.	NO_INFO
E5: More precise data gathered from satellite radar measurements reveal an accelerating rise of 7.5cm (3.0in) from 1993 to 2017, which is a trend of roughly 30cm (12in) per century.	NO_INFO

Table 1: An example claim ("C") and associated evidence passages ("Ek") from Climate-Fever ("REFU" = REFUTES; "NO_INFO" = NOT_ENOUGH_INFO).

2 Related Work

Fact checking is the task of assessing whether a textual claim is true, based on a corpus or knowledge base. Conventionally, the task is performed manually by human experts (Hassan et al., 2015). However, manual efforts do not easily scale (Elazar et al., 2021), leading to increasing attention in automatic fact checking (Wang, 2017; Alhindi et al.,

[1]The code associated with this paper is available at https://github.com/ruixing76/ClimateChange-ExpGen

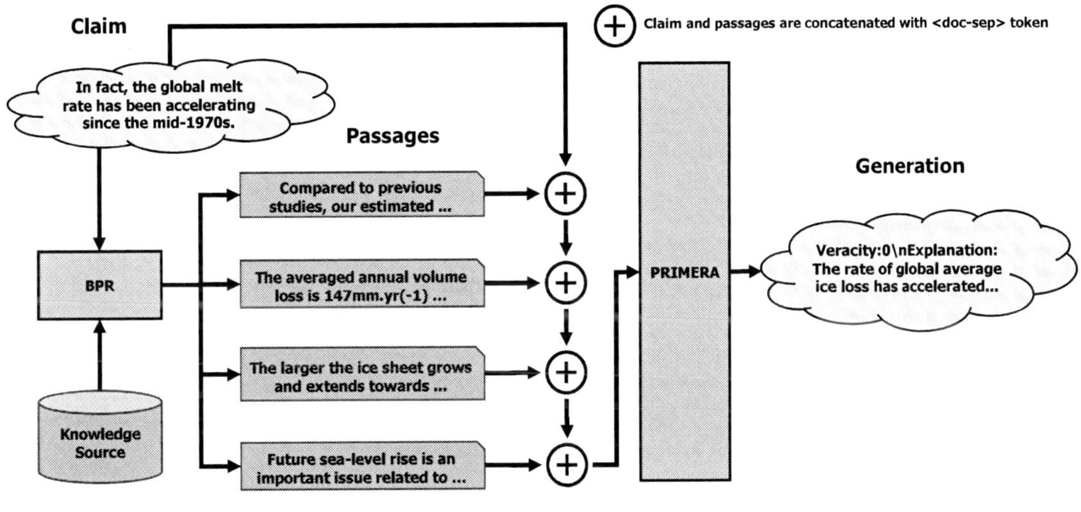

Figure 1: Overview of our method. First the claim is used as input to `BPR` to retrieve top-k claim-relevant passages (k is an adjustable hyperparameter, in this example k=4). Then the claim and passages are concatenated with `<doc-sep>` tokens for input to `PRIMERA`. Finally `PRIMERA` generates explanations together with veracity labels.

2018; Xu et al., 2019; Stammbach and Neumann, 2019; Atanasova et al., 2020). Debunking simply by assigning a *false* label to the claim is not persuasive, and can even reinforce mistaken beliefs (Lewandowsky et al., 2012). As such, it is necessary for automated fact-checking methods to provide explanations to support model predictions. For example, Popat et al. (2018) used attention-based methods to highlight salient excerpts from evidence articles, and Gad-Elrab et al. (2019) adopted knowledge bases to mine explanations. Atanasova et al. (2020) framed explanation generation as a joint classification and extractive summarization task. During generation, the model selects sentences from retrieved documents as explanations.

Separately, there has been recent work on extracting parameterized knowledge from large language models (Roberts et al., 2020), as well as augmenting them using external knowledge sources through retrieval augmentation (Karpukhin et al., 2020; Lewis et al., 2020; Yamada et al., 2021). Here, a claim or question is used to retrieve documents, which are fed into the generator as additional inputs, as a means of extending and domain-adapting large language models without additional pre-training.

There has also been recent work on the applications of NLP to the domain of climate science. Bhatia et al. (2021b) explored automatic classification of neutralization techniques in discourse relating to climate change/science. Diggelmann et al. (2020) introduced Climate-Fever as a novel dataset for veracity prediction. The closest work to our own is that on explanation generation by Bhatia et al. (2021a), which is based on fusion in decoder (Izacard and Grave, 2021), a sequence-to-sequence model that takes as input the claim and passages sourced through retrieval augmentation (Karpukhin et al., 2020; Yamada et al., 2021).

Unlike prior work, we first approach the task via multi-document summarization (Zhang et al., 2020a; Liu and Lapata, 2019; Liao et al., 2018), with a focus on the claim; as such, our approach can be interpreted as query-focused summarization. Specifically, we adopt `PRIMERA` (Xiao et al., 2022), a state-of-the-art pre-trained encoder–decoder model for multi-document summarization.

3 Data

There are two key data components in our task: (1) an external knowledge source from which we retrieve documents; and (2) paired claim–explanation data, to serve as the input (claim) and output (explanation).

For the external knowledge source, we use climate science-related abstracts from PubMed and reports from the Intergovernmental Panel on Climate Change ("IPCC"). IPCC reports are written by a mix of scientists, experts, and policy makers and provide scientific, technical, and socio-economic knowledge on climate change and options to mitigate its impacts. We sample climate science-related publications using MeSH descriptors.

Climate-Fever (Diggelmann et al., 2020) contains 1,535 claims relating to climate change. See Table 1 for an example, wherein each evidence item is labelled as SUPPORTS, REFUTES, or NOT_ENOUGH_INFO with respect to the claim. These are used to label each claim as SUPPORTS (= at least one evidence item is SUPPORTS and all others are NOT_ENOUGH_INFO), REFUTES (= at least one evidence item is REFUTES and all others are NOT_ENOUGH_INFO), NOT_ENOUGH_INFO (= all evidence items are NOT_ENOUGH_INFO), or DISPUTED (= a mixture of SUPPORTS and REFUTES evidence items). Each claim has multiple evidence items, and we create multiple claim–evidence instances for each *congruent* evidence item.[2] We discard DISPUTED claims in this work.

In our framework, the claim serves as the input for us to query the knowledge source to retrieve related documents, and the evidence constitutes the *explanation* that we want to generate as output.

4 Method

In Figure 1, we present an overview of our method, which is made up of two components: (1) a document retriever; and (2) a generator. Given a claim c_i, the retriever retrieves k passages $\{p_1, p_2, ..., p_k|c_i\}$ from the knowledge source, based on which the generator generates a veracity label y_i along with explanation e_i.[3] The generator is an encoder–decoder model which jointly processes the retrieved passages and claim in the form of an abstractive summarization model.

We adopt Binary Passage Retriever (BPR) (Yamada et al., 2021) as the retriever. BPR is a memory efficient version of dense passage retriever (Karpukhin et al., 2020). It first uses two independent BERT (Devlin et al., 2019) encoders to encode question and passages into continuous embeddings and then incorporates a hashing layer to reduce computational cost for similarity calculation. BPR is trained with a multi-task objective over two tasks: effective candidate generation based on binary codes and accurate reranking based on continuous vectors. We use the official release of BPR[4] which was pre-trained on Natural Questions (Kwiatkowski et al., 2019) without fine-tuning, and consider each claim as the query to retrieve top-*k* relevant passages from our knowledge source.

For the generator, we adopt PRIMERA (Xiao et al., 2022) to generate explanations, where the input is the claim concatenated with the top-*k* retrieved passages. PRIMERA is designed for multi-document summarization with Entity Pyramid Masking, a novel pre-training strategy to select and aggregate salient information from multiple documents. PRIMERA uses Longformer (Beltagy et al., 2020) as its encoder, and replaces standard full self-attention with sparse self-attention, i.e. it features a combination of local attention (self-attention between tokens in a narrow context window) and global attention (selected tokens that attends to all other words).

We structure the input by adding <doc-sep> (a special token denoting a document separator) between passages, and concatenating them with the claim with another <doc-sep> token. Moreover, we prepend claims and passages with the special prefix <CLAIM:> and <PASSAGE:> tokens respectively (to provide explicit indication of their functions). By default, PRIMERA assigns global attention only to <doc-sep> tokens. We extend this idea by adding extra global attention to the *claim words* and the two special prefix tokens (<CLAIM:> and <PASSAGE:>). This is to better focus the model on the claim. We also perform veracity prediction by generating veracity labels together with explanations, following Bhatia et al. (2021b). That is, the output takes the form of Veracity:[lab]\nExplanation:[exp], where [lab] is the veracity label and [exp] is the generated explanation.

5 Experiments

As our baseline, we compare against Bhatia et al. (2021a) who use a retrieval-augmented generation framework to jointly perform veracity prediction and explanation generation using fusion in decoder (Izacard and Grave, 2021) and model it as question answering task. Note that in their approach a claim is concatenated with *each* passage and these claim–passage pairs are encoded separately — so as to reduce the computational overhead due to full self-attention — before they are fed to the decoder. Our approach, on the other hand, frames the task as query-focused multi-document summarization, and the use of PRIMERA means we can use the concatenated claim and all passages as input due

[2] Using Table 1 as an example, we would create 3 claim–evidence instances (the 4th and 5th evidence items are discarded as they have different labels to the claim).

[3] To clarify, the veracity label is the claim label and the explanation is an evidence in Climate-Fever (Table 1).

[4] https://github.com/studio-ousia/bpr

CLAIM: About 60% of the warming observed from 1970 to 2000 was very likely caused by the above natural 60-year climatic cycle during its warming phase.
LABEL: `REFUTES`
GEN: In the scientific literature, there is an overwhelming consensus that global surface temperatures have increased in recent decades and that the trend is caused mainly by human-induced emissions of greenhouse gases.
REF: It is extremely likely (95-100% probability) that human influence was the dominant cause of global warming between 1951-2010.

CLAIM: That humans are causing the rise in atmospheric CO2 is confirmed by multiple isotopic analyses.
LABEL: `SUPPORTS`
GEN: Human activity since the Industrial Revolution has increased the amount of greenhouse gases in the atmosphere, leading to increased radiative forcing from CO2, methane, tropospheric ozone, CFCs, and nitrous oxide.
REF: While CO2 absorption and release is always happening as a result of natural processes, the recent rise in CO2 levels in the atmosphere is known to be mainly due to human (anthropogenic) activity.

Table 2: Example generated explanations with `P-full`. CLAIM=claim text, LABEL=claim label, GEN=generated explanation, REF=reference explanation.

Model	B-Score	R-1	R-L	Accuracy
`FiD`	0.26	0.25	0.22	0.55
`P-claim`	0.29	0.29	0.24	0.56
`P-full`	**0.32**	**0.33**	**0.28**	**0.60**

Table 3: Explanation generation and veracity prediction performance: B-Score=BERTScore, R-1=ROUGE-1 and R-L=ROUGE-L.

to its sparse attention mechanism. To clarify, the main difference between our model and Bhatia et al. (2021a) lies in the generator, as both models use `BPR` as the retriever. In terms of evaluation metrics we use ROUGE (Lin, 2004) and BERTScore (Zhang et al., 2020b) for assessing generation quality, and accuracy for veracity prediction.

5.1 Overall performance

Table 3 shows the results for Bhatia et al. (2021a) (`FiD`) vs. two variants of our method: (1) `PRIMERA` that uses only claim as input (`P-claim`); and (2) `PRIMERA` that uses both claim and retrieved passages as input (`P-full`). `P-full` outperforms the baseline model by a margin of 5–6%, and `P-claim` also outperforms the baseline by a margin of 2–4%, indicating that `PRIMERA` is a better model for our task. Table 2 presents some explanations generated by `P-full`. We can see that these generated examples constitute plausible explanations.

5.2 Error Analyses

Automatic evaluation metrics have well-known limitations (Koto et al., 2022), so we additionally perform manual analysis of 50 samples from `P-full` that have the lowest ROUGE-1 scores. We categorize four types of errors including *claim-copying* (14%), *insufficient explanation* (56%), *hallucination* (10%), and *no errors* (20%) and present some examples in Table 4. *Claim-copying* refers to directly copying claims as explanations, which lacks explanatory power. *Insufficient explanations* contain relevant keywords but are overall implausible. *Hallucination* means generated explanations gives the impression of being fluent and natural but are unfaithful or nonsensical to the source documents. And lastly, *no errors* are situations where the explanations are good but due to low lexical overlap they receive low ROUGE scores.

Based on the proportion of these error categories, degenerative behaviour (*claim-copying* and *hallucination*) is low, and the main issue is the inability of our model to generate convincing explanations (*insufficient explanations*), which is a hard problem.

To better understand the underlying causes of *insufficient explanations*, we further analyse these examples. We hypothesise two possible causes: (1) the retrieved passages do not contain enough or relevant information (i.e. a retriever problem) and (2) the model is unable to reason or summarise over multiple passages (i.e. a generator problem). Our analysis reveals that the former is the main cause (21/28 samples), where the retrieved passages are not always relevant even though they share some keywords with the claim. This problem is exacerbated if the claim is complex and contains many important keywords, which makes the retrieved passages more noisy. Ultimately, our findings suggest that perhaps more focus should be put on improving the retriever, as it appears to be the main bottleneck in the system.

Error Type	Generation	R-1
Claim Copying	**CLAIM:** 'Global warming' is a myth — so say 80 graphs from 58 peer-reviewed scientific papers published in 2017. **LABEL:** `SUPPORTS` **GEN:** It is a myth — so say 80 graphs from 58 peer-reviewed scientific papers published in 2017. **REF:** Delingpole has engaged in climate change denialism; in 2009 he wrote of "The conspiracy behind the Anthropogenic Global Warming myth.	0.11
Insufficient Explanation	**CLAIM:** For instance, wind turbines kill birds and insects, and palm-oil plantations destroy the biodiversity of the rain forests. **LABEL:** `SUPPORTS` **GEN:** Tropical rain forests are known for their biodiversity and natural resources, and are considered key to the functioning of modern-day global climate. **REF:** Thousands of birds, including rare species, have been killed by the blades of wind turbines, though wind turbines contribute relatively insignificantly to anthropogenic avian mortality.	0.12
Hallucination	**CLAIM:** Climate change need not endanger anyone. **LABEL:** `REFUTES` **GEN:** Climate change does not endanger anyone, especially low-income people and those with limited economic resources. **REF:** Given the potential threat to marine ecosystems and its ensuing impact on human society and economy, especially as it acts in conjunction with anthropogenic global warming, there is an urgent need for immediate action.	0.11
No Error	**CLAIM:** Earth's changing climate is a critical issue and poses the risk of significant environmental, social and economic disruptions around the globe. **LABEL:** `SUPPORTS` **GEN:** Impacts include the direct effects of extreme weather, leading to injury and loss of life. **REF:** If no mitigating actions are taken, significant disruptions in the Earth's physical and ecological systems, social systems, security and human health are likely to occur.	0.13

Table 4: Error analysis on `P-full` CLAIM=claim text, LABEL=claim label, GEN=generated explanation, REF=reference explanation, R-1=ROUGE-1. R-1 is calculated between GEN and REF.

5.3 Analyzing different global attention

We next perform an ablation study with different forms of global attention in the encoder:[5]

- `P-full`: Our proposed model with global attention on special tokens and claim words.
- `−sep`: Global attention on claim words, special claim, and passage tokens only.
- `−claim`: Global attention on `<doc-sep>` only (default setting in Xiao et al. (2022)).
- `−all`: No global attention on any tokens (local attention only).

As shown in Table 5, `P-full` has the best performance. `−claim` has (marginally) lower performance than `−sep`, suggesting that the claim words are particularly important to the task. To better understand `P-full` vs. `−claim` (default `PRIMERA` configuration), we manually examine the quality of their generated explanations and observe that the latter is more likely to produce claim-copying errors and explanations that are inconsistent with the predicted veracity label. This indicates that the additional global attention helps the model to focus on claims to generate better and more consistent explanations.

[5]Note that sparse attention is only used for self-attention in the encoder; cross-attention from the decoder always uses full attention to the encoder inputs.

Setting	B-Score	R-1	R-L	Accuracy
`P-full`	0.31	0.33	0.28	0.60
`−sep`	0.30	0.33	0.28	0.57
`−claim`	0.29	0.31	0.26	0.59
`−all`	0.30	0.31	0.26	0.58

Table 5: Global attention results. B-Score=BERTScore, R-1=ROUGE-1 and R-L=ROUGE-L

6 Conclusion

In this work, we tackle the problem of claim veracity prediction and explanation generation in the domain of climate change. We use PubMed and IPCC reports as a knowledge source, and frame explanation generation as a query-focused summarization task and use `PRIMERA` as our generation model. Quantitative and qualitative analyses demonstrate that our proposed model improves the quality of generated explanations, and that additional global attention on the claim tokens is helpful.

References

Tariq Alhindi, Savvas Petridis, and Smaranda Muresan. 2018. Where is your evidence: Improving fact-checking by justification modeling. In *Proceedings of the First Workshop on Fact Extraction and Verification (FEVER)*, pages 85–90.

William R. L. Anderegg, James W. Prall, Jacob Harold, and Stephen H. Schneider. 2010. Expert credibility in climate change. *Proceedings of the National Academy of Sciences*, 107(27):12107–12109.

Pepa Atanasova, Jakob Grue Simonsen, Christina Lioma, and Isabelle Augenstein. 2020. Generating fact checking explanations. In *Proceedings of the 58th Annual Meeting of the Association for Computational Linguistics*, pages 7352–7364. Association for Computational Linguistics.

Iz Beltagy, Matthew E. Peters, and Arman Cohan. 2020. Longformer: The long-document transformer. *arXiv:2004.05150*.

Shraey Bhatia, Jey Han Lau, and Timothy Baldwin. 2021a. Automatic claim review for climate science via explanation generation. *CoRR*, abs/2107.14740.

Shraey Bhatia, Jey Han Lau, and Timothy Baldwin. 2021b. Automatic classification of neutralization techniques in the narrative of climate change scepticism. In *Proceedings of the 2021 Conference of the North American Chapter of the Association for Computational Linguistics: Human Language Technologies*, pages 2167–2175, Online. Association for Computational Linguistics.

Jacob Devlin, Ming-Wei Chang, Kenton Lee, and Kristina Toutanova. 2019. BERT: Pre-training of deep bidirectional transformers for language understanding. In *Proceedings of the 2019 Conference of the North American Chapter of the Association for Computational Linguistics: Human Language Technologies, Volume 1 (Long and Short Papers)*, pages 4171–4186, Minneapolis, Minnesota. Association for Computational Linguistics.

Thomas Diggelmann, Jordan Boyd-Graber, Jannis Bulian, Massimiliano Ciaramita, and Markus Leippold. 2020. CLIMATE-FEVER: A dataset for verification of real-world climate claims. *CoRR*, abs/2012.00614.

Yanai Elazar, Hongming Zhang, Yoav Goldberg, and Dan Roth. 2021. Back to square one: Artifact detection, training and commonsense disentanglement in the winograd schema. In *Proceedings of the 2021 Conference on Empirical Methods in Natural Language Processing*, pages 10486–10500. Association for Computational Linguistics.

Mohamed H. Gad-Elrab, Daria Stepanova, Jacopo Urbani, and Gerhard Weikum. 2019. Exfakt: A framework for explaining facts over knowledge graphs and text. In *Proceedings of the Twelfth ACM International Conference on Web Search and Data Mining*, WSDM '19, page 87–95, New York, NY, USA. Association for Computing Machinery.

Naeemul Hassan, Chengkai Li, and Mark Tremayne. 2015. Detecting check-worthy factual claims in presidential debates. In *Proceedings of the 24th ACM International on Conference on Information and Knowledge Management*, CIKM '15, page 1835–1838, New York, NY, USA. Association for Computing Machinery.

Gautier Izacard and Edouard Grave. 2021. Leveraging passage retrieval with generative models for open domain question answering. In *Proceedings of the 16th Conference of the European Chapter of the Association for Computational Linguistics: Main Volume*, pages 874–880, Online. Association for Computational Linguistics.

Vladimir Karpukhin, Barlas Oguz, Sewon Min, Patrick Lewis, Ledell Wu, Sergey Edunov, Danqi Chen, and Wen-tau Yih. 2020. Dense passage retrieval for open-domain question answering. In *Proceedings of the 2020 Conference on Empirical Methods in Natural Language Processing (EMNLP)*, pages 6769–6781, Online. Association for Computational Linguistics.

Fajri Koto, Timothy Baldwin, and Jey Han Lau. 2022. FFCI: A framework for interpretable automatic evaluation of summarization. *Journal of Artificial Intelligence Research*, 73.

Tom Kwiatkowski, Jennimaria Palomaki, Olivia Redfield, Michael Collins, Ankur Parikh, Chris Alberti, Danielle Epstein, Illia Polosukhin, Jacob Devlin, Kenton Lee, Kristina Toutanova, Llion Jones, Matthew Kelcey, Ming-Wei Chang, Andrew M. Dai, Jakob Uszkoreit, Quoc Le, and Slav Petrov. 2019. Natural questions: A benchmark for question answering research. *Transactions of the Association for Computational Linguistics*, 7:452–466.

Stephan Lewandowsky, Ullrich K. H. Ecker, Colleen M. Seifert, Norbert Schwarz, and John Cook. 2012. Misinformation and its correction: Continued influence and successful debiasing. *Psychological Science in the Public Interest*, 13(3):106–131. PMID: 26173286.

Patrick Lewis, Ethan Perez, Aleksandra Piktus, Fabio Petroni, Vladimir Karpukhin, Naman Goyal, Heinrich Küttler, Mike Lewis, Wen-tau Yih, Tim Rocktäschel, Sebastian Riedel, and Douwe Kiela. 2020. Retrieval-augmented generation for knowledge-intensive NLP tasks. In *Advances in Neural Information Processing Systems*, volume 33, pages 9459–9474. Curran Associates, Inc.

Kexin Liao, Logan Lebanoff, and Fei Liu. 2018. Abstract Meaning Representation for multi-document summarization. In *Proceedings of the 27th International Conference on Computational Linguistics*, pages 1178–1190, Santa Fe, New Mexico, USA. Association for Computational Linguistics.

Chin-Yew Lin. 2004. ROUGE: A package for automatic evaluation of summaries. In *Text Summarization Branches Out*, pages 74–81, Barcelona, Spain. Association for Computational Linguistics.

Yang Liu and Mirella Lapata. 2019. Hierarchical transformers for multi-document summarization. In *Proceedings of the 57th Annual Meeting of the Association for Computational Linguistics*, pages 5070–5081, Florence, Italy. Association for Computational Linguistics.

Diego Mollá, Christopher Jones, and Vincent Nguyen. 2020. Query focused multi-document summarisation of biomedical texts. In *CLEF (Working Notes)*.

Kashyap Popat, Subhabrata Mukherjee, Andrew Yates, and Gerhard Weikum. 2018. DeClarE: Debunking fake news and false claims using evidence-aware deep learning. In *Proceedings of the 2018 Conference on Empirical Methods in Natural Language Processing*, pages 22–32. Association for Computational Linguistics.

Adam Roberts, Colin Raffel, and Noam Shazeer. 2020. How much knowledge can you pack into the parameters of a language model? In *Proceedings of the 2020 Conference on Empirical Methods in Natural Language Processing (EMNLP)*, pages 5418–5426, Online. Association for Computational Linguistics.

Abeed Sarker, Diego Mollá, and Cécile Paris. 2013. An approach for query-focused text summarisation for evidence based medicine. In *Conference on Artificial Intelligence in Medicine in Europe*, pages 295–304. Springer.

Dominik Stammbach and Guenter Neumann. 2019. Team DOMLIN: Exploiting evidence enhancement for the FEVER shared task. In *Proceedings of the Second Workshop on Fact Extraction and VERification (FEVER)*, pages 105–109.

William Yang Wang. 2017. "liar, liar pants on fire": A new benchmark dataset for fake news detection. In *Proceedings of the 55th Annual Meeting of the Association for Computational Linguistics (Volume 2: Short Papers)*, pages 422–426, Vancouver, Canada. Association for Computational Linguistics.

Wen Xiao, Iz Beltagy, Giuseppe Carenini, and Arman Cohan. 2022. PRIMERA: Pyramid-based masked sentence pre-training for multi-document summarization. In *Proceedings of the 60th Annual Meeting of the Association for Computational Linguistics (Volume 1: Long Papers)*, pages 5245–5263, Dublin, Ireland. Association for Computational Linguistics.

Brian Xu, Mitra Mohtarami, and James Glass. 2019. Adversarial domain adaptation for stance detection. *arXiv preprint arXiv:1902.02401*.

Ikuya Yamada, Akari Asai, and Hannaneh Hajishirzi. 2021. Efficient passage retrieval with hashing for open-domain question answering. In *Proceedings of the 59th Annual Meeting of the Association for Computational Linguistics and the 11th International Joint Conference on Natural Language Processing (Volume 2: Short Papers)*, pages 979–986, Online. Association for Computational Linguistics.

Jingqing Zhang, Yao Zhao, Mohammad Saleh, and Peter J. Liu. 2020a. PEGASUS: Pre-training with extracted gap-sentences for abstractive summarization. In *Proceedings of the 37th International Conference on Machine Learning*.

Tianyi Zhang, Varsha Kishore, Felix Wu, Kilian Q. Weinberger, and Yoav Artzi. 2020b. BERTScore: Evaluating text generation with BERT. In *International Conference on Learning Representations*.

A Appendix

<s> CLAIM: 97 % consensus on human - ca used global warming has been dispro ven <doc-sep> PASSAGE: Since the mid - 19 th century , human activities have increased greenhouse gases such as carbon dioxide , methane , and nit rous oxide in the Earth 's atmosphere that resulted in increased average temperature . The effects of rising temperature include soil degradation , loss of productivity of agricultural land , desert ification , loss of biodiversity , degradation of ecosystems , reduced fresh - water resources , acid ification of the oceans , and the disruption and depletion of strat osp heric ozone . All these have an impact on human health , causing non - commun icable diseases such as injuries during natural disasters , malnutrition during famine , and increased mortality during heat waves due to complications in chronically ill patients . Direct exposure to <doc-sep> With a documented increase in average global surface temperatures of 0 . 6 degrees C since 1975 , Earth now appears to be warming due to a variety of clim atic effects , most notably the casc ading effects of greenhouse gas emissions resulting from human activities . There remains , however , no universal agreement on how rapidly , region ally , or asymm etr ically the planet will warm or on the true impact of global warming on natural disasters and public health outcomes . Most reports to date of the public health impact of global warming have been anecdotal and retrospective in design and have focused on the increase in heat - stroke deaths <doc-sep> Global air surface temperatures increased by about 0 . 6 degrees C during the 20 th century , but as Z w iers and Weaver discuss in their Perspective , the warming was not continuous . Two distinct periods of warming , from 1910 to 1945 and since 1976 , were separated by a period of very gradual cooling . The authors highlight the work by St ott et al ., who have performed the most comprehensive simulation of 20 th century climate to date . The agreement between observed and simulated temperature variations strongly suggests that forcing from anthrop ogenic activities , moder ated by variations in solar and volcanic forcing , has been the main driver of <doc-sep> Recent reconstruct ions of Northern Hemisphere temperatures and climate forcing over the past 1000 years allow the warming of the 20 th century to be placed within a historical context and various mechanisms of climate change to be tested . Compar isons of observations with simulations from an energy balance climate model indicate that as much as 41 to 64 % of pre anthrop ogenic (pre - 18 50) dec adal - scale temperature variations was due to changes in solar irrad iance and volcan ism . Removal of the forced response from reconstructed temperature time series yields residual s that show similar variability to those of control runs of coupled models , thereby lending support to the <doc-sep> The most pronounced warming in the historical global climate record prior to the recent warming occurred over the first half of the 20 th century and is known as the Early Tw ent ieth Century W arming (ET CW). Understanding this period and the subsequent slowdown of warming is key to dis ent angling the relationship between dec adal variability and the response to human influences in the present and future climate . This review discusses the observed changes during the E TC W and hypotheses for the underlying causes and mechanisms . Attribution studies estimate that about a half (40 - 54 %; p > . 8) of the global warming from 1901 to 1950 was <doc-sep> </s>

Figure 2: Visualization of attention weights on model input

A.1 Analyzing attention weights

Attention weights can provide insights into what the model focuses on during learning, and how it affects generation. We visualize attention strength on tokens in our model input in Figure 2. Darker shades indicate higher weights on corresponding words. We analyse the (summed) cross-attention weights on the input words at the final decoding step, and observe that our model tends to: (1) produce strong attention on the claim words and `<doc-sep>` tokens; and (2) focus on relevant words in the passages.

A.2 Implementation Details

We split Climate-Fever into training, validation and test sets which yields 963 training, 83 validation and 332 test instances. We trained `PRIMERA` with the following settings: number of retrieved passages = 5, batch size = 1 with gradient accumulation = 4, max input text length = 1,024 and max generated output length = 150. We use Adam optimizer, learning rate = 1e-5 with a linear scheduler, weight decay = 0.01, and total steps = 8,000 with warmup steps = 400. We evaluate our model on validation set every 500 steps. Following previous work (Bhatia et al., 2021a), we use ROUGE scores (ROUGE-1 and ROUGE-L) and rescaled BERTScore to evaluate the performance of explanation generation and classification accuracy (ACC) for veracity prediction.

Zhangzhou Implosives and Their Variations

Yishan Huang, Gwendolyn Hyslop

Linguistics Department
University of Sydney
yishan.huang@sydney.edu.au; Gwendolyn.hyslop@sydney.edu.au

Abstract

As a typologically rare phenomenon, the airstream mechanism of glottalic ingressive is employed phonemically in Zhangzhou Southern Min, a Sinitic dialect spoken in Southern China. Their realisations are observed to be highly diverse, with 11 phonetic variants ([ɓ, ɗ, ɠ, m, n, ŋ, β, lʷ, ɣʷ, ɠ̪, ɠʲ]) that can be derived from 3 implosives (/ɓ, ɗ, ɠ/). Such dynamic allophonic variation occurs as a consequence of regressive impacts from subsequent nasal [Ṽ], labial-velar [u, w], and palatal [i, j] segments. Several phonetic processes can be generalized, comprising labialisation, nasalisation, lenition, laminalisation, dentalisation and palatalization, which trigger alternation on the airstream mechanism, change the manner of articulation or place of articulation, and result in diverse outputs that can be characterized using phonological rules. This study directly strengthens our understanding of the phonology and phonetics of implosives in this dialect while contributing convincing empirical data to the typology of phonation as a special linguistic phenomenon in natural languages. It also sheds important light on how human languages can be encoded in a complicated way far beyond our general assumptions and expectation.

Keywords: Implosives, allophonic variation, phonological rule, Zhangzhou

1 Introduction

Human languages exploit various dimensions to characterise consonants, which comprise place of articulation, manner of articulation, nasality, laterality, phonation, voicing status of the glottis, aspiration, and airstream mechanism, among others (Bickford & Floyd, 2006). Each dimension can further classify consonants into several different sub-categories. For example, the airstream mechanism can group consonants into pulmonic egressive, glottalic egressive (ejective), glottalic ingressive (implosive), and velaric ingressive (click), which are lexically observed around the world, depending on where the airstream is initiated, lungs, glottis, or tongue, and in which direction the airstream flows, outward or inward (Bickford & Floyd, 2006).

The Sinitic dialect of Zhangzhou Southern Min, spoken in the South Fujian province of Mainland China, is found to employ two types of airstream mechanisms in its consonantal system. In addition to the general type of pulmonic egressive, three implosive sounds (/ɓ, ɗ, ɠ/) are synchronically used to distinguish lexical items However, it may be because of their special mechanism that is only found in 13% of the world's languages, and the continuous motion of organ apparatus in speech production, the realisations of implosive phonemes are observed to be highly diverse, with eleven variants being derived at the surface level, covering five different places of articulation, and four types of the manner of articulation, as shown in Table 1.

Onset	Labial	Dental	Alveolar	Palatal -velar	Velar
Implosive	[ɓ]	[ɗ̪]	[ɗ]	[ɠ^j]	[ɠ]
Nasal	[m]		[n]		[ŋ]
Fricative	[β]				[ɣ^w]
Lateral			[l^w]		

Table 1: Phonetic variants of Zhangzhou implosives

Such an intriguing linguistic phenomenon has not received any attention in the literature until Huang (2018; 2019; 2020) firstly documented the existence of implosives in this dialect. As an extension to explore their nature, this article is designed to systematically explore and discuss the phonology and phonetic variation of implosives in Zhangzhou Southern Min. It aims to address three research questions (a) what has motivated such diverse allophonic variation of implosives; (b) how these phonetic outputs can be derived from their underlying representation, and (c) how the observed variation can be interpreted using the distinctive feature theory. It is hoped to broaden and deepen our knowledge of implosives and their variation in this Southern Min variety, while contributing important empirical data to the typology of the airstream mechanism and sound changes in the world's languages.

2 Zhangzhou and Syllables

2.1 Zhangzhou Speech

Zhangzhou is a prefecture-level city in the south of Fujian province in South-eastern China, covering an area of approximately 12,600 square kilometers and a registered population of about 5.10 million (Huang, 2018). The colloquial language spoken by native speakers is Southern Min, known as Hokkienese. It is mutually intelligible with other Southern Min varieties of Xiamen, Quanzhou and Taiwan, but is entirely unintelligible with other Chinese dialects, such as Mandarin, Hakka, and Cantonese. Because a certain degree of regional variation can be perceived in the sound system among its eleven administrative areas, this study specifies the locality on the urban districts of Longwen and Xiangcheng that are conventionally considered to be representative of Zhangzhou speech (e.g., Ma, 1994; ZZG, 1999).

2.2 Zhangzhou Syllables

A template of C(G)V(X) can be generalised from the synchronic data of Zhangzhou speech in which onset and nucleus are compulsory while glide and coda are optional to occur in a syllable (Huang 2019; 2020). Table 2 summarises the phoneme inventory for individual syllable components. As indicated, Zhangzhou possesses a relatively small onset inventory of 15 phonemes, but their contrasts involve various places of articulation (labial, alveolar, velar, pharyngal and glottal) and manners of articulation (aspiration, voicing, fricative, airstream mechanism). The components of the nucleus system are diverse comprising oral vowels, nasal vowels, and syllabic nasals. Prevocalic glides occupy an independent status, whereas, because of their being less productive, postvocalic glides are grouped into one type of syllable codas that incorporate obstruent and nasal stops. Four syllable types—CV, CGV, CVC, and CGVC—can be generalised as illustrated in Table 3 in which lexical tones are transcribed using Chao (1930)'s notational system with 5 representing the highest pitch level and 1 the lowest.

Component		Phoneme
Onset	C	p, p^h, ɓ, t, t^h, ɗ, k, k^h, ɠ, ts, ts^h, s, z, ħ, ʔ
Glide	G	j, w
Nucleus	V	i, e, ɛ, ɐ, ɔ, ɵ, u, ĩ, ɛ̃, ɐ̃, ɔ̃, m̩, ŋ̍
Coda	X	j, w, m, n, ŋ, p, t, k

Table 2. Phoneme inventory for Zhangzhou syllables

Syllable	Example 1	Example 2
CV	/ʔɔ35/ 'dark'	/ɗĩ22/ 'year'
CGV	/sjɐ51/ 'write'	/kwɐ35/ 'song'
CVC	/sim35/ 'heart'	/kɐw22/ 'monkey'
CGVC	/kwɐj35/ 'obedient'	/tsjɐp41/ 'juice'

Table 3. Examples of syllable types in Zhangzhou

3 Zhangzhou Implosives

3.1 Zhangzhou Plosives

As many as 60% of Zhangzhou onset phonemes are oral plosives, which can be characterised in several different ways. They can be classified into bilabial (/p, p^h, ɓ/), alveolar (/t, t^h, ɗ/), and velar plosives (/k, k^h, ɠ/) in accordance with where the oral constriction is created. Among those onsets sharing an identical place of articulation, a neat three-way contrast comprising voiceless aspirated (/p^h, t^h, k^h/), voiceless unaspirated (/p, t, k/), and voiced plosives (/ɓ, ɗ, ɠ/) can be identified. Similarly, the onsets can be grouped into pulmonic egressives (/p, p^h, t, t^h, k, k^h/) and glottalic ingressives (/ɓ, ɗ, ɠ/) (known as implosives) with respect to where and in which direction the airstream is initiated in the vocal tract. Table 4 illustrates the nine oral plosives in this dialect.

Table 4. Examples of Zhangzhou oral plosives

Onset		Example 1	Example 2
Labial	/p/	/pi51/ 'compare'	/piŋ22/ 'friend'
	/pʰ/	/pʰi51/ 'scab'	/pʰiŋ22/ 'comment'
	/ɓ/	/ɓi51/ 'rice'	/ɓiŋ22/ 'bright'
Alveolar	/t/	/ti51/ 'resist'	/tiŋ22/ 'pavilion'
	/tʰ/	/tʰi51/ 'store'	/tʰiŋ22/ 'stop'
	/ɗ/	/ɗi51/ 'you'	/ɗiŋ22/ 'zero'
Velar	/k/	/ki51/ 'point	/kiŋ22/ 'lift up'
	/kʰ/	/kʰi51/ 'tooth'	/kʰiŋ22/ 'jade'
	/ɠ/	/ɠi51/ 'speech'	/ɠiŋ22/ 'welcome'

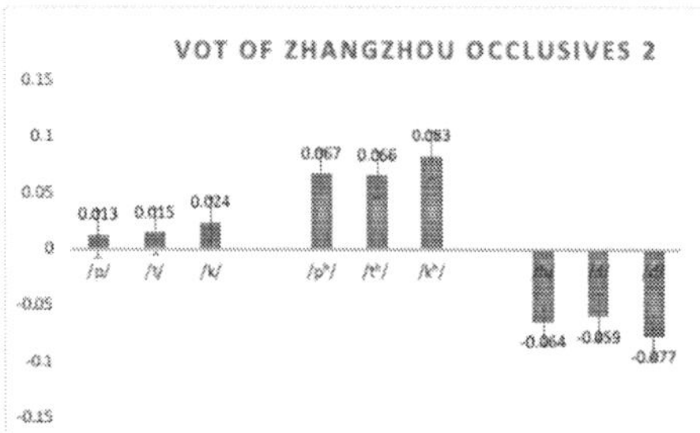

The plosives can also be well distinguished in terms of the phonetic parameter of VOT (voice onset time), which is defined as the time between the release of an oral constriction for the plosive production and the onset of vocal fold vibration to produce vocalic segment (Abramson & Whalen 2017). This can be seen in Figure 1, which is derived from quantifying 1147 samples (=6 tokens * 9 plosives * 21 speakers) based on the empirical data that the first author collected in the urban districts of Zhangzhou city in 2015.

Figure 1: VOT distribution of Zhangzhou plosives.

As shown, the voiceless unaspirated plosives (/p/, /t/, /k/) consistently show positive values slightly above zero from 0.013 ms to 0.024 ms, because the vocal folds vibrate for subsequent vowel/glide production immediately after the oral constriction is released. The voiceless aspirated stops (/pʰ, tʰ, kʰ/) show steep positive values from 0.067 ms to 0.083 ms because, after the plosive releases, there is a period for the articulation of aspiration, causing a delay in the onset of vocal fold vibration. Contrastively, those implosives (/ɓ, ɗ, ɠ/) present steep negative values between -0.077 ms and -0.064 ms because the vocal folds start vibrating before the oral constriction is released.

3.2 Comparison with Prior Work

Zhangzhou has received extensive documentation on its segmental system, but all prior works (Dong 1959; Lin 1992; Ma 1994; FJG 1998; ZZG 1999) do not document any implosive sound until Huang's preliminary finding (2018; 2019; 2020) start using such a concept. Instead, the three implosive sounds /ɓ, ɗ, ɠ/ are conventionally documented as /b, l, g/, which appears not to be supported in synchronic data. All auditory impressions and acoustic manifestations, along with the observation of the articulatory gesture of native speakers in the field site, show that related tokens are seldom pronounced with voiced pulmonic plosives [b] and [g], though the alveolar lateral [l] can be perceived on a certain occasion as an allophonic variant of alveolar implosive /ɗ/, which will be discussed in a later section. Figure 2 illustrates the waveforms and spectrograms of three implosives of different places of articulation from a 58-year-old male speaker WYF.

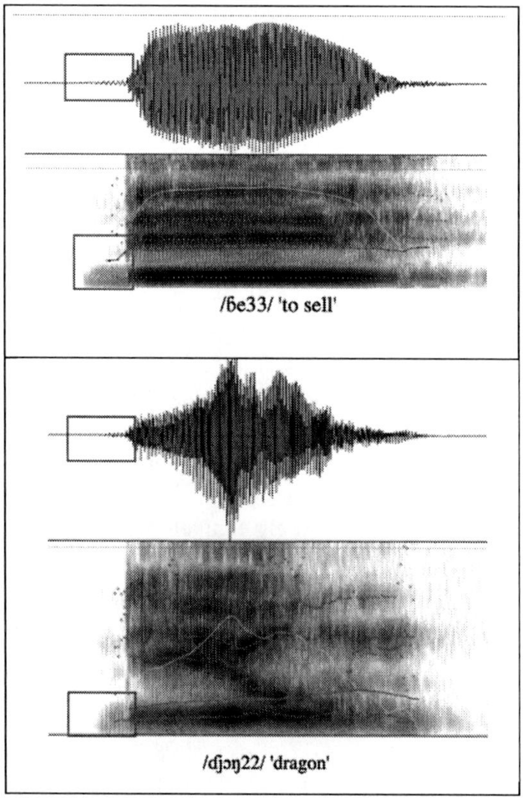

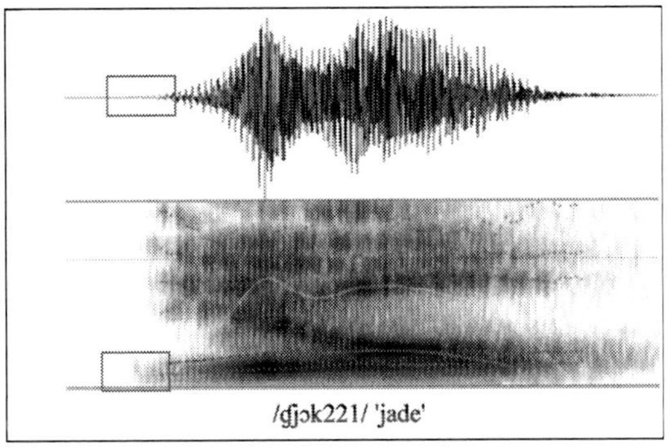

Figure 2: Spectrograms and waveforms of implosives in Zhangzhou Southern Min (WYF, male).

As seen, a voice bar can be seen at the bottom of each spectrogram of the three examples, signifying the vibration of vocal folds before the production of subsequent vocalic segments. As well as this, the amplitude of waveforms gradually increases from the beginning of the voicing till the oral release, indicating a glottalic ingressive mechanism. This is because, during the articulation, the larynx is lowered, causing the supra-laryngeal cavity to be enlarged while the oral closure is maintained. A growing amplitude of waveform has been cross-linguistically reported to be a typical indicator for implosive sounds, such as in Bantu (Velde et al. 2019), and Chaozhou Chinese (Cun, 2010).

4 Allophonic Variation of Implosives

While having a relatively small size of onset inventory, the realizations of individual phonemes in Zhangzhou are found to be diverse, motivated by various factors, resulting in several variants at the surface level. For example, as indicated in Figure 3, the bilabial implosive /ɓ/ is weakened to a voiced bilabial fricative [β] when it precedes the rounded back vowel [u], shifted to the labial nasal [m] before nasal vowels, while realized as an implosive [ɓ] elsewhere. Similarly, the alveolar implosive /ɗ/ is found to have four variants of [ɗ̠, lʷ, n, ɗ], while the velar implosive /ɠ/ is realised differently with four variants of [ɠʲ, ɣʷ, ŋ, ɠ].

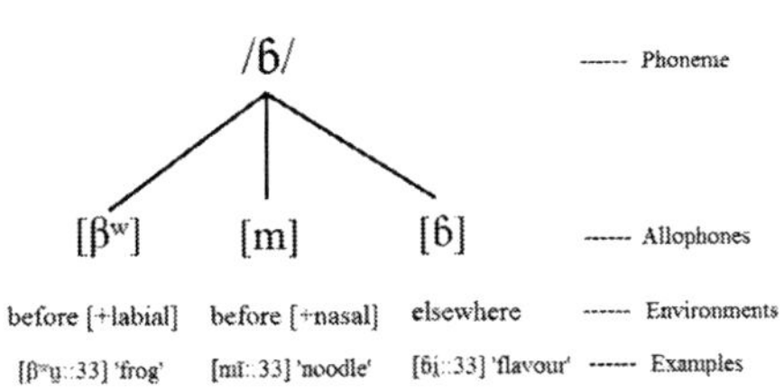

Figure 3: Allophonic variants of labial implosive /ɓ/.

Though phonetically very different, the variants of the implosive phonemes are in complementary distribution, and their occurrences are predictably conditioned by three main factors comprising the palatal [i] and[j], the bilabial ([u]), and the nasality feature of nasal vowels [Ṽ], as summarized in Table 5. This section is to discuss how eleven allophones are derived from only three implosives and what has motivated such a rich variation.

Impl.	**/_[i, j]**	**/_[u, w]**	**/_[Ṽ]**	**Elsewhere**
/ɓ/	[ɓ]	[β]	[m]	[ɓ]
/ɗ/	[ɗ̠]	[lʷ]	[n]	[ɗ]
/ɠ/	[ɠʲ]	[ɣʷ]	[ɠ]	[ɠ]

Table 5. Allophonic variants of Zhangzhou implosives.

4.1 Nasal-Conditioned Variation

Contrastive nasal consonants are absent in the onset inventory of Zhangzhou speech, but they are perceivable in certain circumstances. The three implosives /ɓ/, /ɗ/, and /ɠ/ are found to be realised as their corresponding homorganic nasal plosives [m], [n], and [ŋ], respectively, before nasal vowels. As illustrated in Table 6, the bilabial and alveolar implosives are underlyingly able to combine with all nasal vowels that can be identified in the data. On the contrary, the volar implosive can only occur before /ɛ̃/ and /ɔ̃/, since there present phonological gaps in its combination with nasal vowels /ẽ/ and /ĩ/ to form attested syllables.

Implosive		Phonemic	Phonetic	Gloss
/ɓ/	[m]	/ɓɛ̃33/	[mɛ̃33]	'scold'
		/ɓɔ̃35/	[mɔ̃35]	'crazy'
		/ɓĩ33/	[mĩ33]	'noodle'
		/ɓẽ35/	[mẽ35]	'mum'
/ɗ/	[n]	/ɗɛ̃35/	[nɛ̃35]	'milk'
		/ɗɔ̃33/	[nɔ̃33]	'two'
		/ɗĩ33/	[nĩ33]	'dye'
		/ɗẽ22/	[nẽ22]	'forest'
/ɠ/	[ŋ]	/ɠɛ̃33/	[ŋɛ̃33]	'stiff'
		/ɠɔ̃51/	[ŋɔ̃51]	'midday'

Table 6. Examples of nasal-conditioned variation

As seen, the derivation from implosives (/ɓ, ɗ, ɠ/) to nasal stops ([m, n, ŋ]) involves changing the airstream mechanism from glottalic ingressive to pulmonic egressive and also changing the manner of articulation from oral plosives to nasal plosives. Such an alternation can be interpreted as an effect of nasalization motivated by the [+nasality] feature of nasal vowels, which is understandable from the articulatory perspective. The articulation of nasal vowels requests a lowered velum to partially block the airstream passing through the oral cavity, which contradicts the articulatory setting for implosive production. Because during the articulation of implosive sounds, the velum has to be raised to completely block off the nasal cavity, whereby the airstream can rush into the mouth before they flow out again to release the oral constriction (Bickford & Floyd, 2006). Thus, for maximum ease of articulation, it appears to be a natural process for implosives to be pronounced as nasal sounds as an impact of the progressive assimilation to their subsequent nasal vowels. This nasalisation can thus be expressed using the rule in (1).

Rule (1). Nasalisation of implosives /ɓ, ɗ, ɠ/

/ɓ, ɗ, ɠ/ → [m, n, ŋ]/_ [Ṽ]

$$\begin{pmatrix}\text{+glottalic}\\ \text{+ingressive}\\ \text{+voice}\end{pmatrix} \longrightarrow \begin{pmatrix}\text{+nasal}\\ \text{-ingressive}\\ \text{+pulmonic}\end{pmatrix} \Big/ \underline{\quad\quad} \begin{pmatrix}\text{+nasal}\\ \text{+vocalic}\\ \text{+pulmonic}\\ \text{-consonantal}\end{pmatrix}$$

4.2 Labial Velar-Conditioned Variation

The realisation of implosive phonemes undergoes substantial changes when they proceed segments of either nucleus or prevocalic glide that feature [+labial] and [+velar]. The bilabial implosive /ɓ/ is realised as its homorganic voiced fricative [β]; the velar one /ɠ/ becomes a voiced labialized velar fricative [ɣʷ]; the alveolar implosive /ɗ/ is observed to change to a labialized lateral approximant [lʷ], as illustrated in Table 7.

Implosive		Phonemic	Phonetic	Gloss
/ɓ/	[β]	/ɓu51/	[βu51]	'dance'
		/ɓu33/	[βu33]	'frog'
		/ɓwi35/	[βwi35]	'smile'
		/ɓwɐ22/	[βwɐ22]	'grind'
/ɗ/	[lʷ]	/ɗu51/	[lʷu51]	'female'
		/ɗu35/	[lʷu35]	'push'
		/ɗwi35/	[lʷwi35]	'money'
		/ɗwɐ22/	[lʷwɐ22]	'spicy'
/ɠ/	[ɣʷ]	/ɠu22/	[ɣʷu22]	'cow'
		/ɠu33/	[ɣʷu33]	'giggle'
		/ɠwɐ51/	[ɣʷwɐ51]	'I'
		/ɠwe22/	[ɣʷwe22]	'moon'

Table 7. Examples of labial-velar-conditioned variation

As seen, the peripheral implosives /ɓ/ and /ɠ/ both involve changing the airstream mechanism from the glottalic ingressive to pulmonic egressive and also changing the manner of articulation from plosive to fricative, while the latter acquires an additional feature [+labial] from its subsequent rounded segment as the output. The derivation can be considered resulting from the effect of the sonorising lenition process. Because of a reduced articulatory effort during the production, the features of the glottalic ingressive airstream mechanism and the complete oral constriction for implosive sounds are deleted, resulting in more sonorant fricatives but with the same place of articulation that can be captured in this labial-velar context. The lenition process can also be referred to as spirantization (Gurevich, 2011).

On the contrary, the alveolar implosive /ɗ/ is not realized as a fricative as its counterparts in different places of articulation, but rather, it is observed to change to a lateral approximant [lʷ] before the labial-velar segments /u/ and /w/, which may be ascribed to two reasons. There already exists a voiced alveolar fricative phoneme /z/ in this dialect. Thus, the phonological awareness of native speakers may make it not to be a premium option to be realized. Another plausible reason may be that, the two voiceless alveolar plosives /t/ and /tʰ/ are perceived being laminalised and labialized over their articulation, because native speakers tend to use their tongue blade, rather than the tongue tip, to create a constriction around the alveolar ridge, as illustrated in Table 8. Thus, it is reasonable to assume that the /ɗ/ phoneme also receives a process of laminalisation. Correspondingly, the derivation from an alveolar implosive /ɗ/ to a labialised lateral approximant [lʷ] could be regarded as a consequence of the coupling effect of lenition, laminalisation and labialization, resulting in the derived sound being more sonorant with a little oral constriction that can be observed in the speaker's articulatory gesture.

Alveolar		Phonemic	Phonetic	Gloss
/t/	[t̻ʷ]	/tu35/	[t̻ʷu35]	'pile'
		/twɐ33/	[t̻ʷwɐ33]	'big'
/tʰ/	[t̻ʰʷ]	/tʰu41/	[t̻ʰʷu41]	'dispute'
		/tʰwɐ35/	[t̻ʰʷwɐ35]	'drag'

Table 8. Examples of laminalisation of alveolar plosives

Thus, because of different places of articulation, the three implosives involve different phonetic processes for their realisation in the labial-velar environment, though they share a commonness of changing the airstream mechanism from the glottalic ingressive to the pulmonic egressive. The deviations can also be captured in terms of rules, as expressed in Rule (2)-(4) below.

Rule 2: Lenition process of /ɓ/

/ɓ/ → [β]/_ [u; w]

$$\begin{bmatrix}\text{+glottalic}\\ \text{+ingressive}\\ \text{+bilabial}\\ \text{+voice}\\ \text{-continuant}\end{bmatrix} \longrightarrow \begin{bmatrix}\text{-glottalic}\\ \text{-ingressive}\\ \text{+bilabial}\\ \text{+voice}\\ \text{+continuant}\\ \text{+pulmonic}\end{bmatrix} \Big/ \_\_\_ \begin{bmatrix}\text{+rounded}\\ \text{+vocalic}\\ \text{+pulmonic}\\ \text{+high}\\ \text{+back}\\ \text{-consonantal}\end{bmatrix}$$

Rule 3: Lenition and labialization of /ɠ/

/ɠ/ → [ɣʷ]/_ [u; w]

$$\begin{bmatrix}\text{+glottalic}\\ \text{+ingressive}\\ \text{+dorsal}\\ \text{+voice}\\ \text{-continuant}\end{bmatrix} \longrightarrow \begin{bmatrix}\text{-glottalic}\\ \text{-ingressive}\\ \text{+dorsal}\\ \text{+rounded}\\ \text{+continuant}\\ \text{+pulmonic}\end{bmatrix} \Big/ \_\_\_ \begin{bmatrix}\text{+rounded}\\ \text{+vocalic}\\ \text{+pulmonic}\\ \text{+high}\\ \text{+back}\\ \text{-consonantal}\end{bmatrix}$$

Rule 4: Lenition, laminalization and labialization of /ɗ/

/ɗ/ → [lʷ]/_ [u; w]

$$\begin{bmatrix}\text{+glottalic}\\ \text{+ingressive}\\ \text{+coronal}\\ \text{+voice}\\ \text{-continuant}\end{bmatrix} \longrightarrow \begin{bmatrix}\text{-glottalic}\\ \text{-ingressive}\\ \text{+coronal}\\ \text{+rounded}\\ \text{+continuant}\\ \text{+pulmonic}\\ \text{+lateral}\\ \text{+distributed}\\ \text{+approximant}\end{bmatrix} \Big/ \_\_\_ \begin{bmatrix}\text{+rounded}\\ \text{+vocalic}\\ \text{+pulmonic}\\ \text{+high}\\ \text{+back}\\ \text{-consonantal}\end{bmatrix}$$

4.3 Palatal-Conditioned Variation

The palatal segments of vowel [i] and glide [j] can also form a palatal environment of [+high, +front, +sonorant] and trigger processes on implosives to have different realizations. The alveolar implosive /ɗ/ is found to be dentalised and becomes [ɗ̪] when it occurs before the segments [i] and [j]. This is observed based on the articulatory gesture of native speaker during the production, whose tongue tip appears not to raise to the alveolar ridge but rather touch the back of the upper incisor to create a constriction. On the contrary, the velar implosive /ɠ/ is palatalized and becomes a fronted sound [ɠʲ]. This velar fronting is predictably natural to occur because of progressive assimilation to the high and front properties of subsequent segments, native speakers are observed moving their tongue forward the hard palate to form a constriction. On the contrary, the bilabial implosive /ɓ/ does not change their realization in this palatal context. This may be ascribed to the fact that, its primary constriction for is created by lips, out of the oral cavity, rendering its place of articulation not easy to be affected.

As seen, unlike other conditioning factors as mentioned above, the two palatal segments do not cause a change in both the airstream mechanism and manner of articulation of related implosives; instead, they only affect the place of articulation of those implosives that are non-bilabial, as illustrated in Table 9. The derivation between /ɗ/ and [ɗ̪] can be stated as being triggered by the process of dentalisation, while the derivation between /ɠ/ and [ɠʲ] is motivated by the process of palatalization or velar fronting. They can be, respectively, expressed using the rules (5) and (6).

Implosive		Phonemic	Phonetic	Gloss
/ɗ/	[ɗ̪]	/ɗi51/	[ɗ̪i51]	'you'
		/ɗjɐ21/	[ɗ̪jɐ21]	'catch'
/ɠ/	[ɠʲ]	/ɠi51/	[ɠʲi51]	'speech'
		/ɠjɐ22/	[ɠʲjɐ22]	'carry'

Table 9. Examples of palatal-conditioned variation

Rule 5: Dentalisation process of /ɗ/

/ɗ/ → [ɗ̪]/_ [i; j]

$$\begin{bmatrix}\text{+glottalic}\\ \text{+ingressive}\\ \text{+coronal}\\ \text{+voice}\end{bmatrix} \longrightarrow \begin{bmatrix}\text{-glottalic}\\ \text{-ingressive}\\ \text{+pulmonic}\\ \text{+distributed}\\ \text{+dental}\end{bmatrix} \Big/ \_\_\_ \begin{bmatrix}\text{+high}\\ \text{+front}\\ \text{+vocalic}\\ \text{-consonantal}\\ \text{+pulmonic}\end{bmatrix}$$

Rule 6: Palatalisation process of /ɠ/

/ɠ/ → [ɠʲ]/_ [i; j]

$$\begin{bmatrix}\text{+glottalic}\\ \text{+ingressive}\\ \text{+dorsal}\\ \text{+voice}\end{bmatrix} \longrightarrow \begin{bmatrix}\text{-glottalic}\\ \text{-ingressive}\\ \text{+pulmonic}\\ \text{+distributed}\end{bmatrix} \Big/ \_\_\_ \begin{bmatrix}\text{+high}\\ \text{+front}\\ \text{+vocalic}\\ \text{-consonantal}\\ \text{+pulmonic}\end{bmatrix}$$

4.4 Elsewhere

The implosives can also occur before the other five non-high oral vowels /e, ɵ, ɛ, ɐ, ɔ/, but are found to be realised as themselves with a glottalic suction initiation, which are thus referred to as unmarked forms. For the bilabial implosive, it is also realised as itself before the palatal segments /i/ and /j/. Examples for the unmarked realization of Zhangzhou implosives are provided in Table 10. Correspondingly, the derivation of implosives in the unmarked environment can also be expressed in rule, as shown in Rule 7.

Rule 7: the unmarked realization of /ɓ, ɗ, ɠ/

/ɓ, ɗ, ɠ/ → [ɓ, ɗ, ɠ]/_elsewhere

$$\begin{bmatrix}\text{+glottalic}\\ \text{+ingressive}\\ \text{+voice}\end{bmatrix} \longrightarrow \begin{bmatrix}\text{+glottalic}\\ \text{+ingressive}\\ \text{+voice}\end{bmatrix} \Big/ \text{ elsewhere}$$

Implosive		Phonemic	Phonetic	Gloss
/ɓ/	[ɓ]	/ɓe33/	[ɓe33]	'sell'
		/ɓɐ41/	[ɓɐ41]	'meat'
		/ɓɛ51/	[ɓɛ51]	'horse'
		/ɓɵ22/	[ɓɵ22]	'do not'
		/ɓɔ51/	[ɓɔ51]	'wife'
		/ɓi51/	[ɓi51]	'rice'
		/ɓjɐt221/	[ɓjɐt221]	'extinguish'
/ɗ/	[ɗ]	/ɗe22/	[ɗe22]	'snail'
		/ɗɐ33/	[ɗɐ33]	'stir'
		/ɗɛ33/	[ɗɛ33]	'catch'
		/ɗɵ41/	[ɗɵ41]	'high'
		/ɗɔ33/	[ɗɔ33]	'road'
/ɠ/	[ɠ]	/ɠe33/	[ɠe33]	'skill'
		/ɠɐk221/	[ɠɐk221]	'music'
		/ɠɛ22/	[ɠɛ22]	'teeth'
		/ɠɵ22/	[ɠɵ22]	'goose'
		/ɠɔ33/	[ɠɔ33]	'five'

Table 10. Examples of unmarked implosive realisation

5 Conclusion

As discussed, Zhangzhou Southern Min employs the airstream mechanism of glottalic ingressive as a contrastive feature in its onset system; but their realisations are highly diverse with eleven phonetic variants that can be derived from three implosive phonemes. The allophonic variation presents regular and predictable patterns under the regressive assimilatory influence of three factors comprising the nasal [Ṽ], labial-velar [u, w], and palatal [i, j] characteristics of subsequent segments. The nasal factor alters the airstream mechanism from glottalic ingressives to pulmonic egressives and changes the manner of articulation to be nasal. The labial-velar factor affects the implosives at different extents depending on their place of articulation. It triggers a lenition process on the bilabial implosive, coupling processes of lenition and labialization on the velar implosive but induces more complex effects on the alveolar implosive involving labialization, laminalisation and lenition. The two non-alveolar implosives are thus changed to their homorganic voiced fricative counterparts, while the alveolar implosive is changed to a lateral approximant. The palatal factor shifts the place of articulation of the two non-labial implosives under the influence of dentalisation or palatalization.

The diverse allophonic variation of implosives in Zhangzhou Southern Min reflects continuous motions of vocal apparatus in the production of human speech sounds, which causes considerable overlapping in articulatory gestures and leads to dynamic physical outputs to individual phonemes (Anderson, 1978; Ohala, 1993). The discussion of this article directly broadens our understanding of the phonetics and phonology of implosives in this dialect, while demonstrating how diverse factors alter their phonetic outputs in terms of airstream mechanism, place of articulation, and manner of articulation. It is hoped to contribute valuable empirical data to the typology of implosives as a special language phenomenon and shed important light on the typology of sound changes that are synchronically motivated.

6 Reference

Abramson, A. S., and Whalen, D. H. 2017. Voice onset time (VOT) at 50: Theoretical and practical issues in measuring voicing distinctions. *Journal of phonetics*, 63, 75–86.

Anderson, Stephen R. 1978. Tone features. In Victoria Fromkin (ed.), *Tone: A linguistic survey*, 133-175. New York: Academic Press.

Bickford, Anita C., and Rick Floyd. 2006. *Articulatory Phonetics: Tools for Analyzing the World's Languages* (4th edition). Dellas, Texas: SIL International.

Chao, Yuanren. 1930. ə sɪstəm əv "toun-lɛtəz" (A system of "tone letters"). *Le Maître Phonétique*, 45. 24–27.

Cun, Xi. 2010. The phonetic cause of sound change from voiceless stops to implosives. *Explorations in Renaissance Culture*, *4*(1), 33-64.

Dong, Tonghe. 1959. *Si ge Minnan fangyan (Four Southern Min varieties)*. Taipei: Zhongyang Yanjiuyuan.

FJG. 1998. *Fujianshegnzhi fangyanzhi (Fujian Province Gazette-Dialect Volume)*. Beijing: Fangzhi Chubanshe.

Gurevich, Naomi. 2011. Lenition. Vol. III, In Marc van Oostendorp, Colin J Ewen and Elizabeth V Hume (eds.), *The Blackwell companion to phonology*, 1559-1575. John Wiley & Sons.

Huang, Yishan. 2018. *Tones in Zhangzhou: Pitch and beyond.* Doctoral dissertation: The Australian National University.

Huang, Yishan. 2019. *Zhangzhou Southern Min: Rhyme tables, Homonyms, Heteronyms, and Vernacular documentation.* Munich, Lincom Europa

Huang, Yishan. 2020. *Zhangzhou Southern Min: Syllables and Phonotactics*. Munich, Lincom Europa

Lin, Baoqin. 1992. Zhangzhou fangyan cihui (Zhangzhou vocabularies). *Fangyan*, 1-3.

Ma, Chongqi. 1994. *Zhangzhou fangyan yanjiu (Studies of Zhangzhou dialect)*. Hongkong: Zongheng Chubanshe.

Ohala, John. 1993. Coarticulation and phonology. *Language & Speech* 36. 155-170.

Velde, Mark Van, Bostoen, Koen, Nurse, Derek, and Philippson, Gerard. The Sounds of the Bantu langauges. In Ian Maddieson, and Bonny Sands. *The Bantu languages Routledge*. Accessed on 15 September 2022. https://www.routledgehandbooks.com/doi/10.4324/9781315755946-3

ZZG. 1999. *Zhangzhou Shizhi Fangyan (Zhangzhou chorography*-dialect). Vol. 49. Beijing: Zhongguo Shehui Kexue Chubanshe.

Evaluating the Examiner: The Perils of Pearson Correlation for Validating Text Similarity Metrics

Gisela Vallejo[1] **Timothy Baldwin**[1,2] **Lea Frermann**[1]
[1]The University of Melbourne [2]MBZUAI
gvallejo@student.unimelb.edu.au,
{tbaldwin,lea.frermann}@unimelb.edu.au

Abstract

In recent years, researchers have developed question-answering based approaches to automatically evaluate system summaries, reporting improved validity compared to word overlap-based metrics like ROUGE, in terms of correlation with human ratings of criteria including fluency and hallucination. In this paper, we take a closer look at one particular metric, QuestEval, and ask whether: (1) it can serve as a more general metric for long document similarity assessment; and (2) a single correlation score between metric scores and human ratings, as the currently standard approach, is sufficient for metric validation. We find that correlation scores can be misleading, and that score distributions and outliers should be taken into account. With these caveats in mind, QuestEval can be a promising candidate for long document similarity assessment.

1 Introduction

Methods which can provide accurate estimates of document content similarity are critical to tasks such as news analysis and fact-checking (Shaar et al., 2020). Researchers have proposed a broad range of metrics to estimate document similarity (Sai et al., 2020), from n-gram overlap metrics such as BLEU (Papineni et al., 2002) and Meteor (Lavie and Agarwal, 2007) for machine translation, and ROUGE (Lin, 2004) for automatic summarisation, to embedding-based metrics such as BERTScore (Zhang et al., 2020) and MoverScore (Zhao et al., 2019). However, these metrics have been shown to rely heavily on superficial features, correlate poorly with human annotations, and perform poorly over longer document pairs (Hanna and Bojar, 2021; Balasubramanian et al., 2020; Kryscinski et al., 2019; Koto et al., 2022).

A more radical recent proposal has been to use question-answering (QA) based models (Wang et al., 2020; Scialom et al., 2021), to automatically generate question–answer pairs from a source document, and estimate similarity by the proportion of questions that can be successfully answered on the basis of the target document. While such approaches were designed to evaluate automatic summarisation in a reference-free manner, i.e., compare a full (long) document with its (short) summary, they can in principle be applied to arbitrary document pairs. In this paper we ask whether the QuestEval method (Scialom et al., 2021) scales to varying-length document pairs, and in particular, can be used to calculate the similarity between same length documents reliably. In other words, we are comparing two evaluation settings: long–short document pairs vs. documents of the same length. In Table 1, we present the different document length scenarios in terms of average length.

Data	Avg. Len. Doc 1	Avg. Len. Doc 2
ABC News	86	86
SemEval	535	535
SummEval	63	359

Table 1: Average document length (words) in each dataset. In the case of SummEval, Doc 1 denotes a summary while Doc 2 the source text.

Consistent with other work on the evaluation of similarity metrics (including the original QuestEval paper), we explore this question by measuring the Pearson correlation between the estimated similarity scores and a gold standard. Pearson correlation is notoriously susceptible to outliers (Sai et al., 2020; Mathur et al., 2020), so in addition to the raw correlation values, we perform detailed analysis of the distribution of the gold and predicted similarity scores (via inspection of scatter plots). We find that reported correlations can be inflated by a small number of outliers, caused by a skewed distribution in the gold standard, and are thus hot fully reflective of the quality of QuestEval.

Our contributions are as follows: (1) we evaluate QuestEval on three different datasets, and demonstrate that it is robust to increasing document lengths; (2) we showcase the perils of presenting Pearson correlation coefficients for metric evaluation in isolation, without examining the raw data distribution; and (3) we suggest visualization strategies which expose possible data biases to the interpretation of raw correlation values.

2 Background

2.1 Evaluating text similarity evaluation

Most common automatic metrics for evaluating summarisation like BLEU and ROUGE, and BERTScore measure lexical overlap. In the case of BLEU and ROUGE, this is based on n-gram overlap, interpolated over different values of n, and with an additional brevity penalty in the case of BLEU. BERTScore, on the other hand, abstracts away from the tokens in calculating similarity based on contextualized embeddings of each token in the respective documents.

While these metrics are computationally inexpensive, they do not penalize critical content divergences (e.g. due to "hallucination" under summarisation: Wang et al. (2020)) or repetitions, and are poor at capturing meaning-critical differences in polarity. Such shortcomings were a large part of the motivation behind QA-based metrics such as QuestEval, which were shown by the authors to be more adept at evaluating factual consistency. We note that subsequent work of Koto et al. (2022) showed that with appropriate model and layer selection, BERTScore is actually superior in evaluating all aspects of summary quality, including factuality. Additionally, unlike the metrics above, QuestEval does not require a reference summary, as it is exclusively based on the consistency between document and generated summary (although varieties of the metric *can* leverage human annotations).

2.2 QuestEval

QuestEval is QA-based pipeline that generates question–answer pairs from a source document, and measures similarity by the proportion of those questions which can be successfully answered based on the target document. While in the context of summarisation evaluation, this is based on the source document and summary, respectively (to test how faithfully the summary captures the content of the source document), this can be applied to document similarity by performing the calculation in both directions and averaged. That is, for a document pair (d_i, d_j), separate scores can be calculated taking each of d_i and d_j as the source document, and the remaining document as the target document.

QuestEval consists of a question generation (QG) and a question answering (QA) model. In question generation, QuestEval selects nouns and named entities as gold-standard answers, and generates questions for them. The model generates questions for each of the nouns and name entities and discards the ones that the QA module is not able to answer correctly. The QuestEval metric comprises two evaluations, which measure whether the summary contains *only* true information (precision), and conversely whether it contains *all* important information (recall). Both the QG and QA components are a fine-tuned version of T5 (Raffel et al., 2020) using SQuAD-v2 (Rajpurkar et al., 2018). Even though SQuAD – where answers are generated based on Wikipedia paragraphs – is not comparable to typical summarization datasets which consist of news articles, the original QuestEval paper showed that the method is robust to the domain shift between component pre-training data and final application. This paper further asks whether QuestEval extends to document similarity assessment more generally, between arbitrary document pairs.

It is worth mentioning that the typical input limit of 512 tokens of pre-trained language models does not affect QuestEval, because the model generates and answers questions based on pre-identified nouns in their *local* context of five sentences. Thus, there is no limit on the document length that QuestEval can be applied to.

3 Experimental Setup

Here, we describe the datasets and evaluation methods we use to test QuestEval's applicability to long documents, as well as reliability across datasets and reference annotations.

3.1 Data

We experiment with three datasets: (1) SummEval, made up of article–summary pairs (long–short); (2) ABC News, consisting of article–article pairs (long–long); and (3) SemEval, also made up of article–article pairs (long–long). In each case, a given document pair is associated with one or more ground-standard labels.

Condition	Measure	Data	r	ρ
Long–Short	Coherence	SummEval	0.22	0.21
Long–Short	Consistency	SummEval	0.41	0.33
Long–Short	Fluency	SummEval	0.30	0.20
Long–Short	Relevance	SummEval	0.35	0.31
Long–Long	Doc Sim	ABC News	0.33	0.10
Long–Long	Doc Sim	SemEval	0.77	0.74

Table 2: Pearson (r) and Spearman (ρ) correlation coefficients for QuestEval scores under different data conditions.

Condition	Measure	Data	r	ρ
Long–Short	Coherence	SummEval	0.22	0.20
Long–Short	Consistency	SummEval	0.37	0.30
Long–Short	Fluency	SummEval	0.25	0.18
Long–Short	Relevance	SummEval	0.33	0.30
Long–Long	Doc Sim	ABC News	<u>0.11</u>	<u>0.06</u>
Long–Long	Doc Sim	SemEval	0.77	0.72

Table 3: Pearson (r) and Spearman (ρ) correlation coefficients, after removing outliers. We underline the most drastic drops.

SummEval (Fabbri et al., 2021) consists of 1600 generated summaries from 16 different models generated for a random sample of 100 articles from the CNN/DailyMail dataset (Hermann et al., 2015), and was used in the original QuestEval publication (Scialom et al., 2021). The average length of each generated summary and source document is 63 and 359 words respectively. Each summary was rated by three experts and five non-experts (crowdworkers) regarding coherence, consistency, fluency, and relevance. In our experiments, we only use the expert ratings for all four dimensions. Note that coherence and fluency are intrinsically intra-document properties, independent of the source document. As such, QuestEval is a slightly odd choice of method, given that it compares the source document with the summary. In line with the original QuestEval paper, however, we include these results based on the hypothesis that there should be some influence on the ability to correctly answer questions if the summary lacks coherence or fluency.

ABC News (Lee et al., 2005) consists of 1225 document-pairs, created by exhaustively pairing 50 news articles taken from the Australian Broadcasting Corporation (ABC) news service. The average article length is 86 words. Each article pair was rated by 8-10 annotators for similarity on a five-point scale from 1 (highly unrelated) to 5 (highly related). In our experiments, we compare QuestEval scores against the average annotated similarity per article pair.

SemEval (Chen et al., 2022) was published as part of SemEval-2022 Task 8: Multilingual news article similarity. The full dataset contains 10K pairs of documents from 10 languages, including both monolingual (two documents in the same language, e.g., English) and cross-lingual (documents in different languages, e.g., English vs. Arabic) pairs. Here we only use the 1348 pairs of the training split where both documents are English.[1] The average article length is 535 words. Document pairs were labeled by trained annotators for a variety of axes of similarity (tone, style, narrative, temporal and geographical range, and entities) as well as overall similarity. Annotations were collected on a four-point scale from 1 (very dissimilar) to 4 (very similar).[2] In our experiments, we include only the *overall* similarity score, which we correlate with QuestEval similarity.

3.2 Validating QuestEval Scores

We obtained QuestEval scores for all three datasets using QuestEval version 0.1.1[3] and calculated the Pearson and Spearman correlation coefficients of the respective gold labels with our QuestEval scores. We report the results in Table 2. It is widely known that correlation scores are susceptible to outliers (Sai et al., 2020; Mathur et al., 2020), rendering the findings less robust. To assess the robustness of observed correlations, we additionally inspect the full distributions of gold ratings and QuestEval scores in Figure 1 in the form of kernel density estimation (KDE) plots, onto which we superimpose the regression line of best fit based on Pearson correlation. We also include the raw scatter plots in Appendix C for comparison.

4 Results

In analysing the results, we investigate: (1) whether QuestEval is document-length agnostic, i.e., scales from the original scenario of article–summary

[1]Noting that the script for reproducing the dataset occasionally failed, so that we evaluate on 74% of the data described in Chen et al. (2022).

[2]The original annotations were collected on the reverse scale (4: most dissimilar), but we flip the scores for consistency with the other results.

[3]The authors provide this link with the source code to reproduce the scores reported in the paper: `https://github.com/recitalAI/QuestEval/releases/tag/v0.1.1`

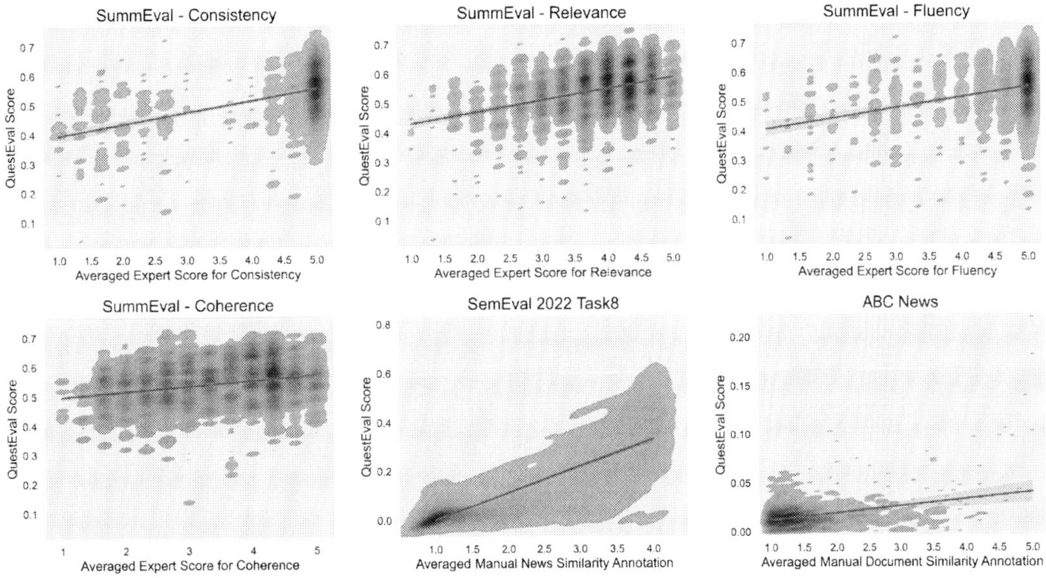

Figure 1: Visualised correlation (heat map of raw data + correlation line) for QuestEval with several human annotated metrics for SummEval, ABC News, and SemEval.

(long–short) similarity to estimating article–article (long–long) similarity in terms of raw Pearson Correlation scores; (2) whether QuestEval correlates with ratings of document similarity, departing from the dimensions of coherence, consistency, fluency, and relevance as originally assessed; and (3) how robust the observed Pearson and Spearman correlations are across all data conditions and ground-truth labels.

QuestEval as a measure of long document similarity The correlation coefficients reported in Table 2 address questions (1) and (2). The top block in the table shows our reproduction of the original QuestEval evaluation setup (Scialom et al., 2021).[4] Our numbers are comparable to the original reported scores, and confirm that QuestEval best captures consistency (i.e,. content similarity) and to a lesser extent accounts for the other three axes of summary quality. The bottom block of Table 2 shows the correlation of QuestEval with the respective manual document similarity scores in the ABC News and SemEval datasets. Both are either close or exceed the best evaluation score obtained for summary evaluation, suggesting that the metric indeed can be employed to estimate long document similarity. However, given the coefficient's high sensitivity to outliers — and consequently the distribution of reference and QuestEval scores — we next assess the robustness of the reported score.

Robustness of QuestEval validation Validating automatic evaluation metrics in terms of their correlation to human labels seems intuitive, however, correlation scores like Pearson are susceptible to outliers. This is particularly pertinent in cases where rank (or label) distributions are skewed, as is often the case when collecting human similarity ratings. Consider the data densities implied for the human quality/similarity ratings in Figure 1, i.e., densities along the x-axis. For most metrics (with the exception of relevance and coherence in SummEval), human labels are concentrated at one end of the spectrum, suggesting that instances labelled with unusual ratings are outliers and to some degree atypical. We can thus achieve high Pearson correlation scores under these highly atypical data conditions.

Conversely, if the outliers were removed, the correlation would drop substantially. Following Mathur et al. (2020), we removed outliers in all datasets based on QuestEval scores x by means of the Median Absolute Deviation (MAD) as shown below:

$$\text{cutoff} < \frac{|x - \text{median}(x)|}{\text{MAD}(x)}$$

[4] Compared to QUESTEVAL$_{W_{\text{uniform}}}$ our coherence, consistency, and relevance scores are 1–2 points lower and fluency scores are 1.3 points higher than those reported in the paper. We also include Spearman, which is not reported in the orginal paper.

Data	Cutoff	# of Outliers
ABC News	5.5	20
SemEval	10	39
SummEval	3.5	16

Table 4: Selected cutoff parameter for each dataset for outliers removal as well as total number of removed outliers.

We selected a different cutoff for each of the datasets, taking as reference box plots, and depict cutoffs and the total amount of outliers in Table 4. Raw scatter plots of the data including removed outliers are illustrated in Figure 2. We report the obtained results in Table 3 and show how the correlations drop for all datasets. The effect is particularly pertinent in the case of ABC News, with a drop of about 22 absolute points in Pearson correlation. Here, the removal of a small number of outliers (similarity > 4.0) would reduce correlation close to zero. On the other hand, for the SemEval 2022 documents, we observe a relatively wide spread of human labels, and correspondingly small impact of removing outliers, and can conclude that the high correlation with QuestEval scores (Table 2) is reliable.

We observe a similar trend for the best-correlated SummEval score of Consistency, for which 89.4% of the data points were labeled with a score $>$ 4.0. SummEval Relevance and Coherence scores are more evenly spread, leading to lower, albeit much more robust, estimates of Pearson correlation. Beyond that, we are aware that Pearson correlation is sensitive to outliers and Spearman correlation is less robust when the distribution happens to have clusters. None of these metrics are perfect and therefore it is crucial to understand the data, plot the distributions in scatter plots and conclude how informative are correlation coefficients.

5 Analysis and Discussion

From our results we can observe that summarisation evaluation metrics and more specifically, QuestEval have utility for tasks beyond summarisation, especially where there is no access to gold human annotations. In our case, we showed that QuestEval scores do correlate with the overall news article similarity scores of SemEval. However, this is not the case for every metric, as we were also able to show with dimensions like document similarity, consistency, and fluency. Moreover, we showed that in isolation Pearson correlation coefficients with human ratings are not a reliable signal for the quality of an evaluation metric, due to their sensitiveness to outliers. We recommend to visualise score distributions in tandem with calculating the correlation to ensure that it is not affected by a minority of outliers. This is consistent with the observations of Mathur et al. (2020) in their analysis of WMT task results. We observed that QuestEval scores are distributed in the range of 0–1 for almost all datasets/measurements except for ABC News, motivating us to look more closely at this dataset. In the Appendix we present some examples with high document similarities but low QuestEval scores. While we are aware that QuestEval values are lower than expected for those examples, the similarity rating is also arguable. For both cases, almost none of the entities overlap in the depicted documents; this could be the reason why QuestEval scores are low. We also propose to take into consideration several correlation coefficients as we show in Table 2. In addition to that, it is also important to understand the data by plotting it to look for useful patterns.

6 Conclusion

In this paper we investigated whether automatic QA-based metrics for summarisation evaluation can be adopted to compare long documents. We also conducted a more detailed evaluation of the robustness of Pearson correlation for similarity metric evaluation, and found that correlation-based metrics need to be validated by plotting and understanding labels and score distributions. In future work, we plan to extend our work to different languages.

References

Sriram Balasubramanian, Naman Jain, Gaurav Jindal, Abhijeet Awasthi, and Sunita Sarawagi. 2020. What's in a name? are BERT named entity representations just as good for any other name? In *Proceedings of the 5th Workshop on Representation Learning for NLP*, pages 205–214, Online. Association for Computational Linguistics.

Xi Chen, Ali Zeynali, Chico Camargo, Fabian Flöck, Devin Gaffney, Przemyslaw Grabowicz, Scott Hale, David Jurgens, and Mattia Samory. 2022. SemEval-2022 task 8: Multilingual news article similarity. In *Proceedings of the 16th International Workshop on*

Semantic Evaluation (SemEval-2022)*, pages 1094–1106, Seattle, United States. Association for Computational Linguistics.

Alexander R. Fabbri, Wojciech Kryściński, Bryan McCann, Caiming Xiong, Richard Socher, and Dragomir Radev. 2021. SummEval: Re-evaluating summarization evaluation. *Transactions of the Association for Computational Linguistics*, 9:391–409.

Michael Hanna and Ondřej Bojar. 2021. A fine-grained analysis of BERTScore. In *Proceedings of the Sixth Conference on Machine Translation*, pages 507–517, Online. Association for Computational Linguistics.

Karl Moritz Hermann, Tomás Kociský, Edward Grefenstette, Lasse Espeholt, Will Kay, Mustafa Suleyman, and Phil Blunsom. 2015. Teaching machines to read and comprehend. In *Advances in Neural Information Processing Systems 28: Annual Conference on Neural Information Processing Systems 2015, December 7-12, 2015, Montreal, Quebec, Canada*, pages 1693–1701.

Fajri Koto, Jey Han Lau, and Timothy Baldwin. 2022. FFCI: A framework for interpretable automatic evaluation of summarization. *Journal of Artificial Intelligence Research*, 73:1553–1607.

Wojciech Kryscinski, Nitish Shirish Keskar, Bryan McCann, Caiming Xiong, and Richard Socher. 2019. Neural text summarization: A critical evaluation. In *Proceedings of the 2019 Conference on Empirical Methods in Natural Language Processing and the 9th International Joint Conference on Natural Language Processing (EMNLP-IJCNLP)*, pages 540–551, Hong Kong, China. Association for Computational Linguistics.

Alon Lavie and Abhaya Agarwal. 2007. METEOR: An automatic metric for MT evaluation with high levels of correlation with human judgments. In *Proceedings of the Second Workshop on Statistical Machine Translation*, pages 228–231, Prague, Czech Republic. Association for Computational Linguistics.

Michael D Lee, Brandon Pincombe, and Matthew Welsh. 2005. An empirical evaluation of models of text document similarity. In *Proceedings of the Annual Meeting of the Cognitive Science Society*, 27.

Chin-Yew Lin. 2004. ROUGE: A package for automatic evaluation of summaries. In *Text Summarization Branches Out*, pages 74–81, Barcelona, Spain. Association for Computational Linguistics.

Nitika Mathur, Timothy Baldwin, and Trevor Cohn. 2020. Tangled up in BLEU: Reevaluating the evaluation of automatic machine translation evaluation metrics. In *Proceedings of the 58th Annual Meeting of the Association for Computational Linguistics*, pages 4984–4997, Online. Association for Computational Linguistics.

Kishore Papineni, Salim Roukos, Todd Ward, and Wei-Jing Zhu. 2002. Bleu: a method for automatic evaluation of machine translation. In *Proceedings of the 40th Annual Meeting of the Association for Computational Linguistics*, pages 311–318, Philadelphia, Pennsylvania, USA. Association for Computational Linguistics.

Colin Raffel, Noam Shazeer, Adam Roberts, Katherine Lee, Sharan Narang, Michael Matena, Yanqi Zhou, Wei Li, and Peter J. Liu. 2020. Exploring the limits of transfer learning with a unified text-to-text transformer. *Journal of Machine Learning Research*, 21:140:1–140:67.

Pranav Rajpurkar, Robin Jia, and Percy Liang. 2018. Know what you don't know: Unanswerable questions for SQuAD. In *Proceedings of the 56th Annual Meeting of the Association for Computational Linguistics (Volume 2: Short Papers)*, pages 784–789, Melbourne, Australia. Association for Computational Linguistics.

Ananya B. Sai, Akash Kumar Mohankumar, and Mitesh M. Khapra. 2020. A survey of evaluation metrics used for NLG systems. *CoRR*, abs/2008.12009.

Thomas Scialom, Paul-Alexis Dray, Sylvain Lamprier, Benjamin Piwowarski, Jacopo Staiano, Alex Wang, and Patrick Gallinari. 2021. QuestEval: Summarization asks for fact-based evaluation. In *Proceedings of the 2021 Conference on Empirical Methods in Natural Language Processing*, pages 6594–6604, Online and Punta Cana, Dominican Republic. Association for Computational Linguistics.

Shaden Shaar, Nikolay Babulkov, Giovanni Da San Martino, and Preslav Nakov. 2020. That is a known lie: Detecting previously fact-checked claims. In *Proceedings of the 58th Annual Meeting of the Association for Computational Linguistics*, pages 3607–3618, Online. Association for Computational Linguistics.

Alex Wang, Kyunghyun Cho, and Mike Lewis. 2020. Asking and answering questions to evaluate the factual consistency of summaries. In *Proceedings of the 58th Annual Meeting of the Association for Computational Linguistics*, pages 5008–5020, Online. Association for Computational Linguistics.

Tianyi Zhang, Varsha Kishore, Felix Wu, Kilian Q. Weinberger, and Yoav Artzi. 2020. BERTScore: Evaluating text generation with BERT. In *8th International Conference on Learning Representations, ICLR 2020, Addis Ababa, Ethiopia, April 26-30, 2020*. OpenReview.net.

Wei Zhao, Maxime Peyrard, Fei Liu, Yang Gao, Christian M. Meyer, and Steffen Eger. 2019. MoverScore: Text generation evaluating with contextualized embeddings and earth mover distance. In *Proceedings of the 2019 Conference on Empirical Methods in Natural Language Processing and the 9th International Joint Conference on Natural Language Processing (EMNLP-IJCNLP)*, pages 563–578, Hong

Kong, China. Association for Computational Linguistics.

A Limitations

We are aware that our analysis may be biased because we focus only on English data. Additionally, due to time constrains we were not able to comprehensively clean the SemEval data, so there may be remnant noise.

B ABC News Examples

See Table 5 for examples where the gold-standard similarity is high but QuestEval score is exceedingly low compared to a sample of documents that are indeed very similar and get high scores from annotations as well as from QuestEval.

C Scatterplots

Figure 2 is a complement to the kernel density plots of Figure 1, and presents the raw scatter plots for the different datasets and removed outliers.

Averaged Similarity: 3.7 – QuestEval Score: 0.0004	
The Bush administration has drawn up plans to escalate the war of words against Iraq, with new campaigns to step up pressure on Baghdad and rally world opinion behind the US drive to oust President Saddam Hussein. This week, the State Department will begin mobilising Iraqis from across North America, Europe and the Arab world, training them to appear on talk shows, write opinion articles and give speeches on reasons to end President Saddam's rule.	The Iraqi capital is agog after the violent death of one of the world's most notorious terrorists, but the least of the Palestinian diplomat's worries was the disposal of Abu Nidal's body, which lay on a slab in an undisclosed Baghdad morgue. Abu Nidal's Fatah Revolutionary Council is held responsible for the death or injury of almost 1000 people in 20 countries across Europe and the Middle East in the three decades since he fell out with Yasser Arafat over what Abu Nidal saw as Arafat's willingness to accommodate Israel in the Palestinian struggle.
Averaged Similarity: 3.9 – QuestEval Score: 0.0003	
U.S. intelligence cannot say conclusively that Saddam Hussein has weapons of mass destruction, an information gap that is complicating White House efforts to build support for an attack on Saddam's Iraqi regime. The CIA has advised top administration officials to assume that Iraq has some weapons of mass destruction. But the agency has not given President Bush a "smoking gun," according to U.S. intelligence and administration officials.	The Iraqi capital is agog after the violent death of one of the world's most notorious terrorists, but the least of the Palestinian diplomat's worries was the disposal of Abu Nidal's body, which lay on a slab in an undisclosed Baghdad morgue. Abu Nidal's Fatah Revolutionary Council is held responsible for the death or injury of almost 1000 people in 20 countries across Europe and the Middle East in the three decades since he fell out with Yasser Arafat over what Abu Nidal saw as Arafat's willingness to accommodate Israel in the Palestinian struggle.
Averaged Similarity: 5.0 – QuestEval Score: 0.182	
An Islamic high court in northern Nigeria rejected an appeal today by a single mother sentenced to be stoned to death for having sex out of wedlock. Clutching her baby daughter, Amina Lawal burst into tears as the judge delivered the ruling. Lawal, 30, was first sentenced in March after giving birth to a daughter more than nine months after divorcing.	Nigerian President Olusegun Obasanjo said he will weep if a single mother sentenced to death by stoning for having a child out of wedlock is killed, but added he has faith the court system will overturn her sentence. Obasanjo's comments late Saturday appeared to confirm he would not intervene directly in the case, despite an international outcry.

Table 5: Examples from ABC News with high gold-standard similarity but very low QuestEval scores compared to an document pair having high scores in both annotations and QuestEval score.

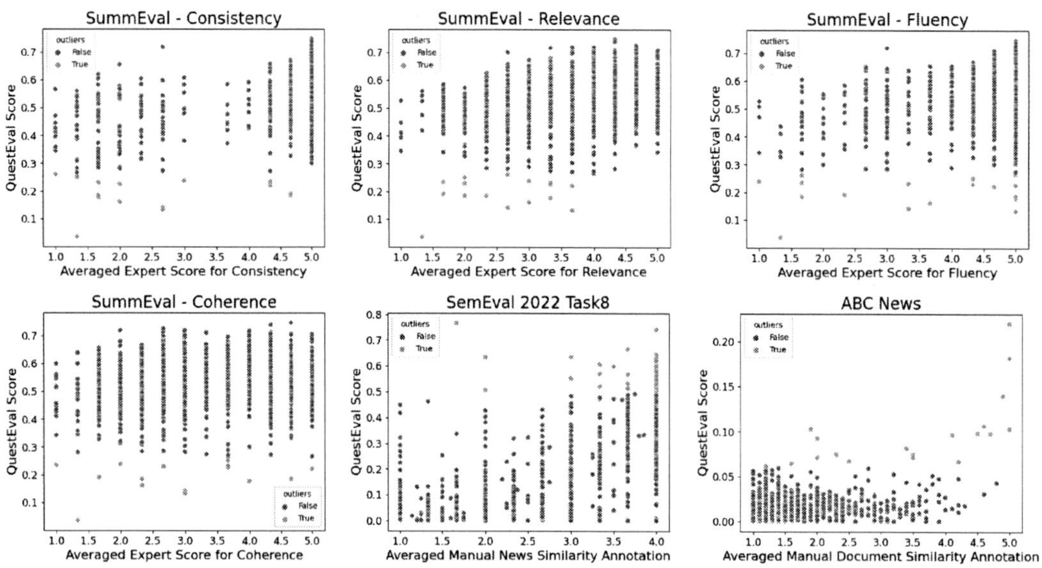

Figure 2: Raw scatter plots of QuestEval vs. gold-standard scores for SemEval, ABC News and SummEval. Data points in orange represent the removed outliers.

Can Language Models Help in System Security? Investigating Log Anomaly Detection using BERT

Crispin Almodovar[1] **Fariza Sabrina**[1] **Sarvnaz Karimi**[2] **Salahuddin Azad**[1]
[1]Central Queensland University, Australia
[2]CSIRO Data61, Sydney, Australia
crispin.almodovar@cqumail.com
{f.sabrina, s.azad}@cqu.edu.au
{sarvnaz.karimi}@csiro.au

Abstract

The log files generated by networked computer systems contain valuable information that can be used to monitor system security and stability. Transformer-based natural language processing methods have proven effective in detecting anomalous activities from system logs. The current approaches, however, have limited practical application because they rely on log templates which cannot handle variability in log content, or they require supervised training to be effective. We propose a novel log anomaly detection approach named LogFiT. It utilises a pretrained BERT-based language model and fine-tunes it towards learning the linguistic structure of system logs. The LogFiT model is trained in a self-supervised manner using normal log data only. Using masked token prediction and centroid distance minimisation as training objectives, the LogFiT model learns to recognise the linguistic patterns associated with the normal log data. During inference, a discriminator function uses the LogFiT model's top-k token prediction accuracy and computed centroid distance to determine if the input is normal or anomaly. Our experiments on three different datasets show that LogFiT is effective.

1 Introduction

Cybercrime costs businesses billions of dollars annually (RiskIQ, 2019; Australia Department of Home Affairs, 2020; International Business Machines, 2022). Log anomaly detection helps to protect businesses' digital infrastructure from cyberattacks by providing the ability to detect abnormal activities, such as network intrusions, from large volumes of event logs generated by networked computer systems.

Recently, approaches based on Deep Learning and Natural Language Processing (NLP) have been applied to address the log anomaly detection problem. A review of the literature indicates that Long Short-Term Memory (LSTM), represented by the DeepLog model (Du et al., 2017), and Transformers, represented by the LogBERT model (Guo et al., 2021), are the deep learning architectures used in the state of the art research in this domain. A practical consideration in log anomaly detection using deep learning is the availability of labeled data to be used in training predictive models. Because of the high cost of preparing labeled data, classification-based approaches such as LogSy (Nedelkoski et al., 2020) are of limited value in production settings. Thus, a majority of log anomaly detection approaches focus on the zero-positive training scenario, in which predictive models are trained in a self-supervised manner using normal log data only (Le and Zhang). Further, Yuan et al. (2021) identifies two general categories of self-supervised models for anomaly detection: (1) forecasting-based, which attempts to predict the next log entry given previous log entries; and (2) reconstruction-based, which recomposes log sequences that have been intentionally corrupted. The DeepLog model adopts the forecasting-based approach, while the LogBERT model uses the reconstruction-based approach.

We focus on log data that consists of sequences of log sentences. A key factor affecting the effectiveness of log anomaly detection models is how well it encodes representations of sequences of log sentences, especially as the content of the log sentences changes over time (Hendrycks et al., 2020; Ott et al., 2021). A common approach is to encode log sentences by first converting them to log templates (Du et al., 2017; Guo et al., 2021). However, this method is shown to negatively affect model effectiveness due to sub-optimal vector representation of the log sequences, and its inability to handle unexpected variability in the content of log sentences over time (Nedelkoski et al., 2020; Le and Zhang, 2021; Wittkopp et al., 2021).

To address the limitations of current approaches, we make the following contributions:

- An anomaly detection model named LogFiT, which uses a fine-tuned pre-trained Bidirectional Encoder Representations from Transformers (BERT)-based Language Model (LM) to learn the linguistic structure and sequential patterns of normal log data. The fine-tuning is done through transfer learning, where a base LM, pre-trained on a large collection of text corpora, is retrained on the normal log data. The use of a pre-trained LM allows LogFiT to generate representations for any sequence of log sentences. Therefore, LogFiT is robust to future changes in the syntactic structure of log sentences.

- A framework and workflow for implementing domain specific LogFiT anomaly detection models. The framework adopts a self-supervised, transfer learning approach based on the Masked Language Modeling (MLM) objective. The model is trained to minimise the cross-entropy loss combined with centroid distance loss. During inference, the model's top-k accuracy and centroid distance are compared against some threshold values to determine whether a log sequence is normal or anomalous. Furthermore, the framework incorporates techniques that are known to speed up model training: discriminative fine-tuning, slanted triangular learning rates, and gradual unfreezing.

2 Related Work

System log data consists of log sentences representing events that occur within computer systems. Several log anomaly detection methods use log parsing as its initial step, in which the log data is converted into a standardised format called "log templates" (Chen et al., 2021; Zhao et al., 2021; He et al., 2021), such that every log sentence can be mapped to a specific log template. The list of log templates thus forms the vocabulary of the model, instead of words or tokens as is typical in NLP. An example of system log data as it is converted to log templates is shown in Figure 1.

The DeepLog and LogBERT approaches are illustrated in Figure 2. In both of these approaches, the input log data is pre-processed to convert them into log sentence templates, which form the *vocabulary* of these models. The input to the model is a sequence of log keys, which are indexes used to look up the corresponding log sentence template from the vocabulary. In the case of DeepLog, the last log key is removed from the input, and the model is trained to predict the missing log key given the previous log keys. In the case of LogBERT, some percentage of log keys are masked in the input, and the model is trained to predict what the masked log keys are.

Some studies (Nedelkoski et al., 2020; Le and Zhang, 2021; Wittkopp et al., 2021) suggest that log templates often result in significant loss of contextual information that is beneficial to a predictive model's performance. The problem with log templates is that it assumes the list of log templates invariant. However, changes in the content of log sentences will naturally happen over time. Thus models that rely on log templates will not be able to map new log sentences to an entry in the list of log templates. Consequently, LogSy (Nedelkoski et al., 2020), Neuralog (Le and Zhang, 2021) and A2Log (Wittkopp et al., 2021) do not use log templates; instead the log data is pre-processed using simple cleanup scripts to remove unnecessary details such as specific IP addresses, file paths, port numbers, and URLs.

Recently, the linguistic capabilities of pretrained LMs such as BERT (Devlin et al., 2019) has been a subject of increasing interest. Several studies have concluded that BERT-based language models learn syntactic and semantic information that can be used to increase the effectiveness of downstream NLP tasks (Jawahar et al., 2020; Lin et al., 2019; Goldberg, 2019; Yenicelik et al., 2020). The LogFiT model therefore leverages a pre-trained BERT LM to accurately "understand" the linguistic structure and sequential properties of normal system logs.

3 Method

LogFiT is trained on normal log data which is first transformed into semantic vectors before being passed to the anomaly detection model. In contrast to DeepLog and LogBERT, the LogFiT model does not require the extraction of log templates during the pre-processing step. By inheriting from a BERT-based language model, LogFiT has the capabilities of an auto-encoder that can reconstruct log data that have been intentionally corrupted via masking. Specifically, LogFiT uses the Longformer (Beltagy et al., 2020) variant of the BERT family of models. The Longformer model allows LogFiT to handle log paragraphs that contain up to 4096 tokens, much higher than BERT's

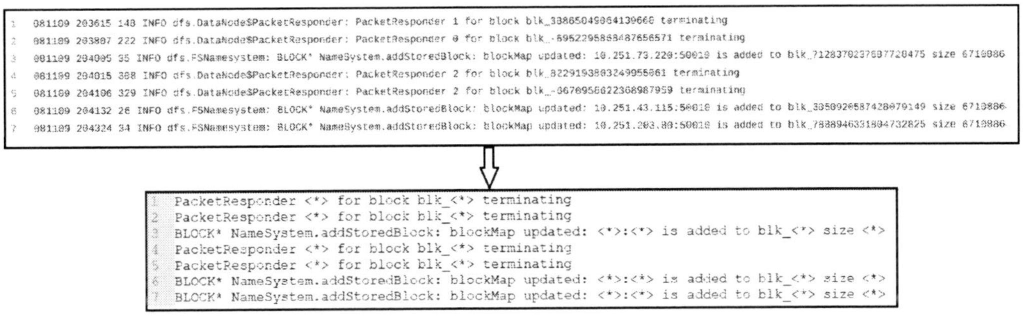

Figure 1: Sample system log data converted to log templates, from the HDFS dataset.

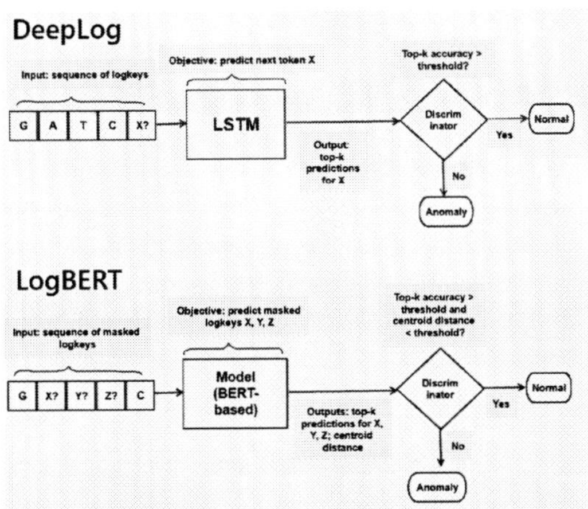

Figure 2: The DeepLog and LogBERT log anomaly detection approaches.

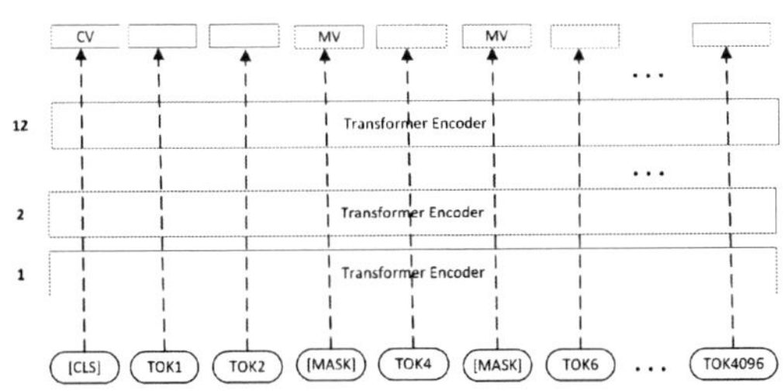

Figure 3: LogFiT Transformer layers.

limit of 512 tokens.

The input to the LogFiT model is a log paragraph consisting of individual log sentences joined together with a line separator character. LogFiT supports up to 4096 tokens, which follows from the limit of the Longformer model. It is noted that the "tokens" in LogFiT differs from the "tokens" in DeepLog and LogBERT - in LogFiT the tokens are words or sub-words, while in DeepLog and LogBERT the tokens are log sentence templates. The output of the final layer of LogFiT are 768-dimension vectors that are the learned contextual representations of the input tokens. Of interest are the **[CLS]** token vector **CV** and the masked token prediction vector **MV**. By convention, in BERT-based models, the [CLS] token is the first token in the input sequence, and is typically used for classification tasks. The **CV** vector corresponds to the representation of the entire log paragraph, while the masked token prediction vectors **MV** correspond to the model's predictions for the masked tokens. At the beginning of each training epoch, the **CV** vector is used to compute the centroid of all normal training data. During training proper, the **CV** vector of each log paragraph is used to compute its distance from the current centroid. In contrast, the **MV** vector is used to compute the masked token prediction loss (cross-entropy loss) following the BERT masked language modeling algorithm. An important detail related to LogFiT's use of Longformer is the use of global attention for the **[CLS]** token and all line separator characters only, while all other tokens are limited to local attention with a window size of 16 to 32 - this value is based on findings discussed in Dai et al. (2022).

3.1 Training Objectives

The LogFiT model is trained in a self-supervised manner using two training objectives:

Objective 1: Masked Language Modeling. This training objective is a variation of the training objective used to pre-train BERT-based language models (Devlin et al., 2019). In this training objective, the model randomly masks up to 75% of the sentences that comprise the log paragraph. The tokens of the log sentences are then masked according to the BERT masking algorithm (80% masked, 10% replaced with a random token, 10% left unchanged). Subsequently the model predicts what the masked tokens are. The intuition behind this training objective is that, for the model to accurately predict the masked tokens, it must learn the contextual relationships of the tokens and the sentences that make up the training data. Thus, the model is thought to gain an understanding of the syntax and semantics of the language domain of normal system logs. Further, because the model is trained on the normal log data, it is expected that the model will be able to learn patterns associated with the normal data and thus distinguish it when the normal data is presented with anomalous data. The masked language modeling training objective is implemented by minimising the cross-entropy loss between the model's predictions of the masked tokens and the correct tokens. Aggregating the cross-entropy loss across all samples in a mini-batch produces the MLM loss and is described by equation 1.

$$Loss_{mlm} = -\frac{1}{b}\sum_{j=1}^{b}\sum_{i=1}^{m} y^{j}_{mask_i} \log(p^{j}_{mask_i}) \quad (1)$$

where b is the mini-batch size, m is the count of masked tokens, y is the true value, and p is the probability of the predicted value.

Objective 2: Centroid Distance Minimisation. This training objective is motivated by the observation that normal log data samples tend to cluster close to each other (Ruff et al., 2019; Nedelkoski et al., 2020; Guo et al., 2021). Therefore, as an additional training objective, the distance of each vectorised log paragraph from the computed centroid of all normal log paragraphs is minimised. The centroid is computed at the start of each epoch to leverage improvements to the model weights from the previous epoch. It has been demonstrated in the works of (Ruff et al., 2019), (Nedelkoski et al., 2020) and (Guo et al., 2021) that the performance of self-supervised log anomaly detection models improves with the addition of this training objective. The centroid distance loss is the mean squared error between the **CV** vector (vectorised log paragraph) and the best centroid computed from the previous training epochs. The centroid is the average of all **CV** vectors of all normal training samples. Additionally during the centroid distance minimisation objective, the q-quantile centroid distance (where q is set to between 0.65 to 0.9 in the experiments) is determined - this distance is then considered as the radius or the hypersphere that encloses all normal samples and is used as threshold value during inference. Equation 2 shows the formula for computing the centroid distance loss for a mini-batch of log data.

$$Loss_{cdist} = \frac{1}{b}\sum_{j=1}^{b}(CV_j - centroid)^2. \quad (2)$$

LogFiT's loss function, shown in Equation 3 is a combination of the cross-entropy loss computed from the masked language modeling objective and the centroid distance loss computed from the centroid distance minimisation objective. The contribution of the centroid distance loss to the final loss value is weighed via hyper parameter cw, which is set to 0.25 in the experiments. The resulting composite loss is then minimised using the Adam optimiser, using hyper parameters recommended by the FastAI framework: momentum $= 0.9$, sqr_momentum $= 0.99$, $\epsilon = 1e - 5$, weight decay $= 0.01$.

$$Loss = Loss_{mlm} + cw * Loss_{cdist}. \quad (3)$$

3.2 Anomaly Detection

The trained LogFiT model can be used to detect anomalous log data because it is trained to recognise normal data. During inference, the input data (in the form of log paragraphs) goes through the same tokenisation, vectorisation, masking, and prediction steps as at training time. Taking inspiration from both DeepLog and LogBERT approaches, LogFiT's anomaly score is composed of two separate scores: the top-k accuracy (with k=5..12) which represents how well LogFiT reconstructs the masked sentences in the input data; and the centroid distance of the CV vector computed by LogFiT for the input data (the centroid is determined during training, based on the average of all CV vectors of all normal log samples). If either of these two scores passes some threshold value then the input data is considered an anomaly. Specifically, if the top k accuracy falls below some threshold (set to between 0.65 and 0.99 in the experiments) or the centroid distance of the CV vector exceeds some multiple of the normal centroid distance (set to between 1.2 to 1.9) computed during training, the input log paragraph is considered an anomaly, otherwise it is considered normal.

Dataset	Avg #W	Avg # S	Unique W
HDFS	176.04	18.63	146
BGL	128.66	15.73	6,046
Thunderbird	1445.70	126.63	15,557

Table 1: Average counts of words (W) and sentences (S) per log paragraph for different datasets.

4 Datasets and Experimental Setup

We use three public datasets: HDFS (Xu et al., 2010), BGL (Oliner and Stearley, 2007) and Thunderbird (Oliner and Stearley, 2007). These datasets are selected because they are used by the baseline models. Some statistics on these datasets are shown in Table 1. There is a noticeable difference in terms of diversity of vocabulary used in these datasets, with HDFS having a very limited vocabulary of only 146 unique words, as opposed to Thunderbird which is more diverse with its vocabulary close to the size of what an adult native English speaker would have, which is approximately 15,000 to 30,000 (Brysbaert et al., 2016).

The HDFS dataset consists of log entries (sentences) that are grouped into sessions, identified by the block ID field. In contrast the BGL and Thunderbird datasets do not have session identifiers, so a time-based grouping of log sentences is used. During deployment LogFiT is intended to be used in an online mode (as opposed to batch) therefore for datasets where the grouping of log sentences is based on time window, the chosen interval is 30 seconds so that a system utilising LogFiT can provide timely feedback to system operators. Each group of log sentences (i.e., a log paragraph) becomes a single sample that is then fed in batches to the models during training, tuning and evaluation.

The datasets are split into training/validation, tuning, and evaluation sets. The training/validation set is created from 6,000 normal samples for training, and 5,000 normal plus 1,000 anomaly samples for parameter tuning. The evaluation set is created from 5,000 normal plus 1,000 anomaly samples. No random shuffling is performed on the datasets - the chronological order of the logs is used; this is to prevent models from "peeking into the future" during training. The evaluation set consists of log data that appear after (in chronological order) the train/validation set.

Implementation Details. LogFiT is implemented using Pytorch (Paszke et al., 2019), FastAI (Howard and Gugger, 2020), and HuggingFace (Wolf et al., 2020).

Evaluation Metrics. To measure the effectiveness of the models, the following metrics are used:

- *Precision* (P) is percentage of correctly detected anomaly samples (TP), among all the anomalies detected by the model as $P = TP / (TP+FP)$.
- *Recall* (R) is percentage of log samples that the model correctly identified as anomaly, over all real anomalies, as $R = TP / (TP+FN)$.
- *F1 Score* ($F1$) is the harmonic mean of the Precision and Recall, as $F1 = 2 * (P*R)/(P+R)$.
- *Specificity* (S) is the percentage of log samples that the model correctly detected as normal, over all real normal samples, as $S = TN/(TN+FP)$.

In practical deployment scenarios a model with high specificity is more valuable, in that it minimises occurrences of false positives or false alarms. A model with high Specificity will accurately identify normal samples, thus if a sample is detected as an anomaly it is highly likely that the sample is really an anomaly. Furthermore, Le and Zhang found that Specificity helps mitigating the effect of imbalanced class distribution.

5 Results and Discussion

Log Anomaly Detection Performance. Table 2 shows the result of running anomaly detection inference using LogFiT, as compared to the metrics obtained when running the publicly available implementations of DeepLog and LogBERT on the same data. The LogFiT model is used to detect anomalous log paragraphs from the HDFS, BGL and Thunderbird datasets. The results show that LogFiT's F1-scores outperform DeepLog and LogBERT on the HDFS and BGL datasets, and comparable to LogBERT on the Thunderbird dataset.

Effect of delaying centroid distance computation. Table 3 shows the effect of a warm-up period of 5 epochs before computing the centroid and the centroid distance loss. LogFiT is trained using three stages of gradual unfreezing (Howard and Ruder, 2018), with five epochs for each stage. The result indicates that a warm-up period negatively affects the model's effectiveness on the HDFS dataset. This could be because LogFiT relies on a pre-trained Longformer which is already

Method	HDFS				BGL				Thunderbird			
	P	R	F1	S	P	R	F1	S	P	R	F1	S
DeepLog	100.0	60.90	75.70	100.0	90.2	70.68	79.25	98.32	65.05	99.4	78.64	89.30
LogBERT	24.02	82.80	37.24	47.62	88.92	88.35	88.63	97.59	91.75	95.7	93.69	98.28
LogFiT (ours)	99.78	90.60	94.97	99.96	98.83	84.70	91.22	99.00	89.90	98.80	94.14	97.78

Table 2: Comparison of anomaly detection effectiveness of different methods in terms of Precision (P), Recall (R), F1 score (F) and Specificity (S) on three log datasets (HDFS, BGL, Thunderbird).

Warm-up	F1	Specificity
No warm-up	94.97	99.96
5-epoch warm-up	87.70	100.0

Table 3: Effect of delaying centroid distance computation on LogFiT/HDFS F1 and specificity.

capable of producing good vector representations of log paragraphs.

Figure 4 shows how the two threshold parameters, top-k token prediction accuracy and centroid distance, contributes to the anomaly decision for the HDFS evaluation set (which consists of 5,000 normal samples and 1,000 anomaly samples). The figure indicates that centroid distance is not an important decision factor for discriminating normal and anomaly HDFS log paragraphs.

Transfer learning. Due to transfer learning, the LogFiT model starts training with an inherited knowledge of the linguistic characteristics of the English language, while neither DeepLog or LogBERT have this benefit. This allows LogFiT training to converge in fewer number of epochs compared to the two baseline models. Furthermore, because LogFiT uses a large pre-trained language model to vectorise log paragraphs, it is more robust to changes in the content of the log data (Nedelkoski et al., 2020; Ott et al., 2021).

Log parsing. Unlike DeepLog, LogBERT and other approaches that depend on a log parsing step, LogFiT works directly with the text data. Figure 5 shows an example of LogFiT's input log paragraph which have been masked according to the BERT masking algorithm, and shows the two criteria (top-k accuracy and centroid distance) used by LogFiT to decide whether the input is normal or an anomaly.

Note that in our initial experiments on the Thunderbird dataset, LogFiT's effectiveness was below that of baselines. This was attributed to the length of the log paragraphs being input to the LogFiT model. After reducing the time window from 60 seconds to 30 seconds, LogFiT's F1 score and specificity were comparable to that of LogBERT. The same reduction in time window was applied to the baselines as well.

Statistical significance. Figure 6 shows the predictions of the LogFiT model compared against the predictions of the LogBERT model on the HDFS dataset, presented in a McNemar contingency table. Applying McNemar's test with continuity correction and a significance level of $\alpha = 0.05$ produces $\chi^2 = 2553.83$ and $P = 0.0$ which confirms that LogFiT performs better than LogBERT.

6 Limitations

Due to the size and computational requirements of the Longformer model, training on log data where the length of a paragraph is longer than 2048 tokens takes a long time to complete. Further, it can be prone to out-of-memory errors even when training on an NVIDIA RTX A6000 with 48 GB of GPU memory. Addressing this limitation will be the subject of a follow up study.

7 Conclusions

Detecting abnormal computer system behavior from the log files that the system generates is an important capability in today's hyper-connected world. Natural language processing techniques and in particular transformer-based models using BERT are investigated for anomaly detection in system logs. We presented a novel log anomaly detection model named LogFiT. The LogFiT model leverages the general knowledge embodied in the pre-trained weights of a BERT-based language model and fine-tuned it to learn the specific linguistic patterns of system logs. LogFiT is trained in a self-supervised manner using only the normal logs and combining two training objectives: Masked token prediction and centroid distance minimisation. It learns to recognise only the linguistic structure of normal system logs and can reconstruct normal log

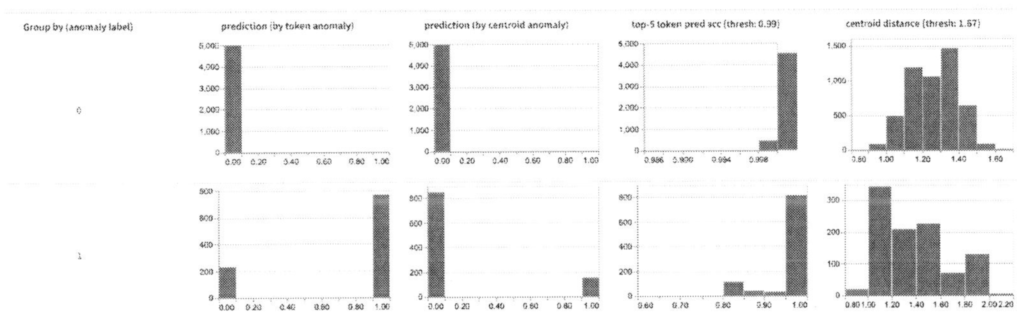

Figure 4: Contribution of each threshold criteria (token prediction accuracy and centroid distance) to the anomaly decision.

log paragraph (masked)	log paragraph (top-1 token predictions)	label	prediction	prediction (top-12 accuracy threshold)	prediction (centroid distance threshold)	top-12 accuracy	centroid distance
<s>synchronized to IPADDR, stratum NUM syn<mask>ized to<mask><mask><mask><mask><mask><m Administrator: Instrumentation Service EventID: NUM Tempera <mask><mask> from<mask><mask><mask>d<mask> synchron<mask><mask><mask><mask><mask><mask><ma <mask><mask><mask><mask><mask><mask><mask><mas [ib_sm_sweep.c:NUM]: No topology change [ib_sm_sweep.c:NUM]: No configuration change required synchronized to IPADDR, stratum NUM synchronized to IPADDR, stratum NUM Administrator: Instrumentation Service EventID: NUM Tempera <mask><mask><mask> peer<mask><mask>d<mask> <mask><mask><mask><mask><mask> Service<mask>ID<m Got trap from peer on fd NUM <mask>chronized<mask><mask><mask><mask><mask><ma <mask><mask><mask><mask><mask> Service<mask><mas Got trap from peer on fd NUM <mask><mask><mask><mask><mask><mask><mask>.<mas <mask><mask><mask><mask><mask><mask><mask><mas Got trap from peer on fd NUM [<mask><mask><mask>_swe<mask><mask>c<mask><mask [ib_sm_sweep.c:NUM]: No configuration change required connection<mask><mask><mask>#<mask> Now running on #NUM#'s privileges. Kerberos TGT authentication as user #NUM# accepted for #NU <mask><mask>NUM#<mask><mask><mask><mask><mask> synchronized to IPADDR, stratum NUM <mask>chron<mask><mask> IP<mask><mask><mask><mas synchronized to IPADDR, stratum NUM</s><pad><pad><pad> ><pad><pad><pad><pad><pad><pad><pad><pad><pad><pad	<s>synchronized to IPADDR, stratum NUM synchronized to IPADDR, stratum NUM Administrator: Instrumentation Service EventID: NUM Tempera Got trap from peer on fd NUM synchronized to IPADDR, stratum NUM [ib_sm_sweep.c:NUM]: ********************** NEW SWEEP *** [ib_sm_sweep.c:NUM]: No topology change [ib_sm_sweep.c:NUM]: No configuration change required synchronized to IPADDR, stratum NUM synchronized to IPADDR, stratum NUM Administrator: Instrumentation Service EventID: NUM Tempera Got trap from peer on fd NUM Administrator: Instrumentation Service EventID: NUM Tempera Got trap from peer on fd NUM synchronized to IPADDR, stratum NUM Administrator: Instrumentation Service EventID: NUM Tempera Got trap from peer on fd NUM [ib_sm_sweep.c:NUM]: ********************** NEW SWEEP *** Administrator: Instrumentation Service EventID: NUM Tempera Got trap from peer on fd NUM [ib_sm_sweep.c:NUM]: No topology change [ib_sm_sweep.c:NUM]: No configuration change required connection from "#NUM#" Now running on #NUM#'s privileges. Kerberos TGT authentication as user #NUM# accepted for #NU User #NUM#, coming from #NUM#, authenticated. synchronized to IPADDR, stratum NUM synchronized to IPADDR, stratum NUM synchronized to IPADDR, stratum NUM</s><pad><pad><pad> ><pad><pad><pad><pad><pad><pad><pad><pad><pad><pad	0	0	0	0	0.99	2.96

Figure 5: An example of LogFiT's input, output prediction, and decision criteria.

	LogBERT correct	LogBERT wrong
LogFiT correct	3130	2784
LogFiT wrong	79	7

Figure 6: McNemar table comparing LogFiT and LogBERT predictions on the HDFS dataset.

data that have been intentionally corrupted. LogFiT flags as anomalies any log sample that it fails to reconstruct. We showed that our method outperform baseline models on the HDFS and BGL datasets, and produces comparable performance on the Thunderbird dataset. Finally, LogFiT is robust to future changes in the syntactic structure of log paragraphs because of its built-in ability to handle out-of-vocabulary tokens.

8 Future Work

The LogFiT model at its core is a BERT-based language model trained to reconstruct normal log data. As such, it can be adapted for use in any log analysis task where the log samples consist of textual description of system events. While the domain and task tackled in this study is system log anomaly detection, LogFiT is intended to be used in the cyber-security domain. In future we focus on applying the LogFiT anomaly detection approach on cyber-security datasets.

References

Australia Department of Home Affairs. 2020. Australia's cyber security strategy 2020.

Iz Beltagy, Matthew E. Peters, and Arman Cohan. 2020. Longformer: The Long-Document Transformer.

Marc Brysbaert, Michaël Stevens, Paweł Mandera, and Emmanuel Keuleers. 2016. How many words do we know? practical estimates of vocabulary size dependent on word definition, the degree of language input and the participant's age. *Frontiers in psychology*, 7:1116.

Zhuangbin Chen, Jinyang Liu, Wenwei Gu, Yuxin Su, and Michael R. Lyu. 2021. Experience Report: Deep Learning-based System Log Analysis for Anomaly Detection.

Xiang Dai, Ilias Chalkidis, Sune Darkner, and Desmond Elliott. 2022. Revisiting Transformer-based Models for Long Document Classification. In *The 2022 Conference on Empirical Methods in Natural Language Processing*.

Jacob Devlin, Ming Wei Chang, Kenton Lee, and Kristina Toutanova. 2019. BERT: Pre-training of deep bidirectional transformers for language understanding. In *The 2019 Conference of the North American Chapter of the Association for Computational Linguistics: Human Language Technologies - Proceedings of the Conference*, pages 4171–4186.

Min Du, Feifei Li, Guineng Zheng, and Vivek Srikumar. 2017. DeepLog: Anomaly detection and diagnosis from system logs through deep learning. In *Proceedings of the ACM Conference on Computer and Communications Security*, pages 1285–1298.

Yoav Goldberg. 2019. Assessing BERT's Syntactic Abilities.

Haixuan Guo, Shuhan Yuan, and Xintao Wu. 2021. LogBERT: Log Anomaly Detection via BERT. *Proceedings of the International Joint Conference on Neural Networks*, 2021-July.

Shilin He, Pinjia He, Zhuangbin Chen, Tianyi Yang, Yuxin Su, and Michael R. Lyu. 2021. A Survey on Automated Log Analysis for Reliability Engineering.

Dan Hendrycks, Xiaoyuan Liu, Eric Wallace, Adam Dziedzic, Rishabh Krishnan, and Dawn Song. 2020. Pretrained Transformers Improve Out-of-Distribution Robustness. In *The 58th Annual Meeting of the Association for Computational Linguistics*, pages 2744–2751.

Jeremy Howard and Sylvain Gugger. 2020. Fastai: A layered api for deep learning. *Information*, 11(2):1–26.

Jeremy Howard and Sebastian Ruder. 2018. Universal language model fine-tuning for text classification. In *Proceedings of the 56th Annual Meeting of the Association for Computational Linguistics*, pages 328–339.

International Business Machines. 2022. Cost of a data breach report 2022.

Ganesh Jawahar, Benoît Sagot, and Djamé Seddah. 2020. What does BERT learn about the structure of language? In *ACL 2019 - 57th Annu. Meet. Assoc. Comput. Linguist. Proc. Conf.*, pages 3651–3657. Association for Computational Linguistics (ACL).

Van-Hoang Le and Hongyu Zhang. Log-based anomaly detection with deep learning: How far are we? In *Proceedings of the 44th International Conference on Software Engineering*, page 1356–1367.

Van-Hoang Le and Hongyu Zhang. 2021. Log-based anomaly detection without log parsing. In *The 36th IEEE/ACM International Conference on Automated Software Engineering (ASE)*, pages 492–504.

Yongjie Lin, Yi Chern Tan, and Robert Frank. 2019. Open Sesame: Getting inside BERT's Linguistic Knowledge. pages 241–253.

Sasho Nedelkoski, Jasmin Bogatinovski, Alexander Acker, Jorge Cardoso, and Odej Kao. 2020. Self-attentive classification-based anomaly detection in unstructured logs. In *Proceedings - IEEE International Conference on Data Mining, ICDM*, volume 2020-Novem, pages 1196–1201. Institute of Electrical and Electronics Engineers Inc.

Adam Oliner and Jon Stearley. 2007. What supercomputers say: A study of five system logs. In *Proceedings of the International Conference on Dependable Systems and Networks*, pages 575–584.

Harold Ott, Jasmin Bogatinovski, Alexander Acker, Sasho Nedelkoski, and Odej Kao. 2021. Robust and Transferable Anomaly Detection in Log Data using Pre-Trained Language Models. *Proceedings - 2021 IEEE/ACM International Workshop on Cloud Intelligence, CloudIntelligence 2021*, pages 19–24.

Adam Paszke, Sam Gross, Francisco Massa, Adam Lerer, James Bradbury, Gregory Chanan, Trevor Killeen, Zeming Lin, Natalia Gimelshein, Luca Antiga, Alban Desmaison, Andreas Köpf, Edward Yang, Zach DeVito, Martin Raison, Alykhan Tejani, Sasank Chilamkurthy, Benoit Steiner, Lu Fang, Junjie Bai, and Soumith Chintala. 2019. PyTorch: An imperative style, high-performance deep learning library. In *Advances in Neural Information Processing Systems*, volume 32. Neural information processing systems foundation.

RiskIQ. 2019. The evil internet minute 2019.

Lukas Ruff, Robert A. Vandermeulen, Nico Görnitz, Alexander Binder, Emmanuel Müller, Klaus-Robert Müller, and Marius Kloft. 2019. Deep Semi-Supervised Anomaly Detection.

Thorsten Wittkopp, Alexander Acker, Sasho Nedelkoski, Jasmin Bogatinovski, Dominik Scheinert, Wu Fan, and Odej Kao. 2021. A2Log: Attentive Augmented Log Anomaly Detection. *HICSS 2022 : Hawaii International Conference on System Sciences.*

Thomas Wolf, Lysandre Debut, Victor Sanh, Julien Chaumond, Clement Delangue, Anthony Moi, Pierric Cistac, Tim Rault, Remi Louf, Morgan Funtowicz, Joe Davison, Sam Shleifer, Patrick von Platen, Clara Ma, Yacine Jernite, Julien Plu, Canwen Xu, Teven Le Scao, Sylvain Gugger, Mariama Drame, Quentin Lhoest, and Alexander Rush. 2020. Transformers: State-of-the-Art Natural Language Processing. In *arXiv preprint arXiv:1910.03771*, pages 38–45.

Wei Xu, Ling Huang, Armando Fox, David Patterson, and Michael I Jordan. 2010. Detecting large-scale system problems by mining console logs. In *ICML 2010 - Proceedings, 27th International Conference on Machine Learning*, pages 37–44.

David Yenicelik, Florian Schmidt, and Yannic Kilcher. 2020. How does BERT capture semantics? A closer look at polysemous words. In *The Third BlackboxNLP Workshop on Analyzing and Interpreting Neural Networks for NLP*, pages 156–162. Association for Computational Linguistics (ACL).

Lun Pin Yuan, Peng Liu, and Sencun Zhu. 2021. Recompose Event Sequences vs. Predict Next Events: A Novel Anomaly Detection Approach for Discrete Event Logs. In *ASIA CCS 2021 - Proc. 2021 ACM Asia Conf. Comput. Commun. Secur.*, volume 1, pages 336–348. Association for Computing Machinery.

Nengwen Zhao, Honglin Wang, Zeyan Li, Xiao Peng, Gang Wang, Zhu Pan, Yong Wu, Zhen Feng, Xidao Wen, Wenchi Zhang, Kaixin Sui, and Dan Pei. 2021. An empirical investigation of practical log anomaly detection for online service systems. In *ESEC/FSE 2021 - Proceedings of the 29th ACM Joint Meeting European Software Engineering Conference and Symposium on the Foundations of Software Engineering*, volume 21, pages 1404–1415.

A Semantics of Spatial Expressions for interacting with unmanned aerial vehicles

Lucas C. F. Domingos
Centro Universitário FEI,
SBC, São Paulo, Brazil
ldomingos@fei.edu.br

Paulo E. Santos
College of Science and Engineering
Flinders University
Adelaide - South Australia
paulo.santos@flinders.edu.au

Abstract

This paper describes an investigation of establishing communication between a quadrotor and a human through qualitative spatial relations allied with an off-the-shelf speech recognition software. The quadrotor used in this research was equipped with GPS, IMU sensors, and radio communication, which was connected to a computer acting as a ground station. The ground station was implemented to interpret the received commands, correctly providing answers to the user according to an underlying qualitative reasoning formalism. The results obtained during the tests show that the error rate related to the answers given by this system was less than five per cent for vertical and radial dimensions. In contrast, commands related to the horizontal extent had an error rate of almost ten per cent.

1 Introduction

Unmanned aerial vehicles (UAV) have been gaining popularity in recent years due to their potential for novel applications (Shakhatreh et al., 2019). One of the most well-known types of UAVs is the quadrotor, owing to their fair cost-benefit and a large number of off-the-shelf programming tools available for application development. Some potential current and future activities involving UAVs include, for instance, mapping large areas (Achtelik et al., 2009), recording movie scenes (Fleureau et al., 2016), and search and rescue missions (Malfaz and Salichs, 2004).

One of the challenges for achieving a large-scale use of UAV applications, however, comes from the need to make more natural the way humans interact with such vehicles, especially for the non-specialised public (Franchi et al., 2012). This issue justified the development of an area of research known as human-robot interaction (HRI). HRI aims to develop strategies for facilitating the interaction with robotic agents in various situations, such as teaching children, rehabilitation, housework and many others. However, HRI is still to be considered in the context of UAV applications. Nevertheless, the most direct way to achieve a high level of communication and understanding between robots and humans is the vocal commands usage to transmit and answer the commands between these agents.

When two people want to talk to each other in everyday situations, they rarely use quantitative information, especially when talking about space and its relations (Aoyama and Shimomura, 2005). For example, when we say to a child to catch something at a table we do not tell the distance in meters or the relative altitude, we just give the basic qualitative information, like if it's close or far, under the table or on it. This observation motivated the present investigation, which aim is to develop new methods of human-robot communication using qualitative information. In general terms, this work aims to bridge the gap in the communication between a human and a quadrotor using speech recognition and a qualitative way of interpreting commands. Ideas from qualitative spatial reasoning (Cohn and Renz, 2008) will be used to provide the basis for this communication.

2 Related Work

The research reported in this paper is related to Qualitative Spatial Reasoning (QSR) (Cohn and Renz, 2008), which is a subfield of Knowledge Representation in AI that aims at the formalisation of spatial knowledge and the development of reasoning methods about this knowledge. In HRI, QSR ideas used a probabilistic model of interactions (Dondrup et al., 2015) based on the Qualitative Trajectory Calculus (QTC) (Van de Weghe et al., 2005). In that work, the robotic agent had to interpret the space around it while making decisions to avoid collisions and interacting with a human operator using qualitative information. More recently, (Perico et al., 2021) presents a multi-robot localisation system based on qualitative spatial information where a sensory-deprived robot was guided to a goal location by other robots by passing high-level spatial commands. Although no human interaction was considered in (Perico et al., 2021), the system presented would be suitable for achieving a human level of representing spatial concepts, as it has the right combination of qualitative representation with probabilistic localisation.

Another relevant work where QTC relations were used to enable autonomous agents to make decisions and predict actions from other agents by using just qualitative information, was presented in (Moratz and Ragni, 2008). Communication using spatial expressions was also considered with the introduction of a new formalism about qualitative location, named Qualitative Ego-Sphere (Rodrigues et al., 2016). The parameters of this formalism were obtained from human trials, and the resulting model was applied to two distinct situations: the first involved the information exchange between two robotic agents, and the second involved the interaction between a robotic agent and a human. As we shall see further in this paper, the Qualitative Ego-Sphere model was used as the basis for the research reported here; however, this idea was extended in the present work by assuming a flying robot as the robotic agent interacting with a human.

Much work has been done recently on deep learning for speech recognition using large language models, such as BERT (Devlin et al., 2019), GPT (Brown et al., 2020) among others (Sun et al., 2022). Although these models show great accuracy in actual language interactions, the semantics of their language constructs is unclear. In contrast, there is a growing interest in the development of formal semantics for spatial expressions, providing a rigorous account for verbal communication (Kelleher and Dobnik, 2022; Richard-Bollans et al., 2020; Rodrigues et al., 2020). This work presents a preliminary application of these ideas in the context of human-robot interaction.

3 Background

This work considers a discretisation of the space around an agent defining the Qualitative Ego-Sphere formalism to obtain successful communication using qualitative information, as presented below.

3.1 Qualitative Ego-Sphere

The qualitative Ego-Sphere (Rodrigues et al., 2016) is a qualitative spatial formalism based on a spherical shape to define the relative position of several points concerning the centre of a virtual sphere around an object, which could be an observer. This defines a qualitative egocentric reference system that can be considered a tridimensional generalisation of the Ternary Point Calculus (Moratz and Ragni, 2008).

To define the Ego-Sphere, the space around the agent (point of view v) is considered a discretised sphere. The first point of analysis is the discretisation of the radial distance relative to the point of reference v, which can be understood as defining regions of space that are referred to as *at*, *near* or *far* (cf. Figure 1). The category *at* is defined as the closest distance to the point of reference, considered as the minimum distance to avoid collisions; *near* is considered as the distance that can be reached by the agent in a short time if the speed is maintained constant, that is, it is a region that is close enough to the agent to be considered its close vicinity; *far* is defined as everything that is at a distance where the agent takes a longer time to reach. These three relations are similar to the human way of conceptualising space and can be understood as part of our commonsense knowledge.

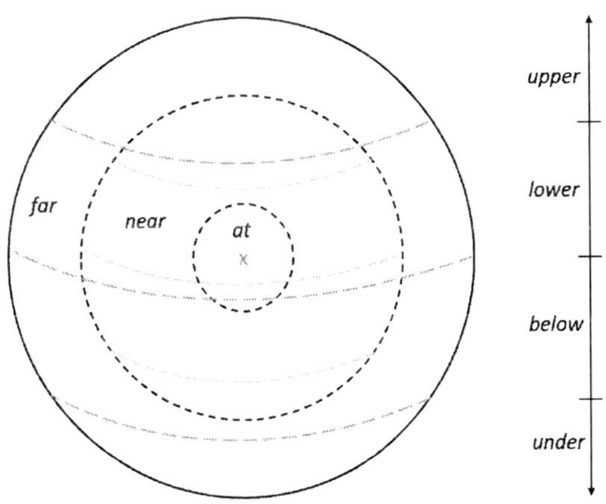

Figure 1: Ego-Sphere related at the point of view v

The second analysis area is divided into four different components called *upper*, *lower*, *below* and *under*, as shown in Figure 1. These components represent the altitude on the vertical level, and they depend directly on the dimensions of the agent: the greater the dimensions of the agent, the greater the distance between the division ranges.

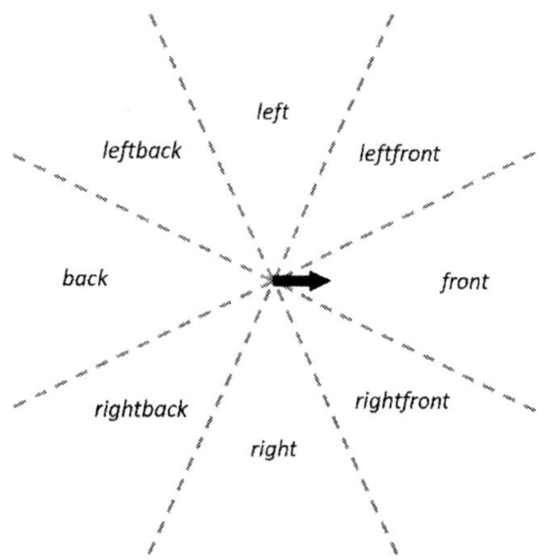

Figure 2: Relative positions regarded to a point of view v

The final subdivision considered in this work is a horizontal representation of directions, which has at its basis the 8-Star Calculus (Renz et al., 2004). This discretisation contains eight distinct regions, that are called *front, left-front, left, left-back, back, right-back, right* and *right-front*, respectively abbreviated as *f, lf, l, lb, b, rb, r* and *rf*. These relations are depicted in Figure 2. Figure 3 shows the resulting model combining all of these relations.

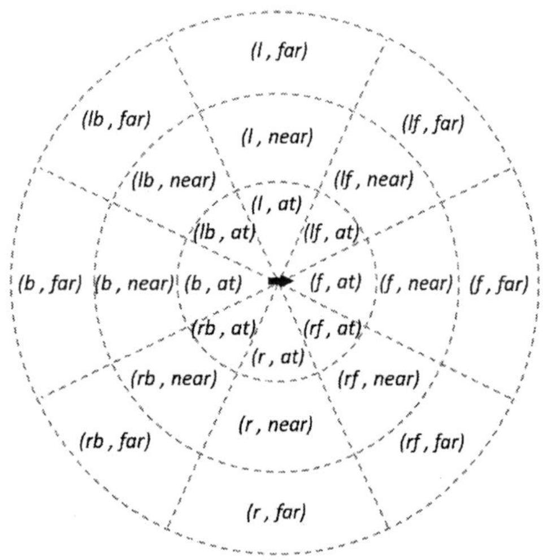

Figure 3: Horizontal relations with Ego-Sphere

An example of the use of the Ego-Sphere resides in the normal actions of daily life, such as the act of a child searching for some object in a dark room. The coordinates to find the object could be given as: "The object is *near*, at your *left side* and *above* you". A child can easily find that object if she follows the commands correctly; the same is expected from a robotic agent when high-level locations, such as "*Near. Left. Upper*", are given.

4 Experimental Setup

The quadrotor used in this research was an Arducopter with an APM 1-2560 board, an IMU board, a radio receiver, two XBee's for the telemetry, and a GPS. The dimension of the vehicle is 64x64x18 cm.

To use the concept of Ego-Sphere applied to this quadrotor, we have to consider that the UAV was the point of view v. The dimensions of the quadrotor were very important for this development, as well as its actuation area, in order to define the qualitative model. In this context, the region *at* was considered as a 1m radius centred at v, because it is the shortest distance to avoid a collision that can be perceived by the UAV GPS system. Similarly, *near* and *far* were considered as 5m and 10m respectively. The vertical discretisations of the sphere, *upper, lower, below* and *under*, received the values 5m, 2m, -2m, -5m, respectively. A new parameter was added to the latter category, the *same* command, as it was necessary to command the robot to stay at its current location. The final category, the horizontal location, was divided equally on the trigonometric circle so that each command would have 45 between adjacent regions in the circle.

The first step of this research was to control the UAV, and for that we used a range of existing software, such as the Ground Control Station (*GCS*), Radio transmitters, mobile apps, and others. We chose a GCS to control our system, as it can be installed on any computer and can have a wide range of peripherals attached to the system. The software used was the Ardupilot Mission Planner[1], and it has all the functions and tools needed for controlling this kind of drone. This software has a very large range of applications, such as support for the autonomous mission, control of all the optional hardware for this model and visual control of the basic functionality needed to fly. Using this software it was not difficult to find the appropriate function to have direct control from the computer.

All the commands sent to the quadrotor were in a specific message type using MAVLink (Meier et al., 2011). The meaning of the prefix MAV is *Micro Air Vehicle*, which is a common element of a large

[1]https://ardupilot.org/planner/

variety of UAV applications. MAVLink protocol is a library used in several programming languages that contain functions to translate and send messages between the vehicle and the control station, in this case, a computer. Thus, this library was a tool needed for the GCS, bringing standard protocol and portability to our code, making it possible to use the same code on other GCS or other software that used the same protocol. The idea of code portability was the main reason to use this protocol. This usage also made it possible to send flying commands using XBee, a radio transmitter/receiver module integrated into the quadrotor attached to the base system.

The first attempt at developing the interface between the control station and the quadrotor was to emulate radio signals from the computer and send them as normal commands by the radio transmitter. However, that was not a good approach, as those radio commands were very specific and did not have any type of support for autonomous flight. An alternative was to control the drone from the specific autonomous commands available in the Mission Planner, and using these commands implies using the full platform of the ground station and all the functionalities present in this software also. To accomplish this task, the Flight Plan tab of the Mission Planner was modified to work with direct commands and not a specific mission, as originally designed. For that, it was necessary to include equations and functions about latitude and longitude coordinates. Equations 1 and 2 describe how this information was used to determine the future trajectory points.

$$
\begin{aligned}
Lat_{end} &= \sin^{-1}(\sin(Lat_{start}) \times \cos\delta + \\
&\quad \cos(Lat_{start}) \times \sin\delta \times \cos\theta) \qquad (1)\\
Long_{end} &= atan2(\sin\theta \times \sin\delta \times \\
&\quad \cos(Lat_{start}), \cos\delta - \\
&\quad \sin(Lat_{start} \times \sin(Lat_{end})) + Long_{start} \qquad (2)
\end{aligned}
$$

In the equations above:

- Lat_{start} is the initial latitude of the drone;
- Lat_{end} is the destination point latitude;
- Long_{start} is the initial longitude of the drone;
- Long_{end} is the destination longitude of the drone;
- δ is the angular distance d/R;
- R is the Radius of the earth;
- θ is the bearing (clockwise from north).

Altitude commands were sent directly by the MAVLink protocol, using the data from the IMU board, which contains a barometer, an accelerometer and a gyroscope; however, distance and direction were sent by latitude and longitude. After receiving GPS signals and calculating the future point, we created the functions to control the Ego-Sphere commands, such as *left, upper* and *near*.

Being able to control the drone directly over the control station, without the radio controller, allowed the implementation of the voice recognition system. We adopted the Microsoft Speech library from Visual Studio (Johnson, 2012) as the basis for the voice recognition system, as this library allowed the processing of voice commands directly from the control station and sending commands to the drone without using the onboard computer in the drone.

The speech recognition module worked well with our functions, serving as the interface between human users and the ground station. The commands listed in the Table 1 were all the basic commands used to control the drone. Besides the basic commands, we have developed the Ego-Sphere commands, as explained above.

Table 1: The basic commands of the voice recognition

Command	***Description***
OK plane	Start the Ego-Sphere commands
Start the engines	Turn on the motors
Stop	Turn off the motors
Take off	Soars to a height of five meters
Down	Land at the same position
Stabilize	Starts the stabilize mode and change the control to the radio controller
Return to Launch	Returns to the initial position and land

All the voice commands used in this work have been adapted to reduce the error rate of recognition.

The voice recognition had great precision without background noise, especially because every word processed by the system was approximated by a previously defined word in the user-defined vocabulary. However, if a spurious sound is similar to one of these words, it can be misclassified as a valid command. To avoid such recognition problems, we configured the library with a confidence precision of 85%, which reduced ambiguity drastically.

A *grammar* class was used as a reference to the voice recognition module so that the application could use the language constraints in the recognition, which increased the hit rate of recognising commands. Four grammatical rules were defined containing different commands categories: the first contained all the basic commands (*Ok plane, start the engines, stop* etc); the second had the horizontal dimension of Ego-Sphere (*left, front, right* etc); the third was defined with vertical dimensions of Ego-Sphere (*upper, lower, under* and *below*) and; the last had the radial distance defined by Ego-Sphere (*at, near* and *far*). For our system to change the grammar at the appropriate time, we needed to establish an order of commands. The order was to call the horizontal references first, then the vertical and finally the distance, all according to the Ego-Sphere definitions. This order is described at Figure 4.

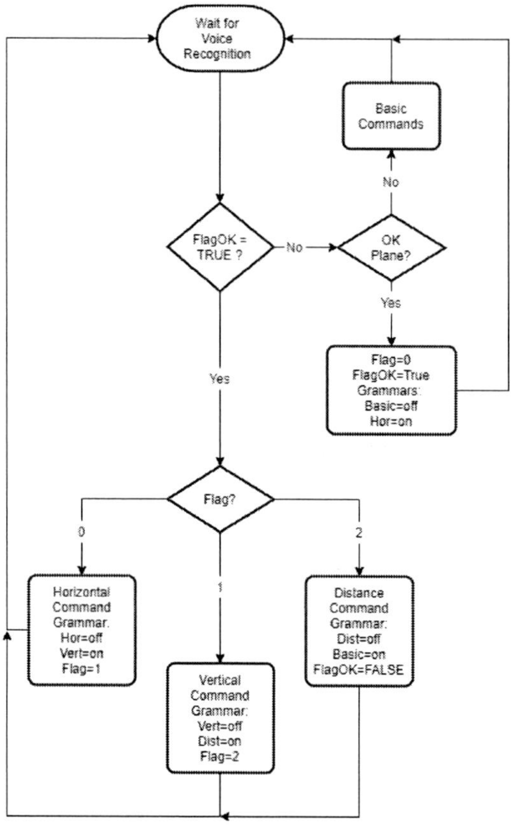

Figure 4: Flowchart of grammar interpretation

5 Results

A flying test was necessary to check if the recognition accuracy would satisfy the project goals and if the tests were consistent when flying with the radio by using direct commands. We found that the autonomous flight had certain issues, such as the stabilisation that was not precise and problems with the altitude holding. So, although the code was entirely developed for the physical platform, the evaluation of the system developed was conducted in a simulated engine, called Flight Gear (Perry, 2004). The usage of Flight Gear gave us a virtual ambient that emulates real flight, so every sensor data was received with precision and every command was sent with minimum delay compared with a real, non-simulated, flight.

The first test was conducted considering the basic commands, whereby we observed that commands with similar sounds, such as *arm* and *disarm* were not possible to be used on this application, because the similarity between these two words generated ambiguity in their recognition. So the major portion of the commands had to be changed to other words, which did not generate any kind of ambiguity. The final version of the basic commands was listed on Table 1.

Testing Ego-Sphere commands took longer than testing the basic commands, due to the complexity of the theory and the number of different words to be recognised. Subsequently, we divided the Ego-Sphere into two identical parts considering its symmetry, passing by the centre in a vertical cut, thus dividing the left side from the right side. For ease, just the left side was used in the experimental evaluation.

After dividing the sphere, four test sessions were executed with thirty complete commands in each one of them, approximately. One complete command was composed of three Ego-Sphere commands, one of each dimension. Every command given to the system was analysed according to the theory described before. Thus, to consider the command successful, we needed to analyse each one of the categories separately. To neutralise the influence of the different combinations of words, every session had the same list of commands executed in a different order, embracing a large range of possibilities. The tests were made on different days with different noise rates, with about 75dB of noise, composed of background voices and ambient sounds. That was made to maintain a realistic noise rate, representing the behaviour that could exist in real situations.

In total, 131 complete commands were tested. A compilation of the results obtained for each category is shown in Table 2. We listed the command's occurrence, evaluating if the voice command was received and interpreted by the ground station with a margin of error lower than five per cent relating to the voice recognition. If the result was outside this margin, the command was ignored and considered wrong.

Command	*Occurrence*	*Right*	*Wrong*
Left	27	25	2
Left front	25	20	5
Front	28	24	4
Left back	29	25	4
Back	22	19	3
TOTAL	131	113	18
Upper	23	23	0
Lower	22	22	0
Same	40	38	2
Below	27	24	3
Under	19	17	2
TOTAL	131	124	7
Far	42	41	1
Near	40	39	1
At	49	45	4
TOTAL	131	125	6

Table 2: Results of the tests

Analysing each one of the lines presented on Table 2 we can see that the *at* command had 4 wrong interpretations of 49 occurrences. Therefore the error rate of *at* command was greater than the other rates in the same category, such as *far* or *near*, which had just one wrong interpretation in each case. On the horizontal dimension, commands consisting of two words had the highest error rate, such as *left-front* and *left-back*, which had five and four wrong interpretations respectively of 25 and 29 occurrences. This was probably due to the existence of two other commands with the same words ending: (*front* and *back*), generating ambiguity. The analysis of the vertical dimension showed that the commands *upper* and *lower* had zero misinterpreted occurrences. That information was relevant when we take into account that the command *upper* and *lower* did not have other similar commands when looking at the phonetic point of view. It shows that the misinterpretation was probably due to noise present in voice recognition, not to the theory involved in the approach. These results showed that the error rate as less than five per cent on the vertical and radial dimensions. In the horizontal dimension, we obtained an error rate of more than ten per cent.

6 Conclusion

In this research, we bridged the gap between qualitative communication in an HRI setting using voice commands and the Qualitative Ego Sphere model as a basis of space qualitative information. The results showed the necessity of increasing the precision of our system, but also that our objective of simplifying the interaction between humans and robots has been achieved.

One of the contributions that can be related to this study is the accessibility improvement of non-specialist users to complex systems, like UAVs - *Unmanned Aerial Vehicles*. Using the approach presented in this paper, everyone able to pronounce the correct sequence of commands is capable of controlling the system successfully, and all the work with stabilisation will be the responsibility of the autonomous system itself. Another important contribution was facilitating the location requests to the quadrotor using quantitative information. In this case, for instance, the vehicle can be requested to go *near* or *far* the objective, using qualitative expressions, without the need of receiving the precise distance and coordinates of the goal location. This can be an advantage in emergency situations, where the answer time may be critical.

The lower error ratio obtained in the tests suggests the efficacy of the method investigated in this paper, but also brings atop the discussion about the equipment used on the system. With more precise instruments, such as using infrared sensors to filter the overall results, and some improvements on the code we can develop a system more consistent and achieve a higher level of communication between humans and a robot.

References

Markus Achtelik, Abraham Bachrach, Ruijie He, Samuel Prentice, and Nicholas Roy. 2009. Autonomous navigation and exploration of a quadrotor helicopter in gps-denied indoor environments. In *First Symposium on Indoor Flight*, 2009. Citeseer.

Kazumi Aoyama and Hideki Shimomura. 2005. Real world speech interaction with a humanoid robot on a layered robot behavior control architecture. In *Robotics and Automation, 2005. ICRA 2005. Proceedings of the 2005 IEEE International Conference on*, pages 3814–3819. IEEE.

Tom Brown, Benjamin Mann, Nick Ryder, Melanie Subbiah, Jared D Kaplan, Prafulla Dhariwal, Arvind Neelakantan, Pranav Shyam, Girish Sastry, Amanda Askell, Sandhini Agarwal, Ariel Herbert-Voss, Gretchen Krueger, Tom Henighan, Rewon Child, Aditya Ramesh, Daniel Ziegler, Jeffrey Wu, Clemens Winter, Chris Hesse, Mark Chen, Eric Sigler, Mateusz Litwin, Scott Gray, Benjamin Chess, Jack Clark, Christopher Berner, Sam McCandlish, Alec Radford, Ilya Sutskever, and Dario Amodei. 2020. Language models are few-shot learners. In *Advances in Neural Information Processing Systems*, volume 33, pages 1877–1901. Curran Associates, Inc.

Anthony G. Cohn and Jochen Renz. 2008. Chapter 13 qualitative spatial representation and reasoning. In Frank van Harmelen, Vladimir Lifschitz, and Bruce Porter, editors, *Handbook of Knowledge Representation*, volume 3 of *Foundations of Artificial Intelligence*, pages 551–596. Elsevier.

Jacob Devlin, Ming-Wei Chang, Kenton Lee, and Kristina Toutanova. 2019. BERT: pre-training of deep bidirectional transformers for language understanding. In *Proceedings of the 2019 Conference of the North American Chapter of the Association for Computational Linguistics: Human Language Technologies, NAACL-HLT 2019, Minneapolis, MN, USA, June 2-7, 2019, Volume 1 (Long and Short Papers)*, pages 4171–4186. Association for Computational Linguistics.

Christian Dondrup, Nicola Bellotto, Marc Hanheide, Kerstin Eder, and Ute Leonards. 2015. A computational model of human-robot spatial interactions based on a qualitative trajectory calculus. *Robotics*, 4(1):63–102.

Julien Fleureau, Quentin Galvane, Francois-Louis Tariolle, and Philippe Guillotel. 2016. Generic drone control platform for autonomous capture of cinema scenes. In *Proceedings of the 2nd Workshop on Micro Aerial Vehicle Networks, Systems, and Applications for Civilian Use*, pages 35–40. ACM.

Antonio Franchi, Cristian Secchi, Markus Ryll, Heinrich H Bulthoff, and Paolo Robuffo Giordano. 2012. Shared control: Balancing autonomy and human assistance with a group of quadrotor uavs. *IEEE Robotics & Automation Magazine*, 19(3):57–68.

Bruce Johnson. 2012. *Professional visual studio 2012*. John Wiley & Sons.

John D. Kelleher and Simon Dobnik. 2022. Distributional semantics for situated spatial language? functional, geometric and perceptual perspectives. In J.-P. Bernardy, R. Blanck, S. Chatzikyriakidis, S. Lappin, and A. Maskharashvili, editors, *Probabilistic approaches to linguistic theory, CSLI Publications*, page 319356. Center for the Study of Language and Information, Stanford university, Stanford, California, USA.

María Malfaz and Miguel A Salichs. 2004. A new architecture for autonomous robots based on emotions. In *Fifth IFAC Symposium on Intelligent Autonomous Vehicles*.

Lorenz Meier, Petri Tanskanen, Friedrich Fraundorfer, and Marc Pollefeys. 2011. Pixhawk: A system for autonomous flight using onboard computer vision. In *Robotics and automation (ICRA), 2011 IEEE international conference on*, pages 2992–2997. IEEE.

Reinhard Moratz and Marco Ragni. 2008. Qualitative spatial reasoning about relative point position. *Journal of Visual Languages & Computing*, 19(1):75–98.

D. H. Perico, P. E. Santos, and R. A. C. Bianchi. 2021. Guided navigation from multiple viewpoints using qualitative spatial reasoning. *Spatial Cognition & Computation*, 21(2):143–172.

Alexander R Perry. 2004. The flightgear flight simulator. In *Proceedings of the USENIX Annual Technical Conference*.

Jochen Renz, Debasis Mitra, et al. 2004. Qualitative direction calculi with arbitrary granularity. In *PRICAI*, volume 3157, pages 65–74.

Adam Richard-Bollans, Luca Gmez lvarez, and Anthony G. Cohn. 2020. Modelling the Polysemy of Spatial Prepositions in Referring Expressions. In *Proceedings of the 17th International Conference on Principles of Knowledge Representation and Reasoning*, pages 703–712.

Edilson J Rodrigues, Paulo E Santos, Marcos Lopes, Brandon Bennett, and Paul E Oppenheimer. 2020. Standpoint semantics for polysemy in spatial prepositions. *Journal of Logic and Computation*, 30(2):635–661.

Felipe Martino Esposito Rodrigues, Paulo E Santos, and Marcos Lopes. 2016. Communication of spatial expressions on multi-agent systems using the qualitative ego-sphere. In *Control and Automation (ICCA), 2016 12th IEEE International Conference on*, pages 25–30. IEEE.

Hazim Shakhatreh, Ahmad H. Sawalmeh, Ala Al-Fuqaha, Zuochao Dou, Eyad Almaita, Issa Khalil, Noor Shamsiah Othman, Abdallah Khreishah, and Mohsen Guizani. 2019. Unmanned aerial vehicles (uavs): A survey on civil applications and key research challenges. *IEEE Access*, 7:48572–48634.

Kaili Sun, Xudong Luo, and Michael Y. Luo. 2022. A survey of pretrained language models. In *Knowledge Science, Engineering and Management: 15th International Conference, KSEM 2022, Singapore, August 68, 2022, Proceedings, Part II*, page 442456, Berlin, Heidelberg. Springer-Verlag.

Nico Van de Weghe, Bart Kuijpers, Peter Bogaert, and Philippe De Maeyer. 2005. A qualitative trajectory calculus and the composition of its relations. In *GeoSpatial Semantics*, pages 60–76, Berlin, Heidelberg. Springer Berlin Heidelberg.

Enhancing the DeBERTa Transformers Model for Classifying Sentences from Biomedical Abstracts

Abdul Aziz, Md. Akram Hossain, and Abu Nowshed Chy
Department of Computer Science and Engineering
University of Chittagong, Chattogram-4331, Bangladesh
{aziz.abdul.cu, akram.hossain.cse.cu}@gmail.com,
and nowshed@cu.ac.bd

Abstract

Evidence-based medicine (EBM) is defined as making clinical decisions about individual patients based on the best available evidence. It is beneficial for making better clinical decisions, caring for patients, and providing information about the therapy, prognosis, diagnosis, and other health care issues. However, it is a challenging task to build an automatic sentence classifier for EBM owing to a lack of clinical context, uncertainty in medical knowledge, difficulty in finding the best evidence, and domain-specific words in medical articles. To address these challenges, ALTA 2022 introduced a task to build automatic sentence classifiers for EBM that can map the content of biomedical abstracts into a set of pre-defined categories. This paper presents our participation in this task where we propose a transformers-based classification approach to identify the category of the content from biomedical abstracts. We perform fine-tuning on DeBERTa pre-trained transformers model to extract the contextualized features representation. Later, we employ a multi-sample dropout strategy and 5-fold cross-fold training to predict the more accurate class labels. Experimental results show that our proposed method achieved competitive performance among the participants.

1 Introduction

Personalized medicine based on the context of primary clinical evidence has become one of the most engaging and promising tasks in biomedical research. To suggest personalized medicine, practitioners require to study a lot of publications of medical science related to patient diagnosis. This kind of study is known as evidence-based medicine (EBM) (Masic et al., 2008) where the decision is taken based on some control traits and evidence including Population (P), Intervention (I), Comparison (C), and Outcome (O), in short PICO.

To automate the EBM process, (Kim et al., 2011) explored a classification task where the sentences are collected from the medical abstracts. As an expansion of this work, ALTA 2022 [1] organized a shared task where they address the control traits as PIBOSO by the inclusion of three new classes including Background (B), Study Design (S), and Other (O) to improve the search performance. Here, Other (O) refers to the sentence with irrelevant content. To demonstrate a clear view of the task definition, we articulate a few examples in Table 1.

Sentence	Label
The aim of this non-randomized study is to evaluate a group of patients treated by VP and KP procedures and to discuss related risks.	[0 0 1 0 1 0]
We evaluated drug effect through physical examinations and symptom scales.	[0 0 0 0 0 1]

Table 1: Example of ALTA 2022 task . Here, labels are population, intervention, background, outcome, study design, and other. The 0 and 1 in the label field denotes its existence in the corresponding sentence.

However, the ambiguous clinical context, the randomness of the medical events, the uncertainty of medical knowledge, and highly domain-specific term make it difficult to automate the classification process of medical abstracts for EBM. We can consider this task as the predecessor of some other well-defined tasks in biomedical research including automatic question answering (Andrenucci, 2008). Prior work has extensively explored feature-

**The first two authors have equal contributions.

[1] http://www.alta.asn.au/events/sharedtask2022/description.html

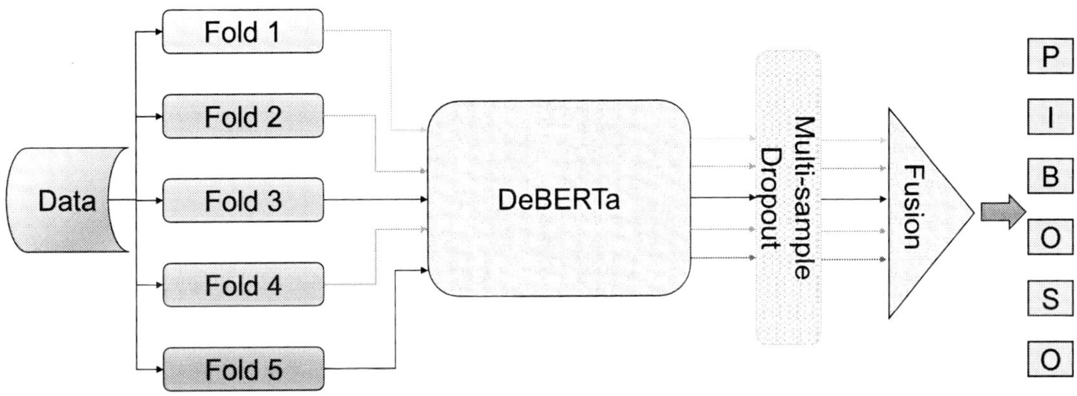

Figure 1: Overview diagram of the proposed system.

based (e.g. lexical and structural features) systems integrated with statistical machine learning (ML) algorithms including support vector machine (SVM), logistic regression, and conditional random fields (CRF) (Amini et al., 2012; Mollá et al., 2012; Sarker et al., 2013). Nevertheless, these approaches are limited to learning complex and ambiguous clinical contexts due to their scattered attention mechanism. Transformer models (Yogarajan et al., 2021) can ameliorate the performance of multi-label natural language processing (NLP) tasks in the medical domain. To overcome the limitations of the prior works and explore the advantages of the transformers model in our proposed system, we fine-tune a SOTA transformers model named DeBERTa (He et al., 2020) integrated with some additional training strategies including the multi-sample dropout and cross-fold training.

We organize the rest of the paper as follows: Section 2 describes our proposed system in the ALTA-2022 automatic labeling medical document abstract into pre-defined classes task whereas, in Section 3, we present our system design with parameter settings along with the results and performance analysis. Finally, we conclude with some future directions in Section 4.

2 Proposed Framework

Transformers models learn the necessary information about the relationship between words effectively. We employed a pre-train transformers model with different training strategies to identify the categories of content from the biomedical abstract. The overview of our proposed transformer-based framework is depicted in Figure 1

For a given biomedical text, we use the DeBERTa transformers model to extract the embedding feature vectors. We fine-tune the DeBERTa model to capture the domain-specific contexts for the biomedical sentence classification task. Later, we apply multi-sample dropout on top of the extracted feature vectors. A classification head averages the feature vectors from multi-sample dropout to predict the confidence of each class. Since a cross-fold training strategy reduce the error rates on class label prediction (Reul et al., 2018; Pikrakis and Theodoridis, 2014), we employ 5-cross-fold training to improve the prediction performances. The predictions obtained from each trained model of each fold are then averaged to determine the final prediction label.

2.1 Transformers Model

Transformers models have the ability to distill long-term dependency and improve the relationship between the words of the sentence. Thus, we fine-tuned the DeBERTa transformers model to extract the contextualized features representation of biomedical sentences.

2.1.1 DeBERTa

DeBERTa (He et al., 2020) stands for decoding-enhanced BERT with disentangled attention. It improves the BERT and RoBERTa models using disentangled attention mechanism and enhanced mask decoder. We used the enhanced version of the DeBERTa model named DeBERTaV3 (He et al., 2021). The DeBERTaV3 model used the ELECTRA style pre-training by replacing mask language modeling (MLM) with the replaced token detection (RTD) strategy where the model is trained as a discriminator to determine whether an input token is either original or replaced by a generator. It also used the gradient-disentangled embedding sharing (GDES) method that shares the embeddings between the generators and the discriminators. However, this sharing is unidirectional where the generator shares its embeddings with the discriminator but the discriminator is restricted to backpropagating the embeddings. This improved DeBERTa model achieved significant performance on downstream tasks. Motivated by this, we employ Huggingface's (Wolf et al., 2019) implementation of *microsoft/deberta-v3-large* checkpoint to extract the feature representation of the sentences. It is composed of 24 transformer blocks, a hidden size of 1024, and 131M parameters with a vocabulary of 128K tokens in the embedding layer.

2.2 Training Strategies

Prior studies suggested different training strategies to improve the performance of the transformers model (Inoue, 2019). Following this, we use two training strategies including the multi-sample dropout and 5-fold cross-fold training.

2.2.1 Multi-sample Dropout

The multi-sample dropout-based training strategy improves the generalization ability and accelerates the training of the base model, which in turn improves the overall performance of the system (Inoue, 2019). In our proposed transformer-based model, we employ this training strategy where we use five dropout samples. Here, we basically duplicate the features vector of the transformer model after the dropout layer, while sharing the weights among these duplicated fully connected layers. To obtain the final loss, we aggregate the loss obtain from each sample and take their average.

2.2.2 Cross-fold Training

To improve the robustness of our model through reducing the error rates during the model training, we use the stratified cross-fold training strategy (Reul et al., 2018; Pikrakis and Theodoridis, 2014; Sechidis et al., 2011). It maintains the proportion of disjoint groups within a population by using samples taken from these groups. Instead of training a model using the full dataset, it basically creates several folds from the training sample and each fold is then used to train the model. It has a great impact on the hyperparameters tuning phase and effectively captures the diversity of contexts related to the task. We use 5-fold stratified multi-label cross-fold training in our method. Finally, we average the predictions attained from each fold to estimate the final prediction score of each class.

3 Experiment and Evaluation

3.1 Dataset Description

The organizers used a benchmark dataset published in DTMBio-2010 (Kim et al., 2011) to evaluate the performance of the participants' systems at the ALTA-2022 shared task. The dataset statistics are summarized in Table 2. The dataset comprises biomedical sentences taken from 1000 biomedical article abstracts. Each sentence is annotated with six categories including population (P), intervention (I), background (B), outcome (O), study design (S), and other (O).

Category	Data
Train	8216
Dev	459
Test	569
Total	9244

Table 2: The statistics of ALTA 2022 dataset.

3.2 Experimental Settings

We now describe the details of our experimental and hyper-parameter settings along with finetuning strategy that we have employed to design our proposed system for the ALTA 2022 shared task.

Parameter	Optimal Value
Learning rate	3e-5
Max-len	128
Number of epochs	5
Batch size	2
Manual seed	4
Number of fold	5
Dropout	0.1, 0.2,..., 0.5

Table 3: Model settings for ALTA-2022 shared task.

We finetune a state-of-the-art Huggingface transformers model named DeBERTa[2] for this task. We used a CUDA-enabled GPU and set the manual seed = 4 to generate reproducible results. The optimal parameter settings of our proposed model based on the development dataset are presented in

[2]https://huggingface.co/microsoft/deberta-v3-large

Team Name	ROC (micro) Score	Team Rank
CSECU-DSG (ours)	0.968750	2nd
Competitive performance of top ranked methods		
Heatwave	**0.987395**	1st
Michaelibrahim	0.963404	3rd
Necva	0.931843	4th
Dmollaaliod	0.910455	5th

Table 4: Comparative performance of our proposed method along with top-performing participants' method (ROC score; Higher is better.)

Table. We used the default settings for the other parameters. In our multi-sample dropout training, we use the dropout range of 0.1 to 0.5. Later, we concatenate the training and development data during our 5-fold cross-fold training phase.

3.3 Evaluation Measure

The ALTA 2022 shared task organizers employed a standard evaluation metric including the receiver operating characteristic (ROC) score to evaluate the participants' system. They calculate the ROC score utilizing the scikit-learn (Pedregosa et al., 2011) roc_auc_score package with micro averaging for ranking the participants' system.

3.4 Results and Analysis

In this section, we analyze the performance of our proposed CSECU-DSG system in the ALTA-2022 biomedical sentence identification shared task. The comparative performance of our proposed CSECU-DSG system on test data against other top-performing participants' systems in are presented in Table 4.

At first, we presented the result of our proposed method and then we added the system performances of other top-ranked participants. Results showed that our proposed system obtained 2nd position in the ALTA-2022 shared task. The best system Heatwave achieved 0.987395 in terms of the primary evaluation metric receiver operating characteristic (ROC) score. Our proposed system obtained a 0.968750 ROC score in the test set. In our proposed CSECU-DSG system, we perform two training strategies including cross-fold training and multi-sample dropout to train the state-of-the-art DeBERTa transformer model. It helps our proposed model to achieve this score.

To further analyze the performance of our model, we estimate the impact of our used training strategies to train the DeBERTa model. The summarized results regarding this analysis on the validation set are presented in Table 5. Here, we have seen that the multi-sample dropout technique improves the performance of the DeBERTa model by 1% while the cross-fold training improves the performance by 1.2% in terms of ROC score. This validates the effectiveness of these training strategies to improve the overall model performances.

Model	ROC Score
DeBERTa	0.95209
DeBERTa+MSD	0.96112
DeBERTa+MSD+ CFT (Ours)	0.971133

Table 5: Performance analysis of individual model used in our proposed CSECU-DSG system. MSD = Multi-sample Dropout; CFT = Cross Fold Training

4 Conclusion and Future Directions

In this paper, we present an approach to labeling a sentence into six predefined classes in medical abstracts using fine-tuned DeBERTa transformers model with various training strategies including the multi-sample dropout and cross-fold training. Experimental results demonstrated the efficacy of our DeBERTa-based proposed method, where the fusion of cross-fold variants approach helped us to obtain competitive performance and ranked 2nd in the ALTA 2022 shared task.

Further research may focus on other SOTA transformers models and a fusion of multiple models in a unified architecture can also be explored. Since the dataset is imbalanced, exploiting the weighted average fusion strategy on different models may capture better contexts for all PIBOSO classes from medical abstracts.

References

Iman Amini, David Martinez, Diego Molla, et al. 2012. Overview of the alta 2012 shared task.

Andrea Andrenucci. 2008. Automated question-answering techniques and the medical domain. *HEALTHINF (2)*, pages 207–212.

Pengcheng He, Jianfeng Gao, and Weizhu Chen. 2021. Debertav3: Improving deberta using electra-style pre-training with gradient-disentangled embedding sharing. *arXiv preprint arXiv:2111.09543*.

Pengcheng He, Xiaodong Liu, Jianfeng Gao, and Weizhu Chen. 2020. Deberta: Decoding-enhanced bert with disentangled attention. *arXiv preprint arXiv:2006.03654*.

Hiroshi Inoue. 2019. Multi-sample dropout for accelerated training and better generalization. *arXiv preprint arXiv:1905.09788*.

Su Nam Kim, David Martinez, Lawrence Cavedon, and Lars Yencken. 2011. Automatic classification of sentences to support evidence based medicine. In *BMC bioinformatics*, volume 12, pages 1–10. BioMed Central.

Izet Masic, Milan Miokovic, and Belma Muhamedagic. 2008. Evidence based medicine–new approaches and challenges. *Acta Informatica Medica*, 16(4):219.

Diego Mollá et al. 2012. Experiments with clustering-based features for sentence classification in medical publications: Macquarie test's participation in the alta 2012 shared task.

Fabian Pedregosa, Gaël Varoquaux, Alexandre Gramfort, Vincent Michel, Bertrand Thirion, Olivier Grisel, Mathieu Blondel, Peter Prettenhofer, Ron Weiss, Vincent Dubourg, et al. 2011. Scikit-learn: Machine learning in python. *the Journal of machine Learning research*, 12:2825–2830.

Aggelos Pikrakis and Sergios Theodoridis. 2014. Speech-music discrimination: A deep learning perspective. In *2014 22nd European signal processing conference (EUSIPCO)*, pages 616–620. IEEE.

Christian Reul, Uwe Springmann, Christoph Wick, and Frank Puppe. 2018. Improving ocr accuracy on early printed books by utilizing cross fold training and voting. In *2018 13th IAPR International Workshop on Document Analysis Systems (DAS)*, pages 423–428. IEEE.

Abeed Sarker, Diego Mollá, and Cécile Paris. 2013. An approach for automatic multi-label classification of medical sentences. In *Proceedings of the 4th International Louhi Workshop on Health Document Text Mining and Information Analysis. Sydney, NSW, Australia*.

Konstantinos Sechidis, Grigorios Tsoumakas, and Ioannis Vlahavas. 2011. On the stratification of multi-label data. In *Joint European Conference on Machine Learning and Knowledge Discovery in Databases*, pages 145–158. Springer.

Thomas Wolf, Lysandre Debut, Victor Sanh, Julien Chaumond, Clement Delangue, Anthony Moi, Pierric Cistac, Tim Rault, Rémi Louf, Morgan Funtowicz, et al. 2019. HuggingFace's Transformers: State-of-the-art Natural Language Processing. *arXiv preprint arXiv:1910.03771*.

Vithya Yogarajan, Jacob Montiel, Tony Smith, and Bernhard Pfahringer. 2021. Transformers for multi-label classification of medical text: an empirical comparison. In *International Conference on Artificial Intelligence in Medicine*, pages 114–123. Springer.

Textstar: a Fast and Lightweight Graph-Based Algorithm for Extractive Summarization and Keyphrase Extraction

David Brock
Dallas College
dbrock@dallascollege.edu

Ali Khan
University of North Texas
alikhan@my.unt.edu

Tam Doan
University of North Texas
tamdoan@my.unt.edu

Alicia Lin
University of North Texas
alicia.y.lin@gmail.com

Yifan Guo
University of North Texas
yifan.guo.3517@gmail.com

Paul Tarau
University of North Texas
paul.tarau@unt.edu

Abstract

We introduce Textstar, a graph-based summarization and keyphrase extraction system that builds a document graph using only lemmatization and POS tagging. The document graph aggregates connections between lemma and sentence identifier nodes. Consecutive lemmas in each sentence, as well as consecutive sentences themselves, are connected in rings to form a "ring of rings" representing the document. We iteratively apply a centrality algorithm of our choice to the document graph and trim the lowest ranked nodes at each step. After the desired number of remaining sentences and lemmas is reached, we extract the sentences as the summary, and the remaining lemmas are aggregated into keyphrases using their context. Our algorithm is efficient enough to process large document graphs without any training, and empirical evaluation on several benchmarks indicates that our performance is higher than most other graph-based algorithms.

1 Introduction

Contemporary natural language processing is mostly done through neural networks. However, this is resource intensive and requires large amounts of data. This can be a problem for languages that are not widely spoken, due to insufficient data for training these models. Even for tasks where neural network based models excel, they are often an overkill. State of the art Transformer-based tools such as BERT (Devlin et al., 2019), GPT-3 (Brown et al., 2020), and even Longformer (Beltagy et al., 2020) have size limits and require hierarchical approaches to long documents. However, graph-based approaches are one-shot algorithms that do not require expensive computational resources to train. The need for a fast graph-based summarizer is also justified as a preprocessor to assist these neural models by enabling them to work on salient smaller subsets of a large document.

To address this insufficiency, we propose Textstar, a lightweight graph-based summarization and keyphrase extraction algorithm that outperforms most other graph-based methods. Our model is language-independent, making it suitable for application to languages with insufficient training data. Additionally, it simultaneously supports keyphrase extraction and summarization. This flexibility, along with its short runtime, opens up possibilities for many applications.

We will start with an overview of our system, as presented in Figure 1. After a document is uploaded, it is pre-processed. Then, each sentence is converted into a connected ring of nodes (Figure 2). Additionally, the sentence IDs are also connected into a ring of nodes. Afterwards, the graph is fed to the Textstar algorithm, which gradually trims out word nodes and sentence ID nodes that have low ranking values. When the graph contains only the desired number of sentence ID nodes or keyword nodes, we feed this information to the postprocessing component. The postprocessing component then converts certain keywords into keyphrases and combines the sentences represented by the sentence ID nodes into a summary.

Our contribution is as follows:

(1) We introduce a novel graph-based algorithm that extracts both summaries and keyphrases at the same time.

(2) We construct textgraphs via the ring-of-rings method.

(3) Our Textstar algorithm is an iterative text graph trimming approach for identifying in one pass the most important sentences and keyphrases.

(4) We show that our system improves the state-of-the-art with respect to other similar graph-based algorithms.

The rest of the paper is organized as follows:

Section 2 overviews related work.

Section 3 describes the algorithm and implementation.

Section 4 provides empirical analysis.

Section 5 analyzes the results and discusses the limitations.

Section 6 concludes the paper.

2 Related Work

Graph-based approaches to text summarization and keyphrase extraction are well-established. TextRank (Mihalcea and Tarau, 2004) and its derivatives are popular unsupervised approaches to text summarization and keyphrase extraction. They utilize graph-based centrality algorithms to score sentences or words with the assumption that sentences or words with the highest centrality scores are expected to have the highest importance in a document. TextRank, in particular, uses the PageRank algorithm (Page et al., 1999) as its scoring mechanism.

Several methods have been proposed that improve the base TextRank algorithm by changing the scoring metric (Barrios et al., 2016) or by changing the construction of the textgraph using salient information about the text or by use of word embeddings.

Bougouin et al. (2013) discover and categorize candidate keyphrases to topics by applying the Hierarchical Agglomerative Clustering algorithm. Then, a weighted complete and undirected graph is generated where nodes represent the topics and weighted edges show the semantic relations of the topics. Keyphrases that best represent each topic are chosen with three criteria: appearing first in the document, appearing most frequently in the document, and being the most similar to other keyphrases in the topic. Then, each topic is ranked by the Textrank algorithm. Choosing the topics with the N highest scores and selecting the most significant keyphrase per topic generates the final set of keyphrases.

Florescu and Caragea (2017) retrieve nouns and adjectives and construct an undirected word graph in which each node is a unique word and the weight of an edge is calculated from the number of bigram co-occurrences in the document. The biased PageRank score of each word is counted by considering both its position and its frequency. The sum of scores of words in each keyphrase generates the keyphrase's score.

Boudin (2018) selects keyphrase candidates and classifies word stems to topics in a manner similar to Bougouin et al. (2013). Then, a complete directed k-partite graph is constructed where each node is a keyphrase, an edge connects 2 different topics, the weight of an edge shows a distance between 2 nodes in the document, and k is the number of topics. In addition, the incoming weight of the first node of each topic is adjusted. Then the TextRank algorithm gives the score for each node, and the N top scoring keyphrases are extracted.

LexRank (Erkan and Radev, 2004) showcases improved summarization by introducing the idea of computed eigenvector centrality. This method constructs a weighted undirected cosine similarity graph cluster from the given multiple documents, where nodes denote sentences and a weighted edge signifies the idf-modified-cosine of 2 nodes. Then, the graph is transferred to an undirected graph which focuses on the salient similar sentences by setting a threshold. The LexRank score of each node is calculated based on eigenvector centrality. The summary is N top scoring sentences.

Most graph-based methods perform either extractive text summarization or automatic keyphrase extraction, but not both. Neural methods have recently been shown to be effective at multi-task natural language processing. However, like graph-based methods, there is little work on neural methods that perform both extractive summarization and keyphrase extraction.

Our approach implements a multi-task approach to summarization and keyphrase extraction by creating a textgraph sharing both sentences and word nodes. We also introduce a different topology for building a textgraph using a ring-of-rings construction for connecting both words in a sentence and sentences among them. At the same time, a new method is used to compute rankings by successive trimming of unimportant nodes until the required number of sentences and keyphrases is reached.

3 Method

Our overall method is shown in Figure 1. The first step of processing a document is to remove words and sentences that are unlikely to contain relevant information. A text graph with a ring-of-rings structure is then constructed using the remaining words and sentences. Using the graph, the core

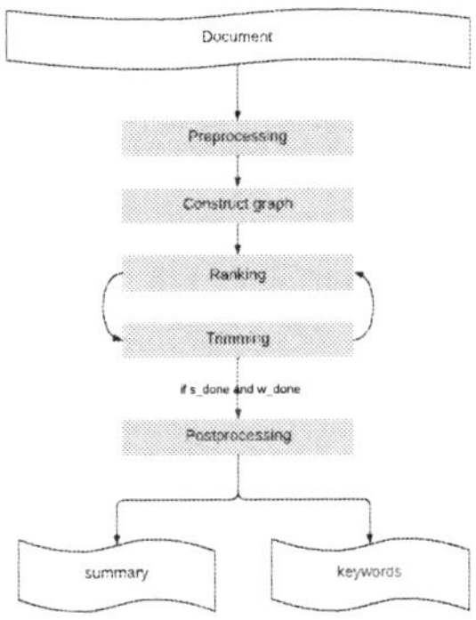

Figure 1: Overview Method

Textstar algorithm works by repeatedly computing a centrality metric and then removing low ranked nodes. This process continues until the desired number of summary sentences and key words is reached. Finally, the word and sentence nodes left in the graph are post-processed to create the final summary and keyphrases.

3.1 Text Preprocessing

Using the NLTK Python package[1] (Bird et al., 2009), we first split the text into sentences (sentence tokenization) and the sentences into words (word tokenization). The words and sentences are filtered to remove those that are unlikely to contain useful information. Sentences are removed if they are too long and/or noisy after the pdftotext translation. We also perform stopword removal. Finally, we also use NLTK to lemmatize the words and apply a basic POS tagging.

3.2 The Ring of Rings Textgraph Construction

We construct the textgraph of the document as a ring of rings meta-structure, in which each sentence is a ring and each sentence is connected to a node in the central ring. This structure allows for the natural encapsulation of information from the document, including word and sentence position in a directed graph. Moreover, the ring structures of words and sentences allow both words and sentences to be connected back to front; this is important because later words/sentences refer to earlier introductions.

[1] https://www.nltk.org/api/nltk.html

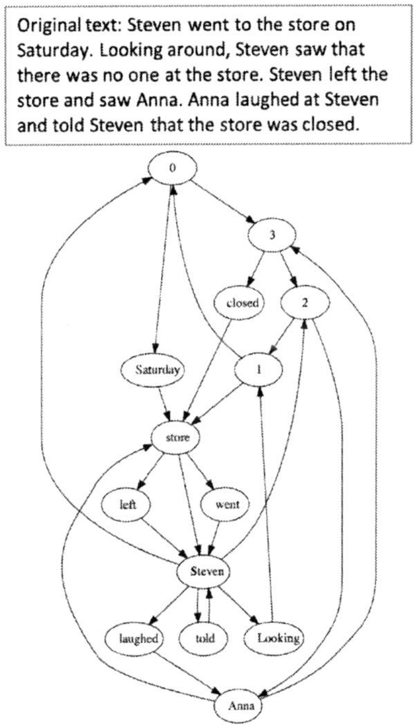

Figure 2: Example Graph

The graph is created from the cleaned and lemmatized text. To facilitate both summarization and keyphrase extraction, the graph's nodes represent both words and sentences. Strings represent words, and sentences are represented by an integer ID.

The cleaned and lemmatized words of a sentence are connected in reverse order, and the sentence's id is connected between the first and last word of the sentence to form a ring. The sentence nodes are also connected in reverse order, and the last sentence node is adjacent to the first sentence node to form the central ring. As a result, a ring of rings with a structure similar to that shown in Figure 3 is formed. An example of the resulting graph of an extremely short text is shown in Figure 2. The ring of sentence ids is shown as the nodes labeled 0 to 3. At the same time, the ring-of-rings torus topology is distorted by the shared occurrences of words such as 'Steven' and 'store' that originate from multiple word rings. Note that some nodes are shared by multiple rings, since some words (e.g. store) are shared by multiple sentences. We also add edges between compounds.

3.3 The Trimming Algorithm

After the graph (containing both word and sentence nodes) is generated, it is passed to the Textstar algorithm. The algorithm first ranks the nodes in the graph using a ranking function. From our tests, the degree centrality ranking function performs best, although Pagerank also works well. The nodes are sorted based on rank and only the highest X percent are kept, where X is a parameter that can be tuned. For summarization, a value of X around 70-80 percent works best, and for keyphrase extraction X can be a bit lower.

This process is then repeated, with the graph being re-ranked and then trimmed. When the number of remaining sentence nodes and word nodes drops below the desired number of summary sentences and key words, respectively, iteration stops.

Algorithm 1: The Textstar Algorithm

```
Input: g: Textgraph of the document
       ranker: ranking algorithm
       sumsize: final number of sentences,
       kwsize: final number of keyphrases,
       trim: percent of lowest ranked
       nodes to remove per step
Result: final_sids, final_kwds
while true do
    ranks ← Ranker(g);
    sids ← ∀x ∈ ranks, if x is a sentence id;
    kwds ← ∀x ∈ ranks, if x is a lemma;
    s_done ← length of sids ≤ sumsize;
    w_done ← length of kwds ≤ kwsize;
    n ← number of nodes in g;
    if not s_done then
        final_sids ← sids;
    end
    if not w_done then
        final_kwds ← kwds;
    end
    if s_done and w_done then
        break;
    end
    split ← trim * n // 100;
    for i = split...n do
        g.remove(ranks[i])
    end
end
```

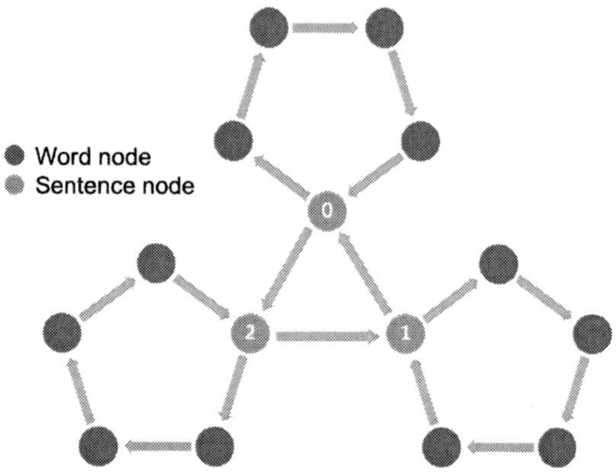

Figure 3: Ring of Rings Structure

3.4 Postprocessing

The summary is generated by taking the remaining sentence nodes from the graph. These nodes have the highest ranks, and the associated sentences from the original text are extracted. To make the summary more readable, the summary sentences are sorted according to the order they appear in the original text.

Similarly, the keyphrases are extracted from the word nodes in the final graph. Only unique word nodes with the highest ranks are taken.

4 Evaluation

We have used the Degree Centrality ranking algorithm, with the summary size and keyphrase size as 6 and the trim percentage set to 80%.

Table 1 provides extractive summarization results on the *arXiv* and *PubMed* datasets. The PubMed dataset, which has 133K scientific documents, is divided into a training set (125,020 documents, 94%); a validation set (3,990 documents, 3 %); and a test set (3,990 documents, 3%). The ArXiv dataset, which contains 215K scientific documents, is distributed between a training set (193,500 documents, 90%); a validation set (10,750 documents, 5 %); and a test set (10,750 documents, 5%).The gold summary of each document in both these datasets is the abstract of the document.(Cohan et al., 2018).

We compare Textstar against well-known extractive graphical algorithms: *LSA* (Steinberger et al., 2004) , *SumBasic* (Vanderwende et al., 2007), and *LexRank* (Erkan and Radev, 2004). We use the results of these algorithms found in Cohan et al. (2018).

Table 2 provides the results for automatic

keyhprase extraction. We evaluate on the following well-known datasets:

- *Inspec*: This dataset contains 2,000 short English texts, which are collected from the Inspec database from between 1998 and 2002. Each piece consists of an abstract, a title, and keyphrases. (Hulth, 2003).

- *SemEval*: This dataset consists of 284 English scientific articles from the ACM Digital Library in four topics: Distributed Systems, Information Search and Retrieval, Distributed Artificial Intelligence, and Behavioral Sciences - Economics. The distribution of each topic is equal. The gold keyphrases were cautiously selected by both authors and readers. (Kim et al., 2010).

Our model is evaluated by f-mesure on the top K keypharses (F1@K). Textstar is compared against the following graph-based keyphrase extraction algorithms: *TextRank* (Mihalcea and Tarau, 2004), *SingleRank* (Wan and Xiao, 2008), *TopicRank* (Bougouin et al., 2013), *PositionRank* (Florescu and Caragea, 2017), and *MultipartiteRank* (Boudin, 2018). The results of *Inspec* and *SemEval2010* for the baseline algorithms are obtained from Liang et al. (2021). Textstar is also comparable to *CopyRNN* (Meng et al., 2017) and outperforms *RNN* (Meng et al., 2017) deep learning model on both the Inspec and SemEval dataset. These results are gained from Meng et al. (2017)

To evaluate these algorithms, we use a Python implementation of the ROUGE (Lin, 2004) metric[2]. Our tests show that we outperform other graph-based algorithms for text summarization on arXiv, and are competitive to LexRank on the PubMed dataset. For keyphrase extraction, we outperform all other graph-based algorithms on all datasets with the exception of the Inspec dataset.

5 Discussion

The experiments show that the algorithm is competitive on benchmarks of both extractive summarization and automatic keyphrase extraction. Whereas separate sentence and word text graphs lose information from the original text, reducing the effectiveness of either task, our multi-task approach takes advantage of the synergies between summarization and keyphrase extraction, allowing for better results than either individually. The important words in a document are strongly correlated to the important sentences. We make use of the relationship between the words and the structure of the document explicitly.

5.1 Limitations

The Textstar algorithm shares its limitations with the larger graph-based family of extractive summarization and keyphrase extraction algorithms:

- performance is usually worse than state-of-the-art of deep learning algorithms
- textgraphs generally do not rely on deeper syntactic and semantic information
- textgraph-based algorithms do not make use of domain knowledge
- extracted summaries are not natural to human readers
- textgraphs generally do not perform well on very short documents

Some of these limitations can be alleviated by bringing in richer syntactic information (e.g., dependency trees) and semantic relations extracted from the text or from knowledge graphs specific to the domain of the document along the lines of Tarau and Blanco (2021).

6 Conclusions

We introduced *Textstar*, a multi-task graph-based extractive text summarization and automatic keyphrase extraction algorithm. By iteratively simplifying the text graph while eliminating the lowest ranked scores as determined by a centrality algorithm, we efficiently determine the most salient sentences and keyphrases. Moreover, by building the textgraphs from both sentence and word nodes, we extract in one pass both summaries and keyphrases.

By aggregating information about word subsequences occurring in a sentence and sentence subsequences occurring in a document, we show that we outperform most other graph-based methods.

While like most other graph-based methods, Textstar's performance does not match that of state-of-the-art deep learning frameworks, Textstar can act as a useful preprocessor to them to

[2] `https://github.com/Diego999/py-rouge`

Algorithm	arXiv			PubMed		
	ROUGE-1	ROUGE-2	ROUGE-L	ROUGE-1	ROUGE-2	ROUGE-L
LSA	29.91	7.42	25.67	33.89	9.93	29.70
SumBasic	29.47	6.95	26.30	37.15	11.36	33.43
LexRank	33.85	10.73	28.99	**39.19**	13.89	**34.59**
Textstar	**38.8**	**12.8**	**32.1**	38.6	**13.9**	32.0

Table 1: Summarization results on PubMed and arXiv dataset.

Algorithm	Inspec		SemEval 2010	
	F1@5	F1@10	F1@5	F1@10
Graph_based Models				
TextRank	27.04	25.08	3.80	5.38
SingleRank	27.79	34.46	5.90	9.02
TopicRank	25.38	28.46	12.12	12.90
PositionRank	**28.12**	32.87	9.84	13.34
Textstar	24.70	**34.70**	**15.20**	**22.80**
Deep Learning Models				
RNN	8.50	6.40	15.70	12.40
CopyRNN	**27.80**	**34.20**	**29.30**	**30.40**

Table 2: Result of keyphrase extraction with metrics F1@5 and F1@10 in Inspec and SemEval 2010 datasets.

accommodate the input size limitations in various neural systems.

Future work is planned to evaluate the use of Textstar as a preprocessor for transformer-based systems that have input-size limitations as well for enhancing the text graph with similarity links between sentence and word embeddings.

References

Federico Barrios, Federico López, Luis Argerich, and Rosa Wachenchauzer. 2016. Variations of the similarity function of textrank for automated summarization.

Iz Beltagy, Matthew E. Peters, and Arman Cohan. 2020. Longformer: The long-document transformer. *arXiv:2004.05150*.

S. Bird, E. Klein, and E. Loper. 2009. *Natural Language Processing with Python: Analyzing Text with the Natural Language Toolkit*. O'Reilly Media.

Florian Boudin. 2018. Unsupervised keyphrase extraction with multipartite graphs. In *Proceedings of the 2018 Conference of the North American Chapter of the Association for Computational Linguistics: Human Language Technologies, Volume 2 (Short Papers)*, pages 667–672, New Orleans, Louisiana. Association for Computational Linguistics.

Adrien Bougouin, Florian Boudin, and Béatrice Daille. 2013. TopicRank: Graph-based topic ranking for keyphrase extraction. In *Proceedings of the Sixth International Joint Conference on Natural Language Processing*, pages 543–551, Nagoya, Japan. Asian Federation of Natural Language Processing.

Tom Brown, Benjamin Mann, Nick Ryder, Melanie Subbiah, Jared D Kaplan, Prafulla Dhariwal, Arvind Neelakantan, Pranav Shyam, Girish Sastry, Amanda Askell, Sandhini Agarwal, Ariel Herbert-Voss, Gretchen Krueger, Tom Henighan, Rewon Child, Aditya Ramesh, Daniel Ziegler, Jeffrey Wu, Clemens Winter, Chris Hesse, Mark Chen, Eric Sigler, Mateusz Litwin, Scott Gray, Benjamin Chess, Jack Clark, Christopher Berner, Sam McCandlish, Alec Radford, Ilya Sutskever, and Dario Amodei. 2020. Language models are few-shot learners. In *Advances in Neural Information Processing Systems*, volume 33, pages 1877–1901. Curran Associates, Inc.

Arman Cohan, Franck Dernoncourt, Doo Soon Kim, Trung Bui, Seokhwan Kim, Walter Chang, and Nazli Goharian. 2018. A discourse-aware attention model for abstractive summarization of long documents. In *Proceedings of the 2018 Conference of the North American Chapter of the Association for Computational Linguistics: Human Language Technologies, Volume 2 (Short Papers)*, pages 615–621, New Orleans, Louisiana. Association for Computational Linguistics.

Jacob Devlin, Ming-Wei Chang, Kenton Lee, and Kristina Toutanova. 2019. BERT: Pre-training of deep bidirectional transformers for language understanding. In *Proceedings of the 2019 Conference of the North American Chapter of the*

Association for Computational Linguistics: Human Language Technologies, Volume 1 (Long and Short Papers), pages 4171–4186, Minneapolis, Minnesota. Association for Computational Linguistics.

G. Erkan and D.R. Radev. 2004. Lexrank: Graph-based lexical centrality as salience in text summarization. *Journal of Artificial Intelligence Research*, 22:457–479.

Corina Florescu and Cornelia Caragea. 2017. PositionRank: An unsupervised approach to keyphrase extraction from scholarly documents. In *Proceedings of the 55th Annual Meeting of the Association for Computational Linguistics (Volume 1: Long Papers)*, pages 1105–1115, Vancouver, Canada. Association for Computational Linguistics.

Anette Hulth. 2003. Improved automatic keyword extraction given more linguistic knowledge. In *Proceedings of the 2003 Conference on Empirical Methods in Natural Language Processing*, EMNLP '03, page 216–223, USA. Association for Computational Linguistics.

Su Nam Kim, Olena Medelyan, Min-Yen Kan, and Timothy Baldwin. 2010. Semeval-2010 task 5: Automatic keyphrase extraction from scientific articles. In *Proceedings of the 5th International Workshop on Semantic Evaluation*, pages 21–26.

Xinnian Liang, Shuangzhi Wu, Mu Li, and Zhoujun Li. 2021. Unsupervised keyphrase extraction by jointly modeling local and global context. In *Proceedings of the 2021 Conference on Empirical Methods in Natural Language Processing*, pages 155–164, Online and Punta Cana, Dominican Republic. Association for Computational Linguistics.

Chin-Yew Lin. 2004. ROUGE: A package for automatic evaluation of summaries. In *Text Summarization Branches Out*, pages 74–81, Barcelona, Spain. Association for Computational Linguistics.

Rui Meng, Sanqiang Zhao, Shuguang Han, Daqing He, Peter Brusilovsky, and Yu Chi. 2017. Deep keyphrase generation. In *Proceedings of the 55th Annual Meeting of the Association for Computational Linguistics (Volume 1: Long Papers)*, pages 582–592, Vancouver, Canada. Association for Computational Linguistics.

Rada Mihalcea and Paul Tarau. 2004. Textrank: Bringing order into text. In *Proceedings of the 2004 conference on empirical methods in natural language processing*, pages 404–411.

Lawrence Page, Sergey Brin, Rajeev Motwani, and Terry Winograd. 1999. The pagerank citation ranking: Bringing order to the web. Technical report, Stanford InfoLab.

Josef Steinberger, Karel Jezek, et al. 2004. Using latent semantic analysis in text summarization and summary evaluation. *Proc. ISIM*, 4(93-100):8.

Paul Tarau and Eduardo Blanco. 2021. Interactive Text Graph Mining with a Prolog-Based Dialog Engine. *Theory Pract. Log. Program.*, 21(2):244–263.

Lucy Vanderwende, Hisami Suzuki, Chris Brockett, and Ani Nenkova. 2007. Beyond sumbasic: Task-focused summarization with sentence simplification and lexical expansion. *Information Processing & Management*, 43(6):1606–1618.

Xiaojun Wan and Jianguo Xiao. 2008. Single document keyphrase extraction using neighborhood knowledge.

Appendix A. Examples of Textstar Output

Below are the results of the Textstar algorithm on a near final version of this paper.

> **Summary:** Our contribution is as follows: (1) We introduce a novel graph-based algorithm that extracts both summaries and keyphrases at the same time. The words and sentences are filtered to remove those that are unlikely to contain useful information. Sentences are removed if they are too long or too noisy after the pdftotext translation. This structure allows for the natural encapsulation of information from the document, including word and sentence position in a directed graph. Moreover, the ring structures of words and sentences allow both words and sentences to be connected back to front; this is important because later words/sentences refer to earlier introductions. The algorithm first ranks the nodes in the graph using a ranking function. Table 1 provides extractive summarization results on the arXiv and PubMed datasets. Moreover, by building the textgraphs from both sentence and word nodes, we extract in one pass both summaries and keyphrases.
>
> **Keyphrases:** *'word', 'node', 'sentence', 'ring', 'document', 'connected', 'score'*

Below are the results of running Textstar on the following few paragraphs from a news article about the *Bloom* deep learning-based language model [3].

> Now there is a true open-source alternative to GPT-3, BigScience Bloom, which is freely available for research and enterprise purposes. Bloom was trained over 117 days at the supercomputing center of the French National Center for Scientific Research and is 176 billion parameters in size. The development involved over 1000 volunteer researchers, organized in the BigScience project, coordinated by Hugging Face, and co-funded by the French government. Bloom can be downloaded for free on Hugging Face and is said to be on par with GPT-3 for accuracy ? and also toxicity. A key difference from GPT-3 is a stronger focus on languages away from the otherwise dominant English language. Bloom can process 46 different languages, including French, Vietnamese, Mandarin, Indonesian, Catalan, 13 Indian languages (such as Hindi) and 20 African languages. BigScience collected numerous new datasets for this and is publishing full details on datasets, development and training of Bloom. The release falls under the Responsible AI License developed by BigScience, which prohibits the use of Bloom in areas such as law enforcement, healthcare, or deception. However, unlike OpenAI, for example, BigScience has no way to effectively prevent misuse because the model is available directly and not through an interface. Bloom is now expected to serve as the foundation for numerous applications and, more importantly, research projects that create alternative AI applications away from the big tech companies.

[3]`https://mixed-news.com/en/bloom-is-a-real-open-source-alternative-to-gpt-3/`

The summary and keyphrases generated by Textstar. The resulting textgraph for this article contains 153 nodes and a fragment of it is shown in Figure 4.

> **Summary:** BigScience Bloom is open science and open source. Bloom was trained over 117 days at the supercomputing center of the French National Center for Scientific Research and is 176 billion parameters in size. The development involved over 1000 volunteer researchers, organized in the BigScience project, coordinated by Hugging Face, and co-funded by the French government. Bloom is now expected to serve as the foundation for numerous applications and, more importantly, research projects that create alternative AI applications away from the big tech companies.
>
> **Keyphrases:** *'National Center', 'Center Scientific', 'Scientific Research', 'Now true alternative', 'volunteer researchers', 'BigScience project'*

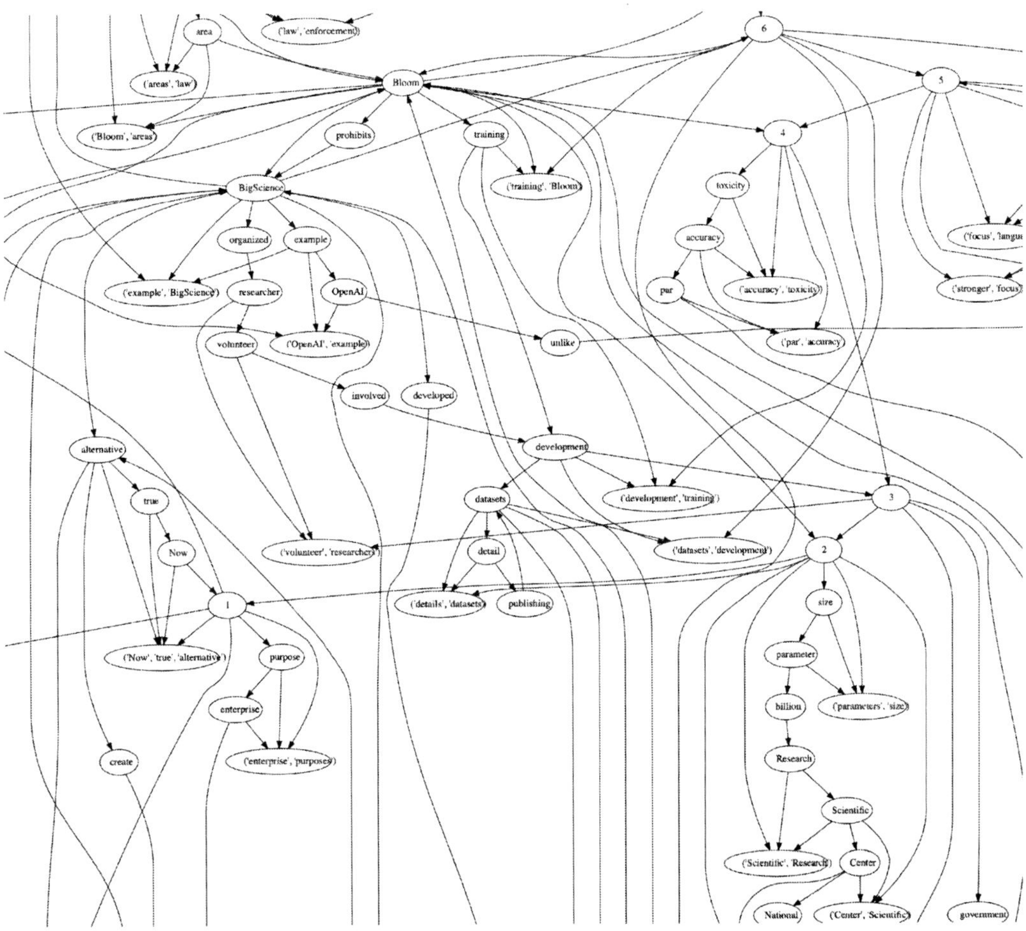

Figure 4: Fragment of the News Article Textgraph

Gap in pagination due to unavailable paper.

Page 178

Overview of the 2022 ALTA Shared task: PIBOSO sentence classification, 10 years later

Diego Mollá
School of Computing
Macquarie University
Sydney, Australia
diego.molla-aliod@mq.edu.au

Abstract

The 2022 ALTA shared task has been running annually since 2010. This year, the shared task is a re-visit of the 2012 ALTA shared task. The purpose of this task is to classify sentences of medical publications using the PIBOSO taxonomy. This is a multi-label classification task which can help medical researchers and practitioners conduct Evidence Based Medicine (EBM). In this paper we present the task, the evaluation criteria, and the results of the systems participating in the shared task.

1 Introduction

Within the practice of Evidence Based Medicine (EBM), the medical practitioner integrates individual clinical expertise with the best external evidence at point of care (Sackett et al., 1996). Finding the best available evidence, however, is increasingly difficult given the large amount of medical publications. For example, at the time of writing, PubMed contains more than 34 million citations for biomedical literature[1]. From 2020 to present, CORD-19, a resource of medical publications about COVID-19, SARS-COV-2, and related coronaviruses, has increased from an initial set of 28,000 papers (Wang et al., 2020) to over 1,000,000[2].

To assist with the task of finding the best available evidence, best EBM practice suggests users to formulate queries that focus on specific aspects of the clinical information sought. PIBOSO (Kim et al., 2011) is a pre-defined set of such aspects of clinical information, and systems participating in the 2012 ALTA shared task classified sentences from medical publications into PIBOSO labels (Amini et al., 2012). In 2022, 10 years later, ALTA has re-visited the task, to find out whether recent advances in machine learning would allow to improve the quality of such classifiers.

This paper presents the results of systems participating in the 2022 ALTA shared task. Section 2 describes the PIBOSO taxonomy. Section 3 briefly mentions related work between the 2012 and the 2022 ALTA shared tasks. Section 4 describes the evaluation framework. Section 5 presents two simple baselines that were made available to the participating teams. Section 6 presents the results and briefly describes the methods of participating systems. Finally, Section 7 concludes this paper.

2 PIBOSO

EBM guidelines recommend the use of structured queries that focus on specific aspects of clinical information (Richardson et al., 1995). One of the most widely used systems is PICO, which defines 4 types of information: ***Population***, for example the number and type of participants in a study; ***Intervention***, such as the treatment applied to the population; ***Comparison*** (if appropriate), for example alternative interventions or placebo; and ***Outcome*** of an intervention.

Different variants and extensions of PICO have been proposed. The ALTA 2012 and 2022 shared tasks use PIBOSO (Kim et al., 2011). This schema removes the ***Comparison*** tag and adds three new tags: ***Background***, ***Study design***, and ***Other***. The PIBOSO tags, as defined by Kim et al. (2011), are:

- *Population*: The group of individual persons, objects, or items comprising the study's sample, or from which the sample was taken for statistical measurement;
- *Intervention*: The act of interfering with a

[1] https://pubmed.ncbi.nlm.nih.gov/, accessed on 15 November 2022.

[2] https://www.kaggle.com/datasets/allen-institute-for-ai/CORD-19-research-challenge, accessed on 15 November 2022.

condition to modify it or with a process to change its course (includes prevention);

- ***Background***: Material that informs and may place the current study in perspective, e.g. work that preceded the current; information about disease prevalence; etc;
- ***Outcome***: The sentence(s) that best summarizes the consequences of an intervention;
- ***Study Design***: The type of study that is described in the abstract;
- ***Other***: Any sentence not falling into one of the other categories and presumed to provide little help with clinical decision making, i.e. non-key or irrelevant sentences.

Different parts of a medical publication may focus on different PIBOSO elements. In practice, each sentence of a PubMed abstract will normally focus on one PIBOSO element, but sometimes a sentence may focus on several (see Table 2 for examples). Thus, systems attempting to determine the PIBOSO labels of a sentence will need to implement multi-label sentence classification. This is the focus of the 2012 and 2022 ALTA shared tasks.

3 Related Work: From 2012 to 2022

The data used in this 2022 shared task is based on the data from the 2012 task (Amini et al., 2012), which is derived from the original NICTA-PIBOSO dataset by Kim et al. (2011). Sentence classification systems participating in ALTA 2012 used approaches based on Conditional Random Field (CRF), Support Vector Machines (SVM), stacked logistic regression, maximum entropy, and random forests. The results of the participating systems are summarised in Table 1.

The following additional research has used the NICTA-PIBOSO dataset for sentence classification. Verbeke et al. (2012) used statistical relational learning. Hassanzadeh et al. (2014) used CRF and a discriminative set of features. Jin and Szolovits (2020) used LSTM plus adversarial training and unsupervised pre-training over large corpora. All of these systems report F1 as the evaluation metric, which is different from the metric used in the ALTA 2012 and ALTA 2022 datasets (Section 4). Even though the F1 and AUC metrics may lead to similar rankings of systems, as observed in the ALTA 2012 shared task (Amini et al., 2012), systems fine-tuned for AUC might not lead to optimal F1 scores. Most notably, systems fine-tuned for AUC do not need to set a classification threshold, and an evaluation using F1 will give very different results depending on the choice of classification threshold.[3]

4 Evaluation Framework

We have been unable to retrieve the labelled test data of the 2012 ALTA shared task. As a consequence, the data for the 2022 shared task is based on the training data from the 2012 shared task, after shuffling the original data and re-numbering the sample IDs. The resulting data has been split into three sets for training, validation, and test.

The documents used in the datasets are abstracts of medical publications published in PubMed. Each abstract contains multiple sentences, and consequently a single PubMed abstract corresponds to several samples in the dataset. To minimise data leakage between the different partitions, the partitions were made based on the abstracts so that all sentences of the same abstract would be in the same partition. Besides preventing data leakage, this partitioning also allows the participating systems to use the context of the other sentences from an abstract during the classification task.

Table 2 shows several samples from the dataset. The table shows that the dataset indicates the PubMed ID, the sentence position in the PubMed abstract, the PIBOSO labels associated with the sentence, and the text of the sentence.

Table 3 shows that the label distributions are not balanced, and most of the labels are ***Background***, ***Outcome***, or ***Other***. All three partitions have a similar label distribution.

The evaluation framework was implemented as a CodaLab competition[4] which consisted of three phases. In the **development phase**, the training and validation data were available but the labels of the validation data were not available. Participant teams were able to make up to 100 submissions to test their systems against the validation data. This phase was not used for the final ranking of the participating systems and ended on the 4th of October 2022. In the **test** phase, the test data

[3]We observed that a system participating in ALTA 2022 obtained very good AUC scores but their F1 score was 0 because the probabilities assigned to each label were lower than the default threshold of 0.5. Probably, a lower threshold would have given a non-zero F1 score for that system.

[4]`https://codalab.lisn.upsaclay.fr/competitions/6935`

System	AUC (test)	F1
Marco Lui (Lui, 2012)	**0.97**	**0.82**
A_MQ	0.96	0.79
Macquarie Test (Molla, 2012)	0.94	0.77
DPMCNA	0.93	0.71
System_Ict (Gella and Long, 2012)	0.93	0.73
Dalibor	0.92	0.73
Starling	0.87	0.79
Mix	0.84	0.74
Benchmarks (Amini et al., 2012)		
- CRF corrected	0.88	0.80
- Naive	0.70	0.55

Table 1: AUC and F1 for the 2012 test set. The best results per column are given in bold. Refer to Section 4 for an explanation of the AUC metric.

PubMed ID	Sentence	Labels	Text
1031546	1	*Population, Intervention*	A 26-year-old subfertile woman ...
1031546	2	*Outcome*	A pregnancy resulted, which ...
1031546	3	*Outcome*	It is suggested that this production ...

Table 2: Annotations corresponding to one PubMed abstract from the training set

	train	val	test
Population	7.11%	7.84%	7.38%
Intervention	6.10%	6.31%	6.15%
Background	21.63%	27.23%	22.67%
Outcome	38.85%	37.25%	35.32%
Study design	2.03%	2.61%	2.46%
Other	29.50%	24.62%	30.75%

Table 3: Label distributions in the data set. The numbers indicate the percentage of sentences that contain the given label. The sum of percentages in each dataset is higher than 100% because a sentence may have multiple labels.

(without labels) was made available and participant teams were able to make up to 3 submissions. This phase was used for the final ranking. In the subsequent phase of **unofficial submissions**, participant systems are able to make an unlimited number of submissions[5] that will be evaluated on the validation data. This phase remains open and new teams are encouraged to participate and make new submissions.[6]

The training data contains 8,216 sentences, the validation data used in the first phase contains 459 sentences, and the test data contains 569 sentences.

Given an input sentence, the output of each participating system must produce, for every PIBOSO label, a number between 0 and 1 that represents the confidence or probability that the label is assigned to the sentence.

The evaluation metric is the micro-average of the Area Under the Receiver Operating Characteristic (ROC) Curve. The ROC curve plots the true positive rate against the false positive rate at various threshold settings for binary classification. We use the micro-average so that labels with more samples are given more importance. The advantage of using this metric instead of metrics such as F1 is that it incorporates the probability scores returned by the system, such that two systems with identical classification predictions but different probability scores will be ranked differently.

5 Baselines

We have provided two simple baselines against which the participating systems can compare. The code for these baselines is publicly available[7]. We

[5]In practice, there is a limit of 999 unofficial submissions.

[6]Read `https://codalab.lisn.upsaclay.fr/competitions/6935` and `http://www.alta.asn.au/events/sharedtask2022/` for details of how to participate.

[7]`https://github.com/altasharedtasks/baselines2022`

System	Category	AUC (test)
Heatwave	Student	**0.9874**
CSECU-DSG	Student	0.9687
Cufe	Open	0.9634
TurkNLP	Student	0.9318
NN baseline		0.9105
NB baseline		0.8769

Table 4: Results of the 2022 ALTA shared task. Metric: Area under the micro-averaged Receiver Operator Characteristics (ROC) curve. Sorted based on AUC (test). The winning team is highlighted in **boldface**.

describe these baselines below.

Naive Bayes (NB). A set of 6 independent Naive Bayes classifiers, one per classification label, has been implemented using scikit-learn. Each sentence is vectorised using tf.idf, and the number of features has been limited to 10,000. Stop words are *not* removed.

Neural Network (NN). A simple Neural Network architecture has been implemented in Keras. The sentences have been vectorised in the same way as with the Naive Bayes baseline. Namely, scikit-learn has been used to obtain the tf.idf of the sentences, and the top 10,000 words have been retained. Stop words are *not* removed. The resulting vectors are fed to a simple neural network consisting of a single dense layer with 6 neurons (one per label), and sigmoid activation. The network does not use dropout. The network has been trained for 70 epochs, batch size 32, and a validation split of 0.2. The choice of number of epochs was determined after examining the loss of the validation split[8].

6 Participating Systems and Results

A total of 3 teams registered in the student category, and 6 teams registered in the open category. Of these, only 5 teams submitted runs in the CodaLab test phase. Table 4 shows the results of the baselines and participating systems for the test phase.

We can observe that all participating teams outperformed the two baselines.

Three of the teams have submitted system descriptions and they are available in the proceedings

[8]Note that the validation split used for training is part of the ALTA training set. This is different from the actual ALTA validation set.

System	AUC (dev)	AUC (test)
NN baseline	0.9091	0.9105
NB baseline	0.8718	0.8769

Table 5: Results of the baseline systems on the development and test sets. Metric: Area under the micro-averaged Receiver Operator Characteristics (ROC).

of the 2022 Australasian Language Technology workshop (ALTA 2022). All three systems incorporated Transformers in their implementations, in particular variants of BERT (Devlin et al., 2018).

Team Heatwave obtained the best results. Their winning system (Fang and Koto, 2022) used an ensemble of BERT-based implementations (BERT, RoBERTa, BioBERT) that classified each sentence with the help of the context of adjacent sentences.

Team CSECU-DSG (Aziz et al., 2022) extended DeBERTa with 5-fold cross-training (creating effectively an Ensemble approach) and multi-sample dropout.

Team TurkNLP (Bölücü and Hepsağ, 2022) extended SciBERT by adding a classification layer that incorporated information from the [CLS] token and the average of SciBERT embeddings.

7 Conclusions

Participation in the 2022 ALTA shared task showed the successful use of Transformer approaches for this task of multi-label classification of abstract sentences from medical publications using PIBOSO. All participating systems outperformed the baselines. Furthermore, the top system outperformed the participating systems of ALTA 2012 (Tables 1 and 4). There is a potential caveat in that the test data used in the 2022 ALTA shared task was different from that of the 2012 ALTA shared task because of the non-availability of the labels of the original 2012 test data. Having said that, given that the test set of the original data was created as a random partition, we would not expect a very large difference in the results. Table 5 shows very small differences between the results of the development and test sets of the Naive Bayes and Neural Networks baselines. In addition, the 2012 shared task (Amini et al., 2012) showed a difference of 0.01 or less between the public and private test partitions in most participating systems. The small differences in the results suggest that an evaluation made with the 2022 test data would produce similar results to an evaluation made with the 2012 test data.

References

Iman Amini, David Martinez, and Diego Molla. 2012. Overview of the ALTA 2012 shared task. In *Australasian Language Technology Workshop 2012: ALTA Shared Task*.

Abdul Aziz, Md. Akram Hossain, and Abu Nowshed Chy. 2022. Enhanding DeBERTa transformers model for classifying sentences from biomedical abstracts. In *Proceedings of the 2022 Australasian Language Technology Workshop, ALTA 2022*, Adelaide, Australia.

Necva Bölücü and Pinal Uskaner Hepsağ. 2022. Automatic classification of evidence based medicine using transformers. In *Proceedings of the 2022 Australasian Language Technology Workshop, ALTA 2022*, Adelaide, Australia.

Jacob Devlin, Ming-Wei Chang, Kenton Lee, and Kristina Toutanova. 2018. BERT: Pre-training of deep bidirectional transformers for language understanding. *arXiv preprint arXiv:1810.04805*.

Biaoyan Fang and Fajri Koto. 2022. Context-aware sentence classification in evidence-based medicine. In *Proceedings of the 2022 Australasian Language Technology Workshop, ALTA 2022*, Adelaide, Australia.

Spandana Gella and Duong Thanh Long. 2012. Automatic sentence classifier for evidence based medicine: Shared task system description. In *Australasian Language Technology Workshop 2012: ALTA Shared Task*.

Hamed Hassanzadeh, Tudor Groza, and Jane Hunter. 2014. Identifying scientific artefacts in biomedical literature: The evidence based medicine use case. *Journal of Biomedical Informatics*, 49:159–170.

Di Jin and Peter Szolovits. 2020. Advancing PICO element detection in biomedical text via deep neural networks. *Bioinformatics*, 36(12):3856–3862.

S. Kim, D. Martinez, L. Cavedon, and L. Yencken. 2011. Automatic classification of sentences to support evidence based medicine. *BMC bioinformatics*, 12:S5.

Marco Lui. 2012. Feature stacking for sentence classification in evidence-based medicine. In *Australasian Language Technology Workshop 2012: ALTA Shared Task*.

Diego Molla. 2012. Experiments with clustering-based features for sentence classification in medical publications: Macquarie Test's participation in the ALTA 2012 shared task. In *Australasian Language Technology Workshop 2012: ALTA Shared Task*.

W. Scott Richardson, Mark C. Wilson, Jim Nishikawa, and Robert S.A. Hayward. 1995. The well-built clinical question: a key to evidence-based decisions. *ACP J Club*, 123:A12–A13.

David L. Sackett, William M. Rosenberg, Jamuir Gray, R. Brian Haynes, and W. Scott Richardson. 1996. Evidence Based Medicine: What it is and what it isn't. *BMJ*, 312(7023):71–72.

Mathias Verbeke, Vincent Van Asch, Roser Morante, Paolo Frasconi, Walter Daelemans, and Luc De Raedt. 2012. A statistical relational learning approach to identifying evidence based medicine categories. In *Proceedings of the 2012 Joint Conference on Empirical Methods in Natural Language Processing and Computational Natural Language Learning*, pages 579–589, Jeju Island, Korea. Association for Computational Linguistics.

Lucy Lu Wang, Kyle Lo, Yoganand Chandrasekhar, Russell Reas, Jiangjiang Yang, Doug Burdick, Darrin Eide, Kathryn Funk, Yannis Katsis, Rodney Kinney, Yunyao Li, Ziyang Liu, William Merrill, Paul Mooney, Dewey Murdick, Devvret Rishi, Jerry Sheehan, Zhihong Shen, Brandon Stilson, Alex Wade, Kuansan Wang, Nancy Xin Ru Wang, Chris Wilhelm, Boya Xie, Douglas Raymond, Daniel S. Weld, Oren Etzioni, and Sebastian Kohlmeier. 2020. Cord-19: The covid-19 open research dataset.

Estimating the Strength of Authorship Evidence with a Deep-Learning-Based Approach

Shunichi Ishihara[1], **Satoru Tsuge**[2], **Mitsuyuki Inaba**[3], **Wataru Zaitsu**[4]
shunichi.ishihara@anu.edu.au, tsuge@daido-it.ac.jp, inabam@sps.ritsumei.ac.jp, w.zaitsu@mejiro.ac.jp

[1] Speech and Language Laboratory, The Australian National University, Canberra, Australia
[2] Department of Information Systems, Daido University, Aichi, Japan
[3] College of Policy Science, Ritsumeikan University, Kyoto, Japan
[4] Department of Psychological Counselling, Mejiro University, Tokyo, Japan

Abstract

This study is the first likelihood ratio (LR)-based forensic text comparison study in which each text is mapped onto an embedding vector using RoBERTa as the pre-trained model. The scores obtained with Cosine distance and probabilistic linear discriminant analysis (PLDA) were calibrated to LRs with logistic regression; the quality of the LRs was assessed by log LR cost (C_{llr}). Although the documents in the experiments were very short (maximum 100 words), the systems reached the C_{llr} values of 0.55595 and 0.71591 for the Cosine and PLDA systems, respectively. The effectiveness of deep-learning-based text representation is discussed by comparing the results of the current study to those of the previous studies of systems based on conventional feature engineering tested with longer documents.

1 Introduction

In forensic science, the likelihood ratio (LR) framework has long been considered the logically and legally correct approach to interpreting the analysis of forensic evidence (Aitken and Stoney, 1991; Aitken and Taroni, 2004; Morrison, 2022; Robertson et al., 2016). The LR framework is standard in DNA typing. The community of forensic text comparison (FTC), commonly known as forensic authorship verification, recently recognised the importance of this framework (Grant, 2022). Despite the importance of the LR framework in forensic science, LR-based studies on textual evidence are still conspicuously rare (Ishihara, 2017, 2021; Ishihara and Carne, 2022).

Many studies claim to be forensic but treat the problem as a usual authorship verification problem. However, there are important differences between conventional and forensic authorship verification. Conventional authorship verification aims to answer a verification problem. Forensic authorship verification aims to assist the fact finder in concluding the case, not answering the problem. Legally, giving an answer to a verification problem (even in a probabilistic term) equates to referring to the ultimate question of 'guilty vs. not guilty', which is only permitted for the fact finder. Logically, forensic scientists without all evidential information of the case cannot estimate the probability of a hypothesis from incomplete evidence. Thus, they cannot logically refer to the ultimate question. However, forensic scientists can logically and legally estimate the strength of evidence via LR (Aitken and Stoney, 1991; Aitken and Taroni, 2004; Robertson et al., 2016).

LR is given in Equation (1). LR is the ratio of two conditional probabilities; one is the probability of evidence (E) given the prosecution hypothesis (H_p) and the other is the probability of the same evidence given the defence hypothesis (H_d).

$$LR = \frac{P(E|H_p)}{P(E|H_d)} \tag{1}$$

The relative strength of the given evidence with respect to the competing hypotheses is reflected in the magnitude of the LR. The greater the LR value is than 1, the stronger support the evidence is considered to provide for the prosecution; the smaller the LR value is than 1, *mutatis mutandis*, for the defence hypothesis. It is very important to note that the LR is not a binary expression of truth.

With an LR estimated as the strength of evidence, the fact finder's belief regarding the hypotheses (quantified as prior odds) is raised to the posterior odds through the Bayesian theorem, as shown in Equation (2).

$$\underbrace{\frac{P(H_p|E)}{P(H_d|E)}}_{\text{posterior odds}} = \underbrace{\frac{P(H_p)}{P(H_d)}}_{\text{prior odds}} \times \underbrace{\frac{P(E|H_p)}{P(E|H_d)}}_{LR} \tag{2}$$

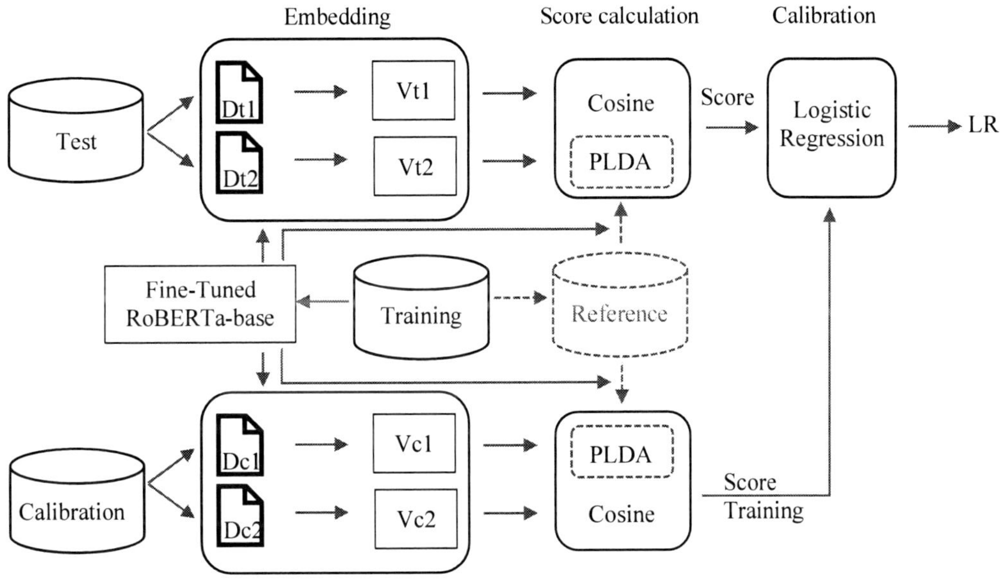

Figure 1: Process of estimating LRs. D{t,c} = (t)est or (c)alibration document; V{t,c} = vectorised (t)est or (c)alibration document; PLDA = probabilistic linear discrimination analysis.

The posterior odds are equivalent to the fact finder's belief regarding the hypotheses given the evidence

Despite the success of deep learning in many natural language processing tasks, a conventional machine learning approach with traditional feature engineering remains effective in authorship verification, particularly for small datasets (Kestemont et al., 2019; Kestemont et al., 2018). Nonetheless, deep-learning-based systems gradually started achieving better verification accuracy than conventional approaches, in particular with a large volume of data (Kestemont et al., 2021; Kestemont et al., 2020; Zhu and Jurgens, 2021). Despite of its clear presence, deep learning has no yet made inroads into the LR-based FTC. This preliminary study looks in the effectiveness of a deep-learning approach in LR-based FTC.

2 Methodology

2.1 Datasets

This study used the dataset of Amazon reviews prepared by Zhu and Jurgens (2021) with minor modifications. They filtered out reviews that are shorter than 50 tokens, and selected authors who contributed at least 5 reviews and at least in two product domains; there are 17 product domains. The text length did not exceed 100 tokens; i.e. max_length = 102.

Table 1 shows the numbers of authors, same author (SA) and different author (DA) comparisons in each dataset. The former is the simulation of the H_p and the latter is that of the H_d. The training and development datasets were used as originally prepared by Zhu and Jurgens (2021). The original test dataset was evenly split into two: one half was used as the test, and the other was used as the calibration dataset.

Dataset	Author	SA	DA
Test	32,124	96,253	96,491
Training	51,398	148,845	149,389
Development	12,849	36,429	36,317
Calibration	32,124	96,253	96,491

Table 1: Numbers of authors and SA/DA comparisons for each dataset.

2.2 Embedding and Fine-Tuning

Stylistic embedding of each text was performed as described by Zhu and Jurgens (2021) and using their tools.[1] They demonstrated the superiority of their system to various deep-learning-based baseline systems.

Each text was mapped into an embedding vector (z) by merging the last hidden states $(= \{h_0, h_1, \cdots, h_n\})$ into a single embedding vector

[1] https://github.com/lingjzhu/idiolect

($= h_o$) by attention pooling. The underlying pre-trained model was RoBERTa (specifically `roberta-base` as the encoder) (Liu et al., 2019). The training was done using the proxy-anchor loss function (Kim et al., 2020) with $\alpha = 30$; $t_s = 0.6$; $t_d = 0.4$; $t_t = t_s + t_d/2$. It is a continuous approximation of the max-margin loss of which the additional parameter enables better control over the penalty magnitude for difficult comparisons. An embedding vector dimension is 768. The hyperparameter values for fine-tuning were set according to Zhu and Jurgens (2021). The batch size was set at 256. Adam optimiser was used with a learning rate of $1e^{-5}$. The models were set to train for five epochs, after which no further improvement in performance was observed.

2.3 Estimating Likelihood Ratios

Estimating LRs for a pair of documents in the form of an embedding vector is illustrated in Figure 1. It is a two-stage process comprising score calculation and calibration.

Two methods were tested for estimating a score for each comparison of documents. One method was based on Cosine distance and the other on probabilistic linear discriminant analysis (PLDA) (Prince and Elder, 2007). The PLDA model used in this study was a two-covariance model. Besides the information regarding the author's unique writing style (x), each embedding vector (h_o) carries some residual noise (ε); for example, noise caused by thematic variations. Thus, h_o can be represented as Equation (3):

$$h_o = x + \varepsilon \quad (3)$$

A Gaussian generative model was assumed for the probability density function for x and ε, which requires a within-author and between-author covariance matrix, respectively. Authors were randomly selected from the training dataset to train the matrices (N = 10,000). A PLDA score was calculated using Equation (4), where z_i and z_j are embedding vectors under comparison.

$$score = \frac{P(z_i, z_j | H_p)}{P(z_i | H_d) P(z_j | H_d)} \quad (4)$$

The scores of the test dataset calculated through the two methods were converted to LRs at the calibration stage using logistic regression, the most common calibration approach for LR-based systems (Morrison, 2013; Ramos and Gonzalez-Rodriguez, 2013). The scores obtained from the calibration dataset were used to train the logistic regression.

2.4 Evaluation

Evaluation metrics based on classification or identification accuracy are not appropriate for assessing the performance of LR-based systems. Such metrics are inappropriate because (1) the category-based classification accuracy does not properly assess the magnitude of LRs (which is continuous), and (2) they implicitly refer to the accuracy of decision making, guilty vs. not guilty; only the fact finders (not forensic scientists or FTC experts) are legally permitted to refer to this ultimate question. The standard evaluation metric for LR-based systems is the log LR cost (C_{llr}) expressed in Equation (5):

$$C_{llr} = \frac{1}{2}\left(\frac{1}{N_{SA}}\sum_{i}^{N_{SA}} \log_2\left(1 + \frac{1}{LR_{SA_i}}\right) + \frac{1}{N_{DA}}\sum_{j}^{N_{DA}} \log_2\left(1 + LR_{DA_j}\right)\right) \quad (5)$$

In Equation (5), N_{SA} and N_{DA} are the numbers of SA and DA comparisons, respectively. LR_{SA_i} and LR_{DA_j} are the i_{th} SA and j_{th} DA linear LRs, respectively. The C_{llr} is the overall average of the costs, which were calculated for all LRs. The closer to $C_{llr} = 0$, the better the performance. If $C_{llr} \geq 1$, it denotes that the evidence is not informative for inference. With the pool-adjacent-violators algorithm, C_{llr} can be decomposed into C_{llr}^{min} and C_{llr}^{cal}, which assess the discrimination and calibration performance of the system, respectively. Thus, $C_{llr}=C_{llr}^{min}+C_{llr}^{cal}$. *EER* is also given for reference. A Tippett plot was used to visualise the magnitude of the derived LRs.

3 Results

The experimental results for the C_{llr}-based metrics are shown in Table 2.

	C_{llr}	C_{llr}^{min}	C_{llr}^{cal}	*EER*
Cosine	0.55595	0.55487	0.00108	0.17263
PLDA	0.71591	0.67159	0.04432	0.21855

Table 2: Experimental results.

Table 2 shows that the Cosine system outperforms the PLDA system in all metrics. The C_{llr}^{cal} values are close to zero, indicating that the derived LRs are well-calibrated for both systems. The PLDA model probabilistically considers the between- and within-author variabilities. Theoretically, the model is expected to suit the authorship verification task. Therefore, it was expected to outperform the Cosine system. The contrary result could be due to the amount of data available for each document—100 words maximum. This finding warrants further study. The Cosine system has been reported as robust against adverse conditions, including the scarcity of data (Ishihara, 2021; Ishihara and Carne, 2022). The derived LRs were plotted as Tippett plots to observe their magnitudes (see Figure 2).

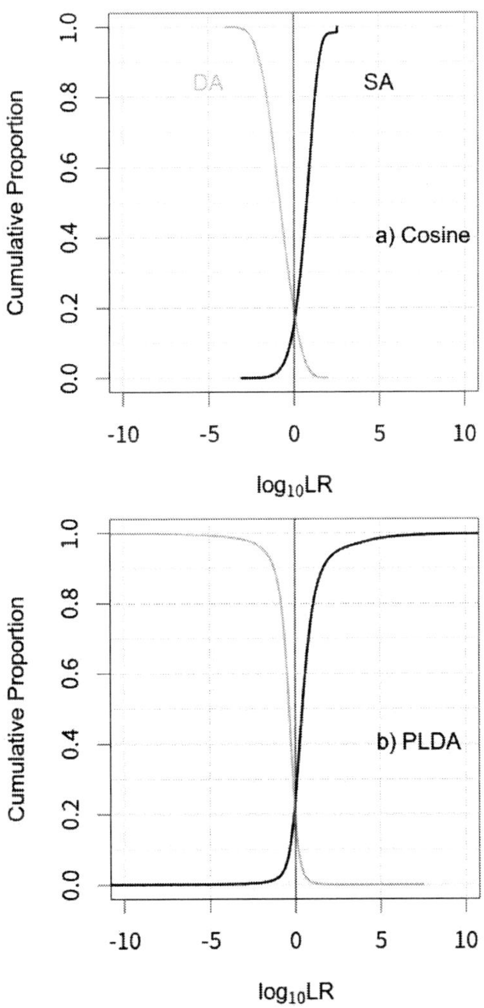

Figure 2: Tippett plots: Panel a) is for the Cosine system and Panel b) is for the PLDA system. The solid black curves = SA LRs and the solid grey curves = DA LRs.

The derived LRs from the Cosine system were conservative in magnitude; most LRs were within the range of the $\log_{10}$LR of ±2.5. Conversely, Figure 2b shows some excessively strong LRs of the PLDA system (e.g., greater than a $\log_{10}$LR of ±10). The strong contrary-to-fact LRs raise concerns. The excessively strong LR values both for the contrary-to-fact comparisons and the consistent-with-fact comparisons indicate the model's instability. Since each document only contains a maximum of 100 words, it is sensible not to have overly strong LRs.

Ishihara (2021) conducted LR-based FTC experiments by measuring the Cosine distance of documents modelled via word unigrams. The target documents were also product reviews for Amazon. Each document was approximately 4 kB in data (approximately 800 words in length)—considerably longer than the current study's (maximum 100 words). Ishihara reported a C_{llr} of 0.70640 as the optimal result. Ishihara's experiments were carried out with the test, reference and calibration datasets, each of which had 720 authors.

Despite the very short documents, the systems tested in this study achieved nearly the same level of performance (Cosine: C_{llr} = 0.55595; PLDA: C_{llr} = 0.71591) as Ishihara's (2021) system based on documents of approximately 800 words (C_{llr} = 0.70640). Although the experiments are not directly comparable, the effectiveness of the deep-learning-based text representation for estimating LRs can be conjectured.

4 Conclusions

In this study, the LRs were estimated by logistic regression calibrating the scores obtained through two systems: one based on Cosine distance and the other on the PLDA model. The documents were mapped on embedding vectors using RoBERTa as the pre-trained model, and the derived LRs were assessed with C_{llr}. Albeit the documents being very short, the systems reached the C_{llr} values of 0.55595 and 0.71591, respectively for the Cosine and PLDA systems. The effectiveness of the deep-learning-based text representation was discussed in comparison to the results of a previous study which was based on the system with conventional feature engineering and longer documents.

Acknowledgements

The authors thank the reviewers for their valuable comments.

References

C. G. G. Aitken and D. A. Stoney. 1991. *The Use of Statistics in Forensic Science*. Ellis Horwood, New York, NY.

C. G. G. Aitken F. Taroni. 2004. *Statistics and the Evaluation of Evidence for Forensic Scientists*. Chichester: John Wiley & Sons, Chichester, 2nd edition.

T. Grant. 2022. *The Idea of Progress in Forensic Authorship Analysis*. Cambridge University Press, Cambridge.

S. Ishihara. 2017. Strength of linguistic text evidence: A fused forensic text comparison system. *Forensic Science International*, 278: 184–197. https://doi.org/10.1016/j.forsciint.2017.06.040.

S. Ishihara. 2021. Score-based likelihood ratios for linguistic text evidence with a bag-of-words model. *Forensic Science International*, 327: 110980. https://doi.org/10.1016/j.forsciint.2021.110980.

S. Ishihara and M. Carne. 2022. Likelihood ratio estimation for authorship text evidence: An empirical comparison of score- and feature-based methods. *Forensic Science International*, 334: 111268. https://doi.org/10.1016/j.forsciint.2022.111268.

M. Kestemont, E. Manjavacas, I. Markov, J. Bevendorff, M. Wiegmann, E. Stamatatos, … M. Potthast. 2021. Overview of the cross-domain authorship verification task at PAN 2021. In *Proceedings of the CLEF 2021 Conference and Labs of the Evaluation Forum*, pages 1–17.

M. Kestemont, E. Manjavacas, I. Markov, J. W. M. Bevendorff, E. Stamatatos, M. Potthast and B. Stein. 2020. Overview of the cross-domain authorship verification task at PAN 2020. In *Proceedings of the CLEF 2020 Conference and Labs of the Evaluation Forum*.

M. Kestemont, E. Stamatatos, E. Manjavacas, W. Daelemans, M. Potthast and B. Stein. 2019. Overview of the cross-domain authorship attribution task at PAN 2019. In *Proceedings of the CLEF 2019 Conference and Labs of the Evaluation Forum*, pages 1–15.

M. Kestemont, M. Tschuggnall, E. Stamatatos, W. Daelemans, G. Specht, B. Stein and M. Potthast. 2018. Overview of the author identification task at PAN-2018: Cross-domain authorship attribution and style change detection. In *Proceedings of the CLEF 2018 Conference and the Labs of the Evaluation Forum*, pages 1–25.

S. Kim, D. Kim, M. Cho and S. Kwak. 2020. Proxy anchor loss for deep metric learning. In *Proceedings of the IEEE/CVF Conference on Computer Vision and Pattern Recognition*, pages 3238–3247.

Yinhan Liu, Myle Ott, Naman Goyal, Jingfei Du, Mandar Joshi, Danqi W. Chen, … Veselin Stoyanov. 2019. *RoBERTa: A robustly optimized BERT pretraining approach. Computing Research Repository*, arXiv:1907.11692. https://doi.org/10.48550/arXiv.1907.11692.

Geoffrey S. Morrison. 2013. Tutorial on logistic-regression calibration and fusion: Converting a score to a likelihood ratio. *Australian Journal of Forensic Sciences*, 45(2): 173–197. https://dx.doi.org/10.1080/00450618.2012.733025.

Geoffrey S. Morrison. 2022. Advancing a paradigm shift in evaluation of forensic evidence: The rise of forensic data science. *Forensic Science International: Synergy*, 5: 100270. https://doi.org/10.1016/j.fsisyn.2022.100270.

Simon J. D. Prince and James H. Elder. 2007. Probabilistic linear discriminant analysis for inferences about identity. In *Proceedings of the 2007 IEEE 11th International Conference on Computer Vision*, pages 1-8.

D. Ramos and J. Gonzalez-Rodriguez. 2013. Reliable support: Measuring calibration of likelihood ratios. *Forensic Science International*, 230(1–3): 156–169. https//dx.doi.org/10.1016/j.forsciint.2013.04.014.

B. Robertson, G. A. Vignaux and C. E. H. Berger. 2016. *Interpreting Evidence: Evaluating Forensic Science in the Courtroom*. Chichester: John Wiley & Sons, Chichester, 2nd edition.

Jian Zhu and David Jurgens. 2021. *Idiosyncratic but not arbitrary: Learning idiolects in online registers reveals distinctive yet consistent individual styles. Computing Research Repository*, arXiv:2109.03158. Version 3. https://arxiv.org/abs/2109.03158v3.

Automatic Classification of Evidence Based Medicine Using Transformers

Necva Bölücü, Pınar Uskaner Hepsağ
Computer Engineering Department
Adana Alparslan Türkeş Science and Technology University
Adana, Turkey
{nbolucu, puskaner}@atu.edu.tr

Abstract

The goal of the shared task is multi-label classification for biomedical records in English used for Evidence-Based Medicine. In this paper, we describe the model based on the Transformer submitted by our team *turkNLP* for the shared task. Our model achieved a Micro ROC score of ≈ 0.93 on the shared task and ranked 5th in the leaderboard.

1 Introduction

The ALTA 2022 shared task[1] is a well-studied Natural Language Processing (NLP) problem which is multi-label sentence classification in biomedical field. The problem is assigning the sentences to one or more labels of the predefined 6 categories for the given dataset which is Evidence-Based Medicine (EBM) dataset presented by Kim et al. (2011).

In this paper, we as a team of *turkNLP* have taken up and proposed a deep learning model based on Transformer (Vaswani et al., 2017) to identify the queries in Evidence-Based Medicine (EBM) presented by Kim et al. (2011) for the ALTA 2022 shared task. Our model concatenates the encoder layer of the Transformer proposed by Vaswani et al (Vaswani et al., 2017) and the embedding of $[CLS]$ token of the BERT model (Kenton and Toutanova, 2019), which is used as the embedding layer of the Transformer model.

The main contribution of this paper is that we investigate the impact of the BERT model on the Transformer for multi-label classification problem. The model has shown an improvement over the Transformer model for multi-label classification, as the concatenation of the embedding of $[CLS]$ token of the BERT model captures the semantic of the whole input, while the Transformer captures the semantic of each word of the input[2].

The rest of the paper is organized as follows: We give the related work on the multi-label classification problem for EBM with the shared task dataset Kim et al. (2011) in Section 2. The proposed model for the problem is given in Section 3 and the experimental setup, results, and detailed analysis of the results are presented in Section 4. Finally, Section 5 concludes the paper with insights on the impact of the proposed model on the multi-label classification problem for EBM and possible future work.

2 Related Work

The first study classifying abstract sentences based on the PIBOSO scheme was conducted by Kim et al. (2011). The NICTA-PIBOSO dataset, the most studied dataset, was also published by Kim et al. (2011). The authors presented a Conditional Random Field (CRF) classifier with lexical (e.g., unigram, bigram), semantic (e.g., metathesaurus), structural (e.g., the position of the words), and sequential (e.g., direct and indirect dependencies on previous sentences) features to assign sentences to predefined labels.

Verbeke et al. (2012) presented a new approach based on $kLog$ (Frasconi et al., 2014), a new language for statistical relational learning with kernels. In the study, the authors extracted features such as PoS tags, lemmas, and dependency labels using BiogaphTA and GENIA dependency parser (Sagae and Tsujii, 2007) and fed them into $kLog$ for the problem. The NICTA-PIBOSO dataset was also the basis of the ALTA 2012 shared task (Amini et al., 2012). Lui (2012) extended the study of Kim et al. (2011) by adding additional features such as PoS n-grams, sentence length etc., and stack the

[1] https://codalab.lisn.upsaclay.fr/competitions/693500

[2] The code is publicly available at https://github.com/adalin16/alta-2022

features with a metalearner to combine multiple feature sets, based on an approach similar to the metalearner of Wolpert (1992). Mollá et al. (2012) presented a model consisting of two stages: (1) using K-means to cluster abstracts according to the actual sentence distribution in the abstract, (2) using clustering results in multi-label classification. Gella and Duong (2012) also used the CRF model with similar features as Kim et al. (2011). The categorization of sentences as structured and unstructured is the main difference compared with previous studies from Kim et al. (2011); Verbeke et al. (2012). If the first sentence in an abstract is a sentence ordering label, the authors categorized the abstract as structured otherwise unstructured. The categorization increased the performance of the problem compared to previous studies.

3 Methodology

Transformer model (Vaswani et al., 2017) is very popular because of its performance in NLP tasks such as sequence tagging (Tsai et al., 2019; He et al., 2020) and machine translation (Wang et al., 2019; Liu et al., 2020). Recently, there are lots of models based on the Transformer (Vaswani et al., 2017) in NLP such as BERT (Kenton and Toutanova, 2019), T5 (Raffel et al., 2020) etc. The success of the Transformer model is processing sequential data in parallel without a recurrent network instead of paying attention to the last state of the encoder, as in Recurrent Neural Networks (RNNs).

In this study, we adopted the encoder of the Transformer model (Vaswani et al., 2017) by extending the model with the pre-trained language models to perform classification by mapping the data to the EBM PIBOSO classes. The architecture of the proposed model is shown in Figure 1.

Let $D = \{S_i, m_i\}_{i=1}^{T}$ denote a set of T samples, where S_i is a sentence and m_i is the corresponding labels "population", "intervention", "background", "outcome", "study design", "other").

The words $\{w_1, w_2, \cdots, w_n\}$ of a sentence are mapped to the corresponding embeddings in the embedding layer, and the positional information E_{pos} is encoded and appended to the text representation and fed into the encoder layer, which consists L identical layers. The output of the Transformer Encoder is the mean of the output of the tokens as given below:

$$T_o = mean(t_1, t_2, \cdots, t_n) \quad (1)$$

We concatenated the output of the Transformer model and the embedding of the $[CLS]$ token as input of the classification layer as defined below.

$$o = T_o \oplus [CLS] \quad (2)$$

In the classification layer, we used the sigmoid function that squeezes the results between 0 and 1, and we used 0.5 as the threshold to convert the probabilities into classes. The formula of the layer is given in Equation 3.

$$\hat{s} = sigmoid(W \cdot o + b) \quad (3)$$

where $\hat{s}$ is the predicted result through the model, W is the weighted matrix, o is the concatenation of the Transformer model and the embedding of the $[CLS]$ token as defined in Equation 2, and b is the bias.

4 Experiments & Results

In this section, we present the details of the dataset, experimental setup, and results.

4.1 Dataset

There are several variants and extensions of the classification PICO (Kim et al., 2011). The dataset called PIBOSO was proposed by Kim et al. (2011), where the tag "comparison" was removed and three new tags "background", "study design", and "other" were added. The PIBOSO dataset has 6 categories namely "background", "population", "Intervention", "outcome", "study design", and "other". Samples taken from train set are given in Table 1.

In the dataset, sentences can have more than one label since it is a multi-label dataset. The train/dev/test size is given in Table 2 with the percentage of sentences annotated with given labels in the train set. The rows sum to more than 100% because a sentence is likely to contain more than one label. Note that "background", "outcome", and "other" received a higher percentage of labels, while "population", "intervention", and "study design" are at least annotated labels in the dataset (Kim et al., 2011).

4.2 Experimental Setting

We implemented the proposed model using the PyTorch library. The Adam optimizer (Kingma and Ba, 2014) was used with an epsilon value of $1e-8$ and the default max grad norm. The BCE loss function was used as the objective function.

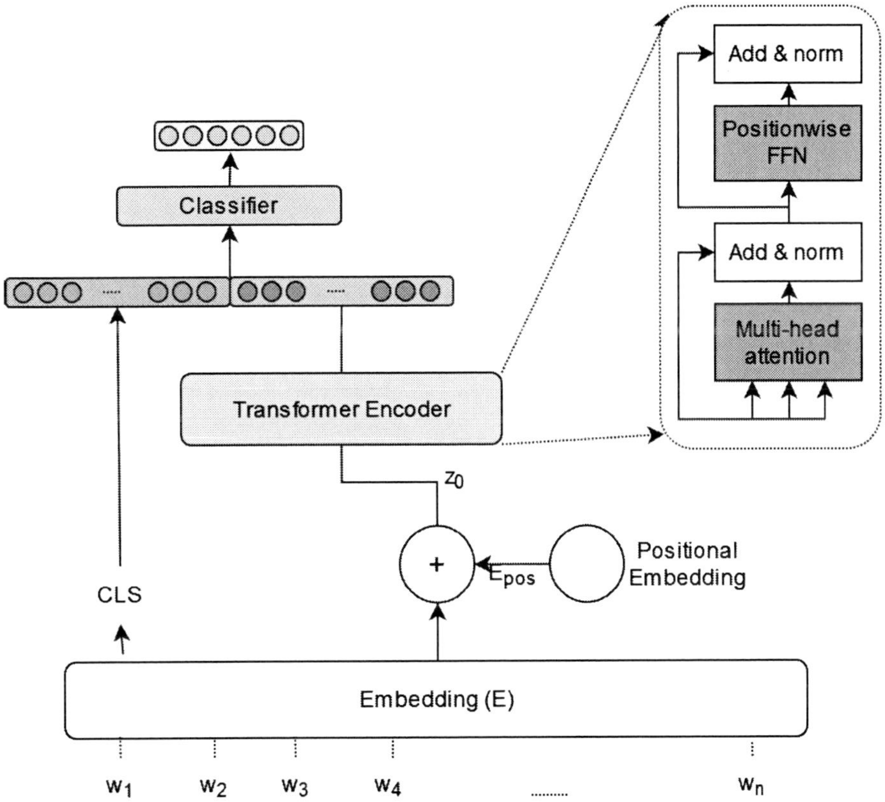

Figure 1: Overview of the architecture for multi-label classification problem

Sentence	population	intervention	background	outcome	study design	other
The response rate was 79.5%.	0	0	0	1	0	0
The average age was 71 years.	1	0	0	0	0	0
This group totaled 410 births.	0	0	0	0	0	1
All of these must be considered.	0	0	1	0	0	0
In an effort to overcome these ···	0	1	1	0	0	0

Table 1: Samples taken from train set of PIBOSO dataset (Kim et al., 2011)

Set	Number
Train	8216
Dev	459
Test	569
Label	**%**
population	7.11
intervention	6.10
background	21.63
outcome	38.85
study design	2.03
other	29.50

Table 2: Percentage of sentences that were annotated with a given label in the dataset

We used BERT (Kenton and Toutanova, 2019) pre-trained language model (SciBERT (Beltagy et al., 2019)[3]) to convert words into embeddings. We finetuned the model using the 0.1 of the train set of the dataset, since the labels of the development set were not revealed in the shared task. The parameters of the model are given in Table 3.

In the shared task, the evaluation metric is the area under the ROC (Receiver Operating Characteristic) curve plotting the fraction of true positives out of positives vs. the fraction of false positives out of the negatives.

4.3 Results

To understand the effect of the concatenation of the embedding of the $[CLS]$ token of the BERT model,

[3]https://huggingface.co/allenai/scibert_scivocab_cased

we conduct experiments with and without it. The Micro ROC scores are given in Table 4. The results show that using the embedding of the $[CLS]$ token improves the results of the Transformer model. The main improvement is due to the fact that embedding of $[CLS]$ token captures the semantic of the entire sentence and provides valuable complementary information for the problem.

HyperParameter	Model
learning rate	1e-4
batch size	16
d_model	1
heads	1
# of layers	1
# of hidden	1
max length	100
dropout	0.1
weight decay	0.1
patience	20

Table 3: Parameter setting of the model

Model	Micro ROC
Transformer	0.87698
Transformer+BERT	0.931843

Table 4: Test Results of the proposed model with base Transformer model

To understand the performance of the model, we generated Precision, Recall, and F_1 scores for each label in the train set of the dataset [4]. The results are shown in Table 5. It can be clearly seen that the result of the label "outcome" which has the best performance of the model. The categories "background" and "other" follow the category "outcome". The categories "population", "intervention", and "study design" show the lowest results of the proposed model. This proves that the model struggles in predicting the "population", "intervention", and "study design" categories. When analyzing the percentage of each categories given in Table 2, there is a correlation between the percentage of the categories and the results.

In Table 6, the results of the proposed model are presented with the results of the teams that participated in the ALTA 2022 shared task[5]. The best Micro ROC score was obtained by `heatwave`. Our model couldn't achieve the highest score, but the result of our model is still competitive with the best result.

Label	Precision	Recall	F_1
population	0.00	0.00	0.00
intervention	0.00	0.00	0.00
background	0.93	0.19	0.31
outcome	0.84	0.83	0.84
study design	0.00	0.00	0.00
other	0.98	0.60	0.75

Table 5: Precision, Recall and F_1 score for each class in the train set

Team Name	Micro ROC
heatwave-2	**0.987395**
heatwave-1	0.983792
CSECU-DSG	0.968750
michaelibrahim	0.963404
turkNLP (Our model)	0.931843
dmollaaliod	0.910455

Table 6: Test Results of multi-label classification using the proposed model and the best results of the ALTA 2022 shared task

5 Conclusion

In this paper, we presented the model of Transformer model augmented with pre-trained language model (Transformer+BERT) on ALTA 2022 shared task in the English language. Experimental results showed that the Transformer+BERT model outperformed the Transformer model. We found that combining the embedding of $[CLS]$ token of the BERT model helps to capture the semantic of the whole sentence and increase the performance of the model. However, this study has also limitations. Our model couldn't perform on the labels with the lower ratio in the dataset. Labels "population", "intervention", and "study design" are difficult to identify despite the performance of the model.

In the future, further improvements can be made in sampling for multi-label classification to handle the imbalanced dataset problem.

[4]The dev and test set labels are not available, we only calculated the Micro ROC score using the `https://codalab.lisn.upsaclay.fr/competitions/6935`

[5]We couldn't compare the results with previous work (Kim et al., 2011; Gella and Duong, 2012; Lui, 2012; Verbeke et al., 2012), since the evaluation metric is different from the previous ALTA 2012 shared task (Amini et al., 2012).

References

Iman Amini, David Martinez, and Diego Molla. 2012. Overview of the ALTA 2012 Shared Task. In *Proceedings of the Australasian Language Technology Association Workshop 2012*, pages 124–129.

Iz Beltagy, Arman Cohan, and Kyle Lo. 2019. Scibert: Pretrained contextualized embeddings for scientific text. *CoRR*, abs/1903.10676.

Paolo Frasconi, Fabrizio Costa, Luc De Raedt, and Kurt De Grave. 2014. klog: A language for logical and relational learning with kernels. *Artificial Intelligence*, 217:117–143.

Spandana Gella and Long Duong. 2012. Automatic sentence classifier using sentence ordering features for event based medicine: Shared task system description. In *Proceedings of the Australasian Language Technology Association Workshop 2012*, pages 130–133.

Zhiyong He, Zanbo Wang, Wei Wei, Shanshan Feng, Xianling Mao, and Sheng Jiang. 2020. A Survey on Recent Advances in Sequence Labeling from Deep Learning Models. *CoRR*, abs/2011.06727.

Jacob Devlin Ming-Wei Chang Kenton and Lee Kristina Toutanova. 2019. BERT: Pre-training of Deep Bidirectional Transformers for Language Understanding. In *Proceedings of NAACL-HLT*, pages 4171–4186.

Su Nam Kim, David Martinez, Lawrence Cavedon, and Lars Yencken. 2011. Automatic classification of sentences to support evidence based medicine. In *BMC bioinformatics*, volume 12, pages 1–10. BioMed Central.

Diederik P. Kingma and Jimmy Ba. 2014. Adam: A Method for Stochastic Optimization.

Xiaodong Liu, Kevin Duh, Liyuan Liu, and Jianfeng Gao. 2020. Very Deep Transformers for Neural Machine Translation. *CoRR*, abs/2008.07772.

Marco Lui. 2012. Feature stacking for sentence classification in evidence-based medicine. In *Proceedings of the Australasian Language Technology Association Workshop 2012*, pages 134–138.

Diego Mollá et al. 2012. Experiments with clustering-based features for sentence classification in medical publications: Macquarie test's participation in the alta 2012 shared task.

Colin Raffel, Noam Shazeer, Adam Roberts, Katherine Lee, Sharan Narang, Michael Matena, Yanqi Zhou, Wei Li, Peter J Liu, et al. 2020. Exploring the limits of transfer learning with a unified text-to-text transformer. *J. Mach. Learn. Res.*, 21(140):1–67.

Kenji Sagae and Jun'ichi Tsujii. 2007. Dependency parsing and domain adaptation with lr models and parser ensembles. In *Proceedings of the CoNLL Shared Task Session of EMNLP-CoNLL*, pages 1044–1050.

Henry Tsai, Jason Riesa, Melvin Johnson, Naveen Arivazhagan, Xin Li, and Amelia Archer. 2019. Small and Practical BERT Models for Sequence Labeling. *CoRR*, abs/1909.00100.

Ashish Vaswani, Noam Shazeer, Niki Parmar, Jakob Uszkoreit, Llion Jones, Aidan N Gomez, Łukasz Kaiser, and Illia Polosukhin. 2017. Attention is all you need. In *Advances in neural information processing systems*, pages 5998–6008.

Mathias Verbeke, Vincent Van Asch, Roser Morante, Paolo Frasconi, Walter Daelemans, and Luc De Raedt. 2012. A statistical relational learning approach to identifying evidence based medicine categories. In *Proceedings of the 2012 Joint Conference on Empirical Methods in Natural Language Processing and Computational Natural Language Learning*, pages 579–589.

Qiang Wang, Bei Li, Tong Xiao, Jingbo Zhu, Changliang Li, Derek F. Wong, and Lidia S. Chao. 2019. Learning Deep Transformer Models for Machine Translation. In *Proceedings of the 57th Annual Meeting of the Association for Computational Linguistics*, pages 1810–1822, Florence, Italy. Association for Computational Linguistics.

David H Wolpert. 1992. Stacked generalization. *Neural networks*, 5(2):241–259.

Context-Aware Sentence Classification in Evidence-Based Medicine

Biaoyan Fang* **Fajri Koto***
School of Computing and Information Systems
The University of Melbourne
{biaoyanf,ffajri}@student.unimelb.edu.au

Abstract

In this paper, we show the effectiveness of before– and after–sentences as additional context for sentence classification in evidence-based medicine. Although pre-trained language models encode contextualized representation, we found that the additional contexts improve sentence classification in terms of ROC (micro) score in the ALTA 2022 shared task. Additionally, averaging the probability of top model predictions boosts the performance, and our results for both public and private test sets officially claim the first rank of the ALTA 2022 shared task.

1 Introduction

Integrating individual clinical expertise and external medicine literature (also known as evidence-based medicine) is the best practice to give care to patients (Sackett et al., 1996; Koto and Fang, 2021). However, obtaining relevant medical literature requires in-depth expertise and can be time-consuming due to the large availability of texts.

A search engine is one of the ways to assist evidence-based medicine, and categorizing sentences in medicine literature based on PICO framework (Kim et al., 2011) can improve the search effectiveness (Amini et al., 2012). PICO mainly consists of four labels: `Population` (P) (i.e. participants in a study); `Intervention` (I); `Comparison` (C) (if appropriate); and `Outcome` (O) (of an Intervention), and can be extended to classes `Background` (B), `Study Design` (S), and `Other` (O) (for sentences that have no relevant content) (Lui, 2012; Kim et al., 2011). The ALTA 2022 shared task uses PIBOSO classes by Kim et al. (2011) and discards `Comparison` (C).

* equal contribution

In previous work, Lui (2012) utilized lexical features (e.g. bag-of-words and part-of-speech) and structural features (e.g. sentence length, sentence heading), and fed them to Naive Bayes, SVM, and logistic regression. By stacking the aforementioned features, Lui (2012) demonstrated the effectiveness of logistic regression for this task.

Our work revisits the PIBOSO-based sentence classification task using current state-of-the-art NLP systems (i.e. pre-trained language models (Devlin et al., 2019; Liu et al., 2019; Clark et al., 2020; Koto et al., 2020)). Similar to Lui (2012), we also use context sentences (i.e. before– and after–sentences) but structure the input to retain the original sequence. Lui (2012) simply used bag-of-words and part-of-speech thus discarding the original sequence information in their features.

We perform context-aware classification using different pre-trained language models including domain-general (Devlin et al., 2019; Liu et al., 2019; Clark et al., 2020) and domain-specific models (Gururangan et al., 2020; Gu et al., 2020; Koto et al., 2021; Fang et al., 2021) with two strategies in the classification layer: (1) single embedding, and (2) average pooling. We showcase that both strategies are competitive and significantly better than heuristic n-gram features (Lui, 2012). We also show that the ensemble method (Koto and Fang, 2021) by averaging probability prediction of top models improves the ROC (micro) scores, and set our submission in this shared task as the winner.

2 Dataset

The ALTA 2022 shared task adopts the data of Kim et al. (2011). In total, there are 9,244 sentences which are split by the shared-task organizers into 8,216/459/569 for training, public test, and private test sets, respectively. Only labels for training data are available, and for conducting experi-

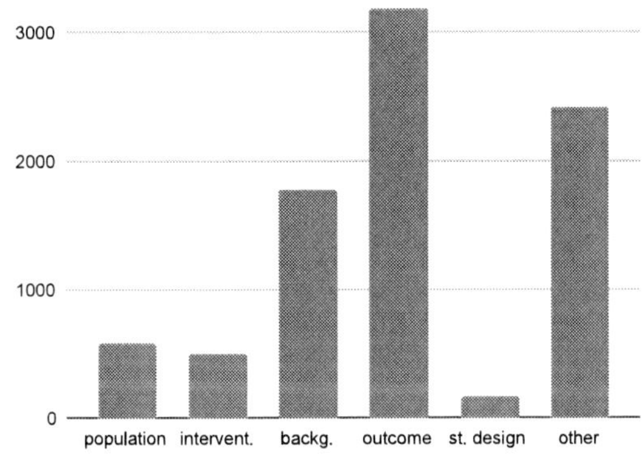

Figure 1: Label distribution of training data.

#document	700
#sentence per document	11.7 ± 6.1
#word per document	210.6 ± 89.1
#word per sentence	17.9 ± 11.2

Table 1: Overall statistics of training data.

ments we randomly sample 768 instances of original training data as the development set and use the remaining for training. The data split ensures that each sentence of a document is in the same set. Please note that we refer `val2022.csv` and `test2022.csv` to the public and private test sets, respectively.

Table 1 shows overall statistics of the training data which consists of 700 documents with 11.7 sentences per document on average. The total number of words per document is 210.6, and each sentence has 17.9 words. There is an imbalanced distribution over the PIBOSO label as described in Figure 1 where `Outcome` is the majority and `Study Design` is the minority class. Please note that this task is a multilabel classification task where one text might consist of more than one label. Further statistics and details regarding the rules of the ALTA 2022 shared task will be described separately by the organizers, and appear alongside this paper.

3 Methodology

In Figure 2, we describe two different approaches for incorporating contextual information: (1) average pooling, and (2) single embedding. Both ways utilize structured input where we added special tokens <nt> and <t> at the beginning of each non-target (context) and target (main) sentence, respectively. We feed this structured text to pre-trained language models and then process the outputs in two aforementioned ways. Specifically, for average pooling, we first use a masking trick to obtain main sentence embedding and context sentence embedding through averaging. We concatenate the two embeddings (the red and green boxes in Figure 2) prior to the classification layer. For the latter, we merely use the corresponding output of token <t> embedding for classification. We argue that the attention mechanism in the transformer (Vaswani et al., 2017) is contextualized to all input tokens, thus encouraging us to test this simpler method.

Our experiments consider domain-general and domain-specific pre-trained language models. It has been shown by previous works (Gururangan et al., 2020; Gu et al., 2020; Koto et al., 2021; Fang et al., 2021, 2022) that domain-general language models are suboptimal for specific domains, and one way to handle this is to use domain-adaptive pre-trained models. In this experiment, we use three domain-general models: BERT (Devlin et al., 2019), RoBERTa (Liu et al., 2019), ELECTRA (Clark et al., 2020), and two domain-specific models: BioBERT from Microsoft (Gu et al., 2020) and DMIS Lab (Lee et al., 2020).[1]

Additionally, we extend the experiments using ensemble learning by averaging probability prediction of top-*k* models. In similar work, Koto and Fang (2021) has demonstrated the efficacy of ensemble learning in evidence-based medicine-related tasks. The ensemble method is better than a single model since it is capable to enhance model robustness on variance and uncertainty.

4 Experiments

4.1 Settings

As stated in Section 3, we use the huggingface Pytorch framework (Wolf et al., 2020) and select 5 models: 1) BERT,[2] 2) RoBERTa,[3] 3) ELECTRA,[4] 4) BioBERT (Microsoft),[5] and 5) BioBERT (DMIS Lab)[6] for our experiments. Each model is finetuned for 50 epochs with a batch size of 48, a learning rate of 1e-5, and a dropout of 0.5. We consider two settings: (1) without context, i.e. not using any

[1] All models can be accessed in `https://huggingface.co/`

[2] `bert-base-uncased`

[3] `roberta-base`

[4] `google/electra-base-discriminator`

[5] `microsoft/BiomedNLP-PubMedBERT-base-uncased-abstract-fulltext`

[6] `dmis-lab/biobert-base-cased-v1.1`

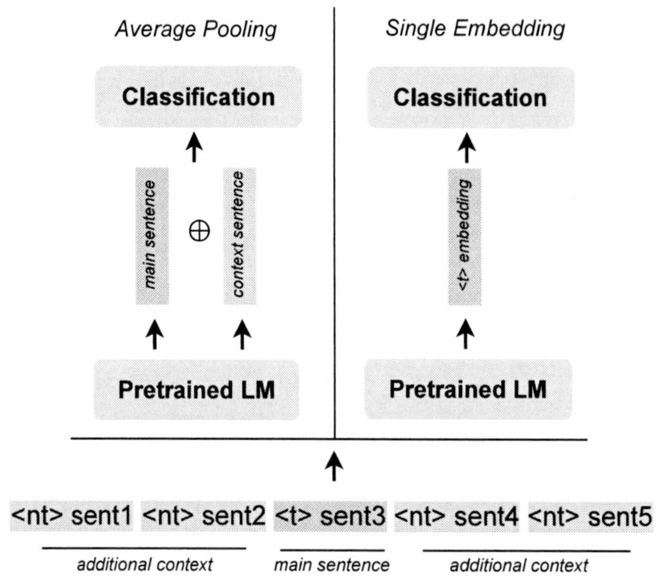

Figure 2: Illustration of our context-aware classification model. `<t>` and `<nt>` are special tokens that differentiate target and non-target (context) sentences in the input.

additional context, and (2) with context, i.e. using 4 sentences (2 before– and after–sentences) as the additional context. Models that achieve the best performance on our development set are used.

For evaluation, we report on ROC (micro), following the ALTA 2022 shared task description.

4.2 Results

We tuned our model hyperparameters based on the development set discussed in Section 2, and evaluate them on public and private test sets. Since participants can use up to 100 submissions for the public test set, we use it to pick our best model and predict the private test set. Overall, we found similar results on both public and private test sets, where the context-aware domain-specific model performs best. In this section, we report the results of the private test set. Results for the public test set can be found in Appendix A.

Table 2 shows ROC (micro) scores of all models over the private test set, with and without context. First, consistent with previous works (Devlin et al., 2019; Koto et al., 2020) that pre-trained language models significantly outperform conventional machine learning methods (i.e. Naive Bayes, Logistic Regression, and SVM), with SVM achieves the ROC (micro) score of 91.7 (4 points lower than BERT). Next, we found that the simple single embedding method tends to result in better ROC (micro) scores than the average pooling, with and without contexts. One possible reason is that average pooling on the sentences might introduce unwanted noise, resulting in lower-performance models. The best individual performance is obtained by BioBERT (Microsoft), with 96.6 and 95.6 ROC (micro) scores under single embedding and average pooling approaches, respectively, indicating the benefits of using domain-specific pre-trained language models for this classification task, thus consistent with previous works (Gururangan et al., 2020; Gu et al., 2020; Koto et al., 2021; Fang et al., 2021).

Also, as stated in Section 3, we explore the importance of additional context, i.e. before– and after–sentences for this task. Table 2 shows consistent improvements of pre-trained language models when incorporating additional context, with a maximum gain achieved by BERT (with average pooling) with 3 absolute ROC (micro) scores. We argue that the improvements might come from a better understanding of the target sentence when additional contexts are provided.

Furthermore, inspired by Koto and Fang (2021), we experimented with the ensemble method to improve model robustness and mitigate the performance variance. Specifically, we ensemble top-k ($k = 3, 4, 5$) models under each setting. Results in Table 2 show that ensemble methods achieve strong performance across different settings, outperforming single pre-trained language models. For better

Model	Without Context		With Context	
	Single Emb.	Ave. Pooling	Single Emb.	Ave. Pooling
Baselines				
Naive Bayes	85.9		–	
Logistic Regression	84.2		–	
SVM	91.7		–	
Pre-trained language models				
BERT	95.4	94.1	97.0	96.7
RoBERTa	96.1	94.9	97.6	97.9
ELECTRA	96.3	95.2	97.6	97.5
BioBERT (Microsoft)	96.6	95.6	97.7	96.2
BioBERT (DMIS Lab)	96.2	95.5	97.3	95.8
Ensemble – averaging Top-k models				
Ensemble (Top-3)	97.0	96.9	98.0	98.1
Ensemble (Top-4)	97.0	96.9	98.0	98.0
Ensemble (Top-5)	97.0	96.7	98.0	98.3
Ensemble – further averaging the Ensemble (Top-k) models of Single Embed. and Ave. Pooling				
Combine of Ensemble (Top-3)	97.3		**98.7**	
Combine of Ensemble (Top-4)	97.3		98.6	
Combine of Ensemble (Top-5)	97.2		98.5	

Table 2: ROC (micro) scores over private test set.

utilization of contextual information, we further average the ensemble top-k models from single embedding and average pooling approaches, achieving further improvements across ensemble top-k models. The best performance, 98.7 ROC (micro) score, is achieved when averaging two ensemble top-3 models and used as our final result.

5 Conclusion

In this paper, we propose a context-aware multi-label sentence classifier in evidence-based medicine. We show the effectiveness of using the additional context, i.e. before– and after–sentences in pre-trained language models, by considering two incorporation approaches, single embedding, and average pooling, which capture different perspectives of additional context. The utilization of the ensemble method further shows the benefits of combining single embedding and average pooling models, achieving the best performance in the ALTA 2022 shared task.

Acknowledgments

In this work, Biaoyan Fang is supported by a graduate research scholarship from the Melbourne School of Engineering, while Fajri Koto is supported by the Australia Awards Scholarship (AAS), funded by the Department of Foreign Affairs and Trade (DFAT), Australia.

References

Iman Amini, David Martinez, and Diego Molla. 2012. Overview of the ALTA 2012 shared task. In *Proceedings of the Australasian Language Technology Association Workshop 2012*, pages 124–129, Dunedin, New Zealand.

Kevin Clark, Minh-Thang Luong, Quoc V Le, and Christopher D Manning. 2020. Electra: Pre-training text encoders as discriminators rather than generators. *arXiv preprint arXiv:2003.10555*.

Jacob Devlin, Ming-Wei Chang, Kenton Lee, and Kristina Toutanova. 2019. BERT: Pre-training of deep bidirectional transformers for language understanding. In *Proceedings of the 2019 Conference of the North American Chapter of the Association for Computational Linguistics: Human Language Technologies, Volume 1 (Long and Short Papers)*, pages 4171–4186, Minneapolis, Minnesota. Association for Computational Linguistics.

Biaoyan Fang, Timothy Baldwin, and Karin Verspoor. 2022. What does it take to bake a cake? the RecipeRef corpus and anaphora resolution in procedural text. In *Findings of the Association for Computational Linguistics: ACL 2022*, pages 3481–3495,

Dublin, Ireland. Association for Computational Linguistics.

Biaoyan Fang, Christian Druckenbrodt, Saber A Akhondi, Jiayuan He, Timothy Baldwin, and Karin Verspoor. 2021. ChEMU-ref: A corpus for modeling anaphora resolution in the chemical domain. In *Proceedings of the 16th Conference of the European Chapter of the Association for Computational Linguistics: Main Volume*, pages 1362–1375, Online. Association for Computational Linguistics.

Yu Gu, Robert Tinn, Hao Cheng, Michael Lucas, Naoto Usuyama, Xiaodong Liu, Tristan Naumann, Jianfeng Gao, and Hoifung Poon. 2020. Domain-specific language model pretraining for biomedical natural language processing.

Suchin Gururangan, Ana Marasović, Swabha Swayamdipta, Kyle Lo, Iz Beltagy, Doug Downey, and Noah A. Smith. 2020. Don't stop pretraining: Adapt language models to domains and tasks. In *Proceedings of the 58th Annual Meeting of the Association for Computational Linguistics*, pages 8342–8360, Online. Association for Computational Linguistics.

Su Nam Kim, David Martinez, Lawrence Cavedon, and Lars Yencken. 2011. Automatic classification of sentences to support evidence based medicine. In *BMC bioinformatics*, volume 12, pages 1–10. BioMed Central.

Fajri Koto and Biaoyan Fang. 2021. Handling variance of pretrained language models in grading evidence in the medical literature. In *Proceedings of the The 19th Annual Workshop of the Australasian Language Technology Association*, pages 218–223, Online. Australasian Language Technology Association.

Fajri Koto, Jey Han Lau, and Timothy Baldwin. 2021. IndoBERTweet: A pretrained language model for Indonesian Twitter with effective domain-specific vocabulary initialization. In *Proceedings of the 2021 Conference on Empirical Methods in Natural Language Processing*, pages 10660–10668, Online and Punta Cana, Dominican Republic. Association for Computational Linguistics.

Fajri Koto, Afshin Rahimi, Jey Han Lau, and Timothy Baldwin. 2020. IndoLEM and IndoBERT: A benchmark dataset and pre-trained language model for Indonesian NLP. In *Proceedings of the 28th International Conference on Computational Linguistics*, pages 757–770, Barcelona, Spain (Online). International Committee on Computational Linguistics.

Jinhyuk Lee, Wonjin Yoon, Sungdong Kim, Donghyeon Kim, Sunkyu Kim, Chan Ho So, and Jaewoo Kang. 2020. Biobert: a pre-trained biomedical language representation model for biomedical text mining. *Bioinformatics*, 36(4):1234–1240.

Yinhan Liu, Myle Ott, Naman Goyal, Jingfei Du, Mandar Joshi, Danqi Chen, Omer Levy, Mike Lewis, Luke Zettlemoyer, and Veselin Stoyanov. 2019. Roberta: A robustly optimized bert pretraining approach. *arXiv preprint arXiv:1907.11692*.

Marco Lui. 2012. Feature stacking for sentence classification in evidence-based medicine. In *Proceedings of the Australasian Language Technology Association Workshop 2012*, pages 134–138, Dunedin, New Zealand.

David L Sackett, William MC Rosenberg, JA Muir Gray, R Brian Haynes, and W Scott Richardson. 1996. Evidence based medicine: what it is and what it isn't.

Ashish Vaswani, Noam Shazeer, Niki Parmar, Jakob Uszkoreit, Llion Jones, Aidan N Gomez, Łukasz Kaiser, and Illia Polosukhin. 2017. Attention is all you need. In *Advances in neural information processing systems*, pages 5998–6008.

Thomas Wolf, Lysandre Debut, Victor Sanh, Julien Chaumond, Clement Delangue, Anthony Moi, Pierric Cistac, Tim Rault, Remi Louf, Morgan Funtowicz, Joe Davison, Sam Shleifer, Patrick von Platen, Clara Ma, Yacine Jernite, Julien Plu, Canwen Xu, Teven Le Scao, Sylvain Gugger, Mariama Drame, Quentin Lhoest, and Alexander Rush. 2020. Transformers: State-of-the-art natural language processing. In *Proceedings of the 2020 Conference on Empirical Methods in Natural Language Processing: System Demonstrations*, pages 38–45, Online. Association for Computational Linguistics.

A Results on Public Test Set

Table 3 shows results across all models on the public test set.

Model	Without Context		With Context	
	Single Emb.	**Ave. Pooling**	**Single Emb.**	**Ave. Pooling**
Baselines				
Naive Bayes	90.9		–	
Logistic Regression	86.2		–	
SVM	91.5		–	
Pre-trained language models				
BERT	96.2	94.6	97.2	97.2
RoBERTa	96.2	95.1	97.5	97.4
ELECTRA	96.1	95.4	97.1	97.8
BioBERT (Microsoft)	96.8	96.1	97.3	97.3
BioBERT (DMIS Lab)	96.0	94.5	97.1	96.5
Ensemble – averaging Top-k models				
Ensemble (Top-3)	96.7	96.7	97.6	98.2
Ensemble (Top-4)	96.8	96.5	97.7	98.1
Ensemble (Top-5)	96.8	96.7	97.8	98.1
Ensemble – further averaging the Ensemble (Top-k) models of Single Embed. and Ave. Pooling				
Combine of Ensemble (Top-3)	97.0		**98.4**	
Combine of Ensemble (Top-4)	97.0		98.3	
Combine of Ensemble (Top-5)	97.1		98.3	

Table 3: ROC (micro) scores over public test set.

Association for Computational Linguistics
209 N. Eighth Street
Stroudsburg, Pennsylvania 18360

CURRAN ASSOCIATES INC.
proceedings.com

ISBN 978-1-7138-9102-4